English Adaptation - Alexander O. Smith
Story Editor - Rich Amtower
Retouch and Lettering - James Lee
Graphic Design - Mark Paniccia
Cover Layout & logo Design - Patrick Hook

Editor - Mark Paniccia
Managing Editor - Jill Freshney
Production Coordinator - Antonio DePietro
Production Manager - Jennifer Miller
Art Director - Matthew Alford
Director of Editorial - Jeremy Ross
VP of Production & Manufacturing - Ron Klamert
President & C.O.O. - John Parker
Publisher & C.E.O. - Stuart Levy

Email: editor@TOKYOPOP.com
Come visit us online at www.TOKYOPOP.com

A 🐾TOKYOPOP® Manga

TOKYOPOP® is an imprint of Mixx Entertainment, Inc.
5900 Wilshire Blvd. Suite 2000, Los Angeles, CA 90036

ISBN: 1-59182-026-X

First TOKYOPOP® printing: June 2003

10 9 8 7 6 5 4 3 2 1

Printed in the USA

SHAOLIN 鈴 SISTERS

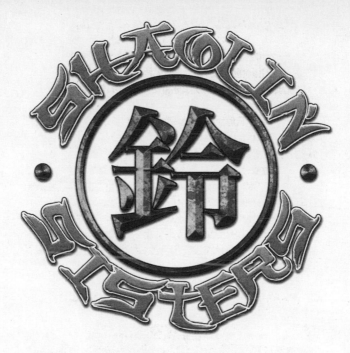

Volume 3

by
Toshiki Hirano
&
Narumi Kakinouchi

TOKYOPOP®
Los Angeles • Tokyo • London

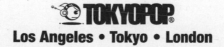

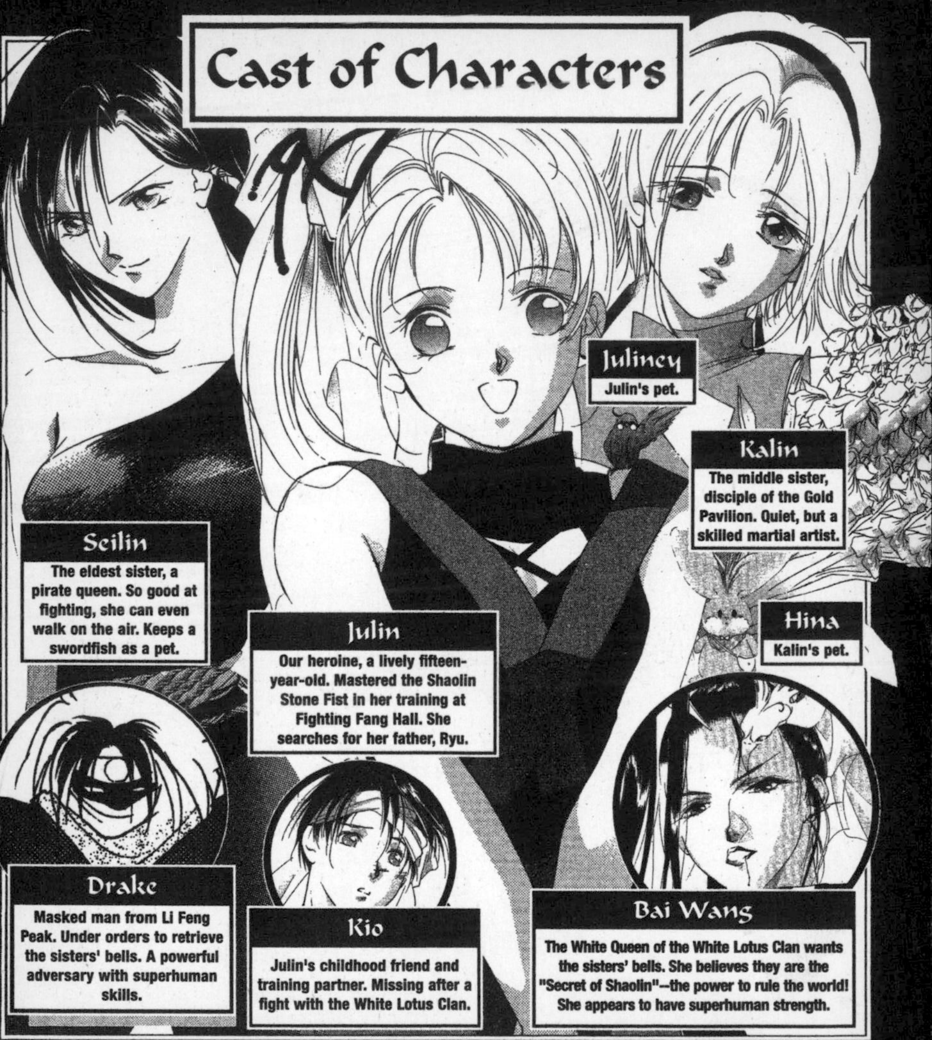
Cast of Characters
Juliney
Julin's pet.
Kalin
The middle sister, disciple of the Gold Pavilion. Quiet, but a skilled martial artist.
Seilin
The eldest sister, a pirate queen. So good at fighting, she can even walk on the air. Keeps a swordfish as a pet.
Julin
Our heroine, a lively fifteen-year-old. Mastered the Shaolin Stone Fist in her training at Fighting Fang Hall. She searches for her father, Ryu.
Hina
Kalin's pet.
Drake
Masked man from Li Feng Peak. Under orders to retrieve the sisters' bells. A powerful adversary with superhuman skills.
Kio
Julin's childhood friend and training partner. Missing after a fight with the White Lotus Clan.
Bai Wang
The White Queen of the White Lotus Clan wants the sisters' bells. She believes they are the "Secret of Shaolin"--the power to rule the world! She appears to have superhuman strength.

STORY SO FAR: It is an age when warriors rule. After an attack by Bai Wang's White Lotus Clan, Julin's master gives his dying breath to impart a secret. Julin learns of her two lost sisters, each possessing a bell like her own, and embarks on a journey of discovery. On the very night that Julin meets her middle sister, Kalin, the White Lotus Clan attacks again. It seems Bai Wang wants the sisters' bells, claiming they are the key to the "Secret of Shaolin"—the power to rule the world! Now the girls are in a race to locate their older sister, the pirate queen, Seilin. Upon discovering and boarding Seilin's vessel, all three bells mystically begin to ring in unison! Seilin, however, is unconvinced of the girls' familial claims and challenges the pair to a test of combat. In the midst of the fight, who should appear but Bai Wang, drawn by the ringing of the bells. Suddenly, another mysterious figure named "Drake" appears and demands that the bells be returned to him. When the dust settles, Drake holds both Kalin and Julin's bells, with Seilin's in the possession of Bai Wang. As our story begins, Kalin and Julin have resolved to get their bells back—even if it means taking on the White Lotus Clan on their home turf.

The sisters, Drake, or Bai Wang: Who will emerge with the key to the "Secret of Shaolin"?

Chapter 11: The Killer's Conscienc

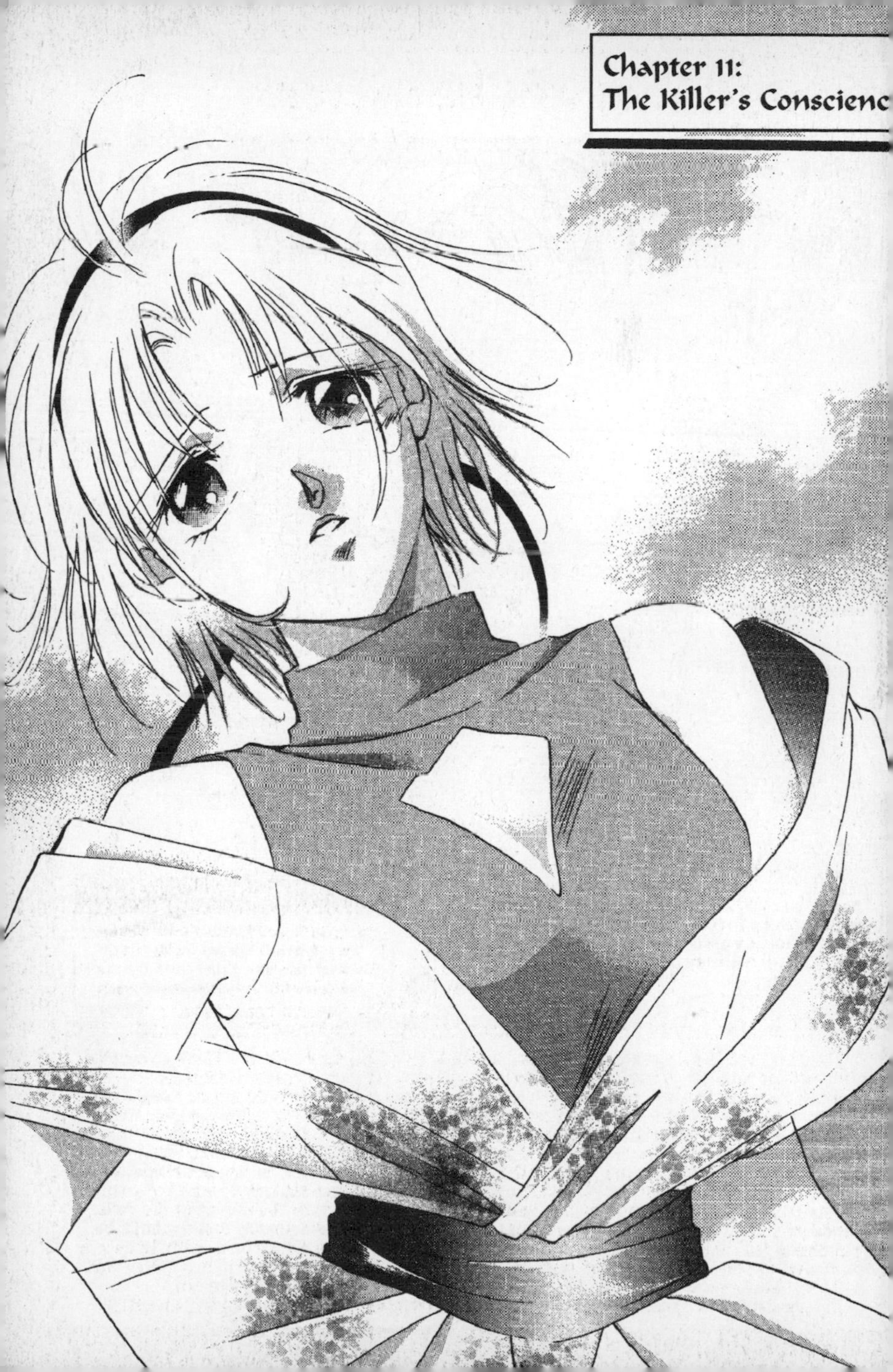

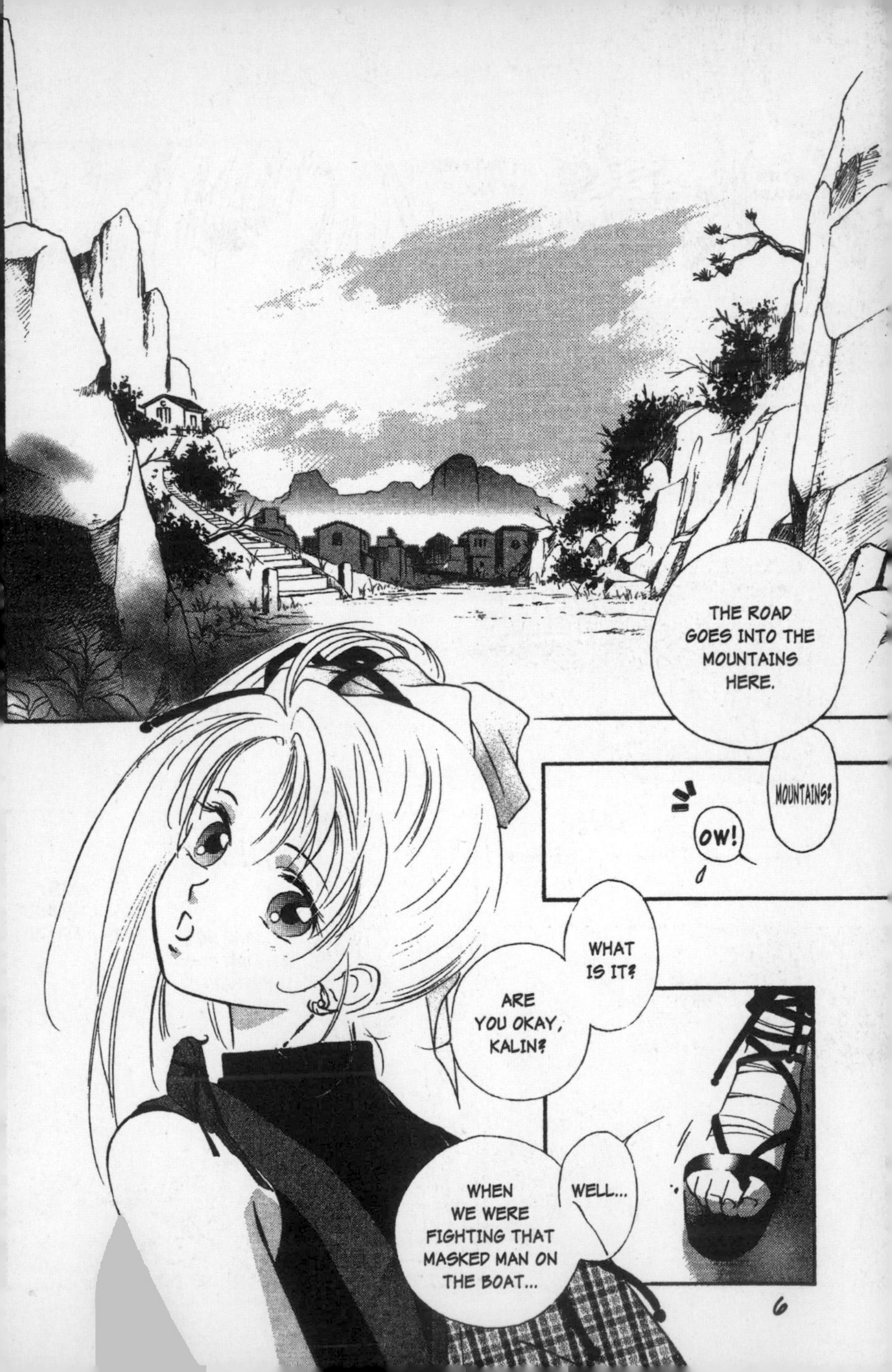
THE ROAD GOES INTO THE MOUNTAINS HERE.
MOUNTAINS?
OW!
WHAT IS IT?
ARE YOU OKAY, KALIN?
WELL...
WHEN WE WERE FIGHTING THAT MASKED MAN ON THE BOAT...

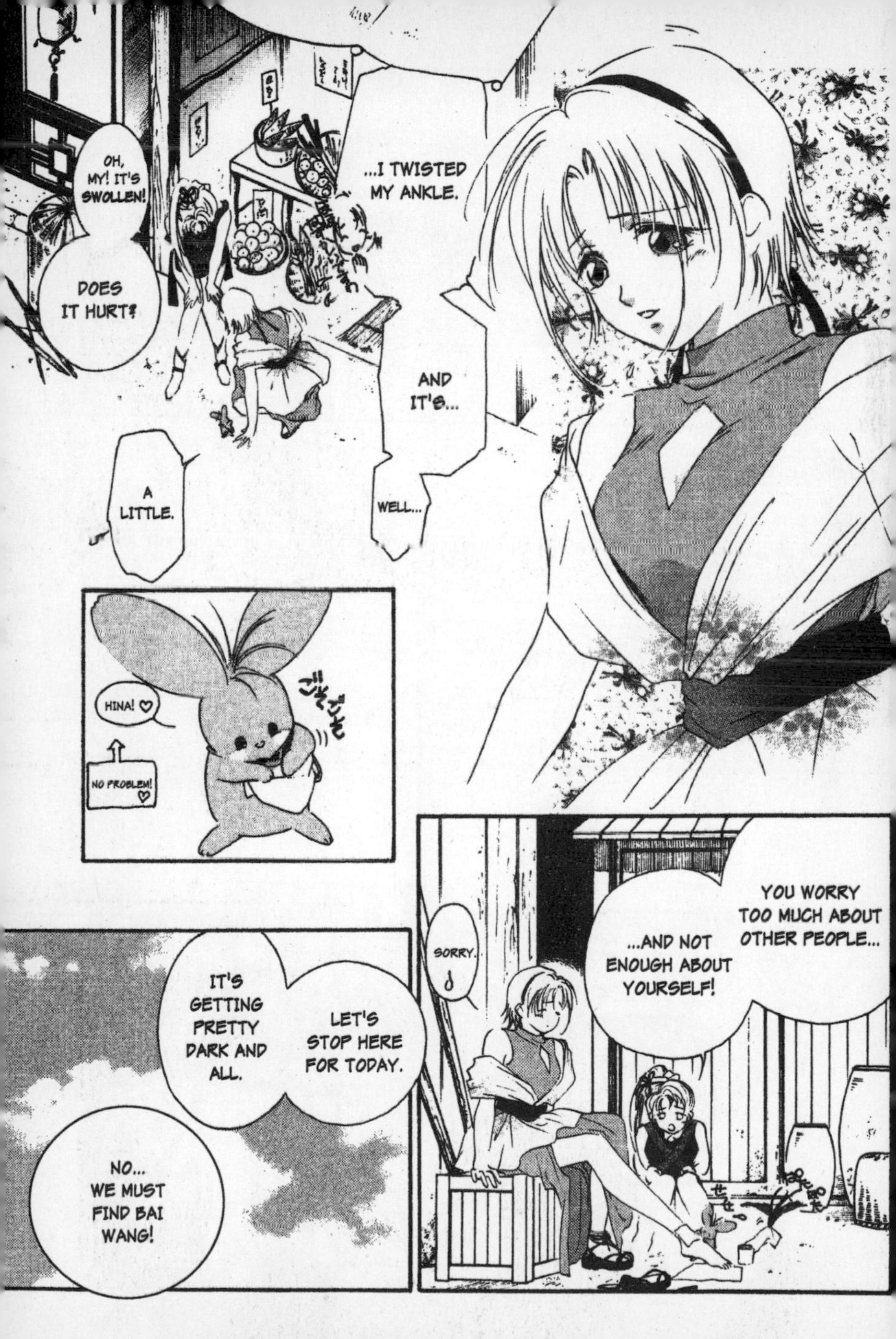
...I TWISTED MY ANKLE.
AND IT'S...
WELL...
OH, MY! IT'S SWOLLEN!
DOES IT HURT?
A LITTLE.
HINA! ♡
NO PROBLEM! ♡
YOU WORRY TOO MUCH ABOUT OTHER PEOPLE...
...AND NOT ENOUGH ABOUT YOURSELF!
SORRY.
IT'S GETTING PRETTY DARK AND ALL.
LET'S STOP HERE FOR TODAY.
NO... WE MUST FIND BAI WANG!

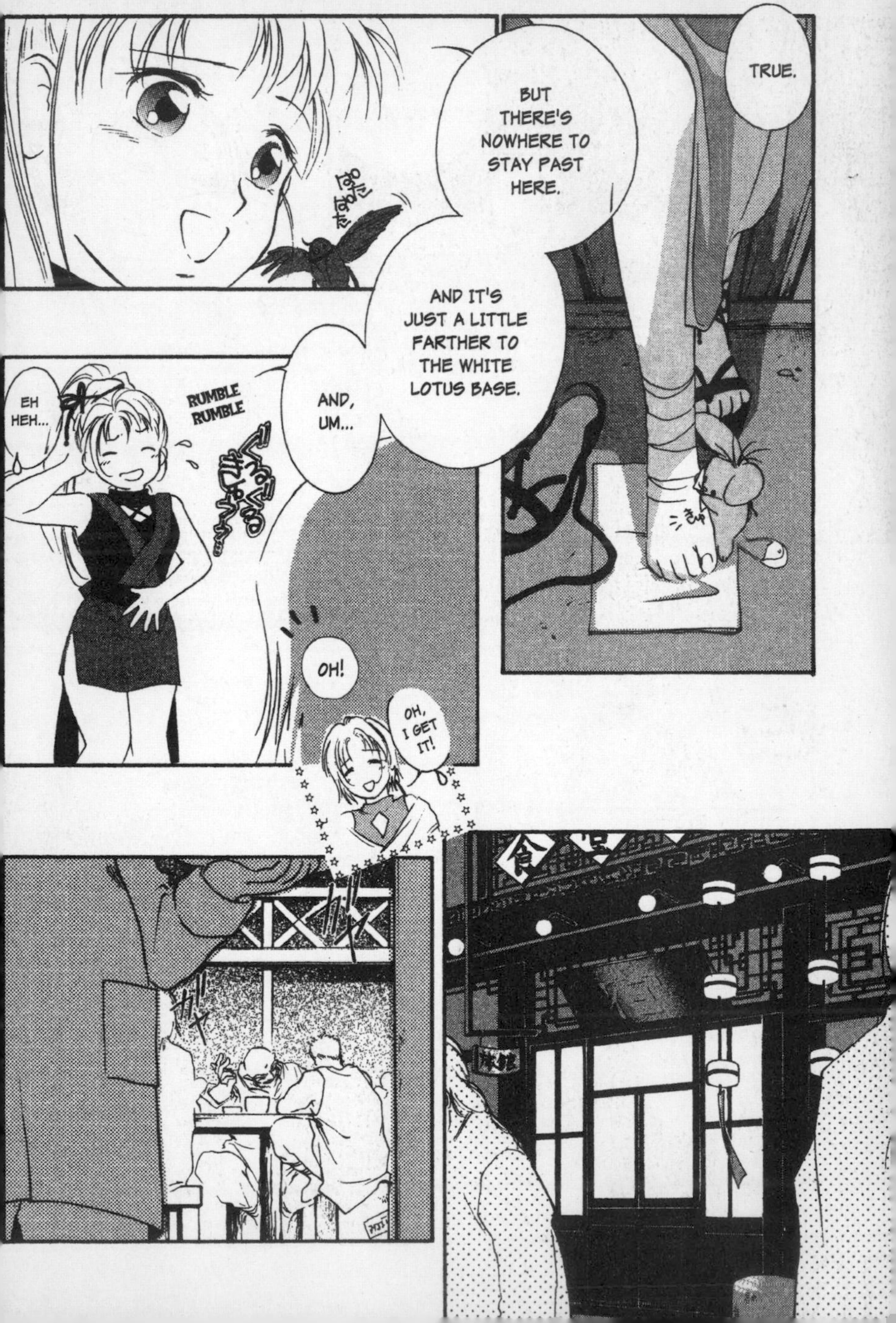
TRUE.
BUT THERE'S NOWHERE TO STAY PAST HERE.
AND IT'S JUST A LITTLE FARTHER TO THE WHITE LOTUS BASE.
AND, UM...
RUMBLE RUMBLE
EH HEH...
OH!
OH, I GET IT!

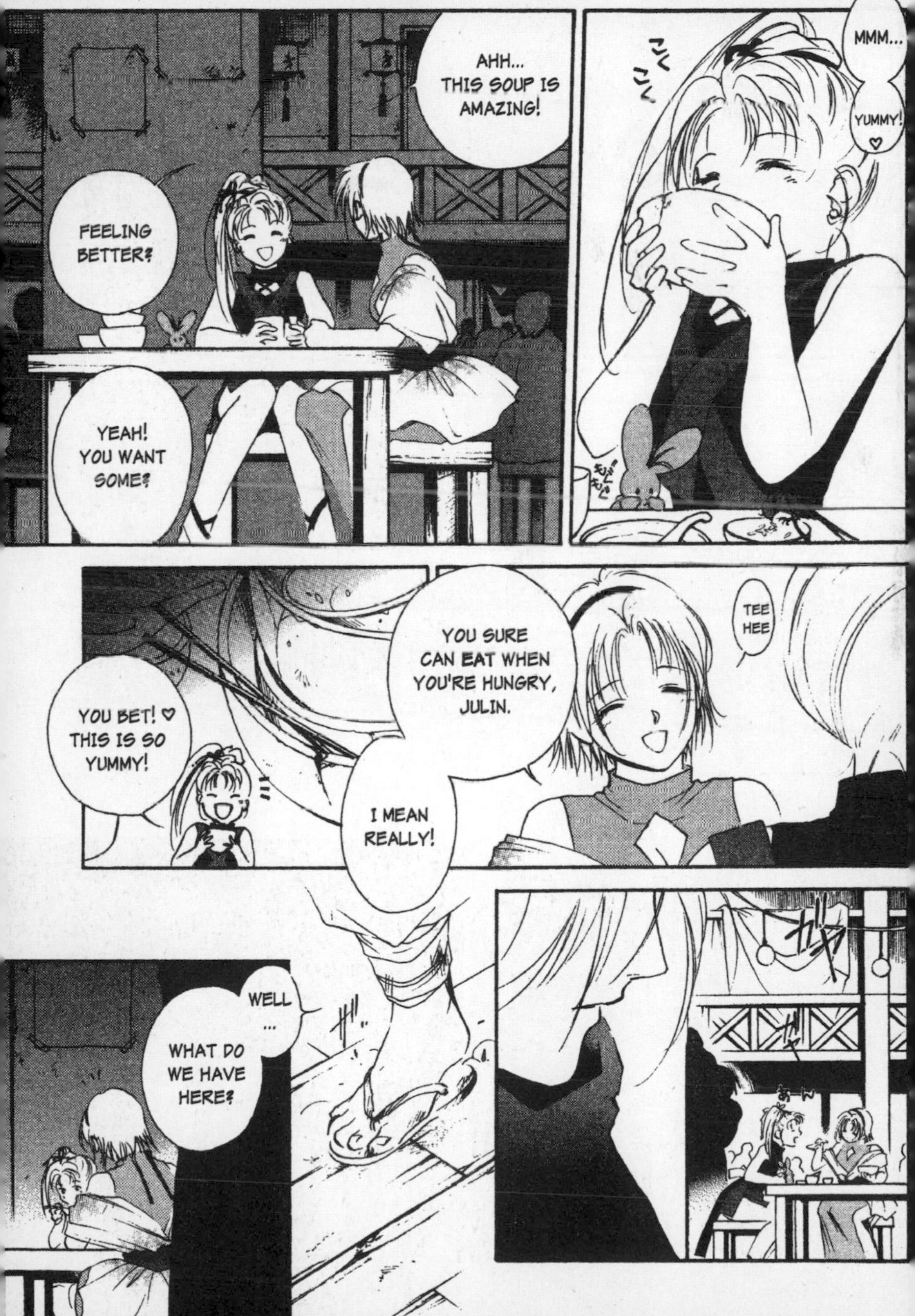
こく こく
MMM...
YUMMY! ♡
AHH... THIS SOUP IS AMAZING!
FEELING BETTER?
YEAH! YOU WANT SOME?
TEE HEE
YOU SURE CAN EAT WHEN YOU'RE HUNGRY, JULIN.
I MEAN REALLY!
YOU BET! ♡ THIS IS SO YUMMY!
WELL ...
WHAT DO WE HAVE HERE?

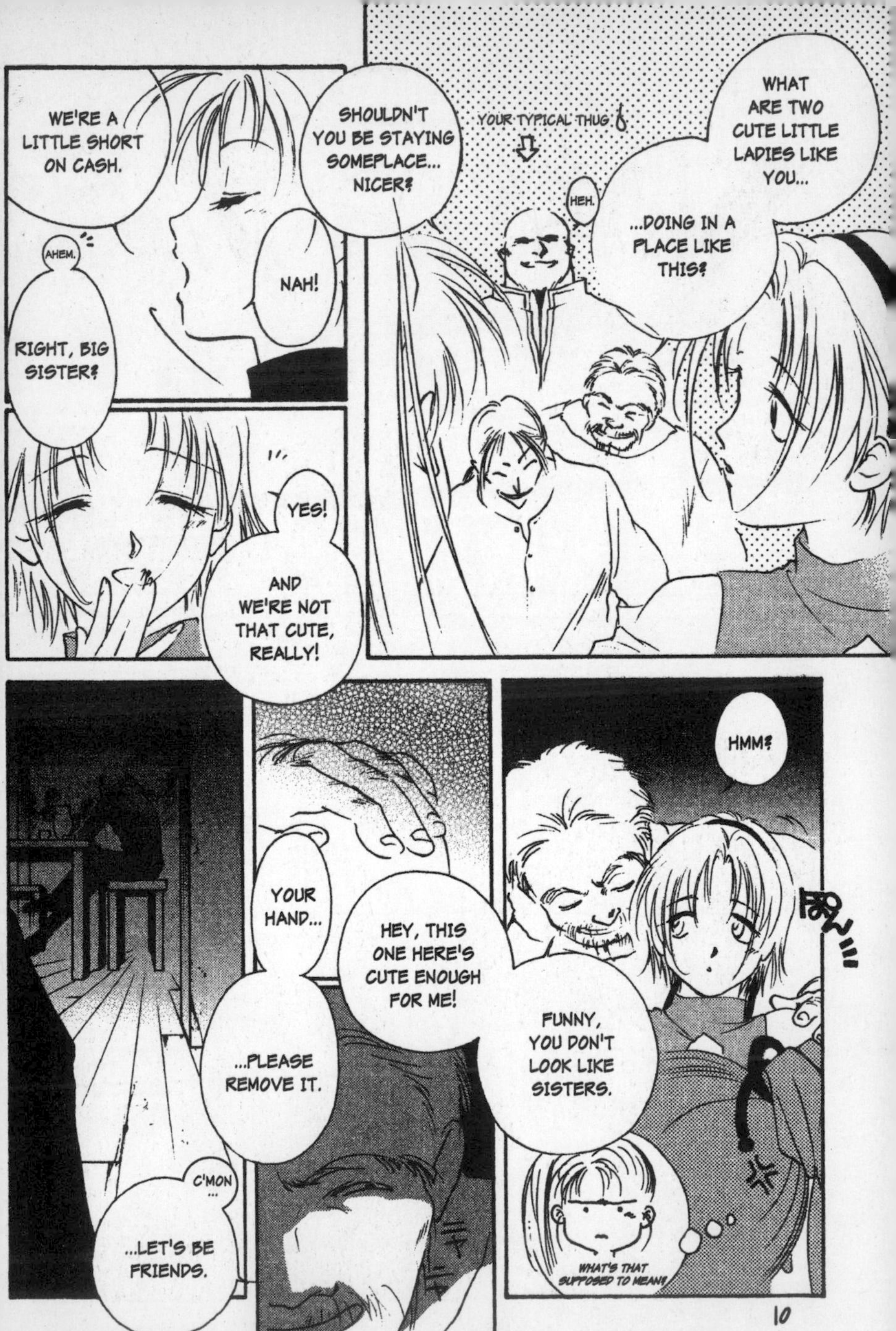
WHAT ARE TWO CUTE LITTLE LADIES LIKE YOU...
...DOING IN A PLACE LIKE THIS?
YOUR TYPICAL THUG
HEH.
SHOULDN'T YOU BE STAYING SOMEPLACE... NICER?
NAH!
WE'RE A LITTLE SHORT ON CASH.
AHEM.
RIGHT, BIG SISTER?
YES!
AND WE'RE NOT THAT CUTE, REALLY!
HMM?
HEY, THIS ONE HERE'S CUTE ENOUGH FOR ME!
FUNNY, YOU DON'T LOOK LIKE SISTERS.
WHAT'S THAT SUPPOSED TO MEAN?
YOUR HAND...
...PLEASE REMOVE IT.
C'MON...
...LET'S BE FRIENDS.

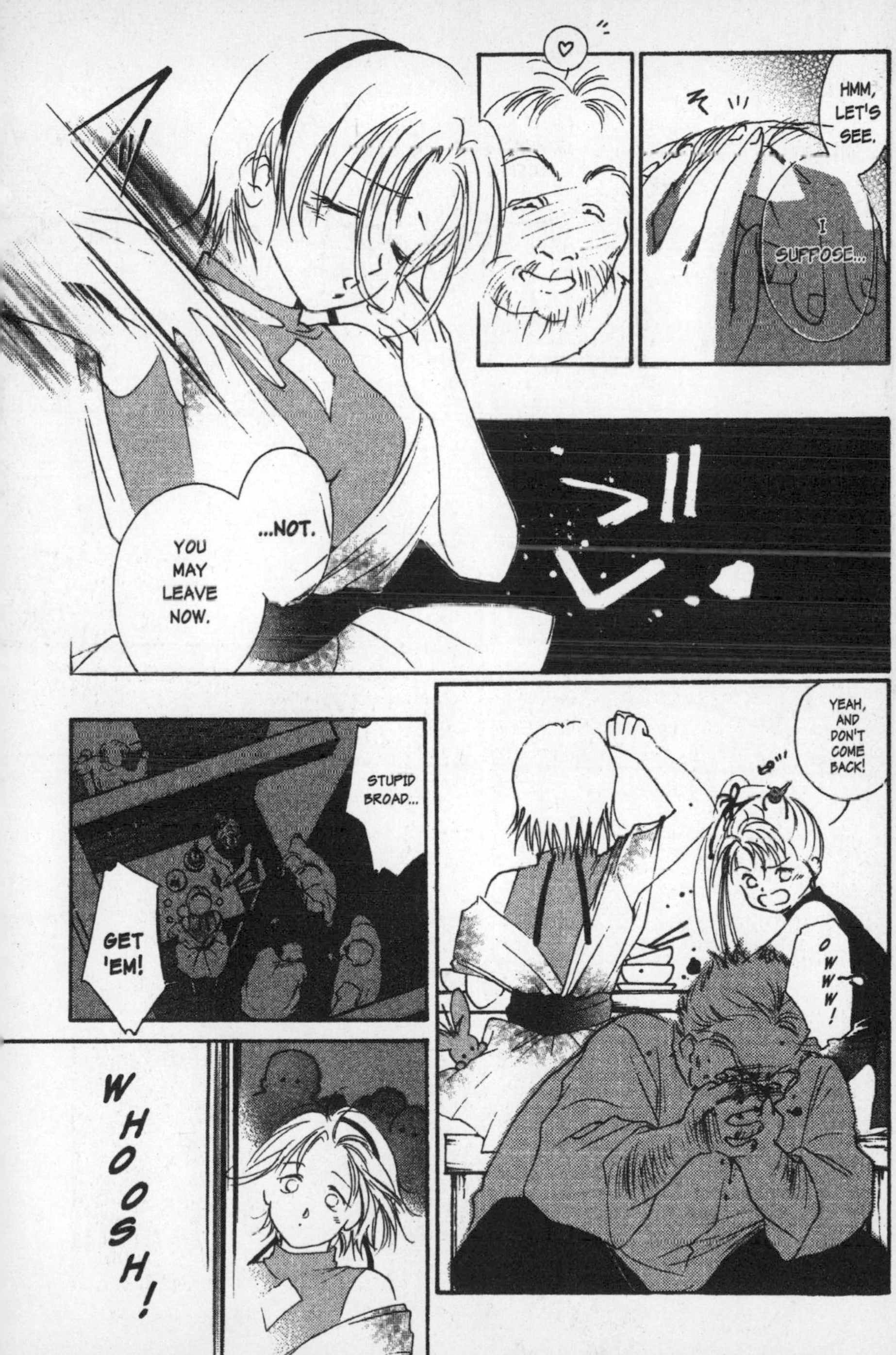
HMM, LET'S SEE.
I SUPPOSE...
...NOT.
YOU MAY LEAVE NOW.
YEAH, AND DON'T COME BACK!
OWWW!
STUPID BROAD...
GET 'EM!
WHOOSH!

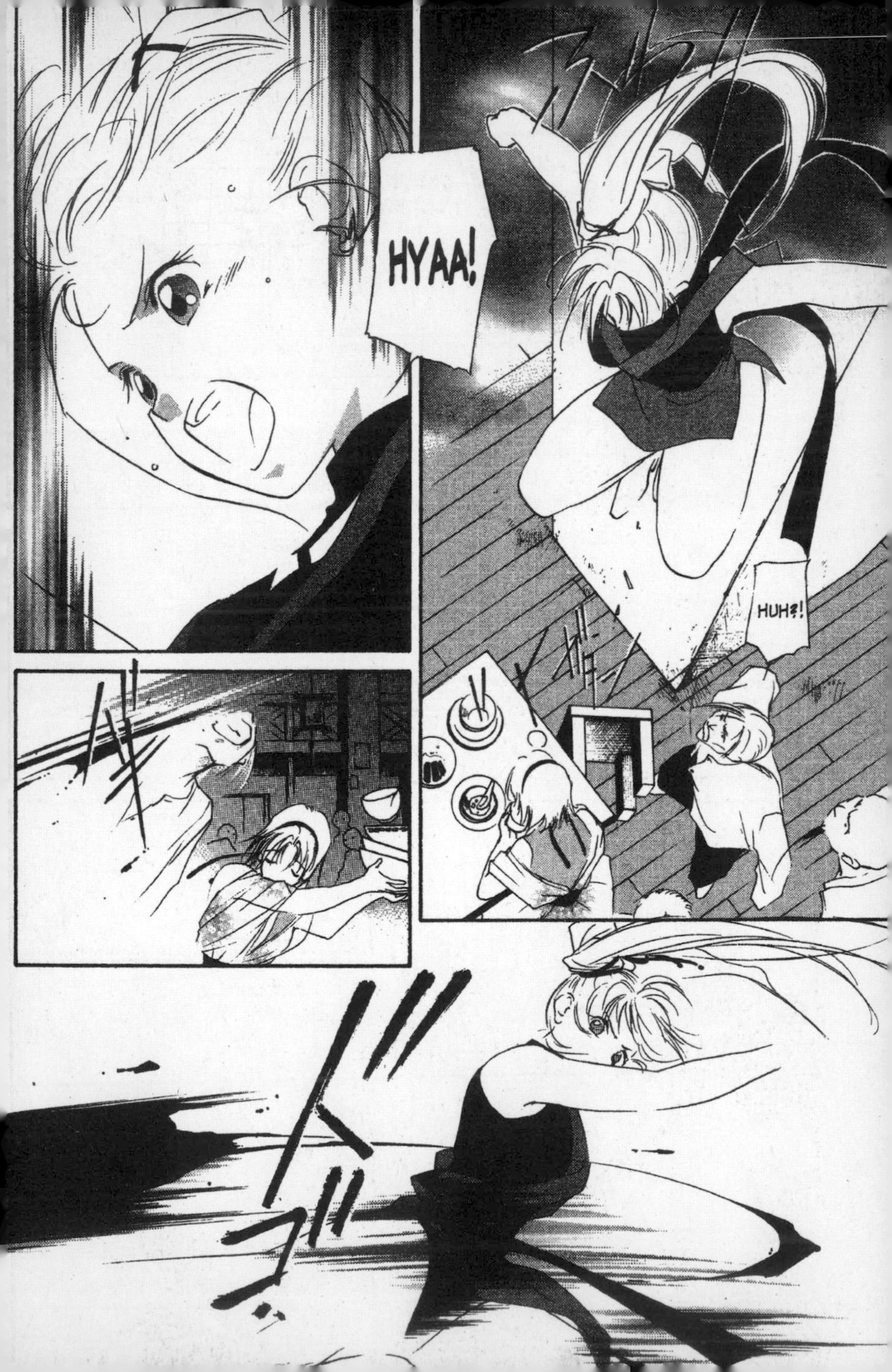
HYAA!
HUH?!

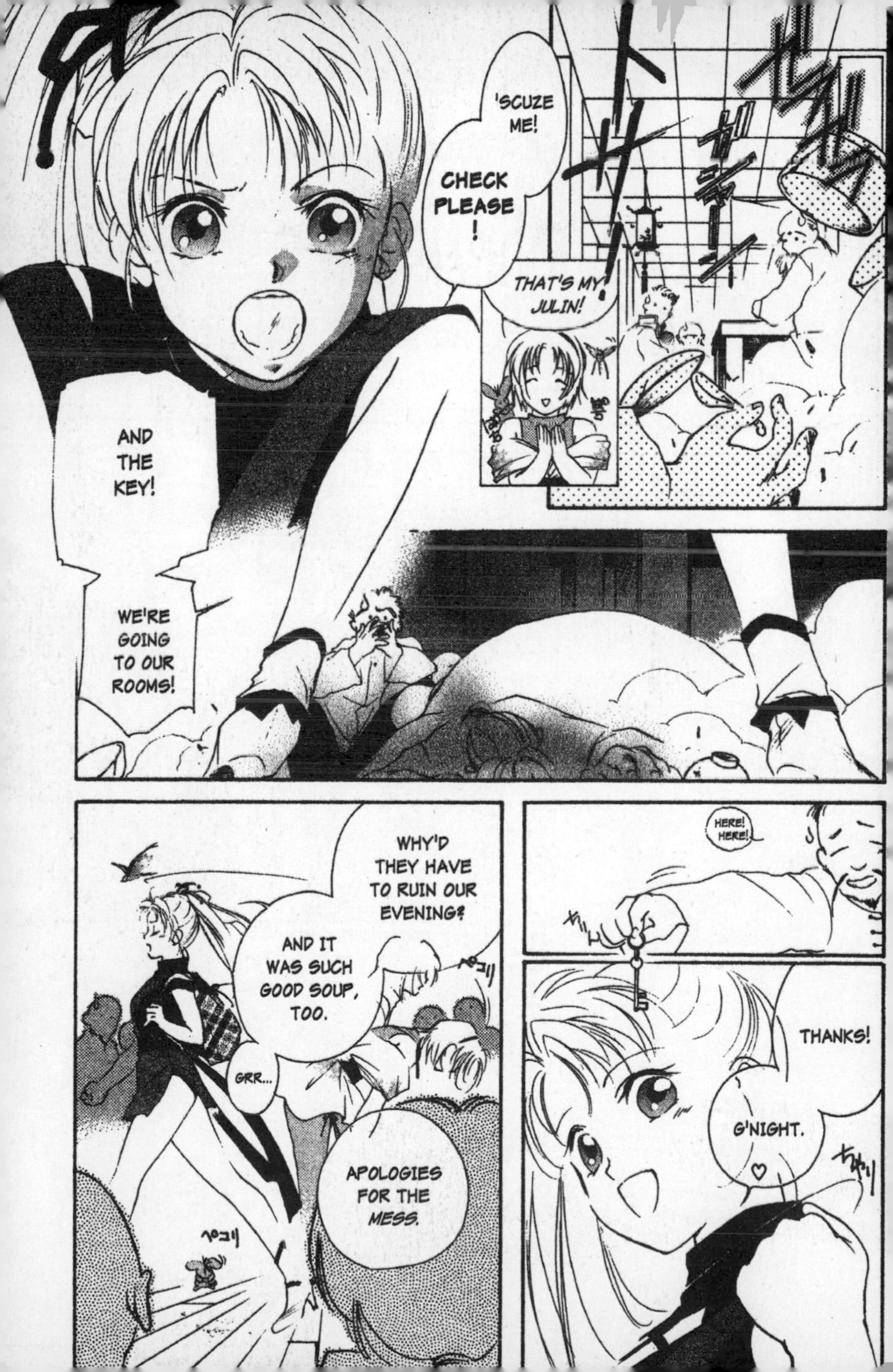
'SCUZE ME!
CHECK PLEASE!
THAT'S MY JULIN!
AND THE KEY!
WE'RE GOING TO OUR ROOMS!
HERE! HERE!
THANKS!
G'NIGHT. ♡
WHY'D THEY HAVE TO RUIN OUR EVENING?
AND IT WAS SUCH GOOD SOUP, TOO.
GRR...
APOLOGIES FOR THE MESS.

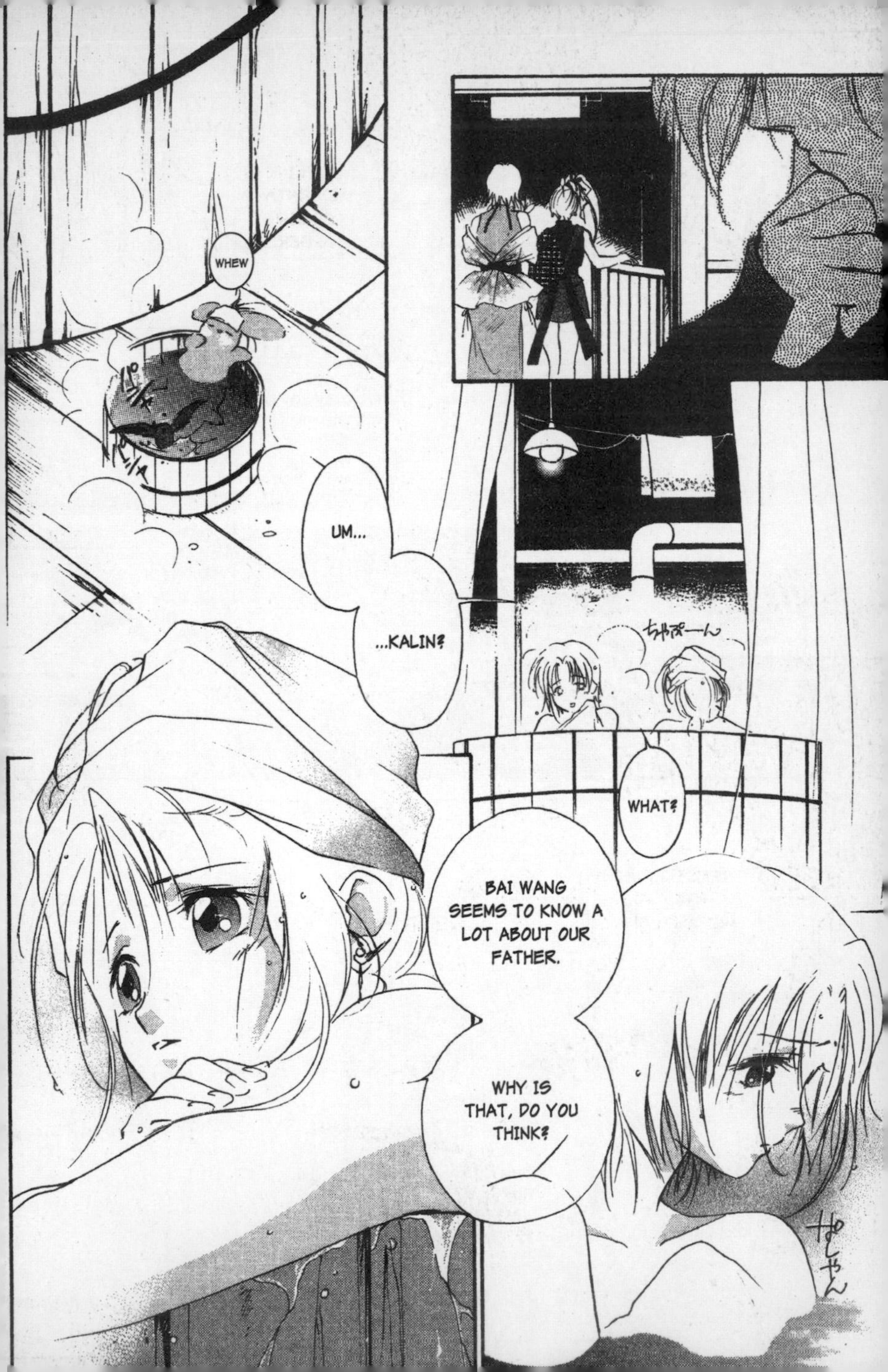
WHEW
UM...
...KALIN?
ちゃぽーん
WHAT?
BAI WANG SEEMS TO KNOW A LOT ABOUT OUR FATHER.
WHY IS THAT, DO YOU THINK?
ぱしゃん

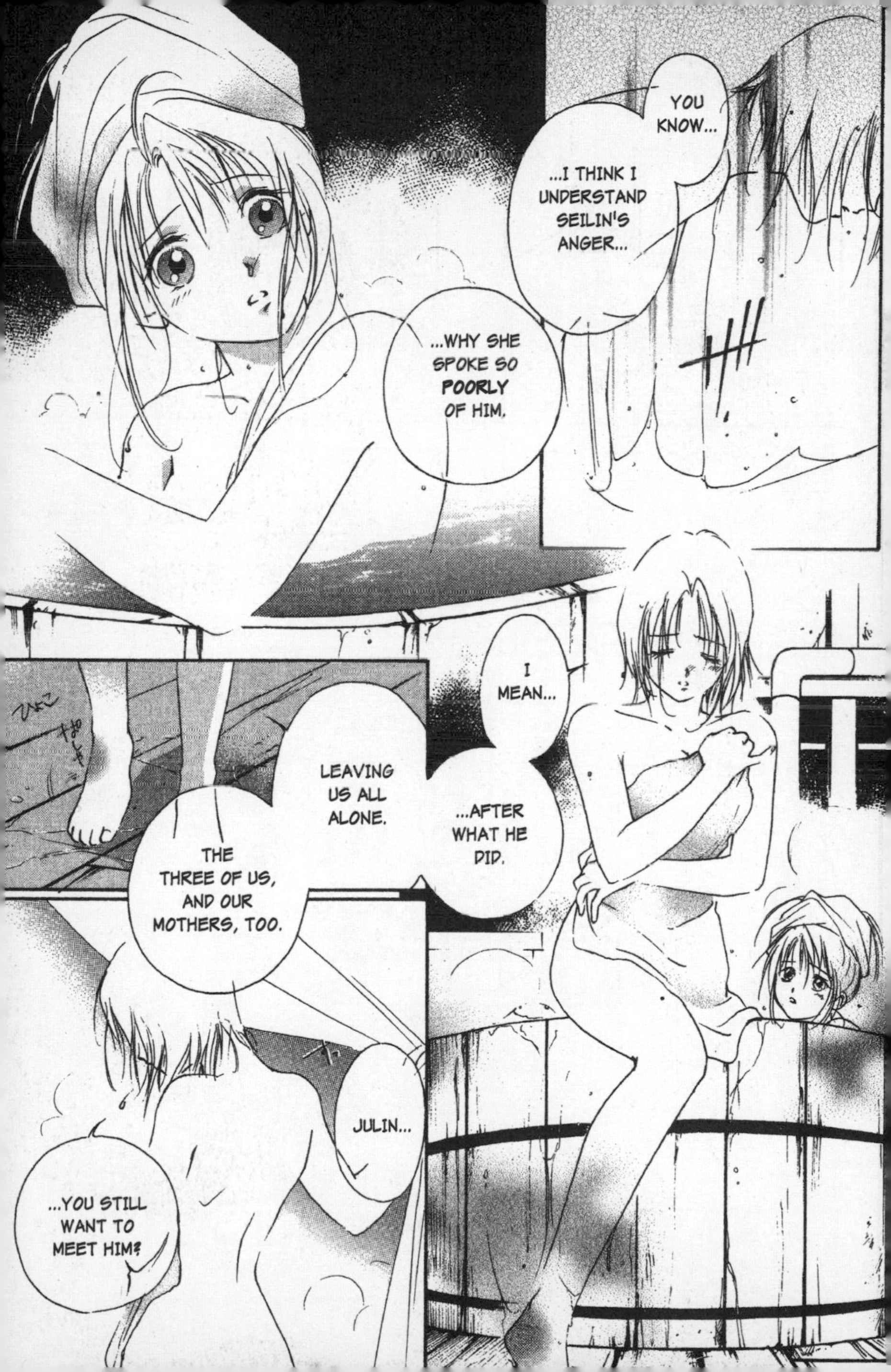
YOU KNOW...
...I THINK I UNDERSTAND SEILIN'S ANGER...
...WHY SHE SPOKE SO POORLY OF HIM.
I MEAN...
...AFTER WHAT HE DID.
LEAVING US ALL ALONE.
THE THREE OF US, AND OUR MOTHERS, TOO.
JULIN...
...YOU STILL WANT TO MEET HIM?

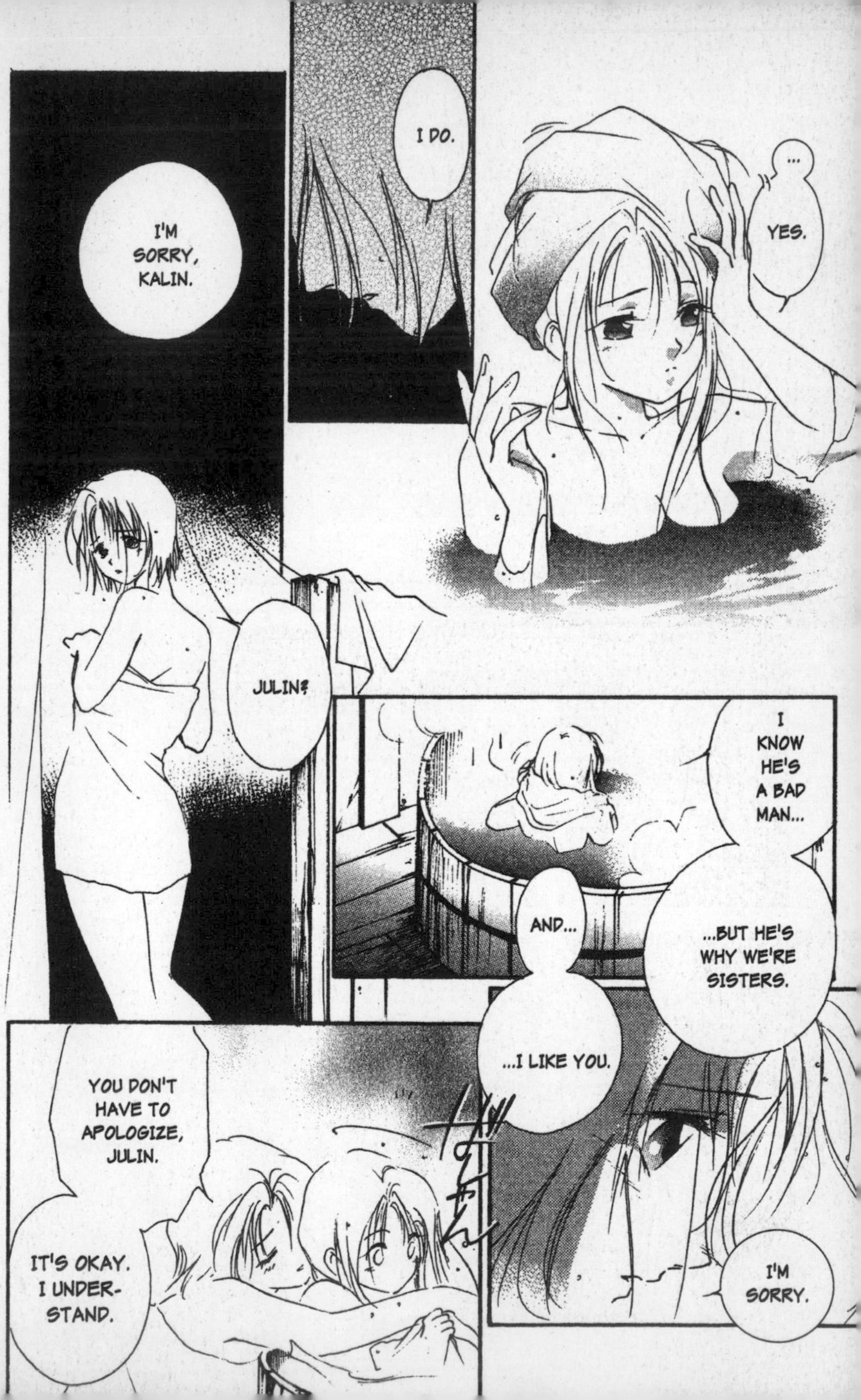
...
YES.
I DO.
I KNOW HE'S A BAD MAN...
...BUT HE'S WHY WE'RE SISTERS.
AND...
...I LIKE YOU.
I'M SORRY, KALIN.
JULIN?
I'M SORRY.
YOU DON'T HAVE TO APOLOGIZE, JULIN.
IT'S OKAY. I UNDER-STAND.

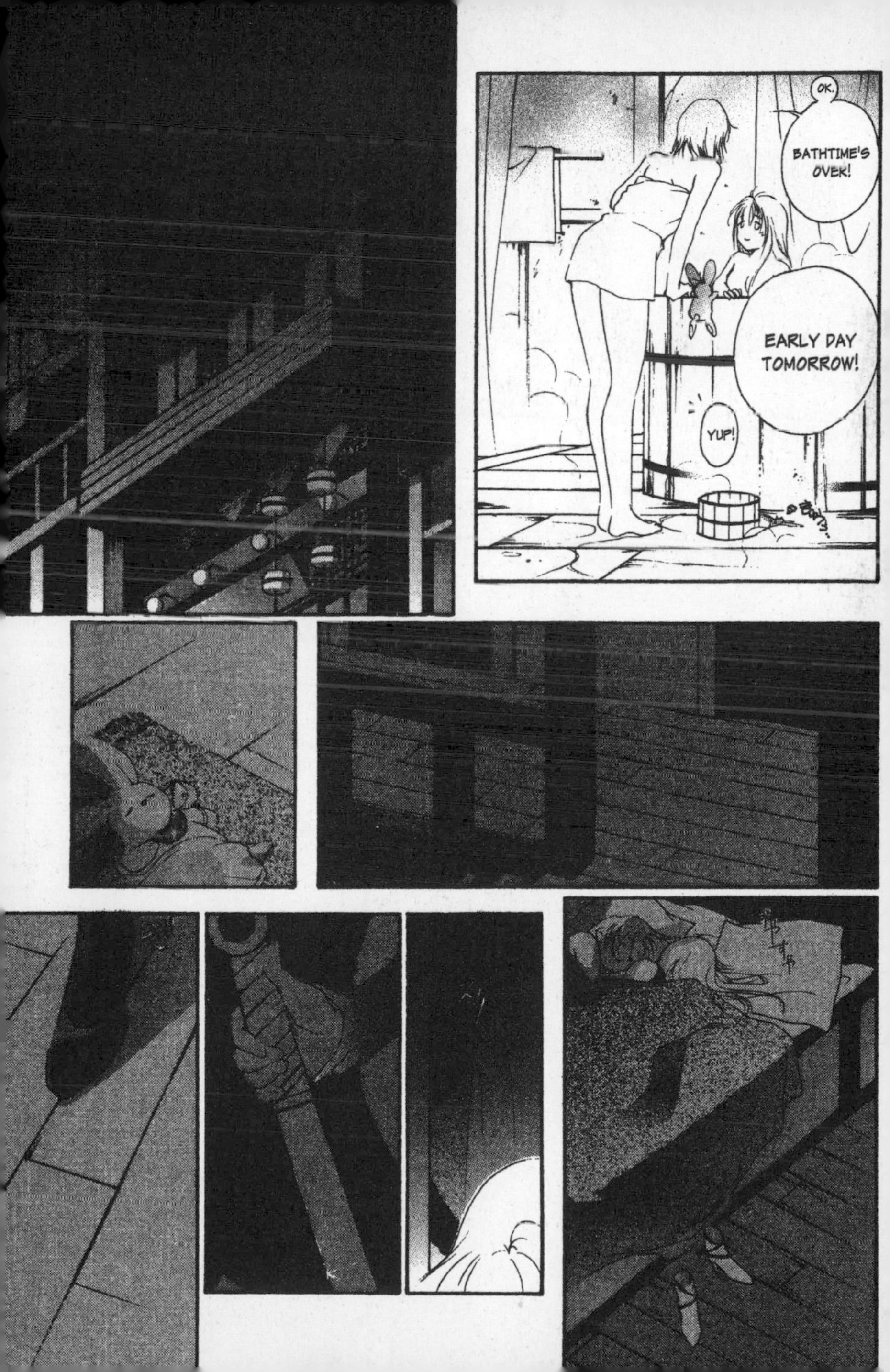
OK.
BATHTIME'S OVER!
EARLY DAY TOMORROW!
YUP!

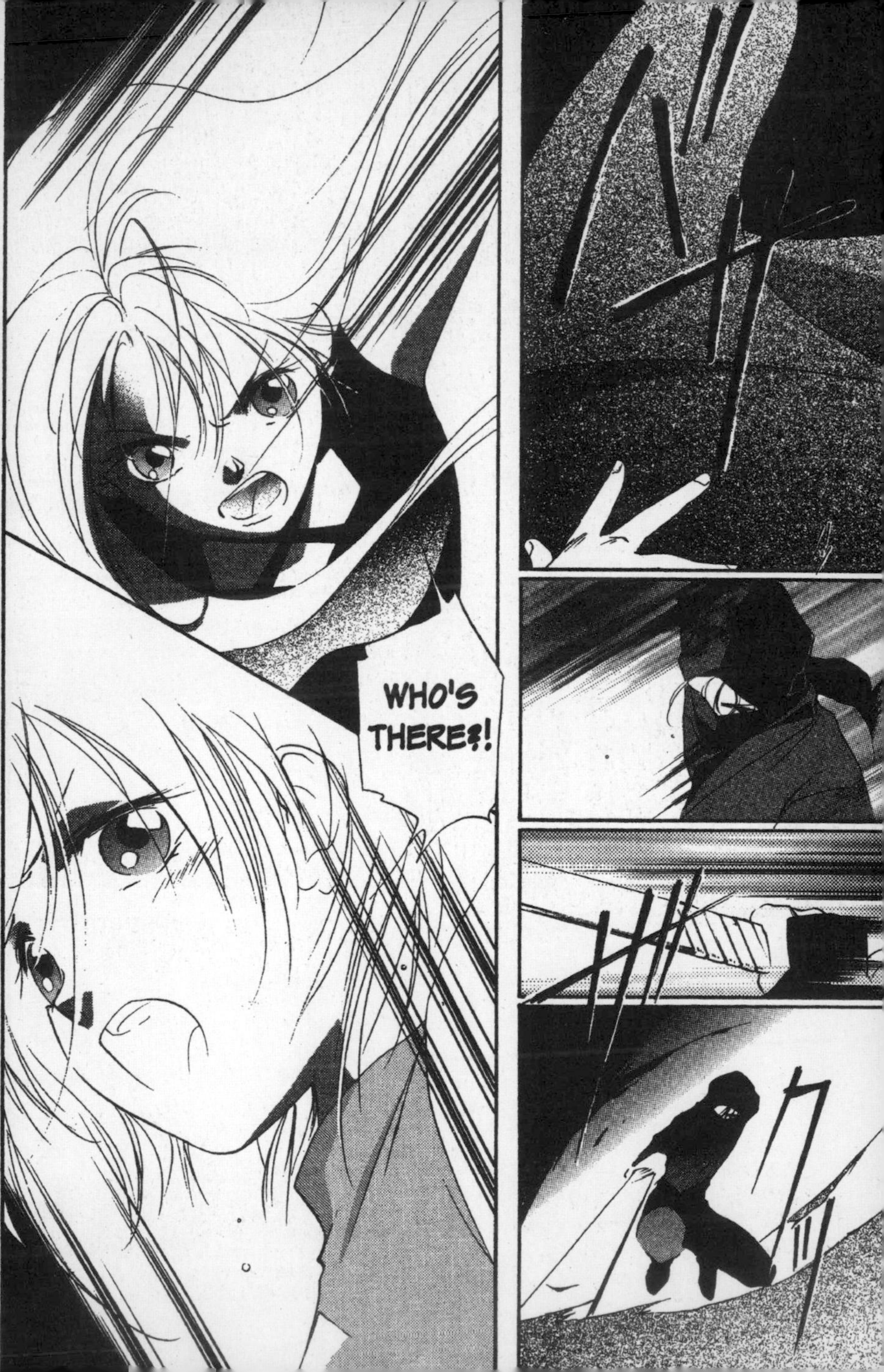
WHO'S THERE?!

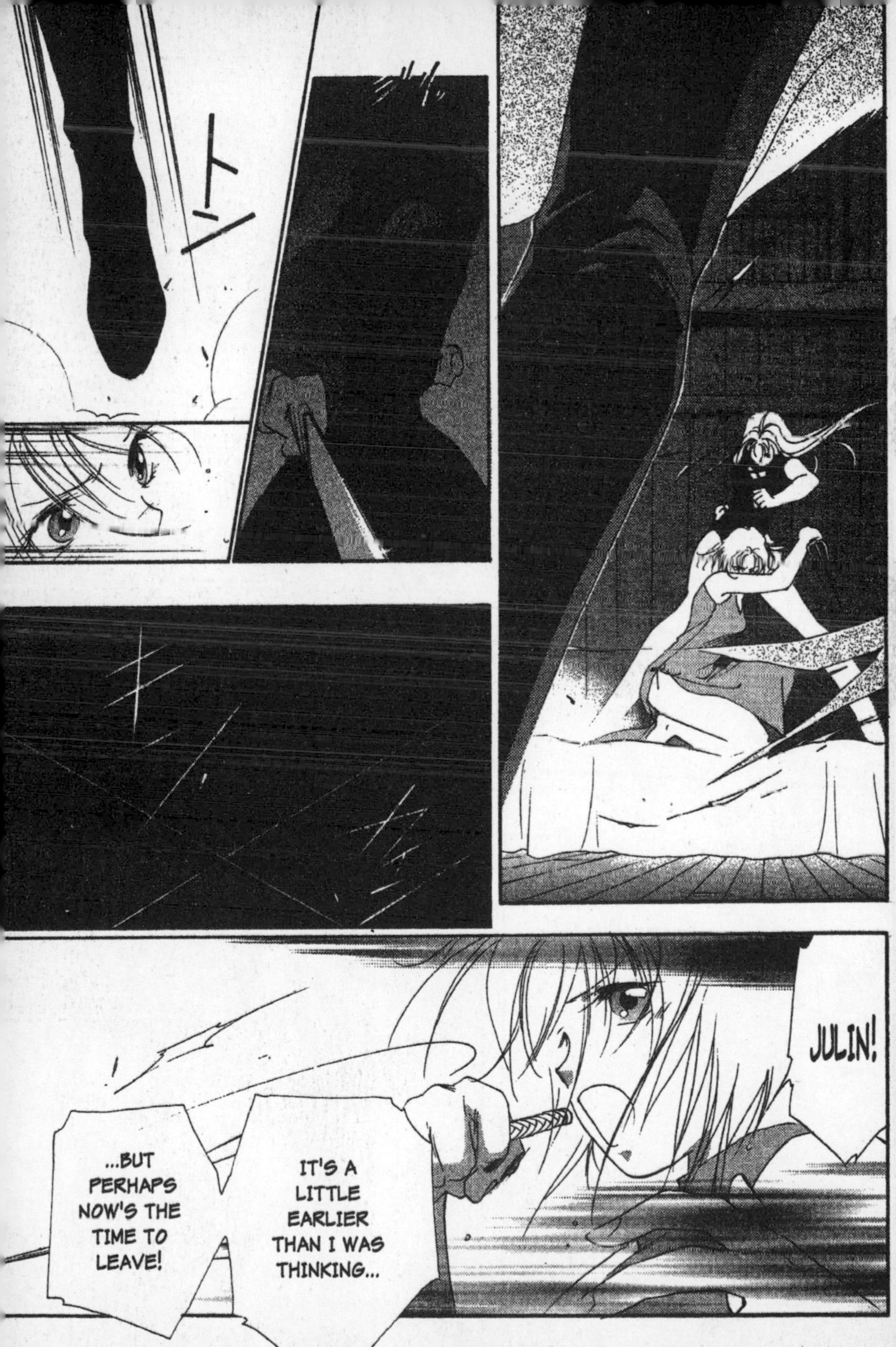
JULIN!
IT'S A LITTLE EARLIER THAN I WAS THINKING...
...BUT PERHAPS NOW'S THE TIME TO LEAVE!

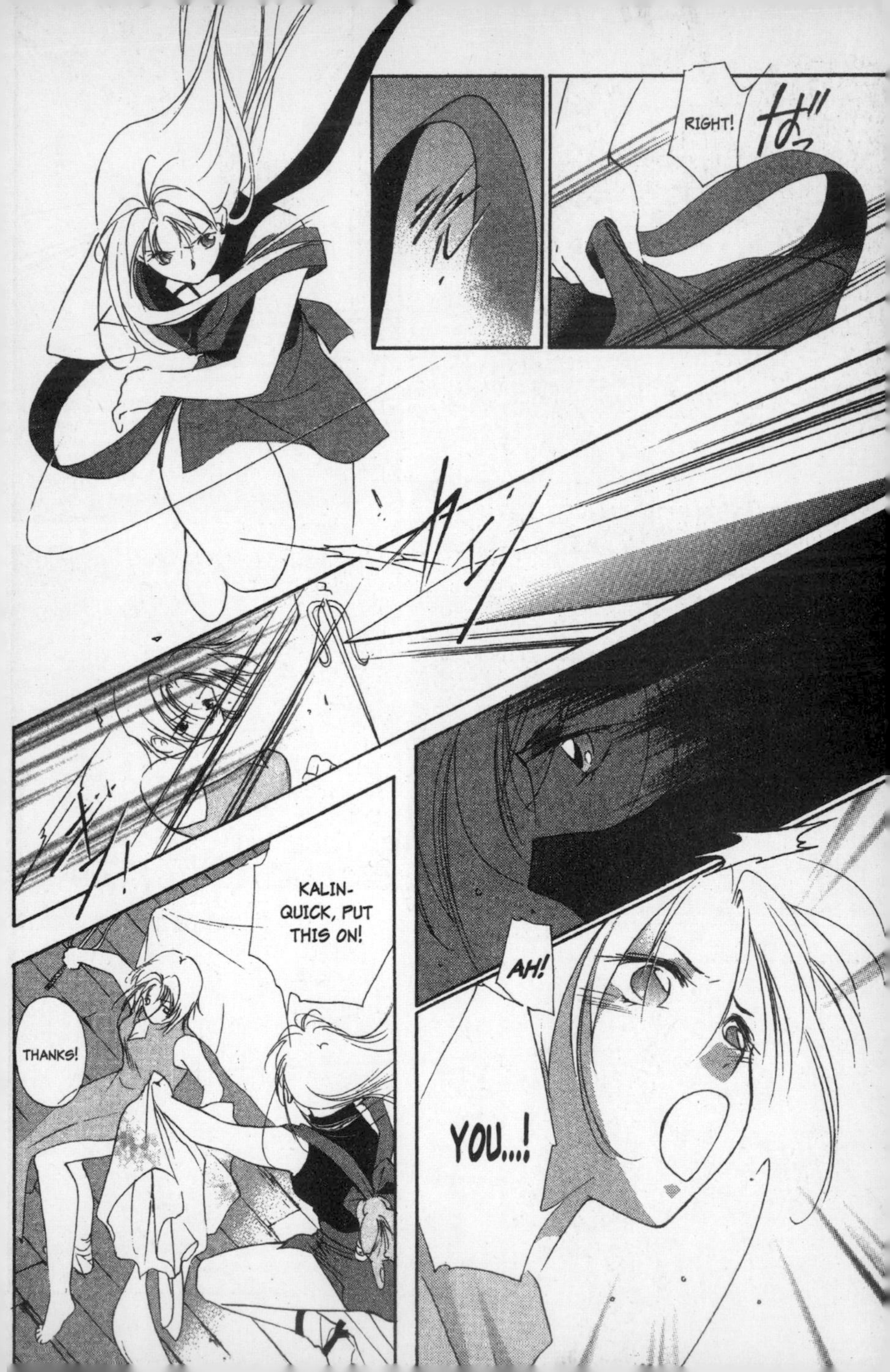
RIGHT!
ばっ
AH!
YOU...!
KALIN-
QUICK, PUT
THIS ON!
THANKS!

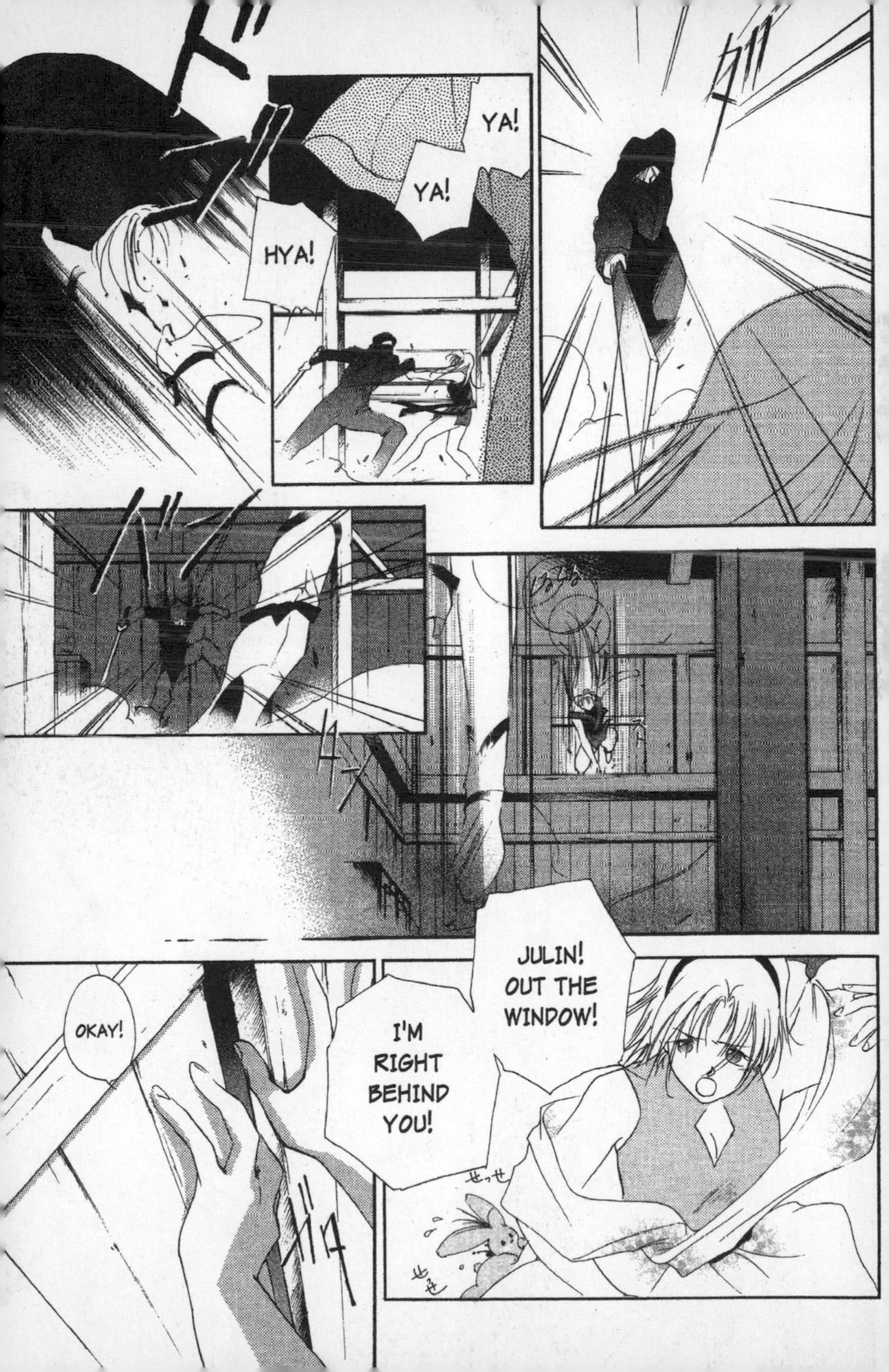
YA!
YA!
HYA!
JULIN! OUT THE WINDOW!
I'M RIGHT BEHIND YOU!
OKAY!

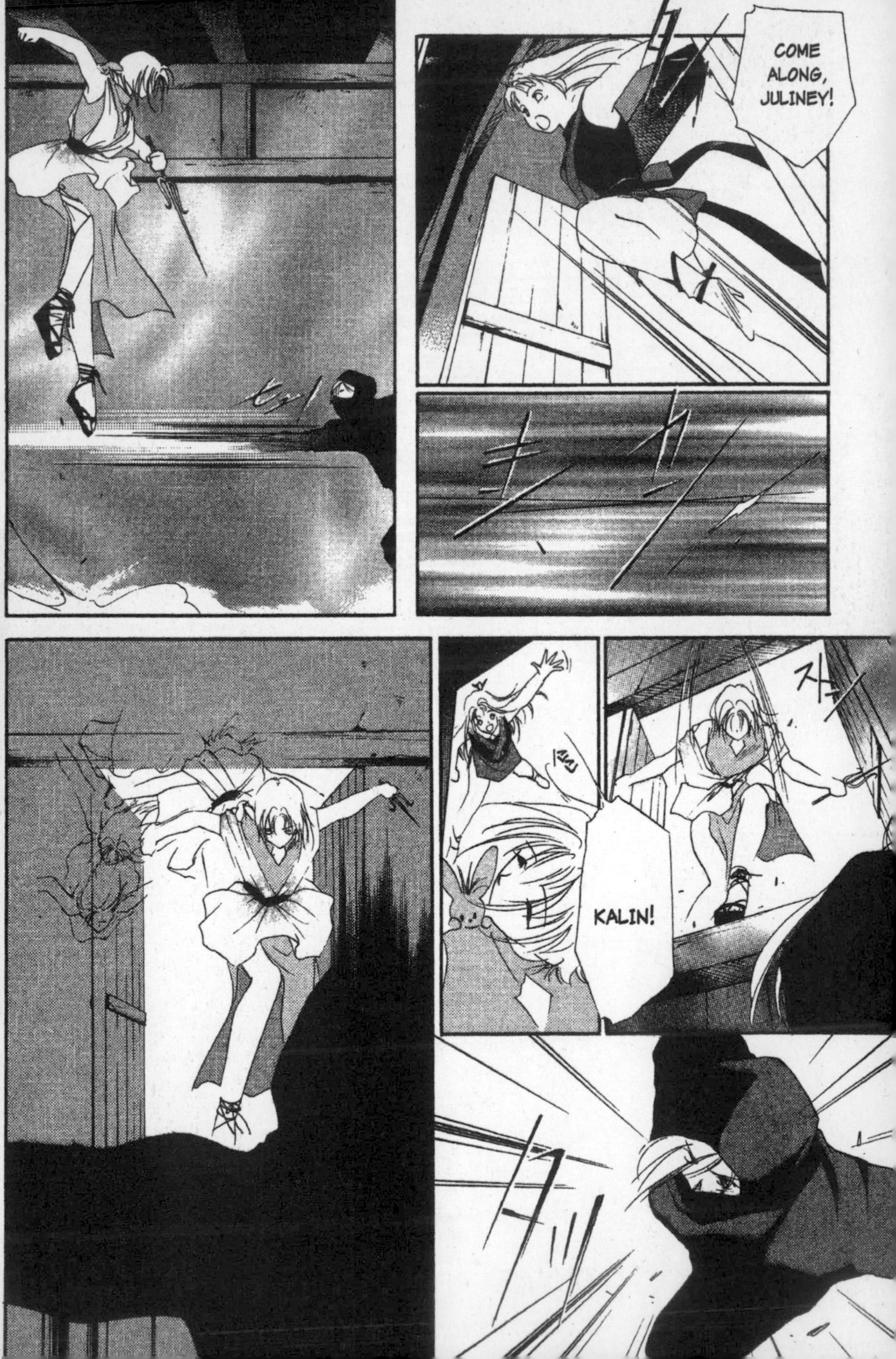
COME ALONG, JULINEY!
KALIN!

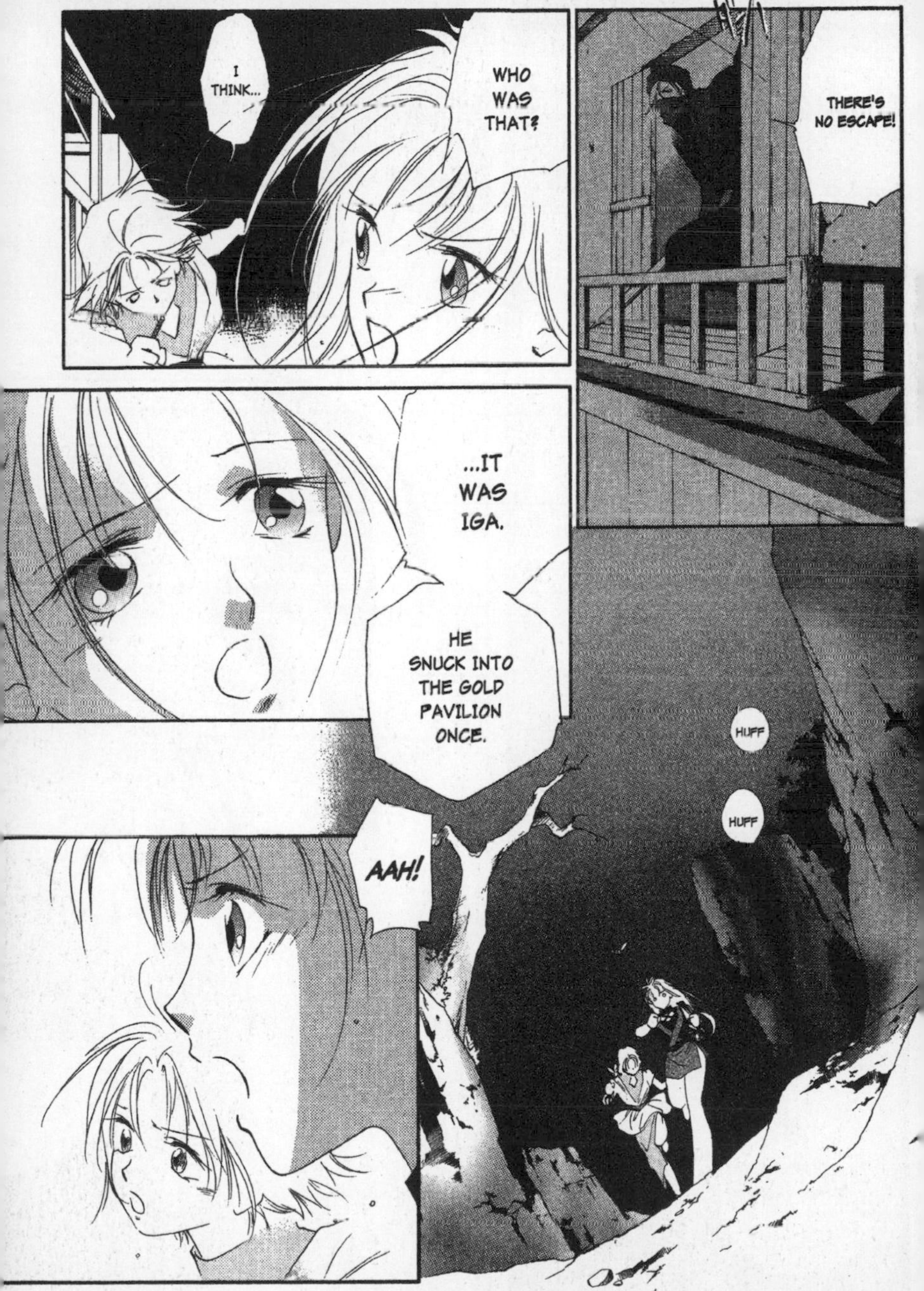
THERE'S NO ESCAPE!
WHO WAS THAT?
I THINK...
HUFF
HUFF
...IT WAS IGA.
HE SNUCK INTO THE GOLD PAVILION ONCE.
AAH!

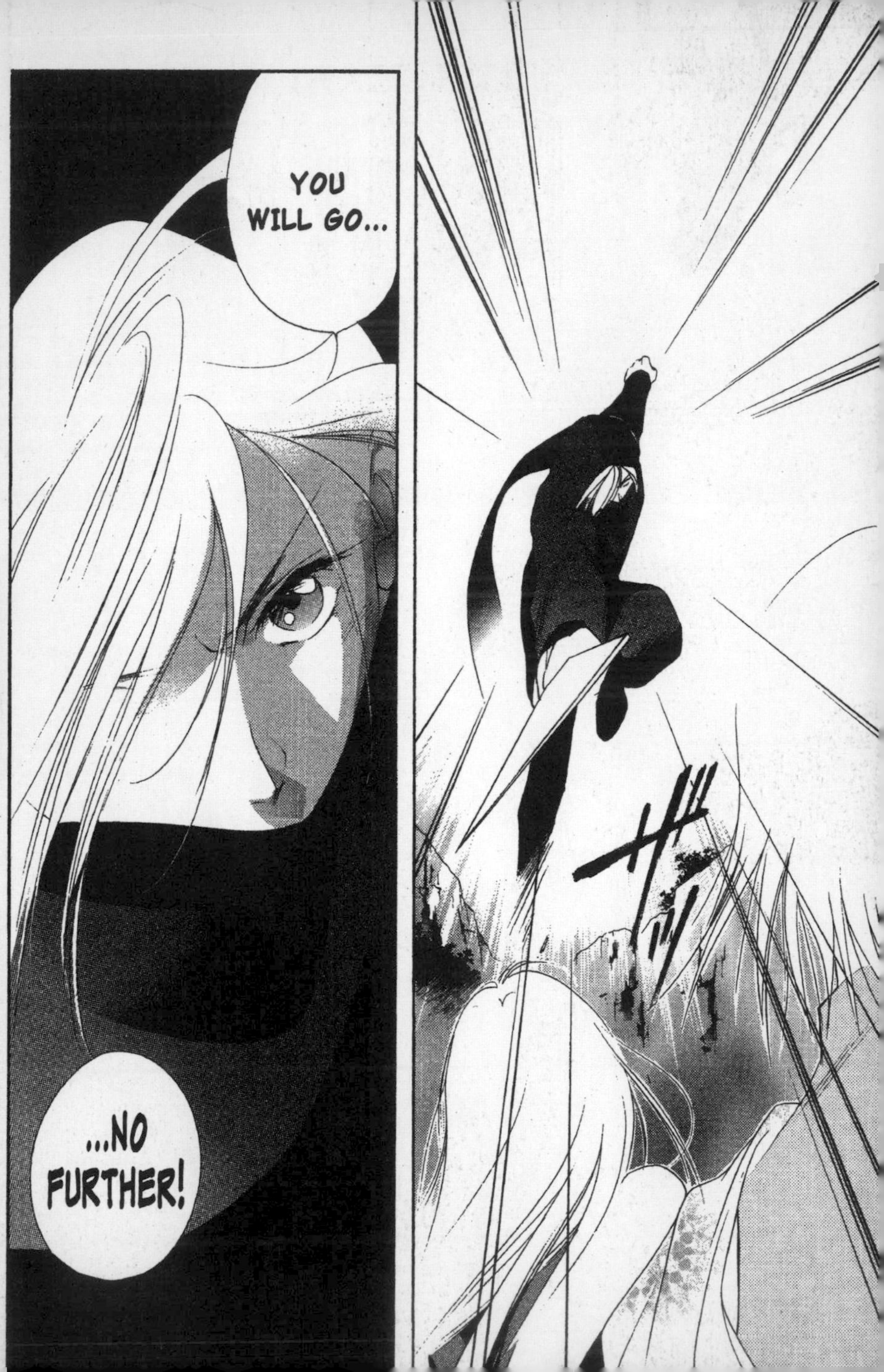
YOU WILL GO...
...NO FURTHER!

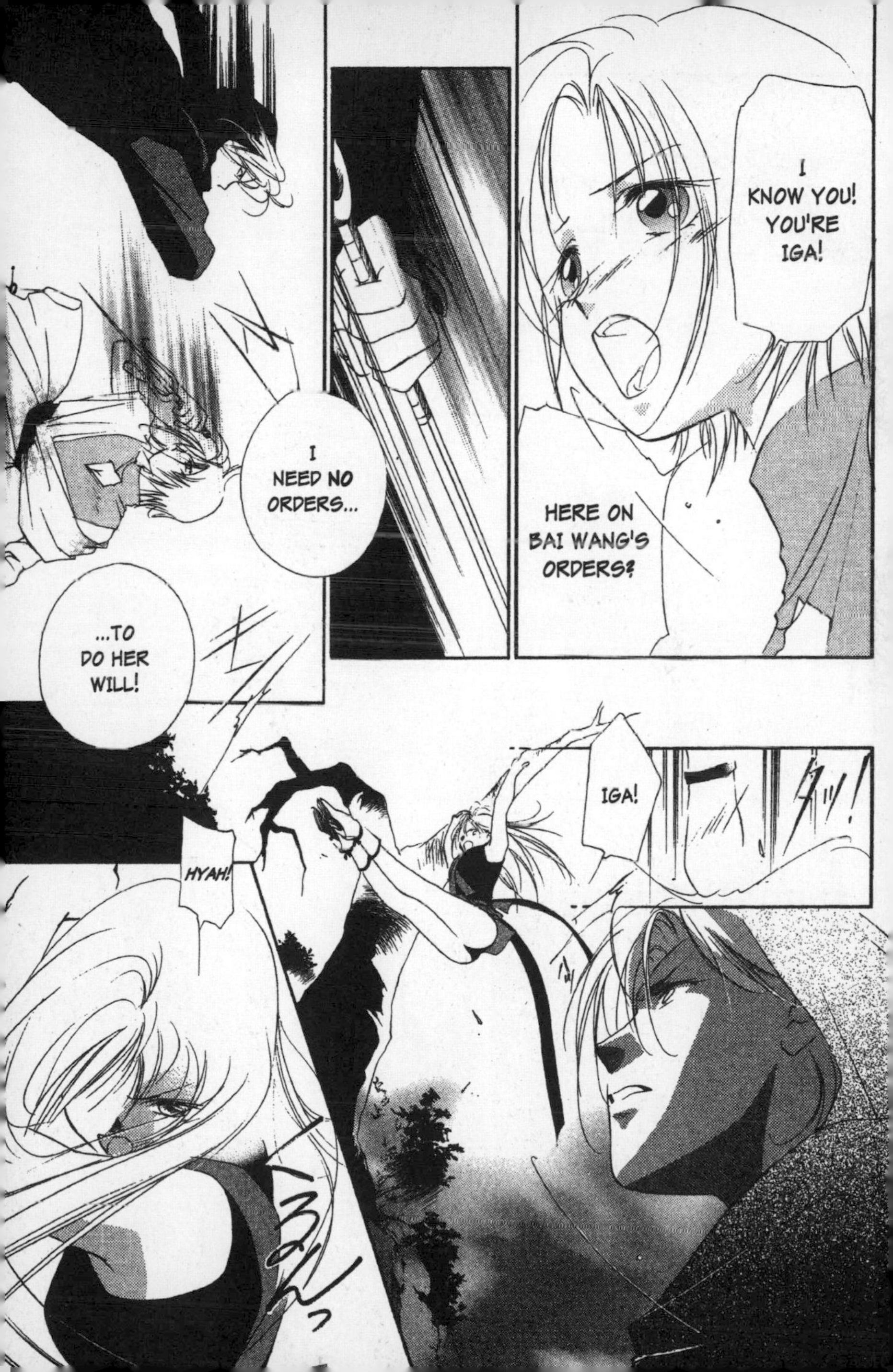
I KNOW YOU! YOU'RE IGA!
HERE ON BAI WANG'S ORDERS?
I NEED NO ORDERS...
...TO DO HER WILL!
IGA!
HYAH!

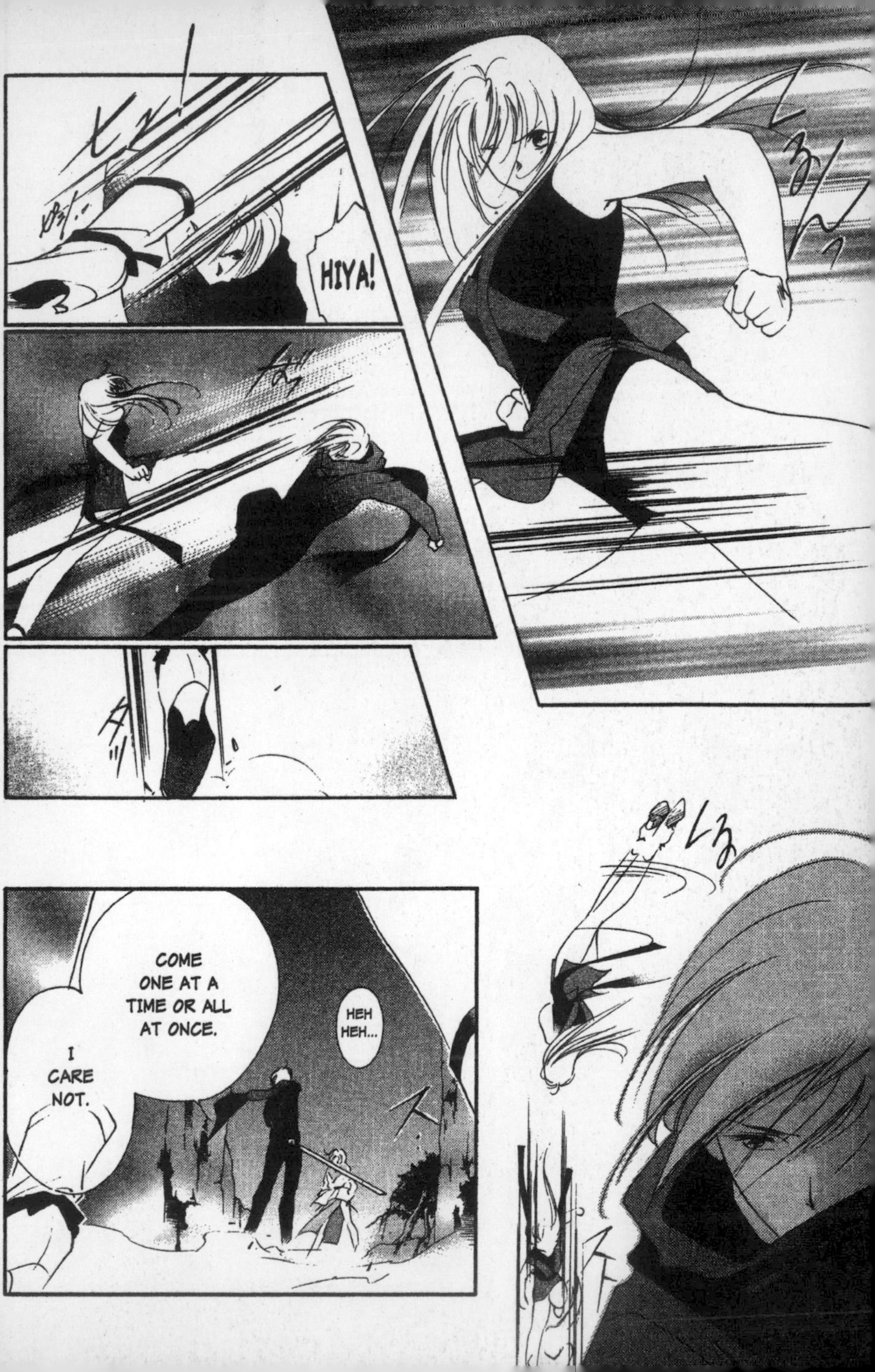
HIYA!
HEH HEH...
COME ONE AT A TIME OR ALL AT ONCE.
I CARE NOT.

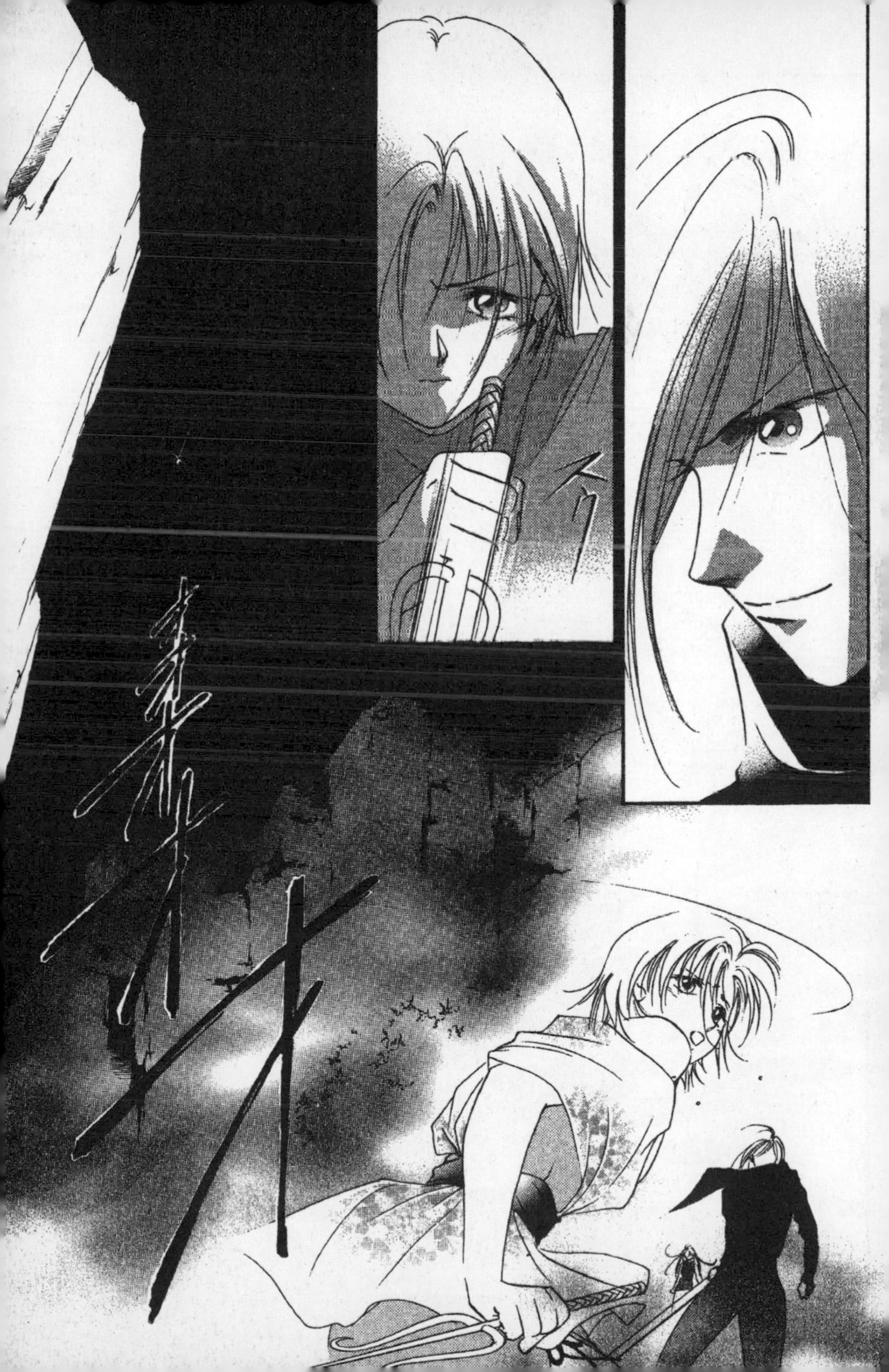

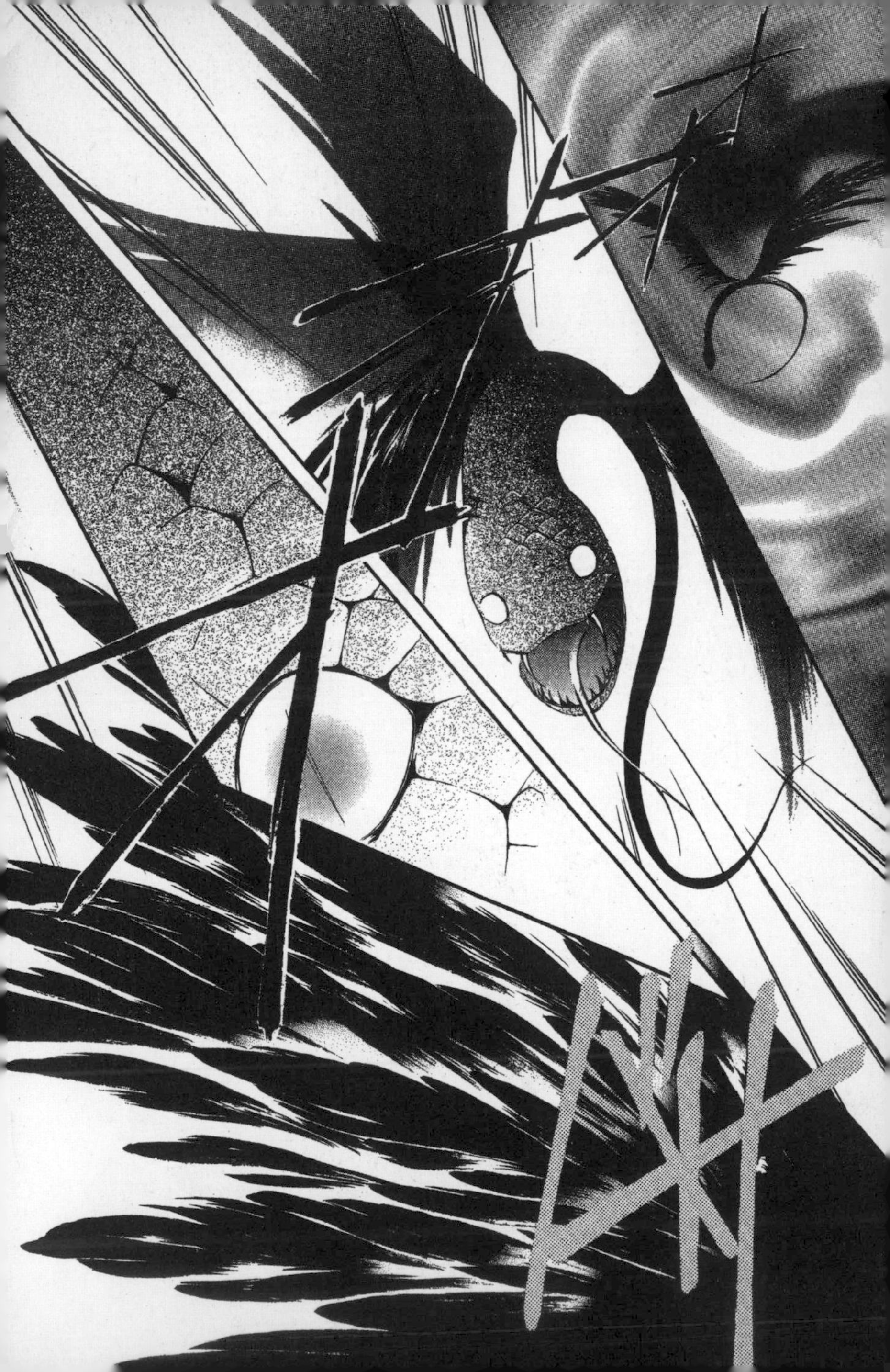

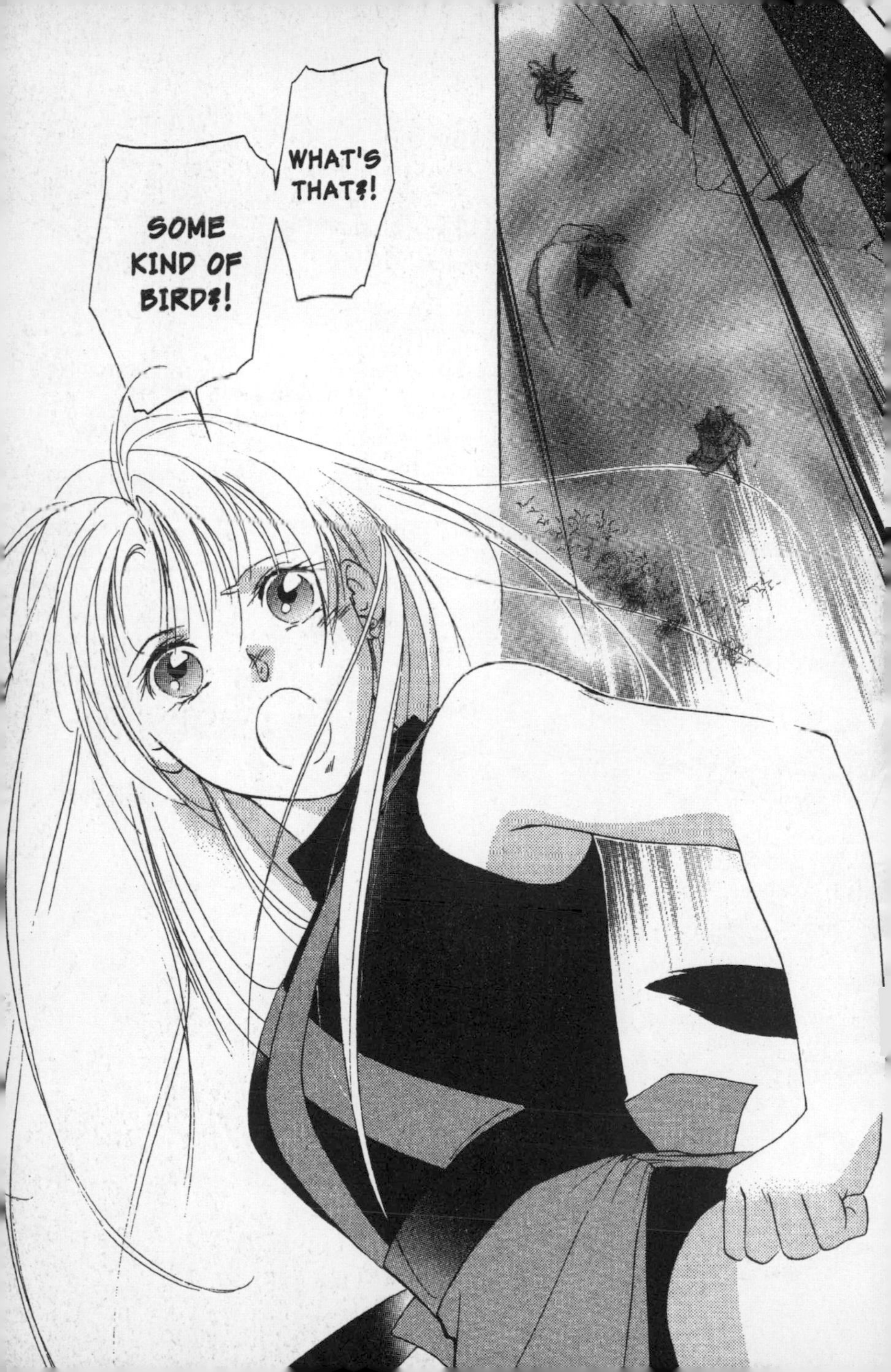
WHAT'S THAT?!
SOME KIND OF BIRD?!

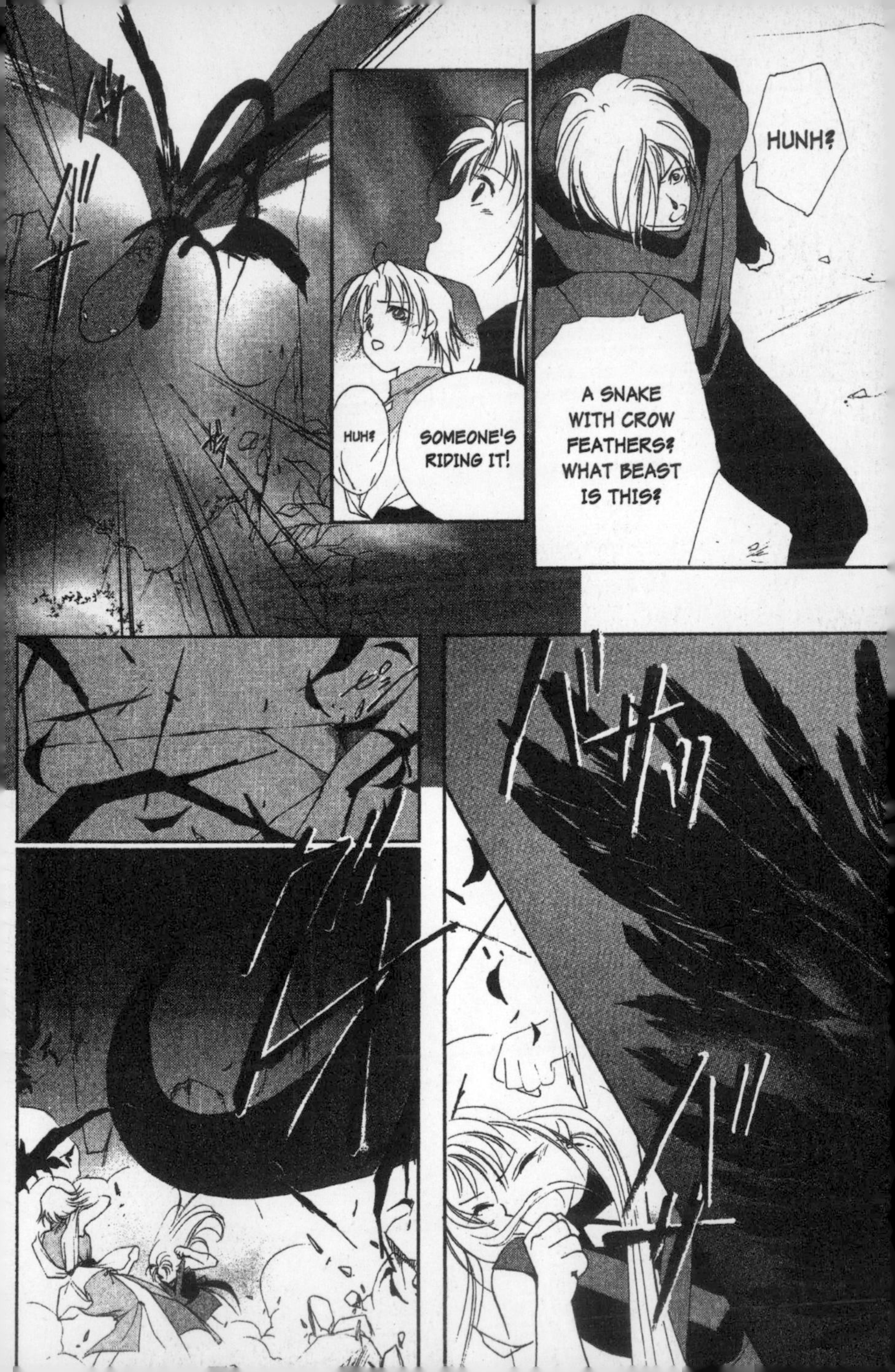
HUNH?
A SNAKE WITH CROW FEATHERS? WHAT BEAST IS THIS?
SOMEONE'S RIDING IT!
HUH?

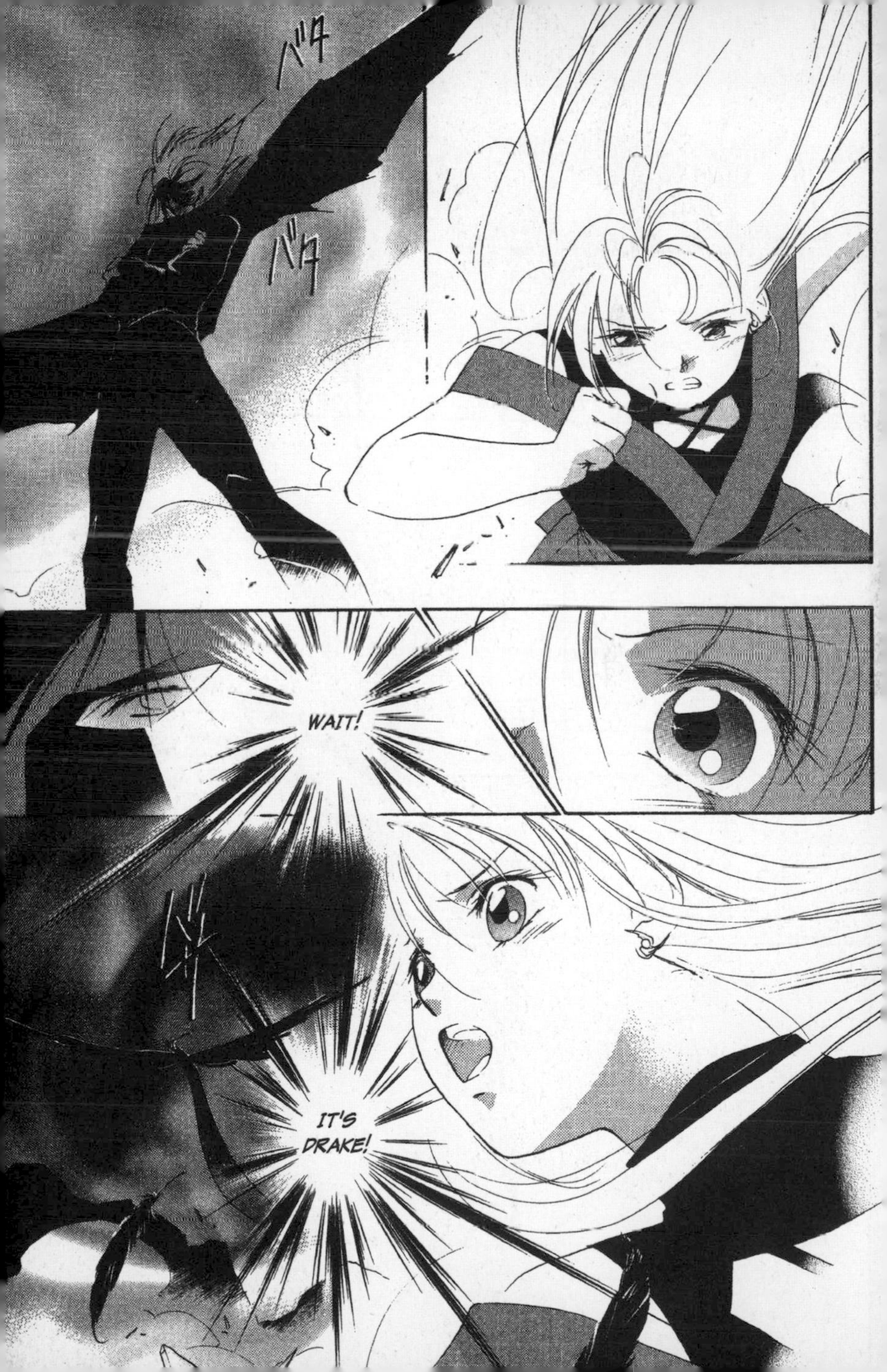
バタ
バタ
WAIT!
IT'S DRAKE!

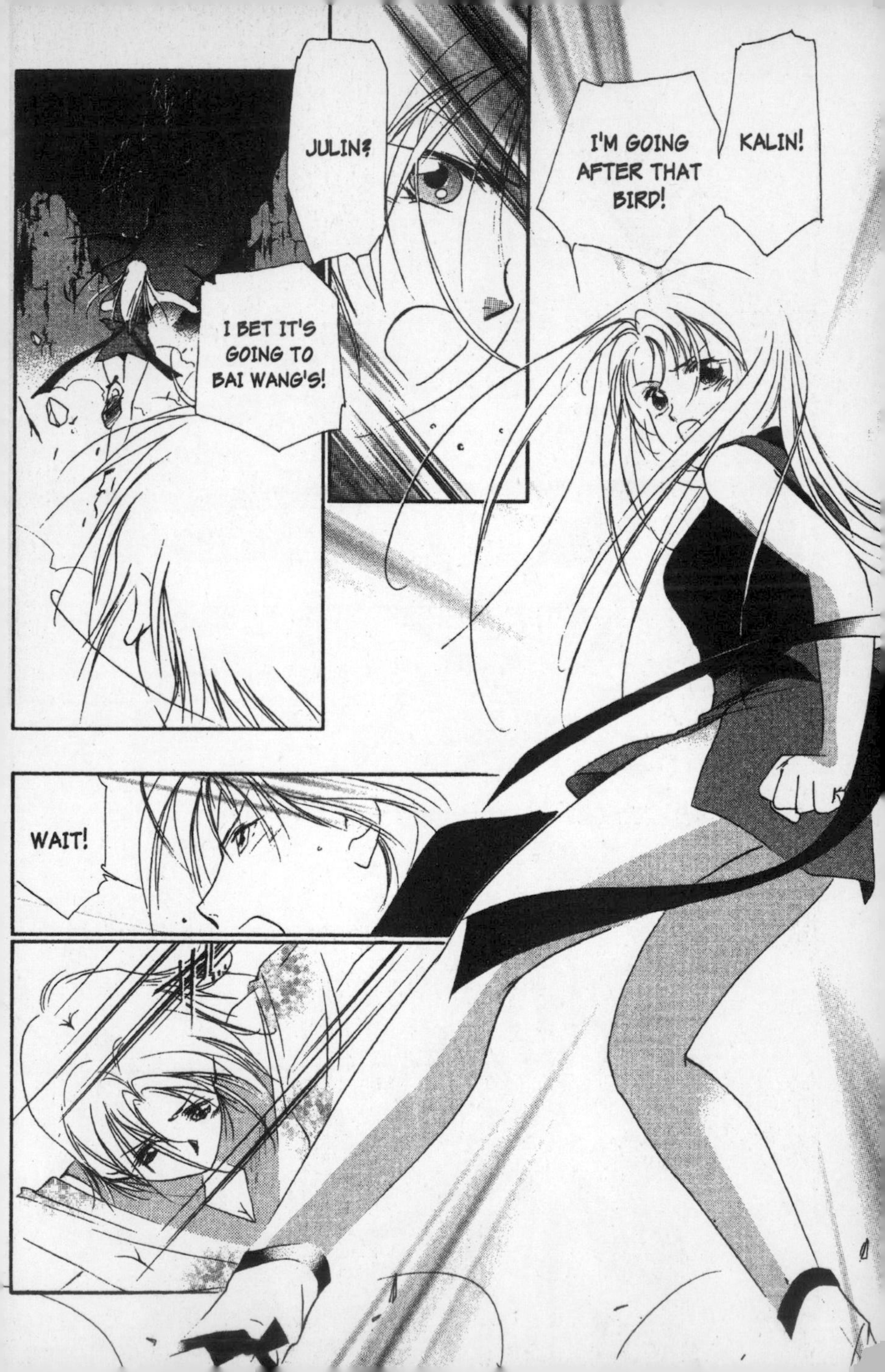
KALIN!
I'M GOING AFTER THAT BIRD!
JULIN?
I BET IT'S GOING TO BAI WANG'S!
WAIT!

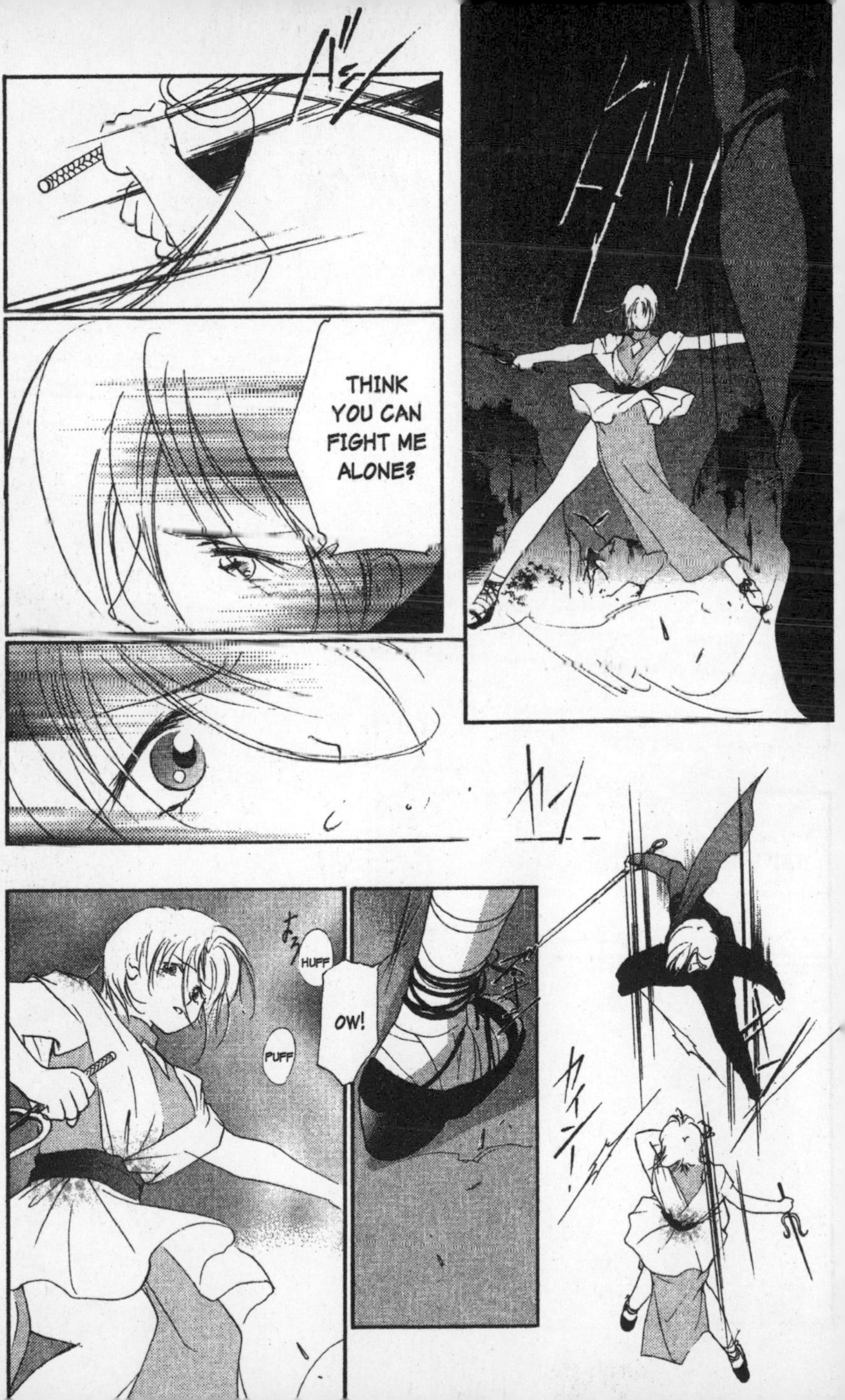
THINK YOU CAN FIGHT ME ALONE?
OW!
HUFF
PUFF

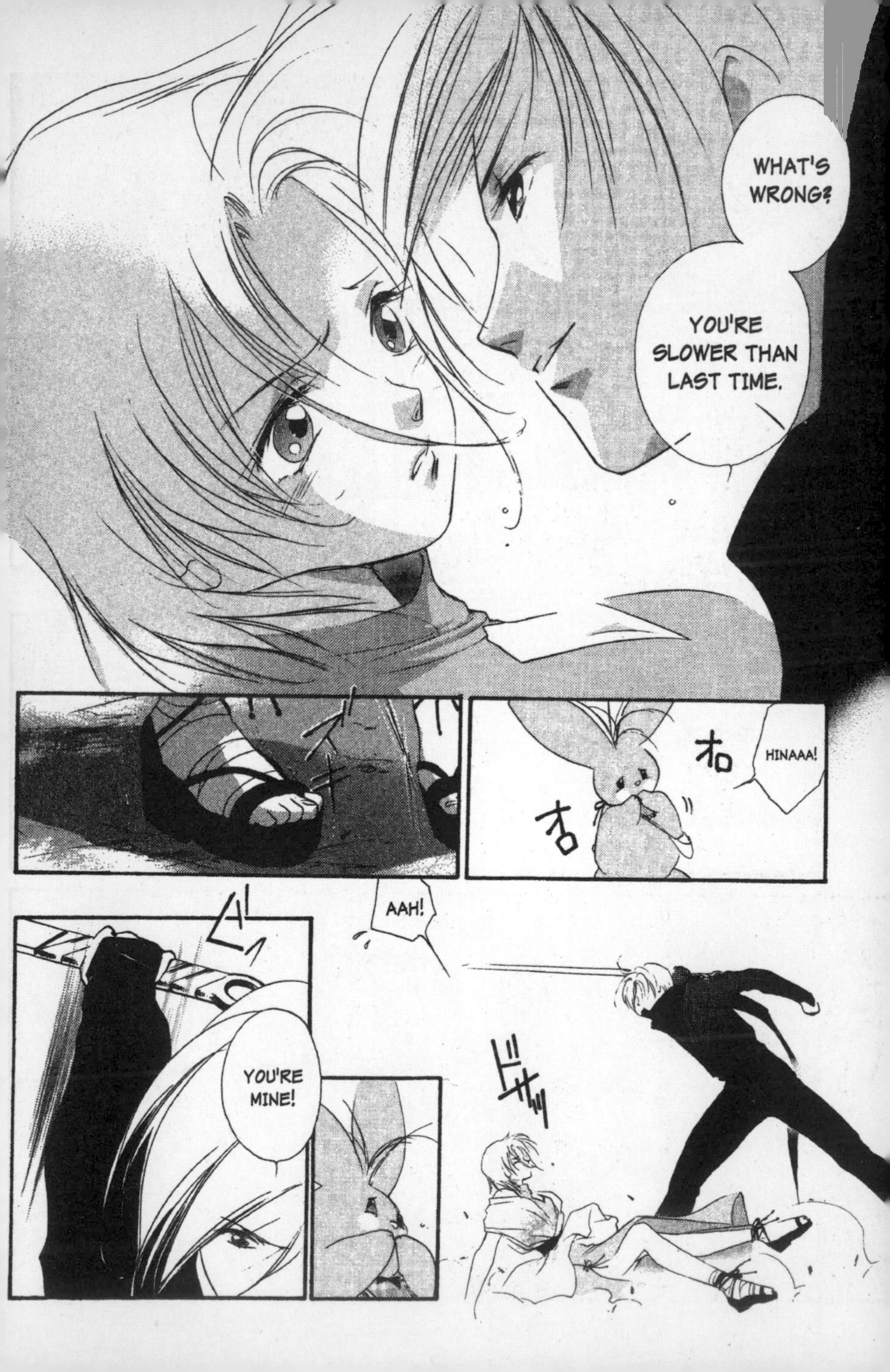
WHAT'S WRONG?
YOU'RE SLOWER THAN LAST TIME.
オロ
オロ
HINAAA!
AAH!
YOU'RE MINE!

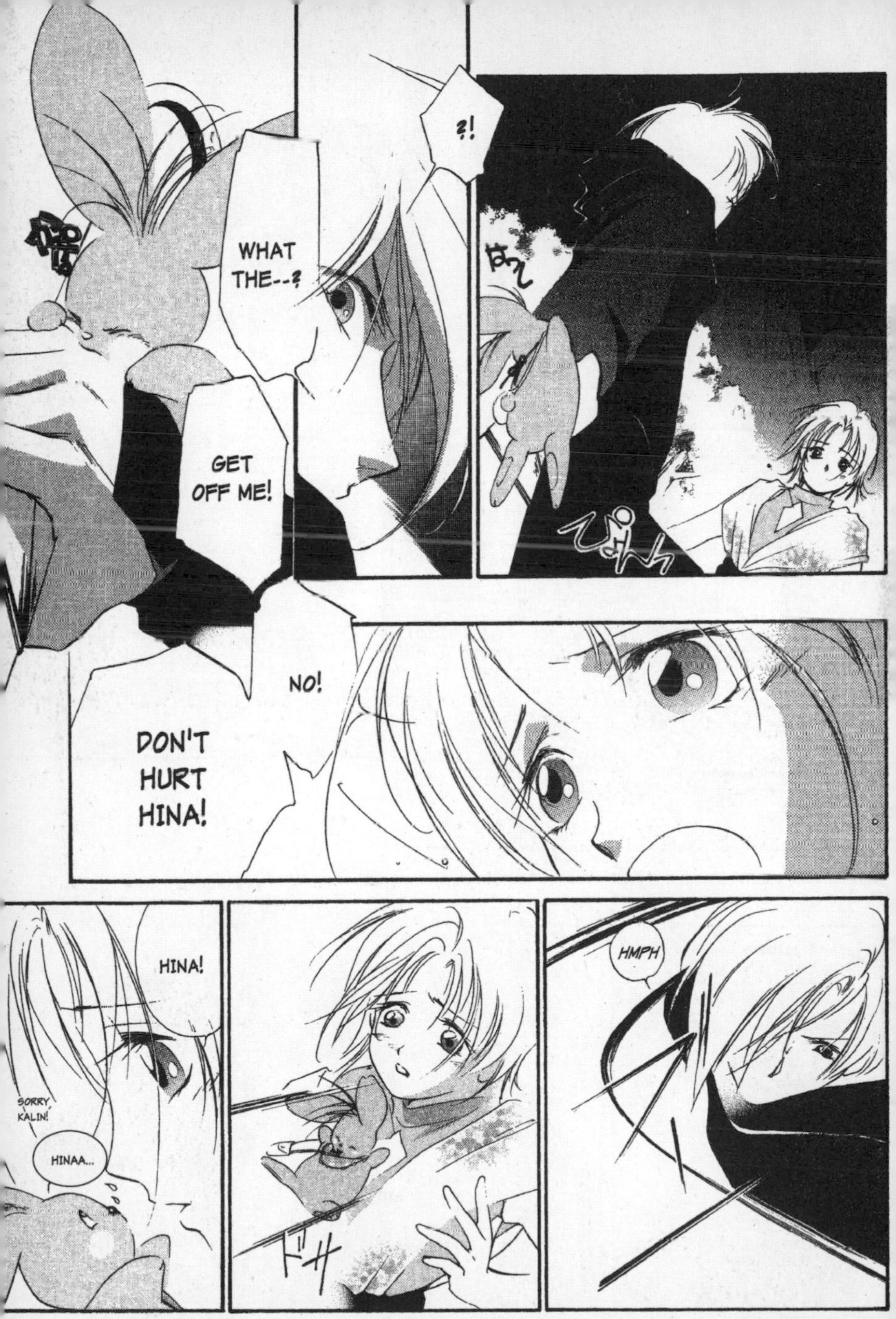
?!
WHAT THE--?
GET OFF ME!
NO!
DON'T HURT HINA!
HMPH
HINA!
SORRY KALIN!
HINAA...

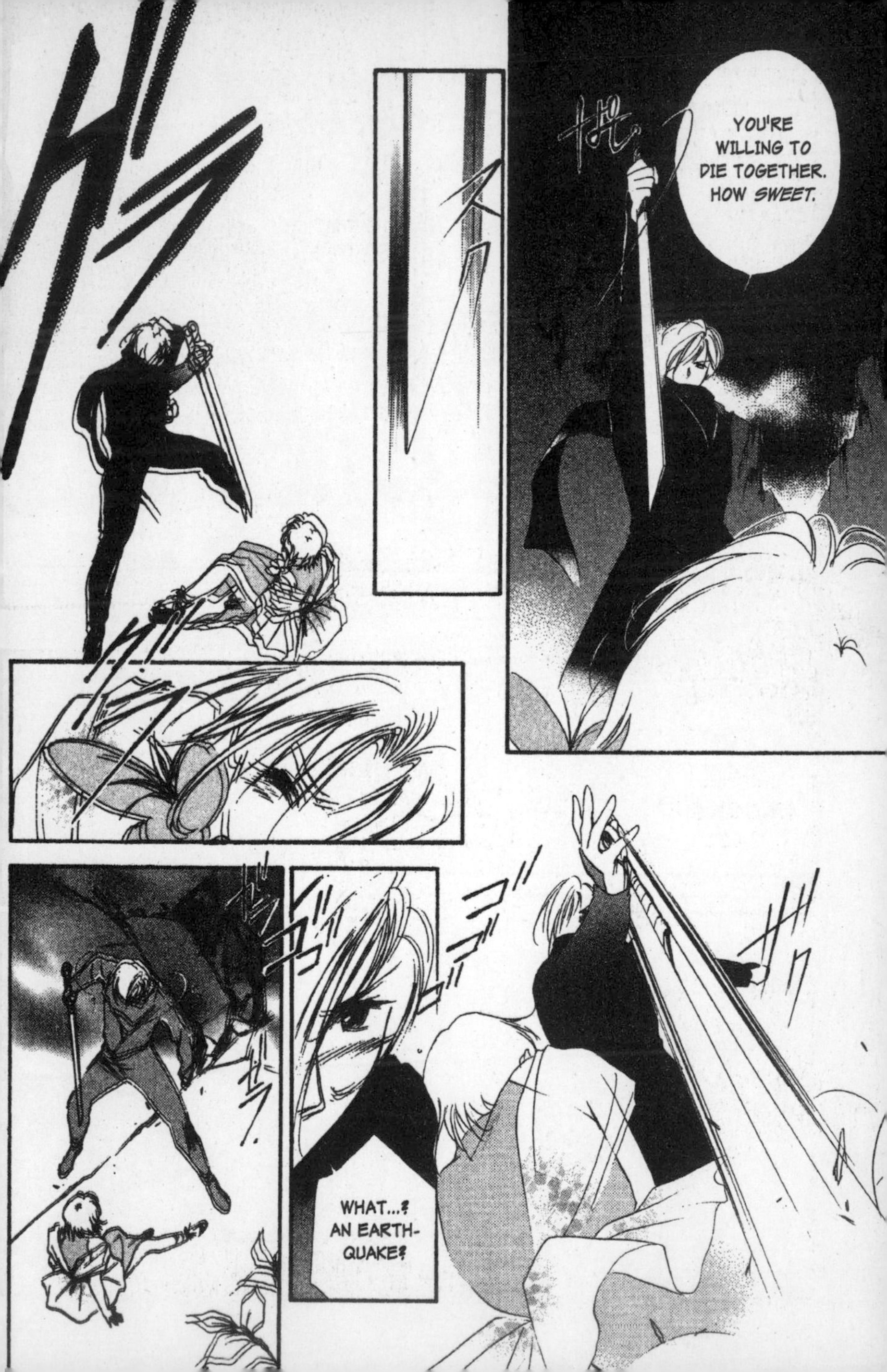
YOU'RE WILLING TO DIE TOGETHER. HOW *SWEET.*
WHAT...? AN EARTH-QUAKE?

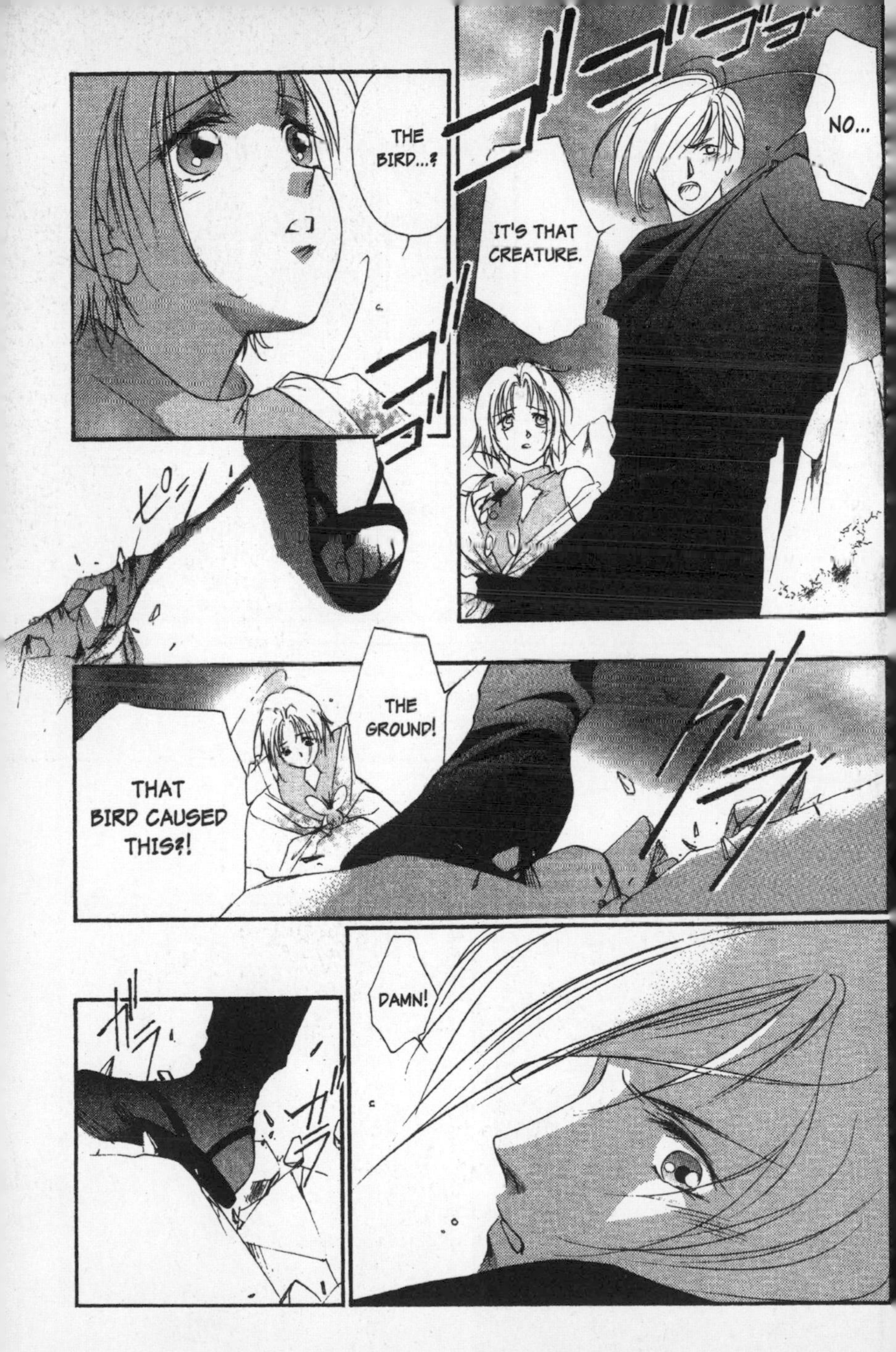
NO...
IT'S THAT CREATURE.
THE BIRD...?
THE GROUND!
THAT BIRD CAUSED THIS?!
DAMN!

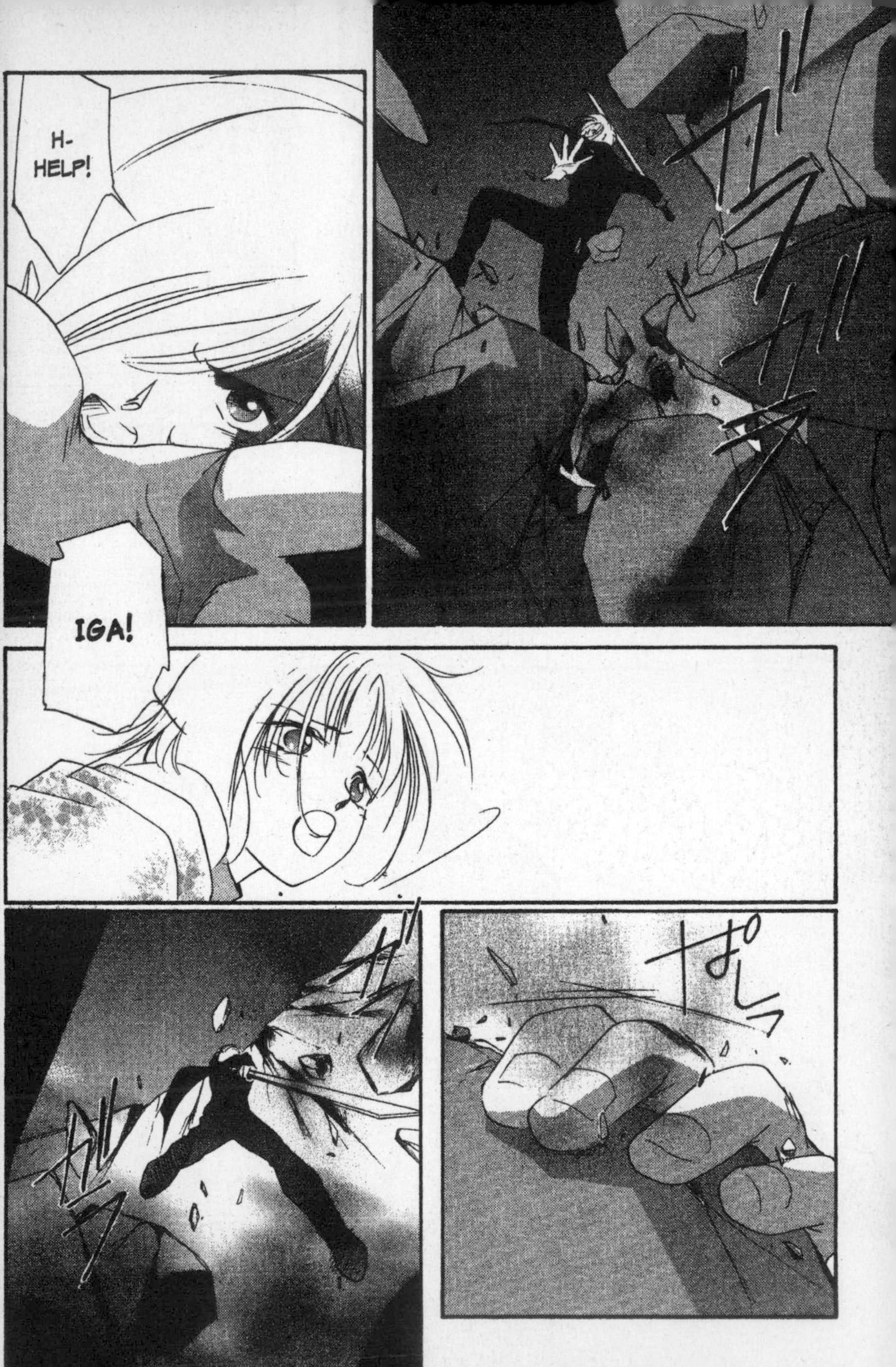
H-
HELP!
IGA!

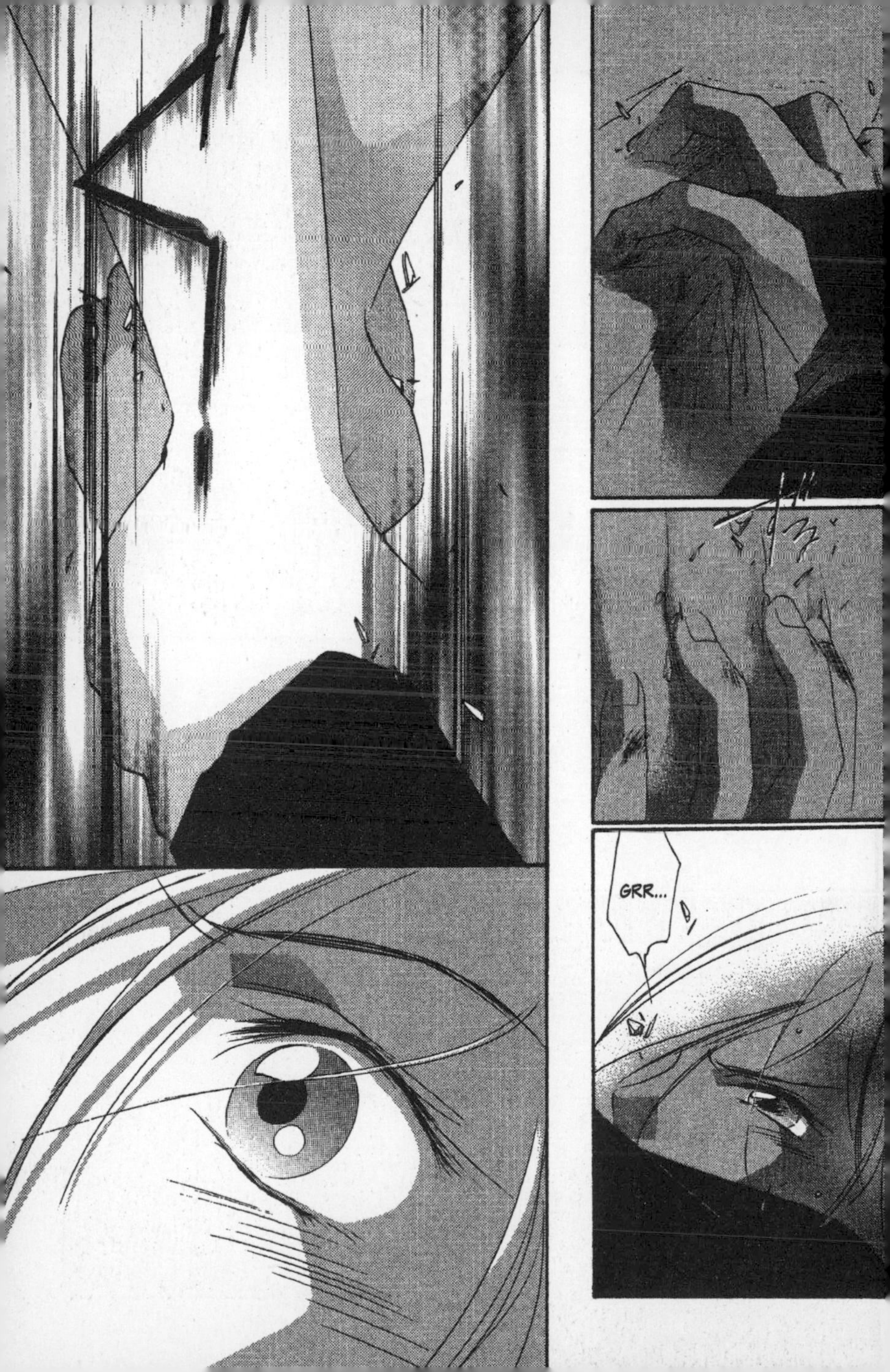
GRR...

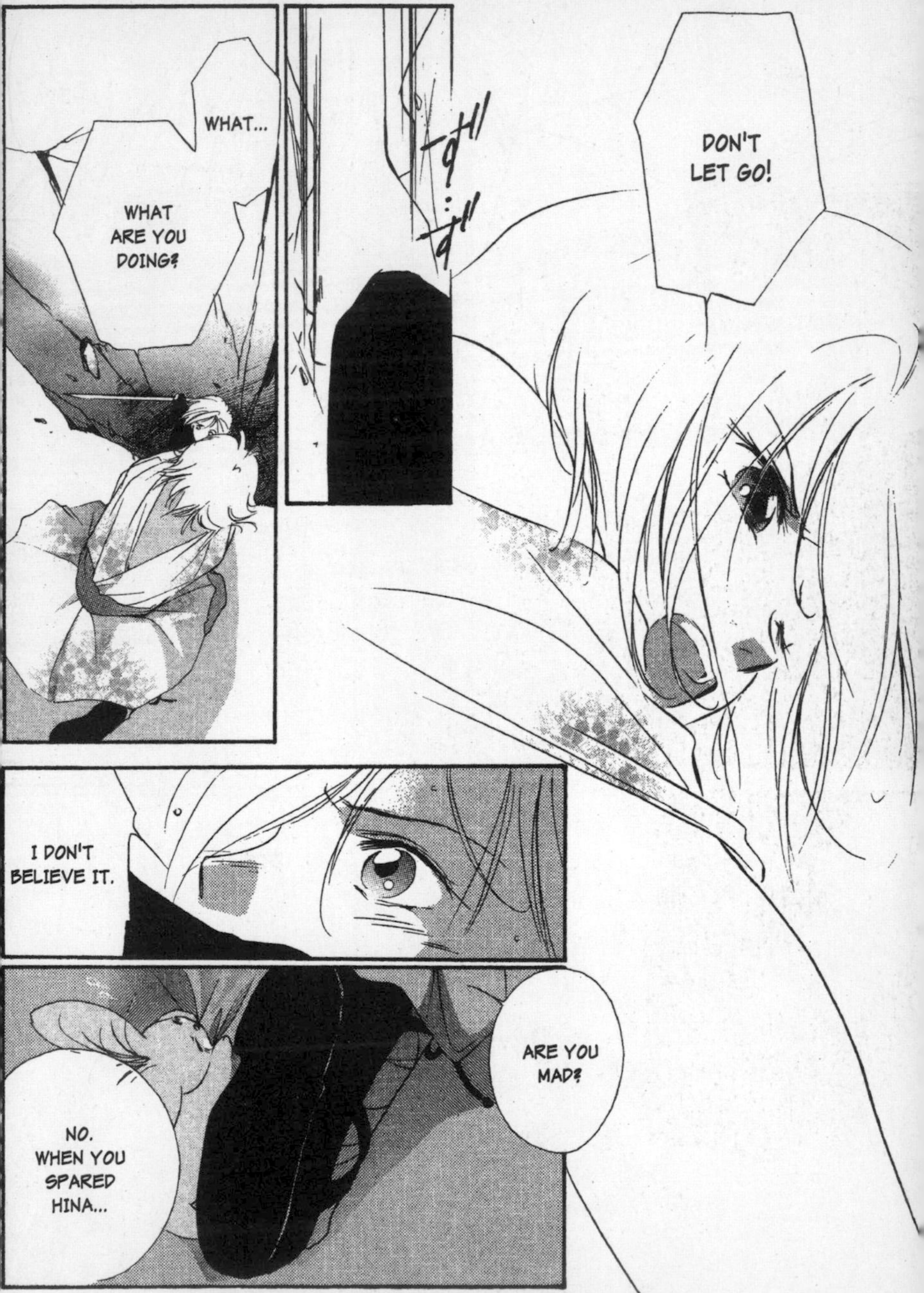
DON'T LET GO!
WHAT...
WHAT ARE YOU DOING?
I DON'T BELIEVE IT.
ARE YOU MAD?
NO. WHEN YOU SPARED HINA...

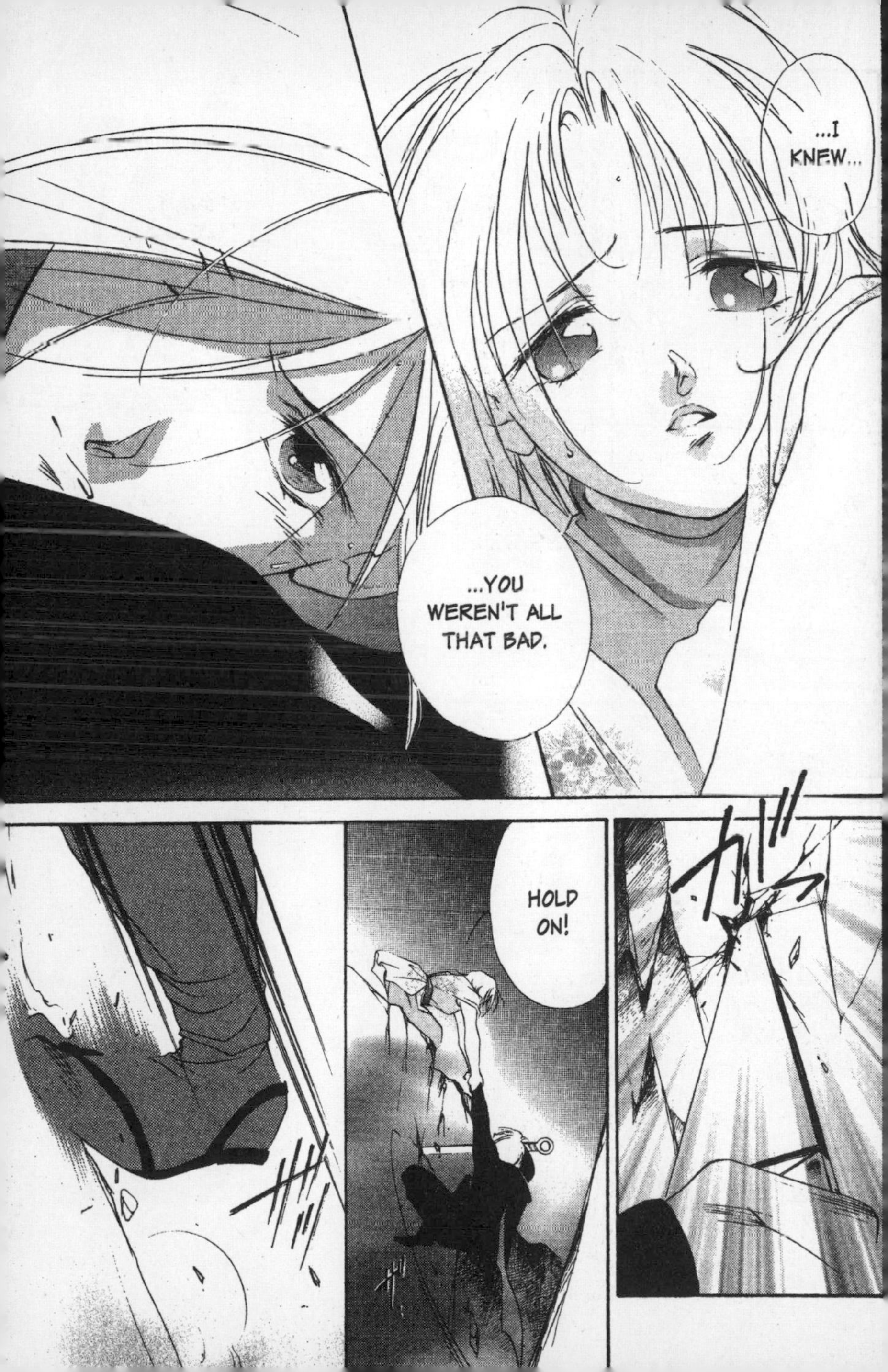
...I KNEW...
...YOU WEREN'T ALL THAT BAD.
HOLD ON!

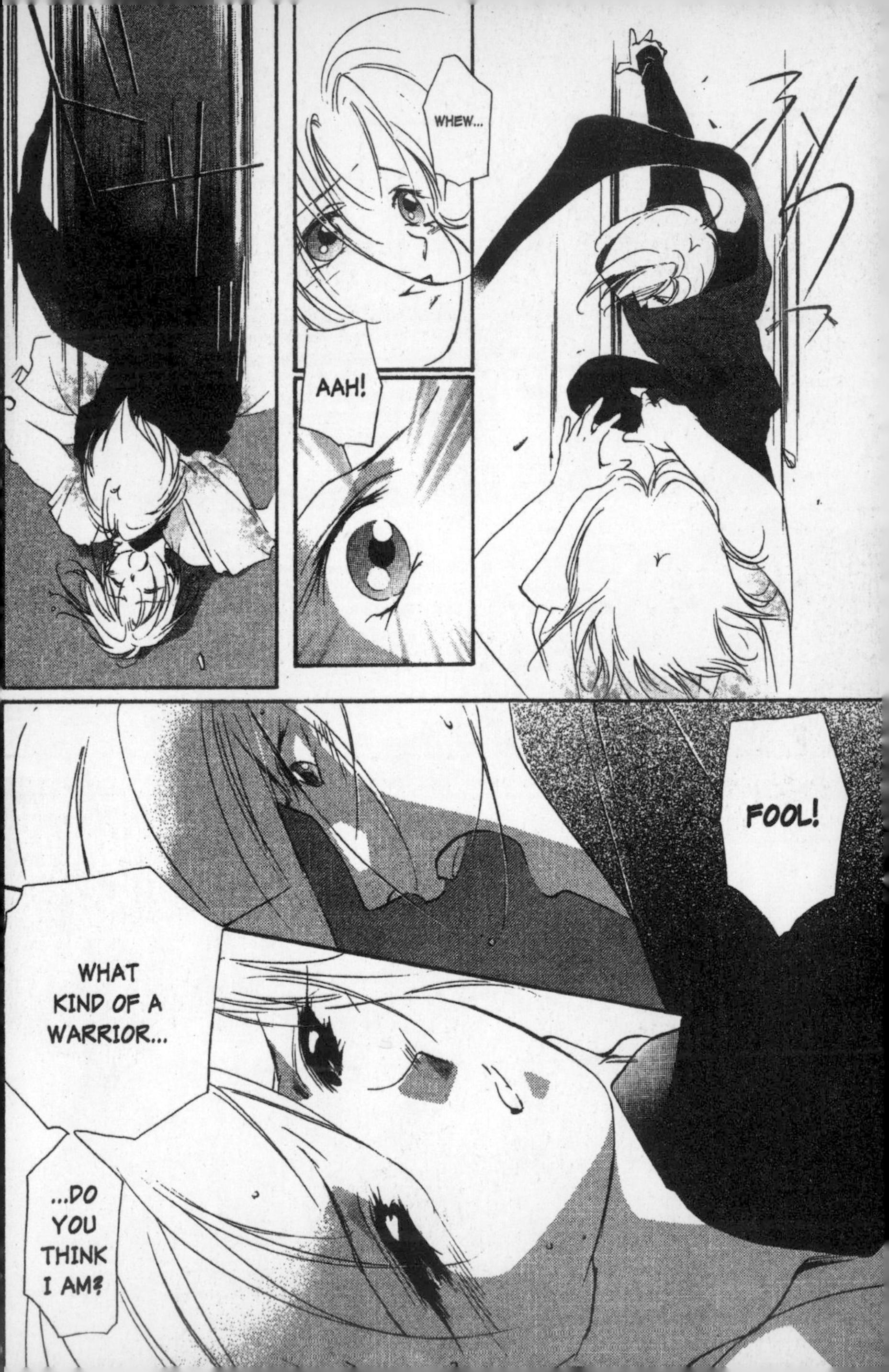
WHEW...
AAH!
FOOL!
WHAT KIND OF A WARRIOR...
...DO YOU THINK I AM?

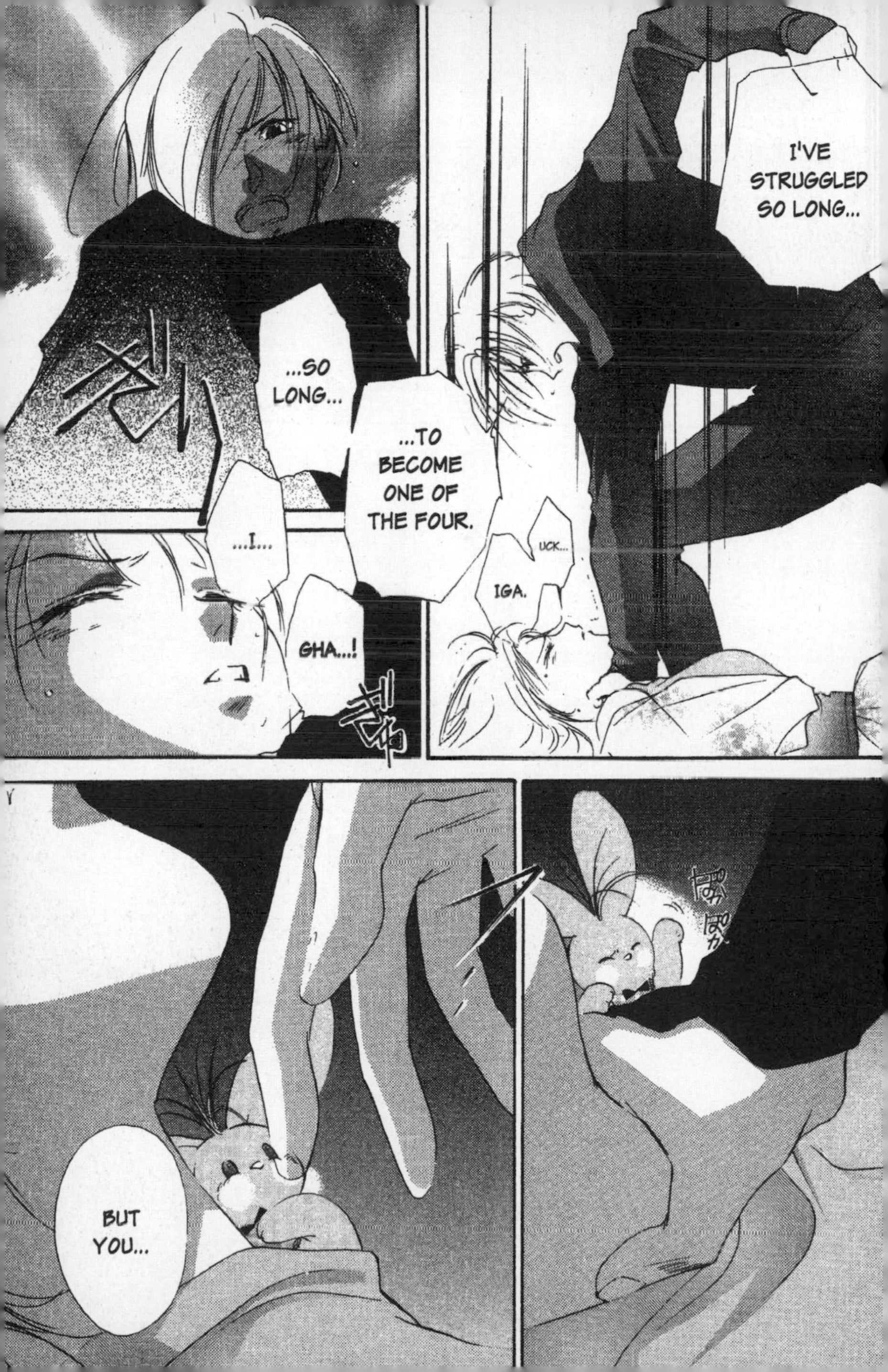
I'VE STRUGGLED SO LONG...
...SO LONG...
...TO BECOME ONE OF THE FOUR.
UCK...
IGA.
...I...
GHA...!
BUT YOU...

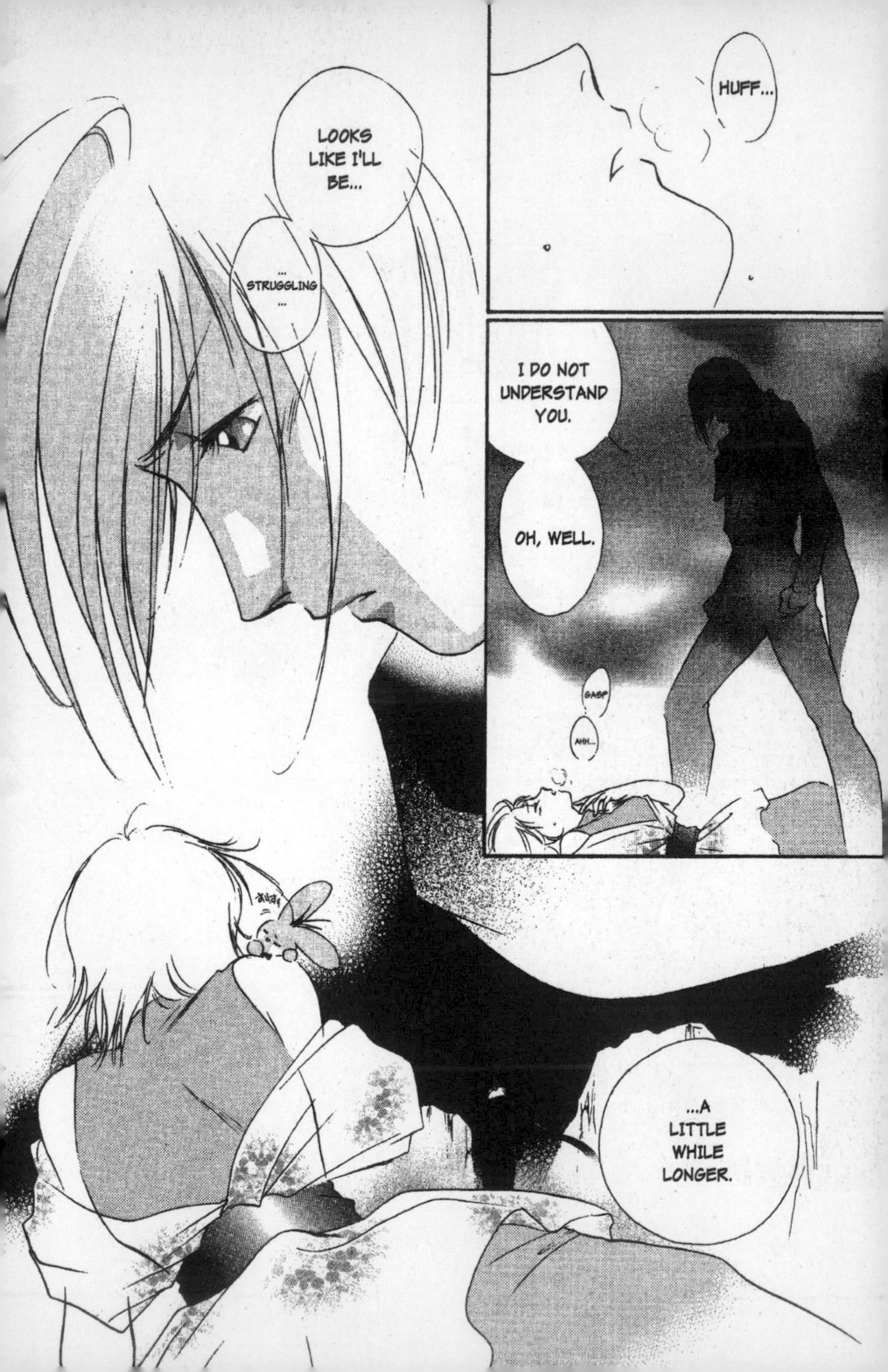
HUFF...
I DO NOT UNDERSTAND YOU.
OH, WELL.
GASP
AHH...
LOOKS LIKE I'LL BE...
... STRUGGLING ...
...A LITTLE WHILE LONGER.

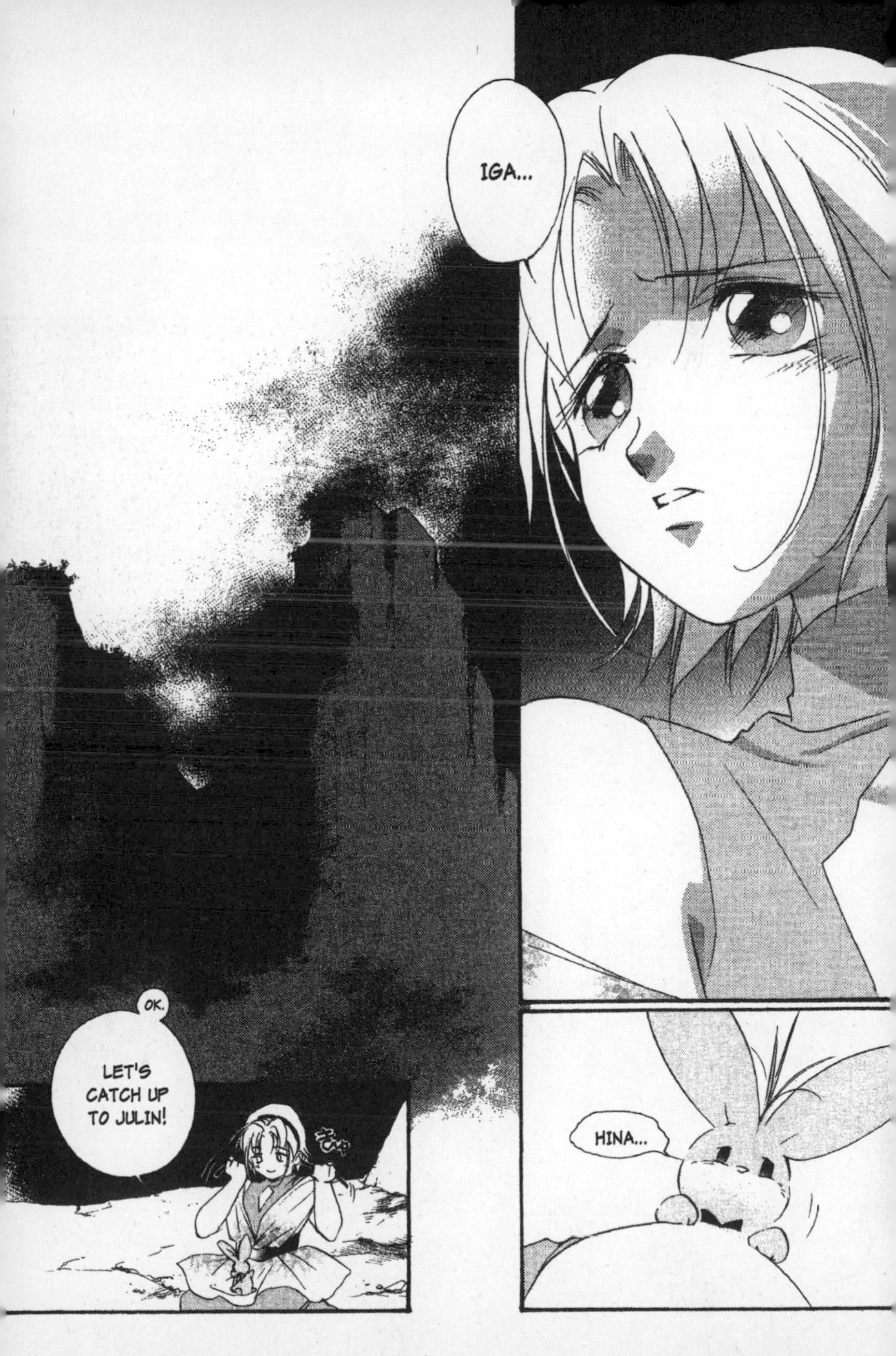
IGA...
HINA...
OK.
LET'S CATCH UP TO JULIN!

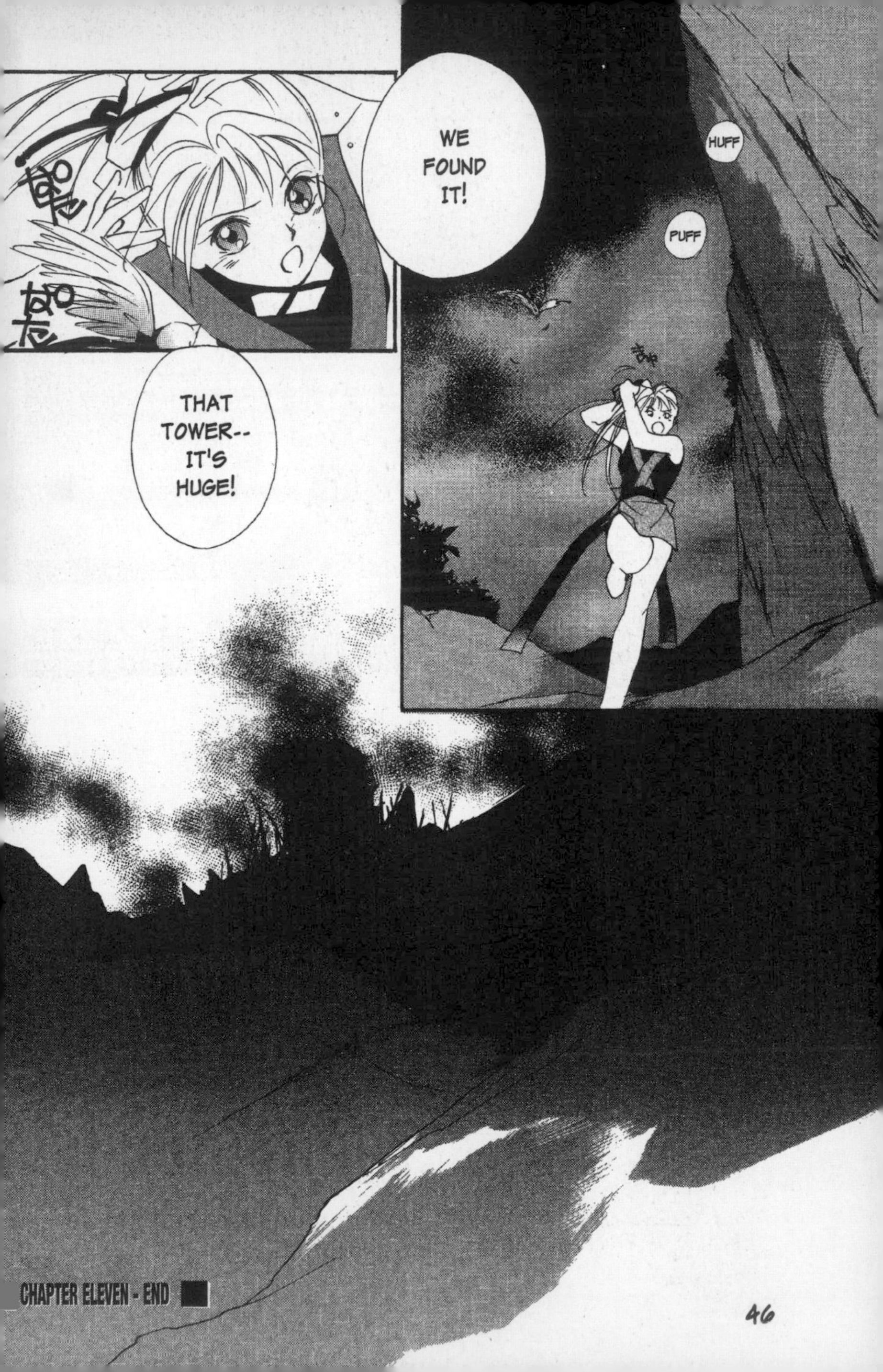
HUFF
PUFF
WE FOUND IT!
THAT TOWER-- IT'S HUGE!
CHAPTER ELEVEN - END

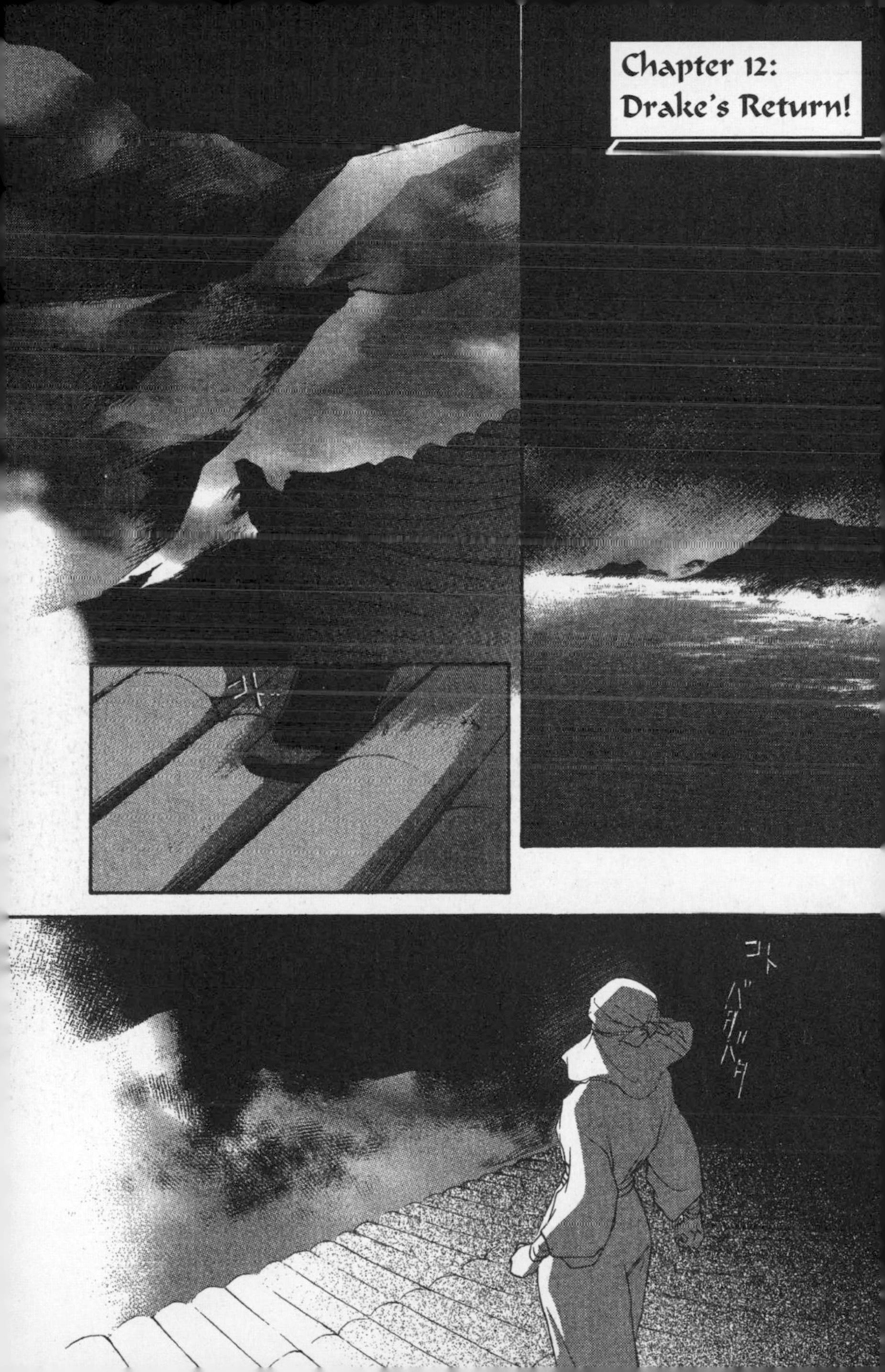
Chapter 12:
Drake's Return!
コト…
コト
バタバタ

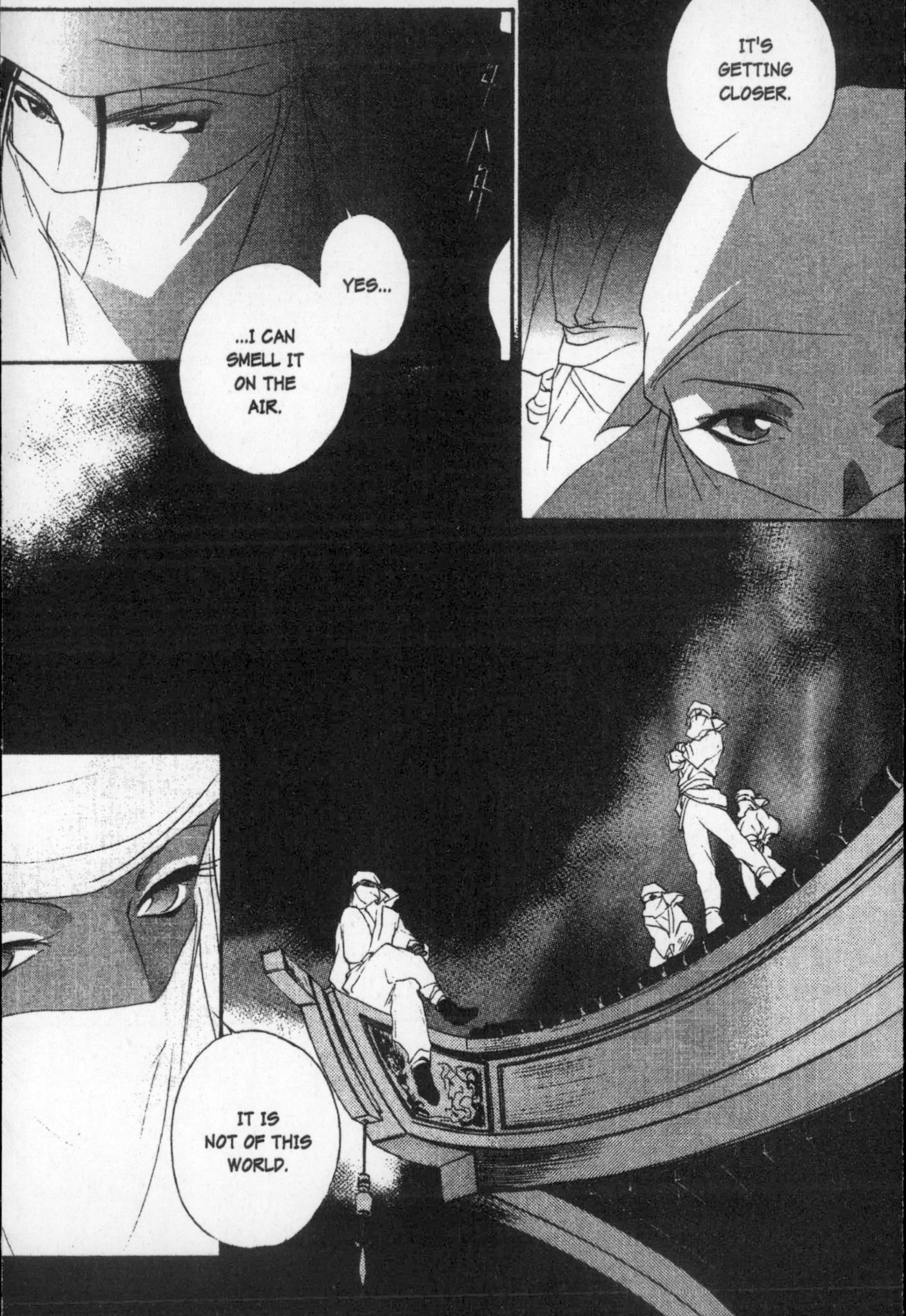
IT'S GETTING CLOSER.
YES...
...I CAN SMELL IT ON THE AIR.
IT IS NOT OF THIS WORLD.

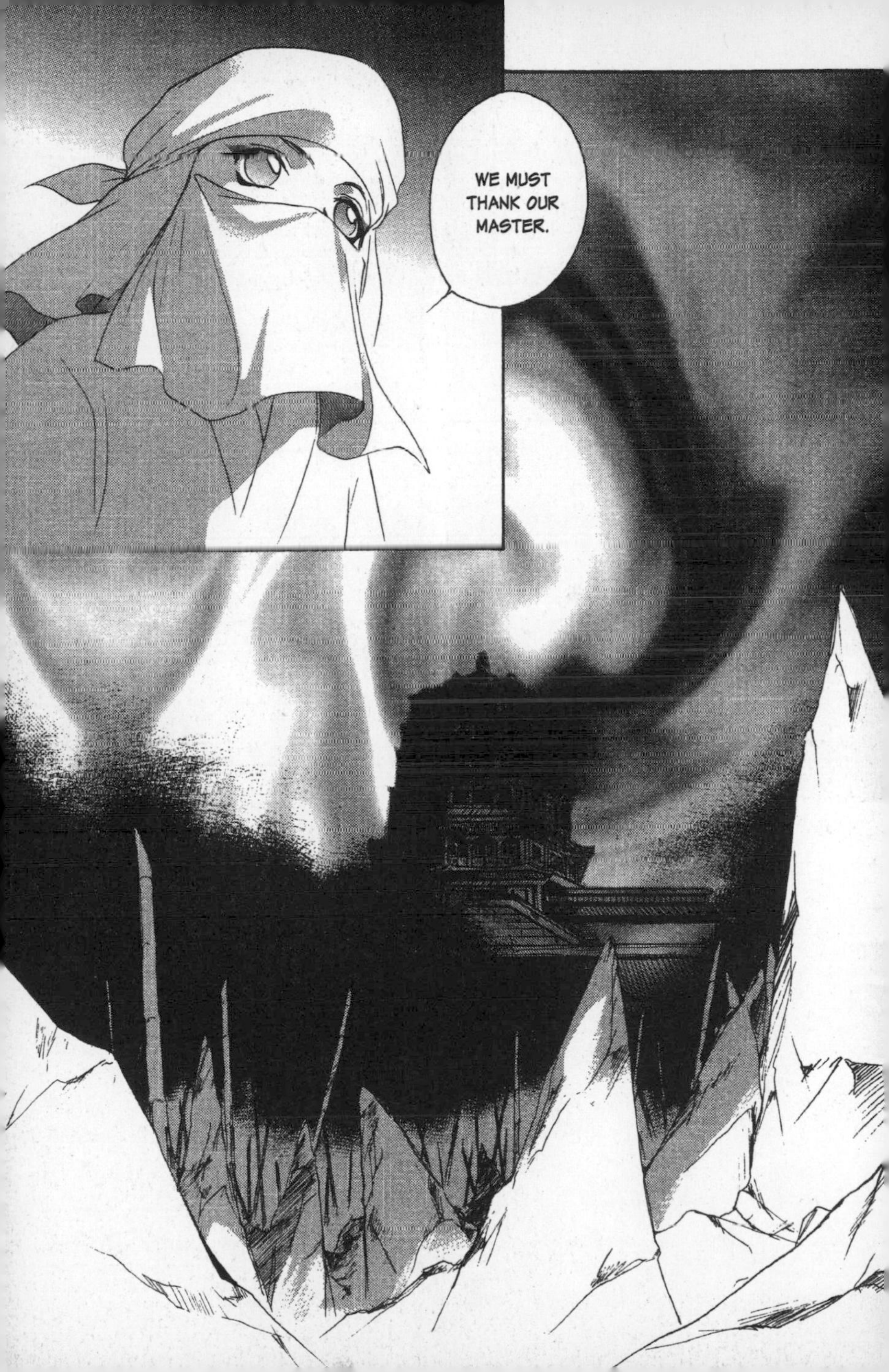
WE MUST THANK OUR MASTER.

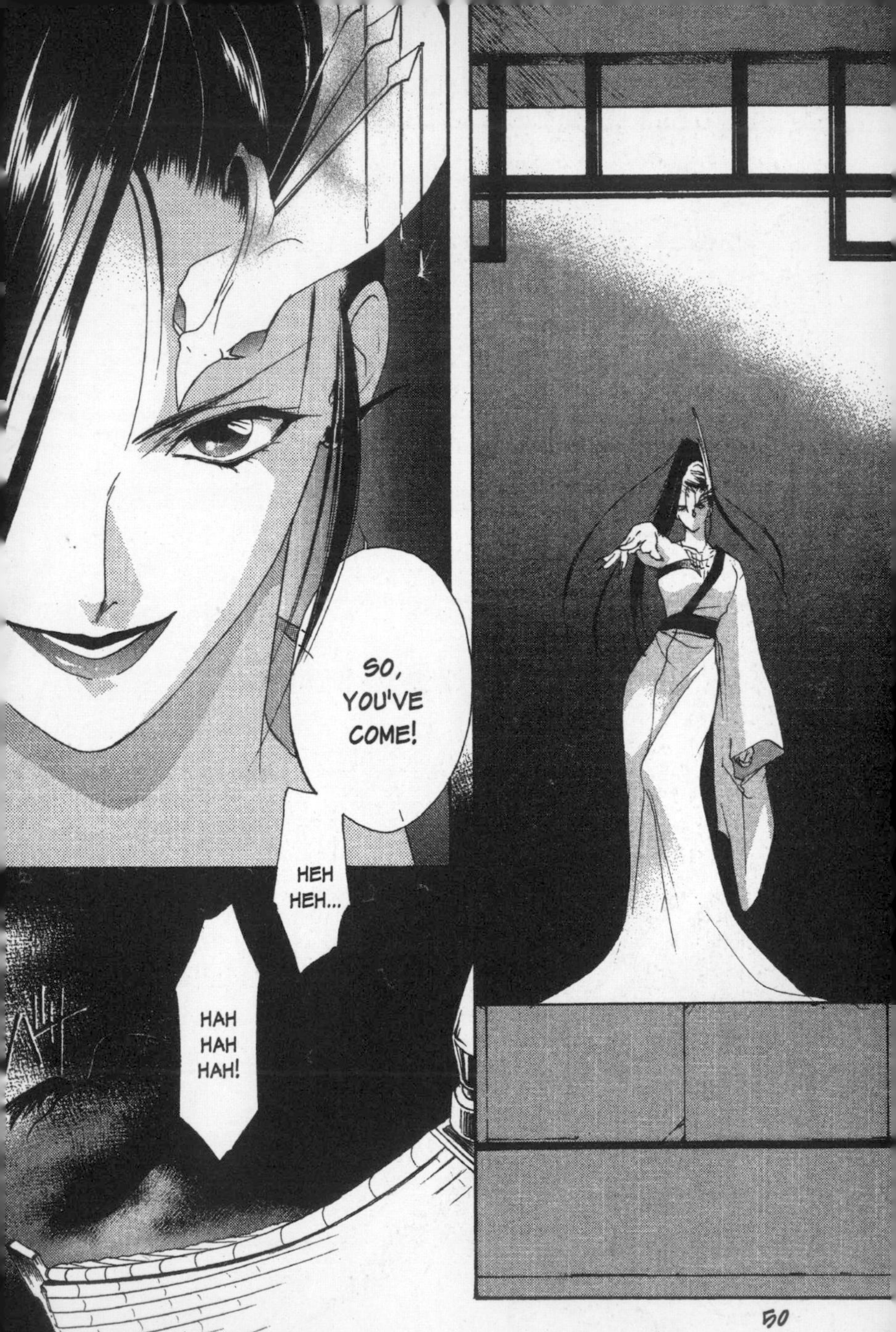
SO, YOU'VE COME!
HEH HEH...
HAH HAH HAH!

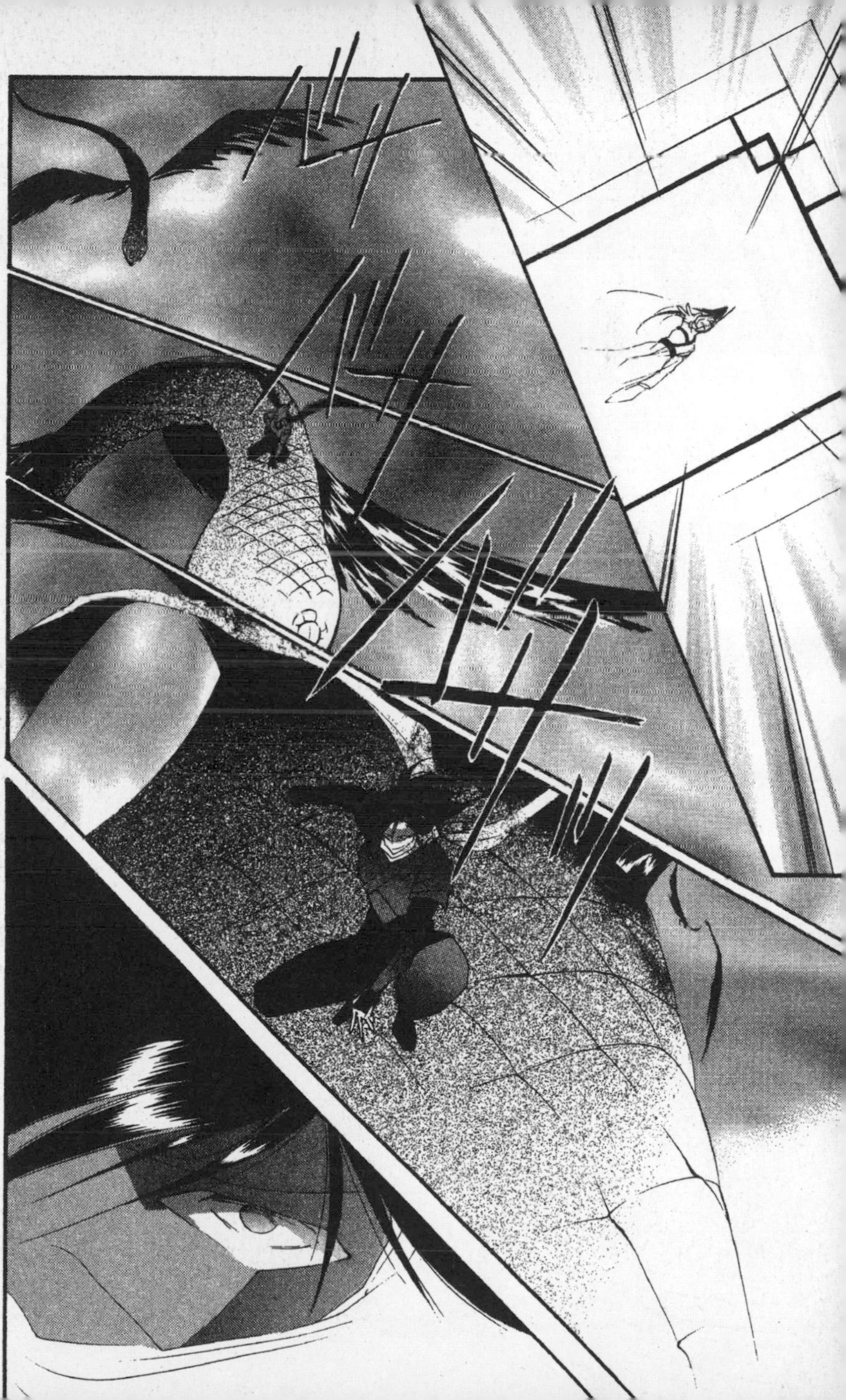

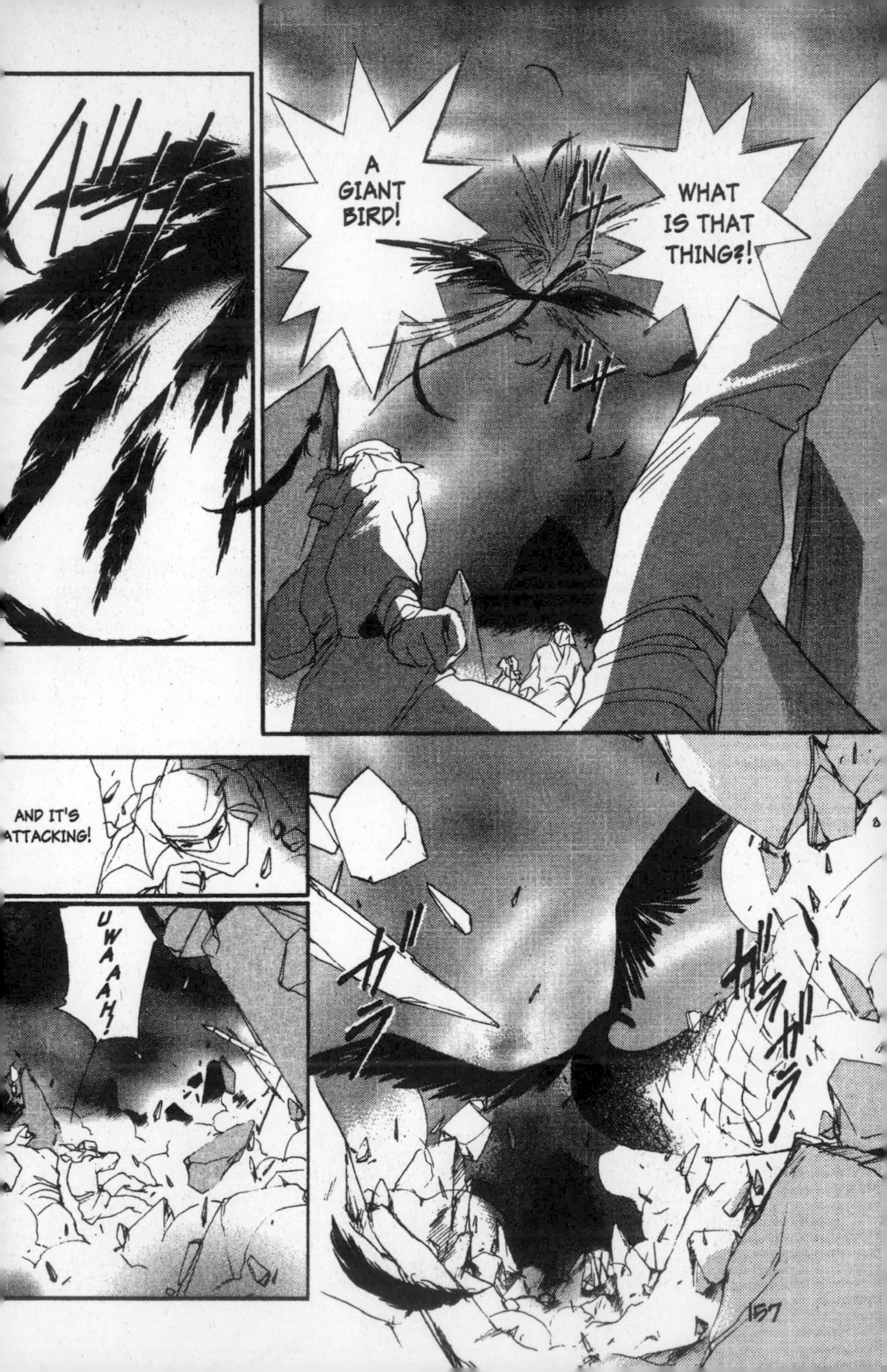
WHAT IS THAT THING?!
A GIANT BIRD!
AND IT'S ATTACKING!
UWAAAAH!

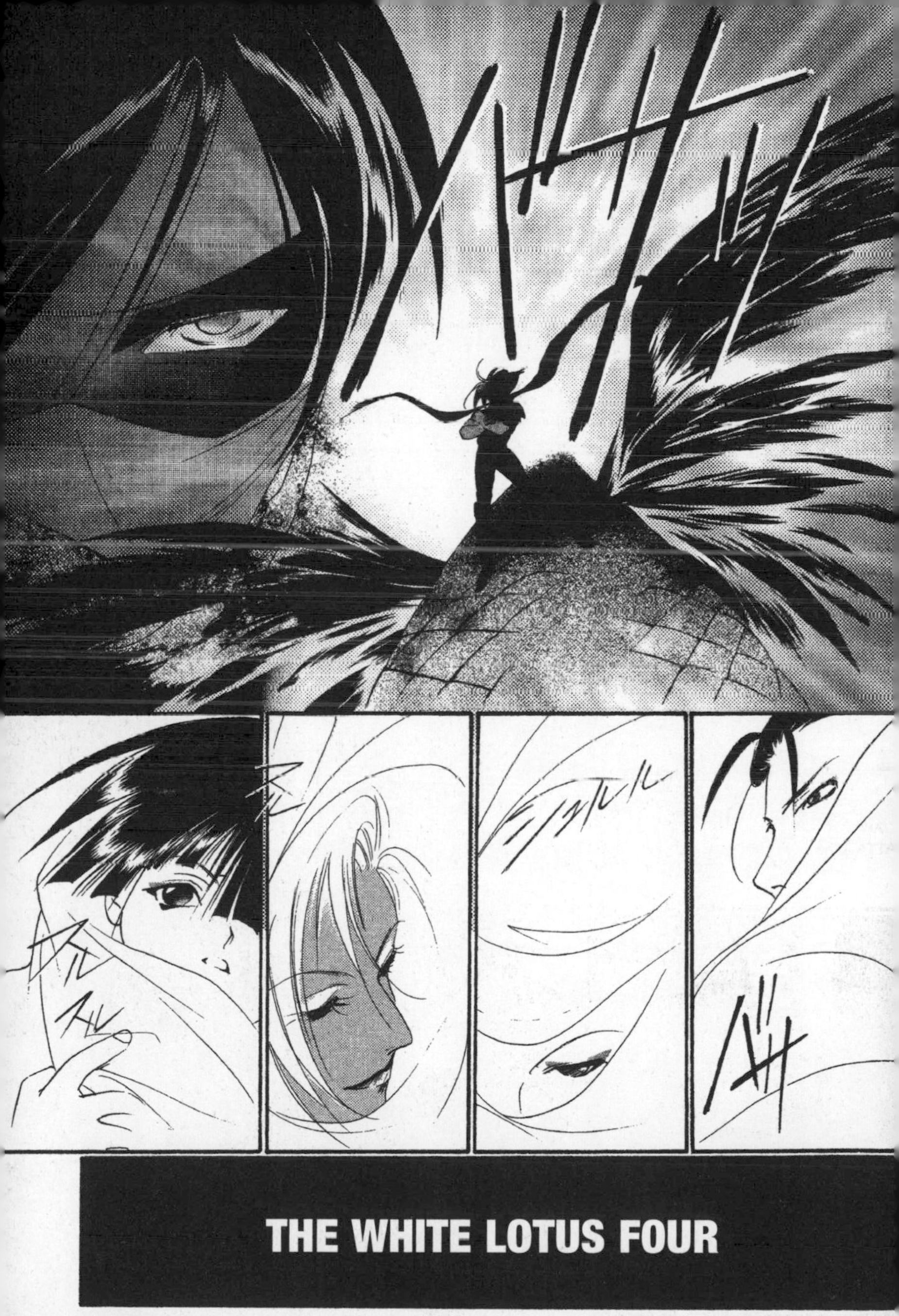

THE WHITE LOTUS FOUR

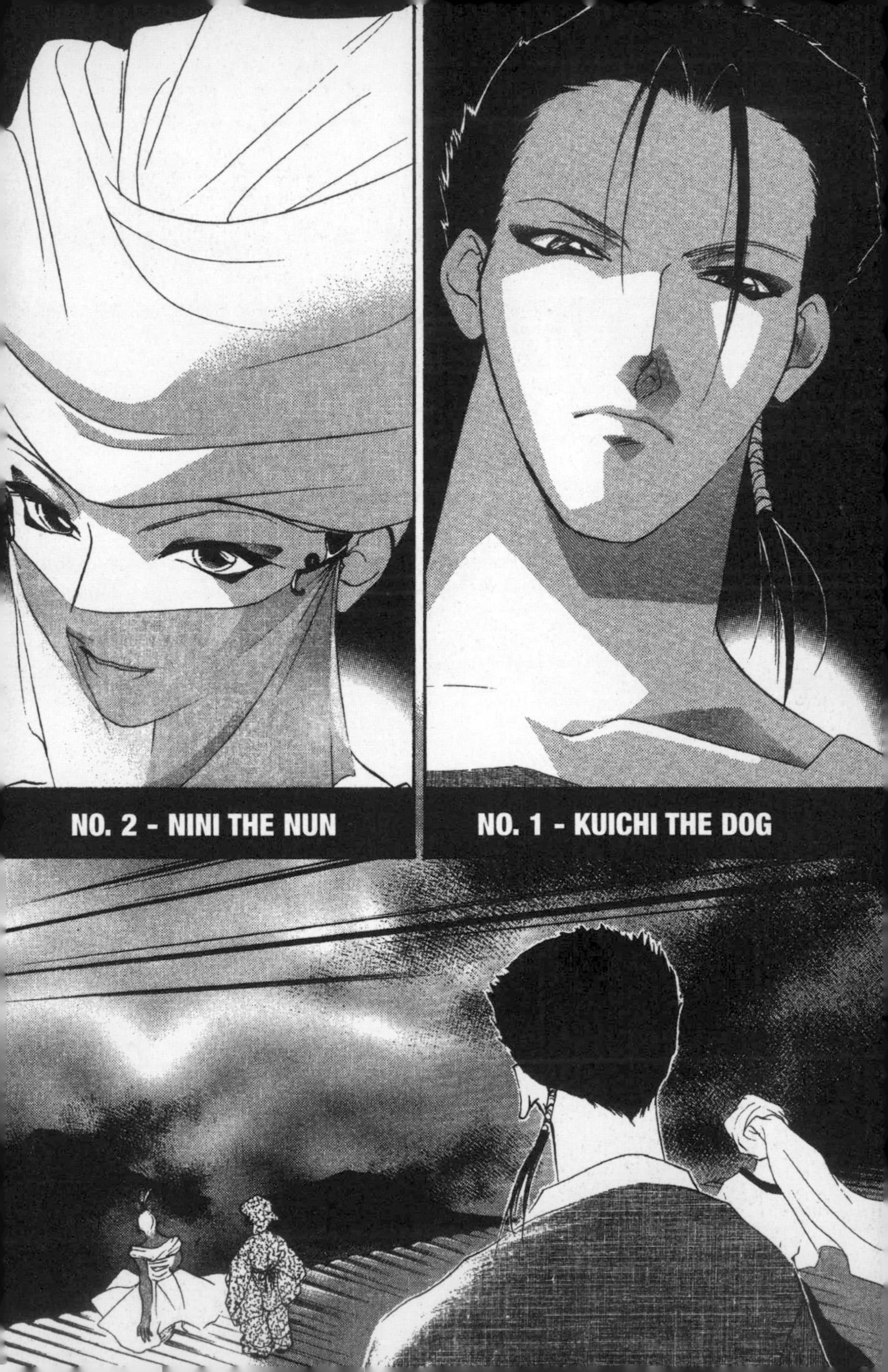
NO. 1 - KUICHI THE DOG
NO. 2 - NINI THE NUN

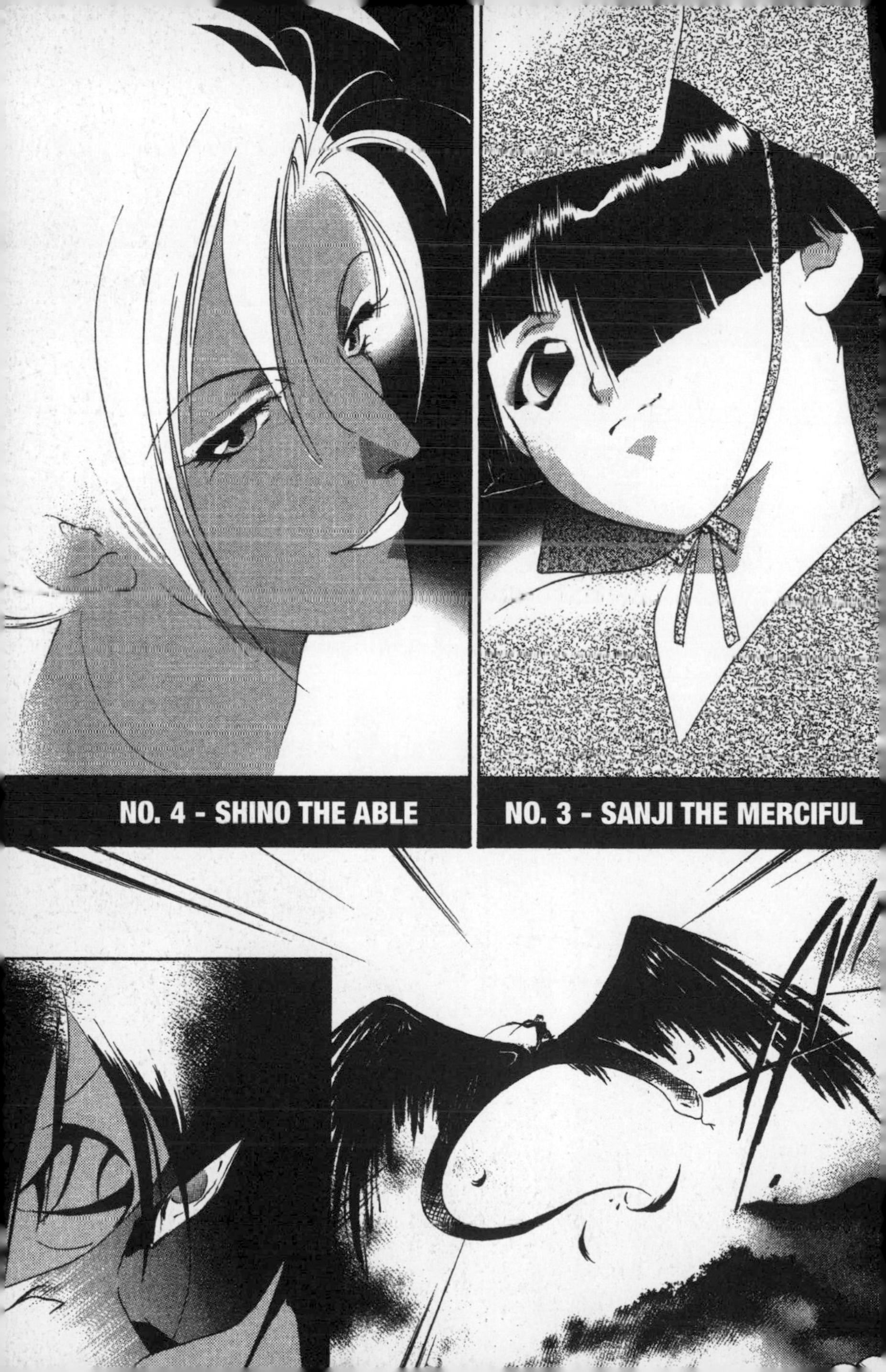
NO. 3 - SANJI THE MERCIFUL
NO. 4 - SHINO THE ABLE

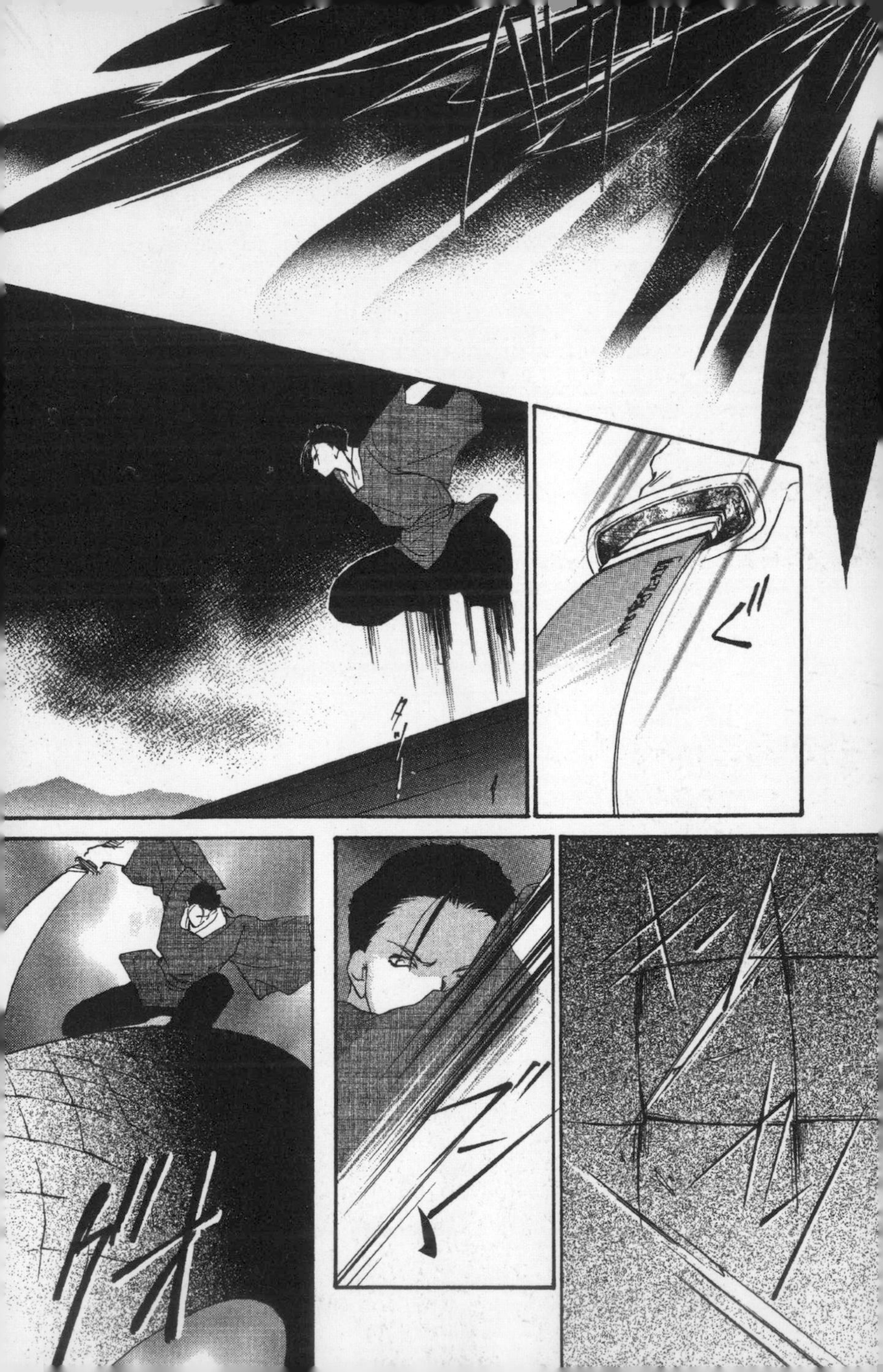
ぐ
ダッ！

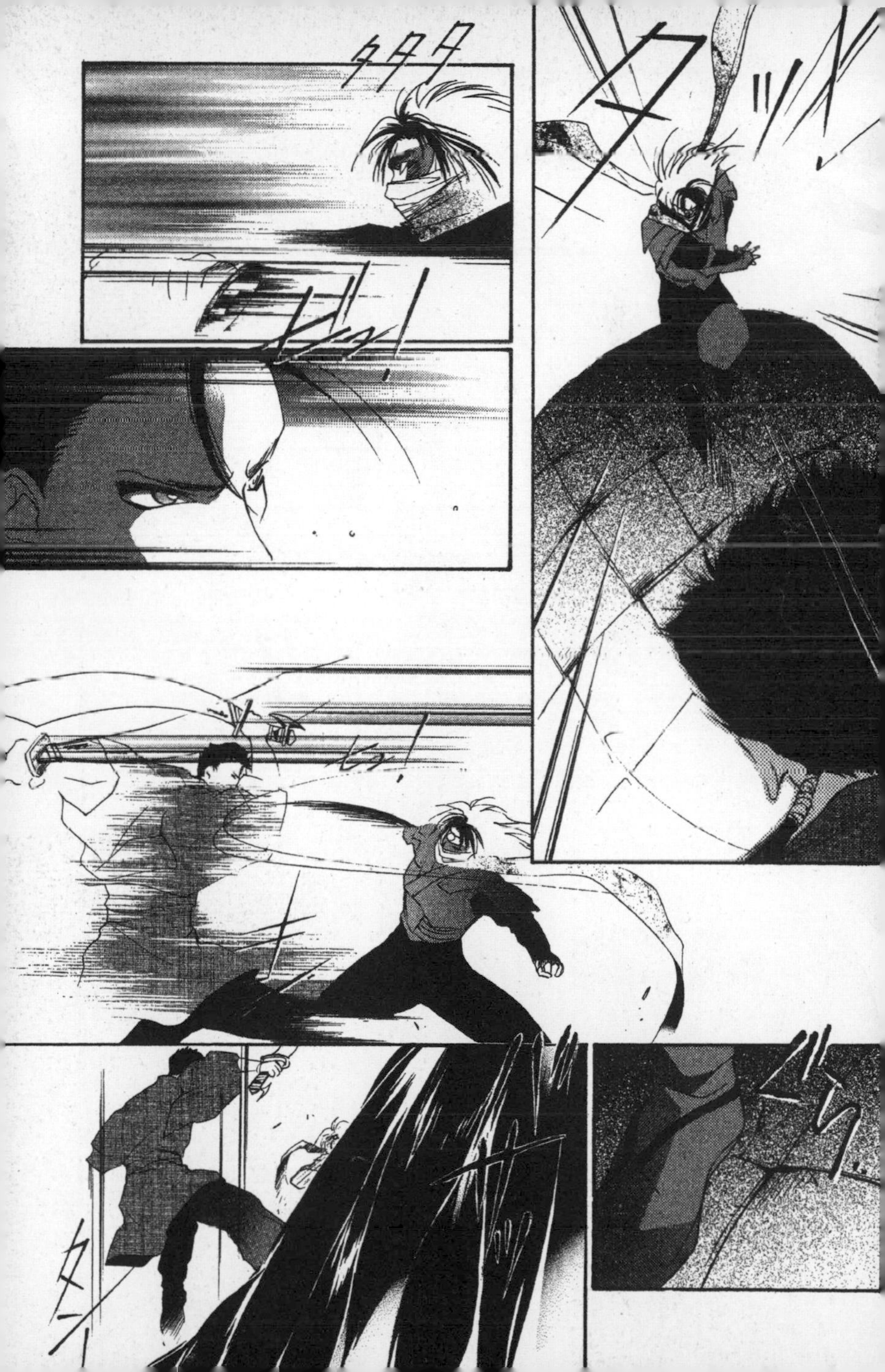

タッ!
タタタ
せっ!
ター

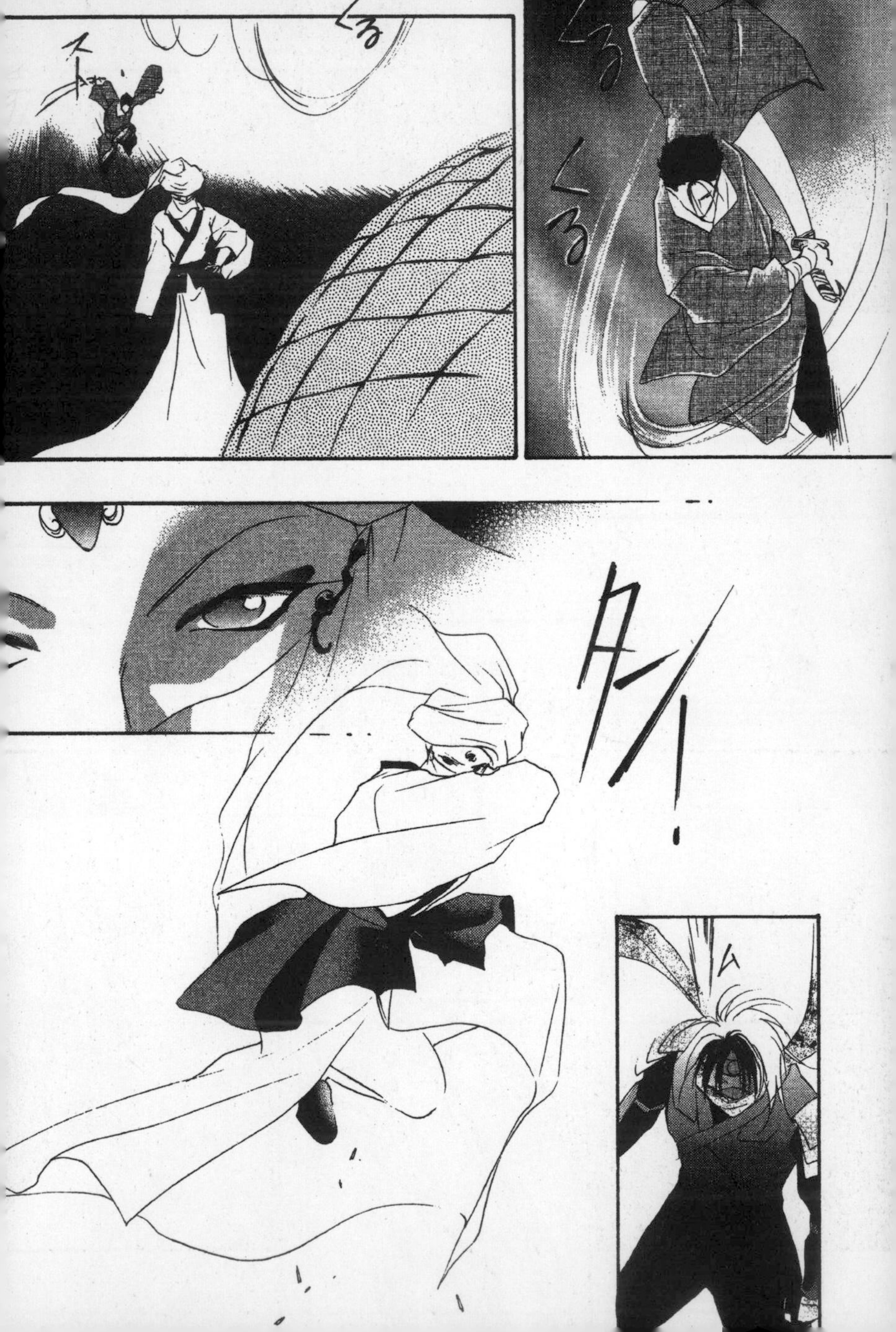
くる
くる
くる
スト
タン!
ム

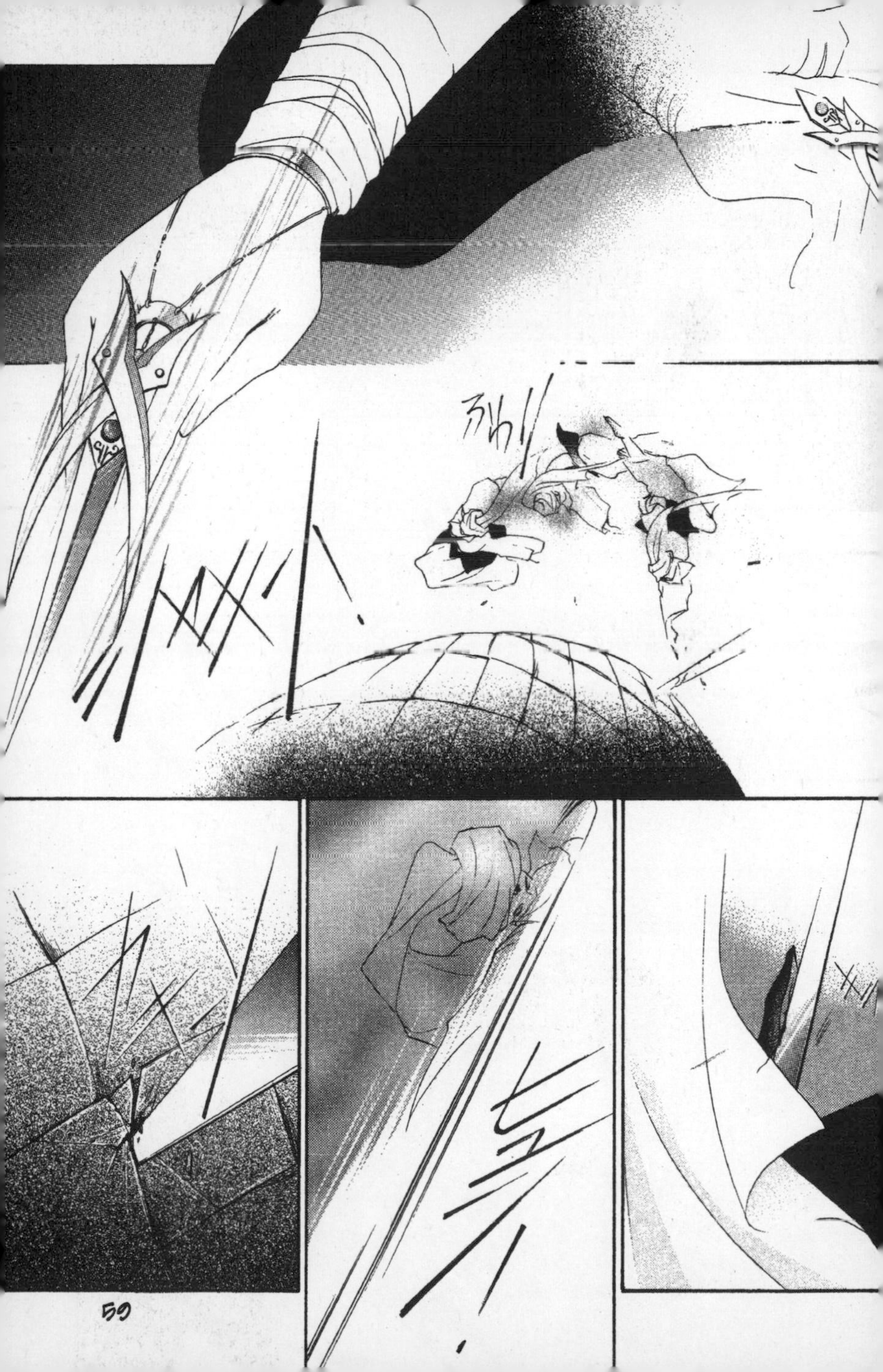
ヒュン!

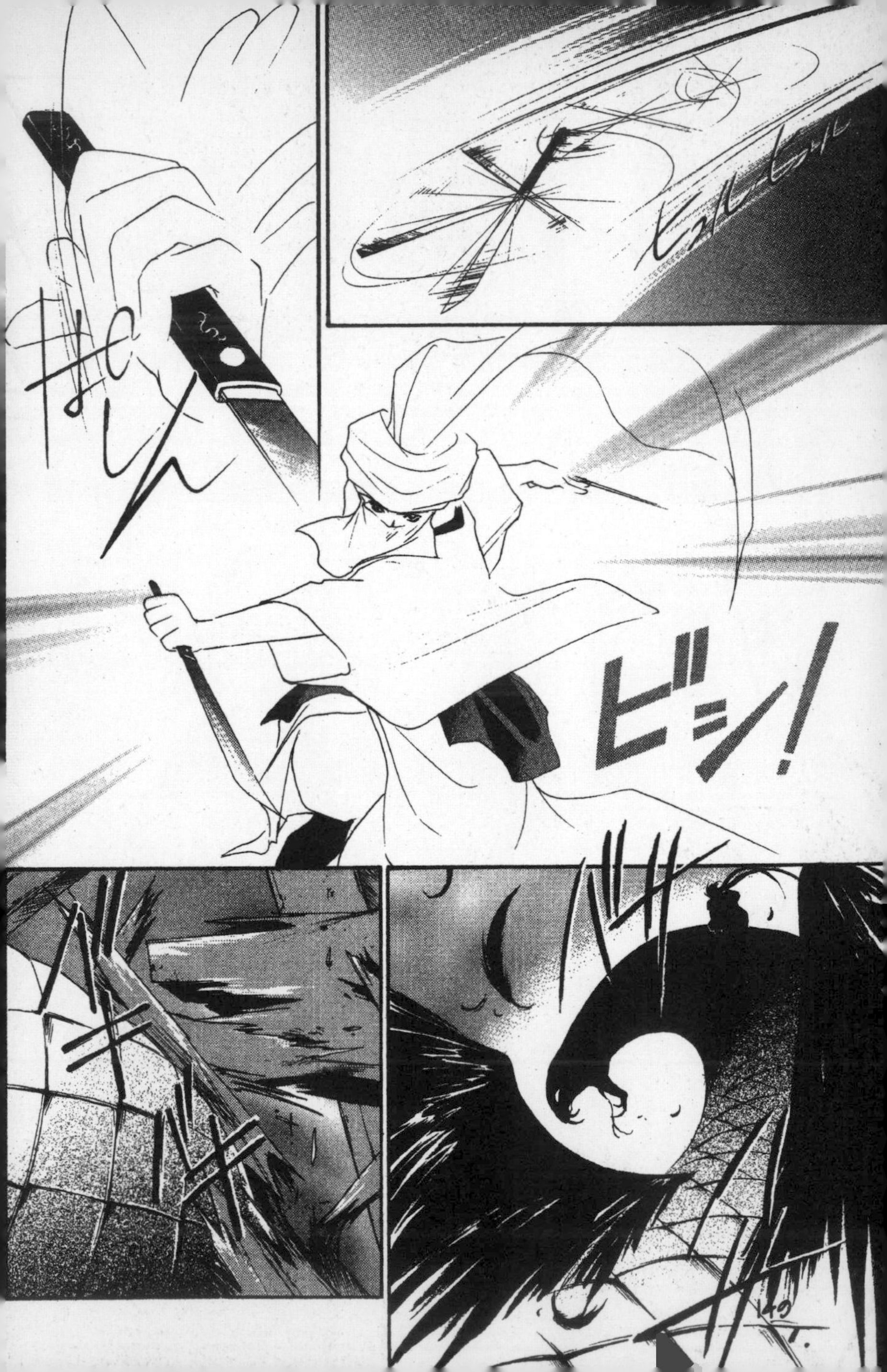
ひゅんひゅん
ぱしん
ビシッ！
バサ
バキ
バキ

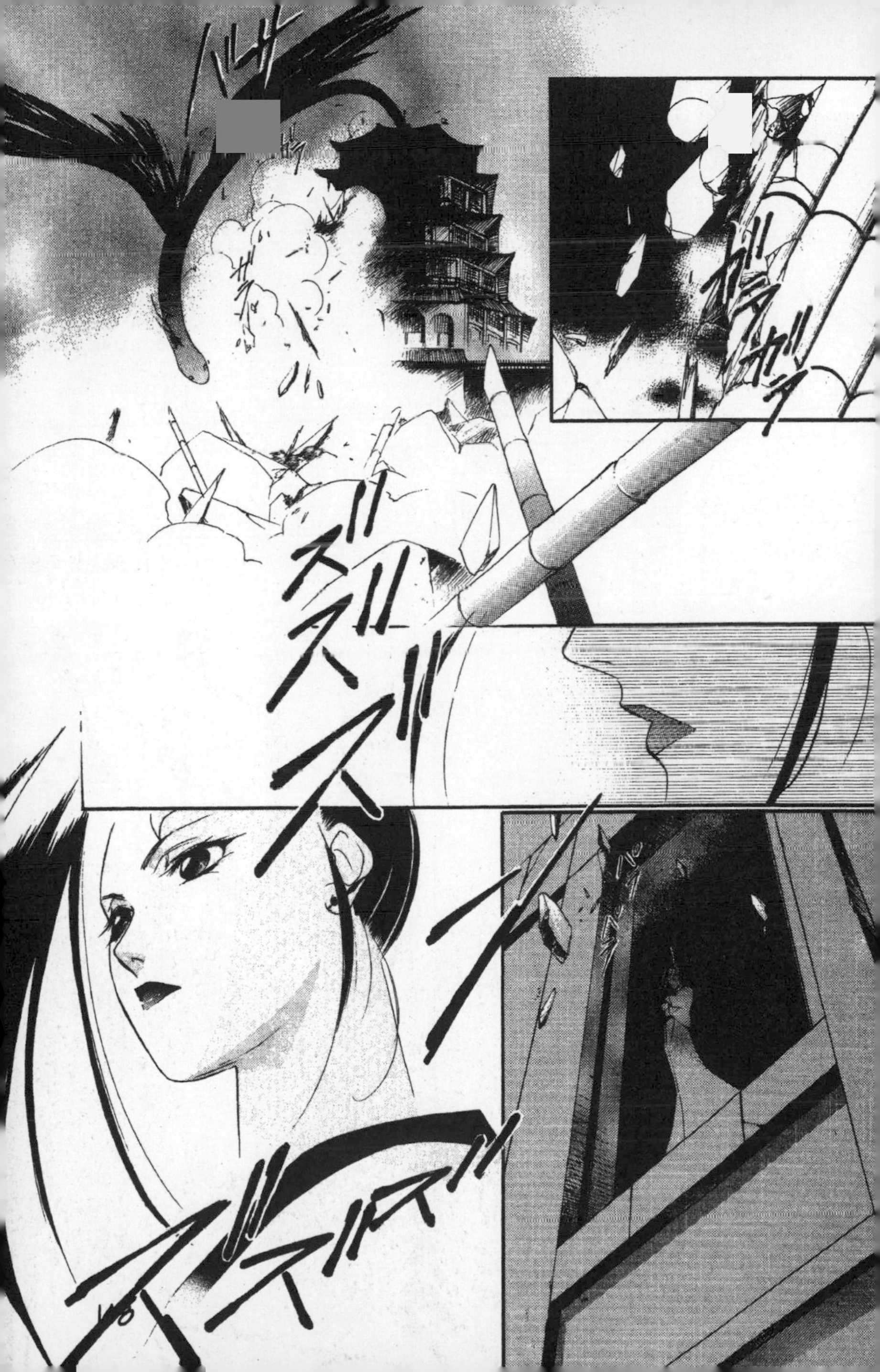

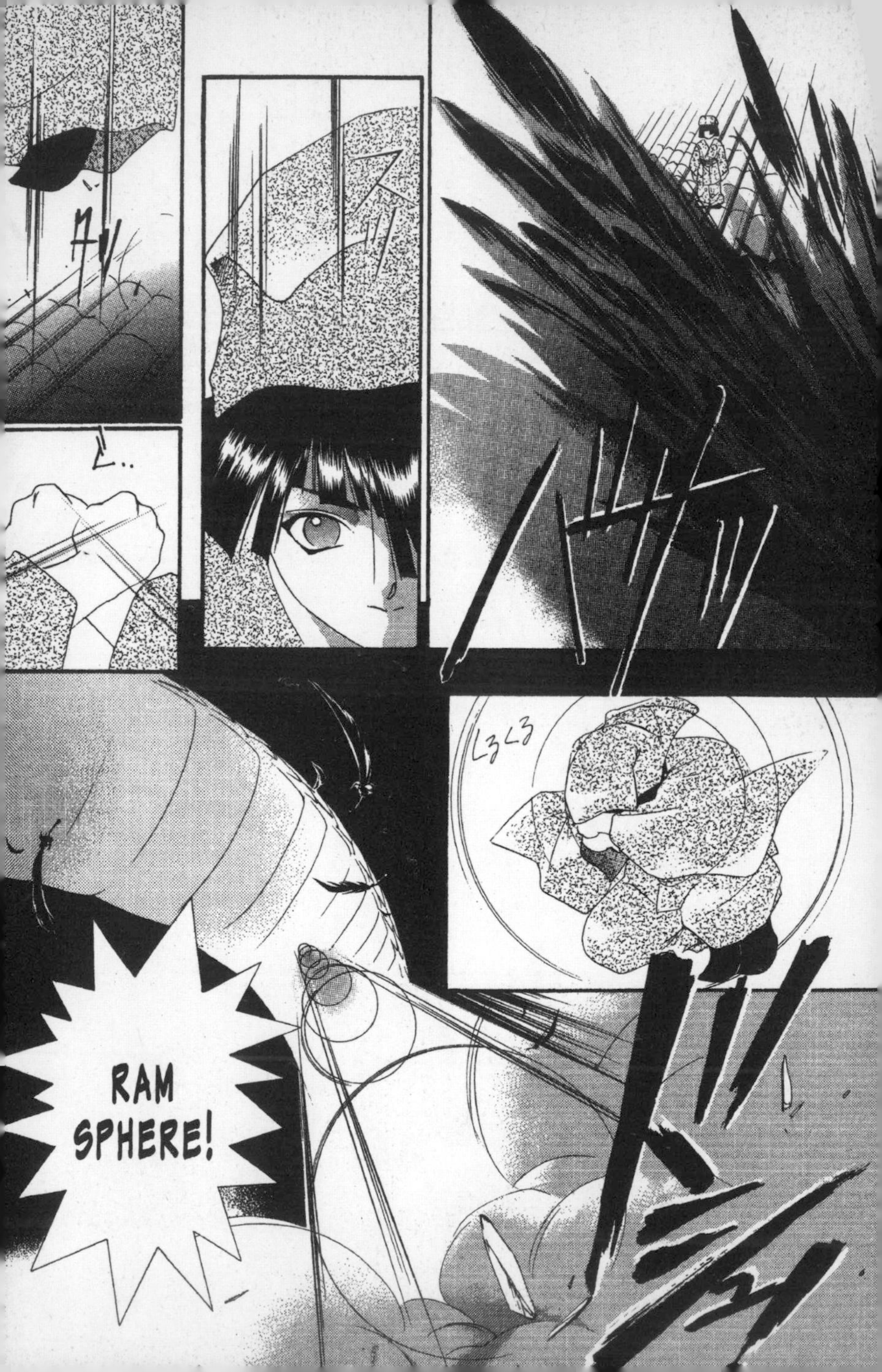
RAM SPHERE!

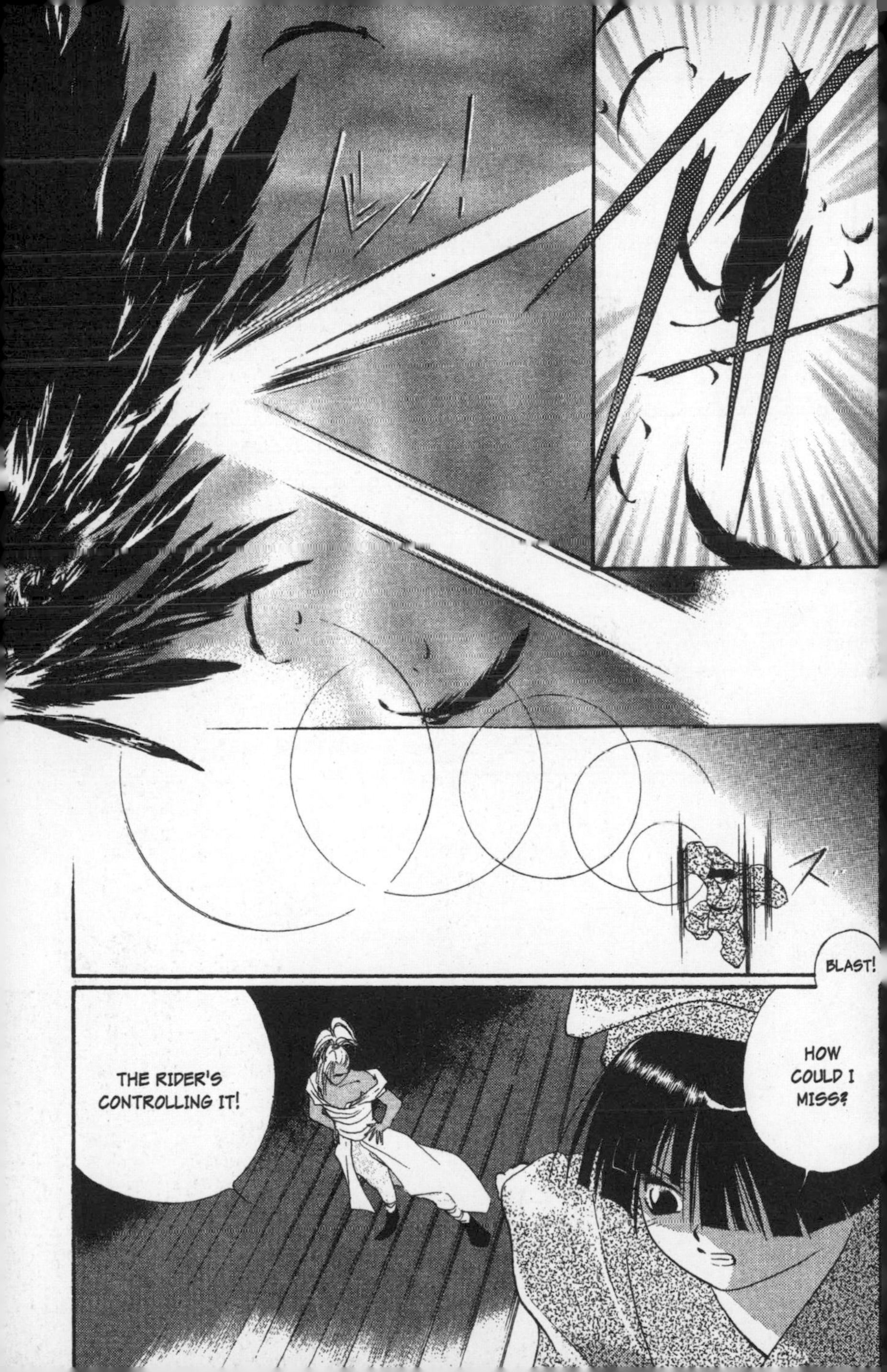
BLAST!
HOW COULD I MISS?
THE RIDER'S CONTROLLING IT!

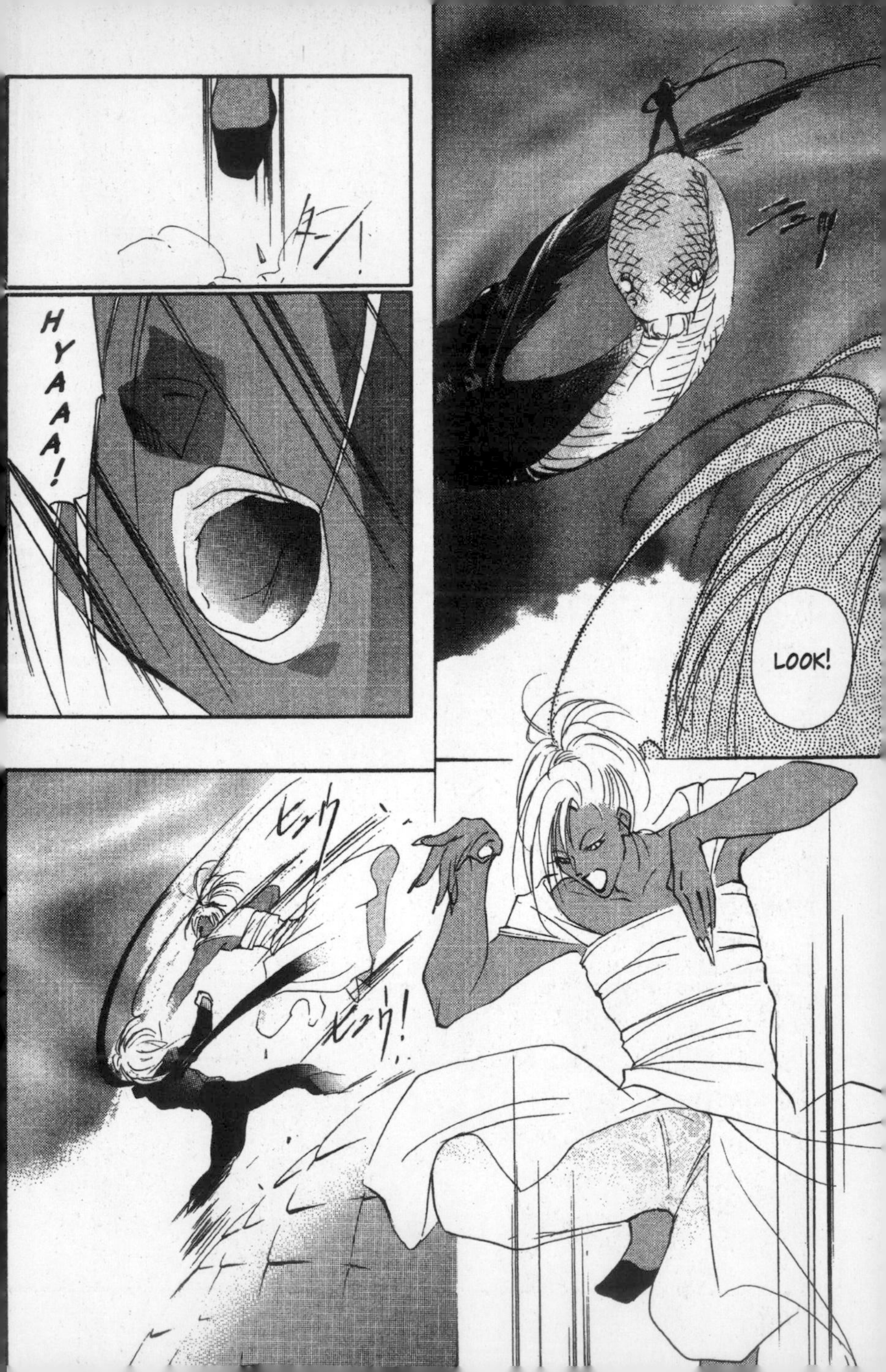
LOOK!
HYAAAA!

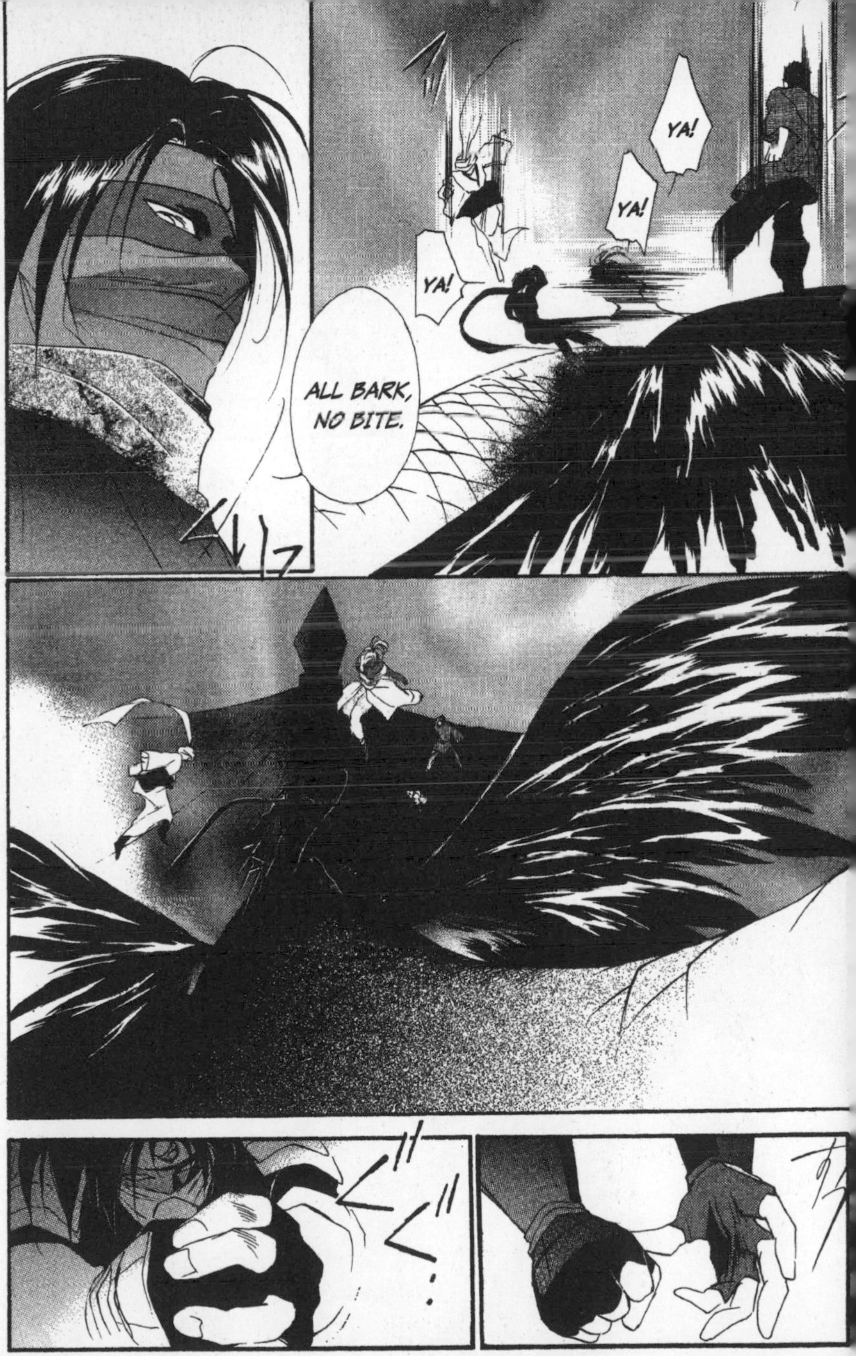
YA!
YA!
YA!
ALL BARK, NO BITE.

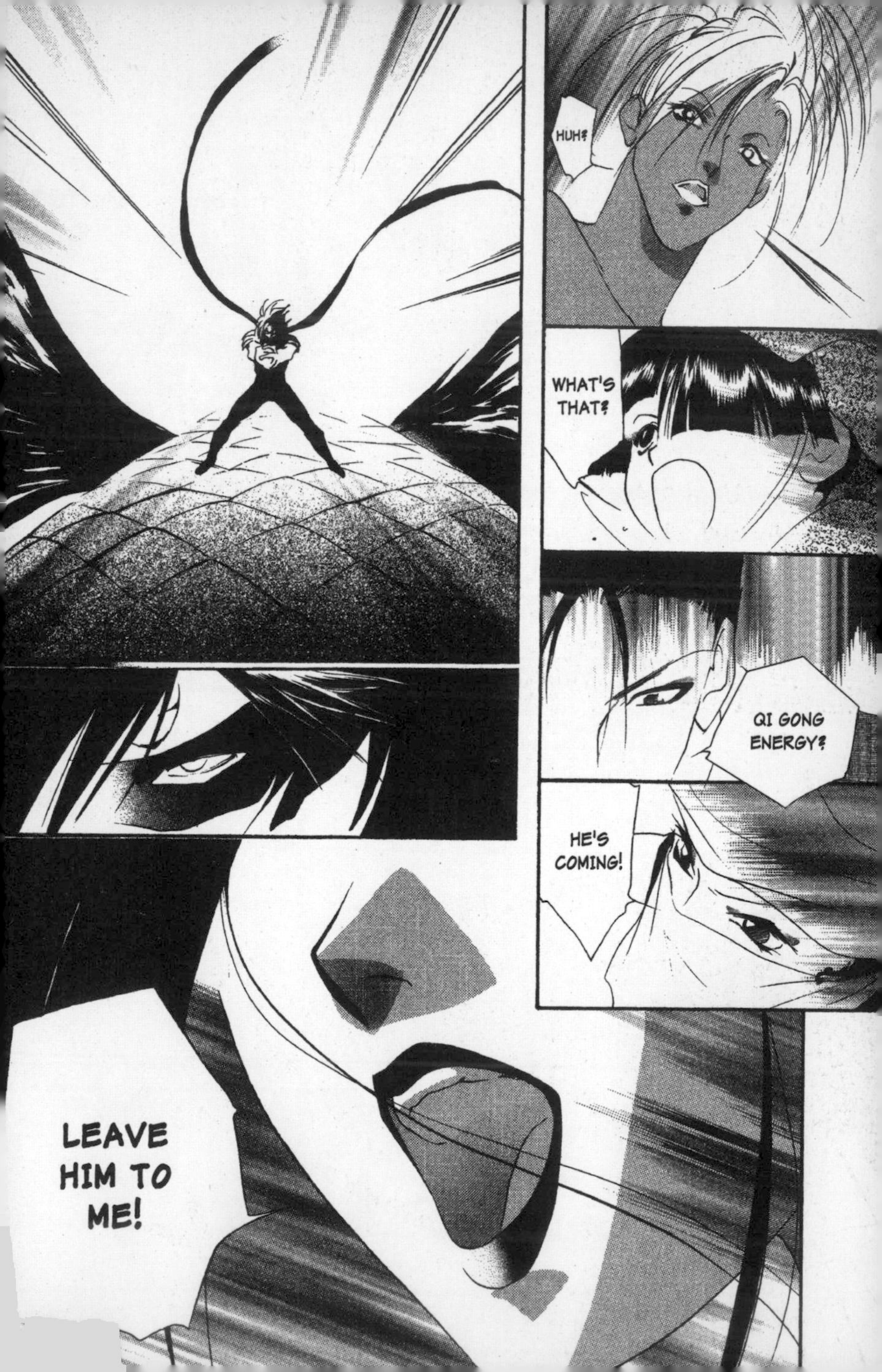
HUH?
WHAT'S THAT?
QI GONG ENERGY?
HE'S COMING!
LEAVE HIM TO ME!

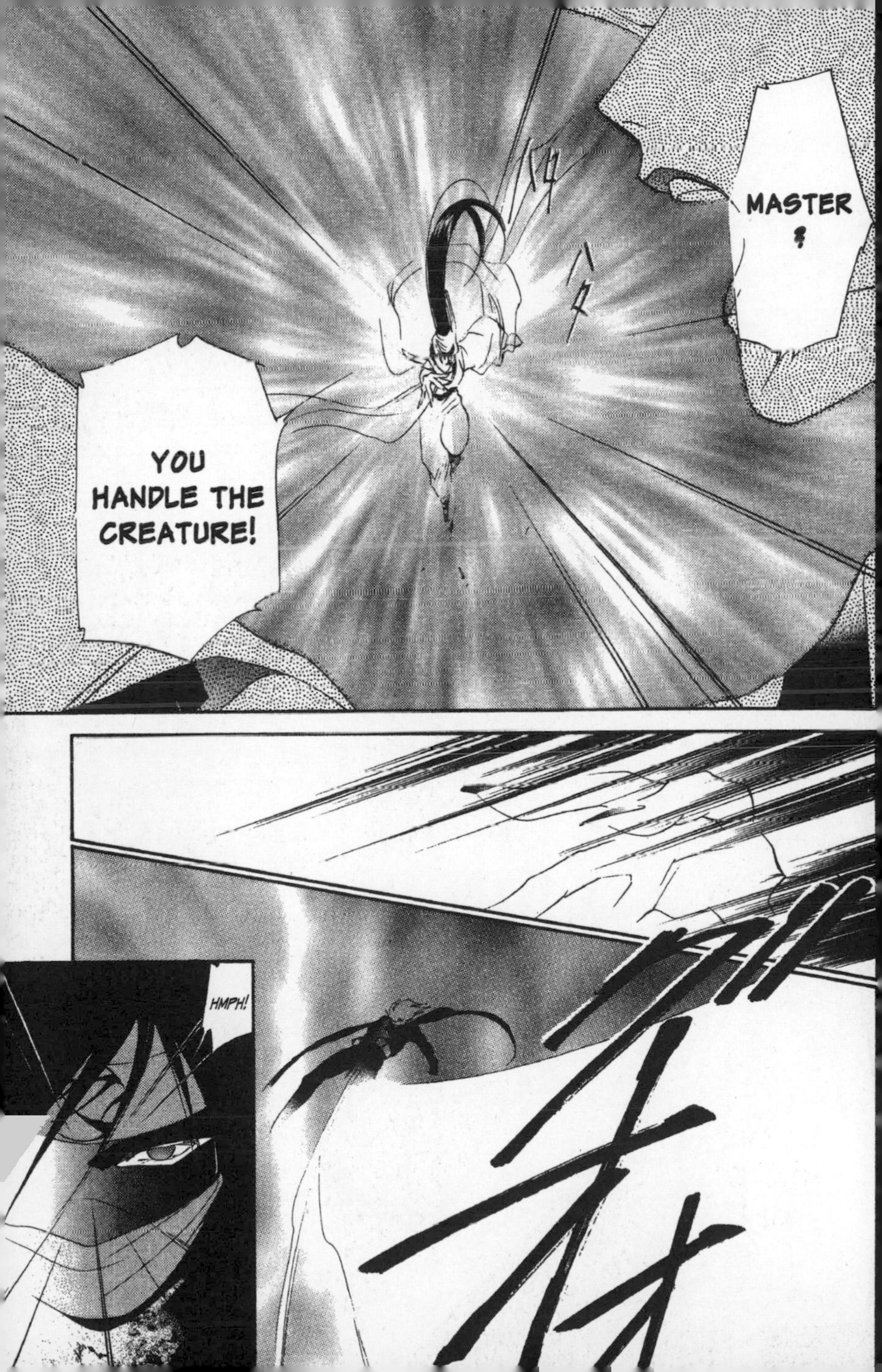
MASTER?
YOU HANDLE THE CREATURE!
HMPH!

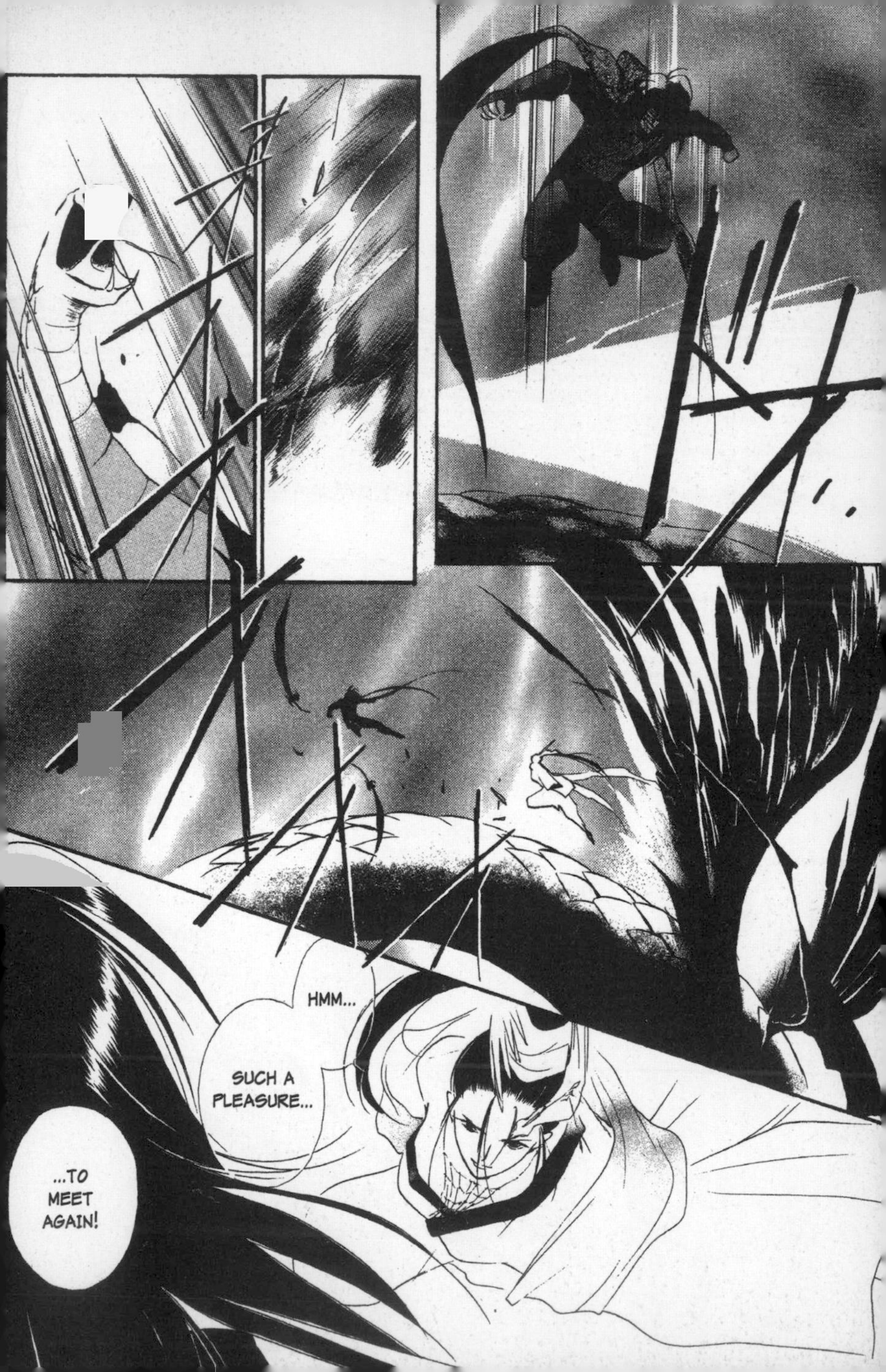
HMM...
SUCH A PLEASURE...
...TO MEET AGAIN!

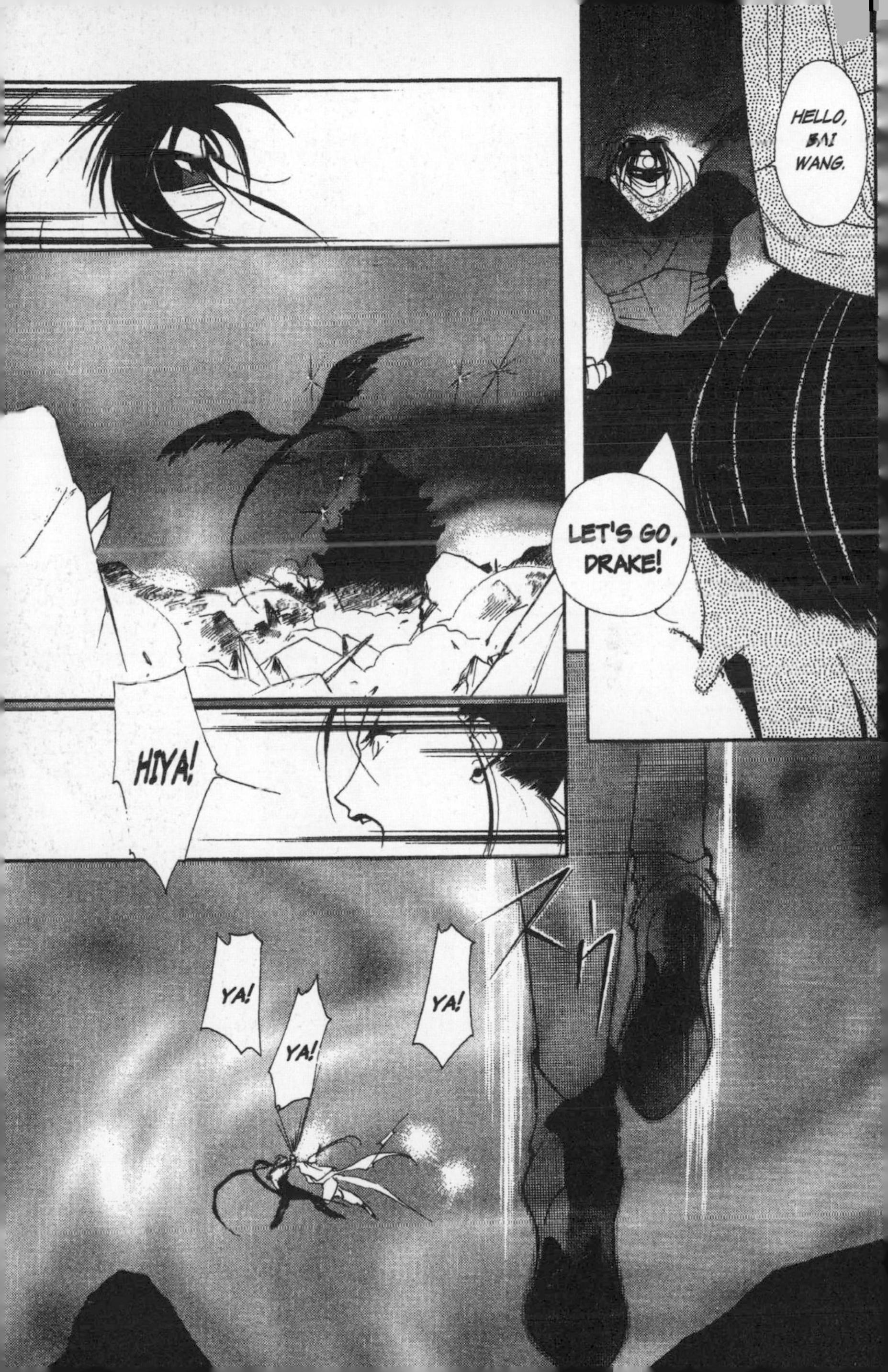
HELLO, BAI WANG.
LET'S GO, DRAKE!
HIYA!
YA!
YA!
YA!

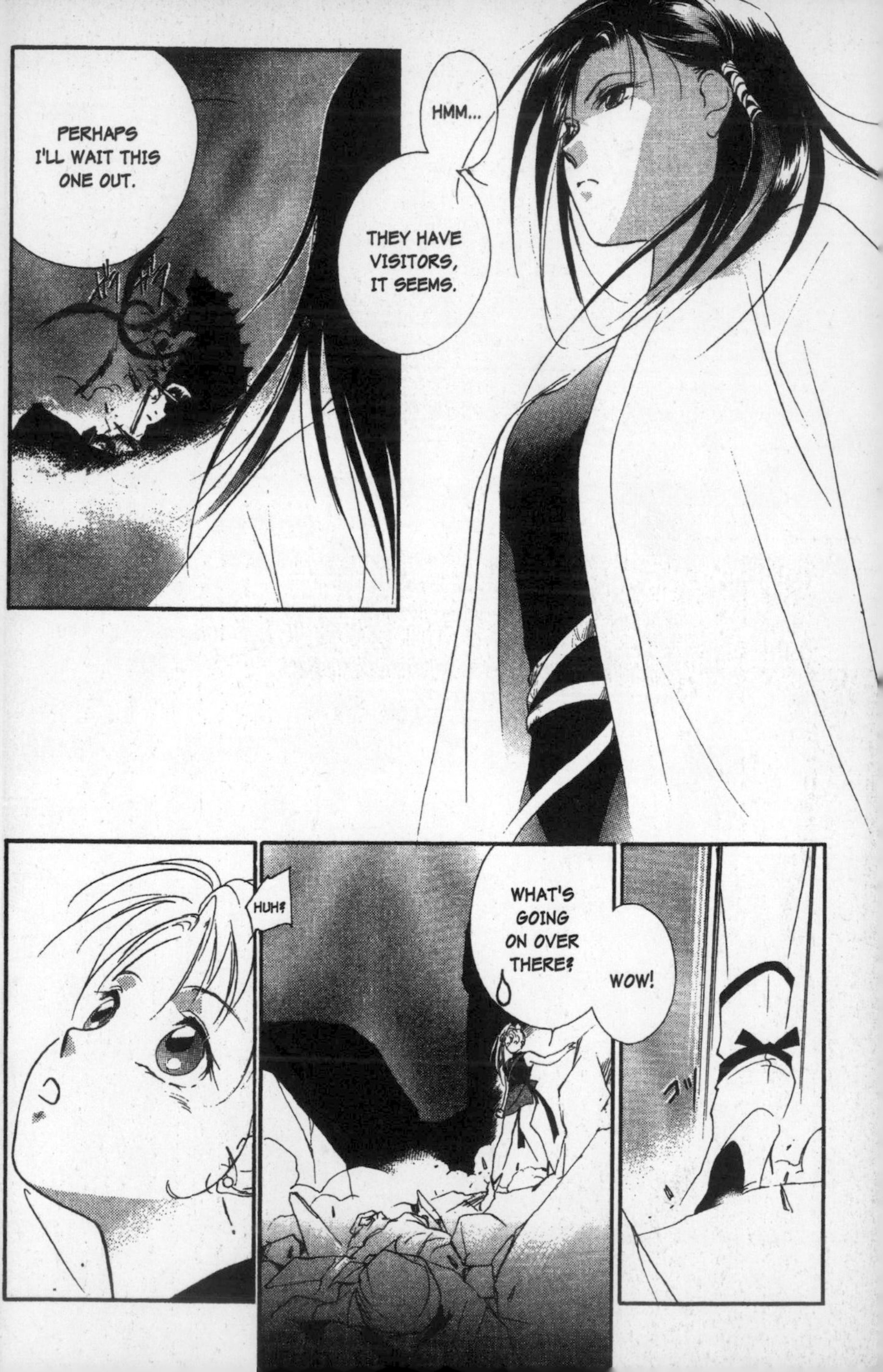
HMM...
THEY HAVE VISITORS, IT SEEMS.
PERHAPS I'LL WAIT THIS ONE OUT.
WOW!
WHAT'S GOING ON OVER THERE?
HUH?

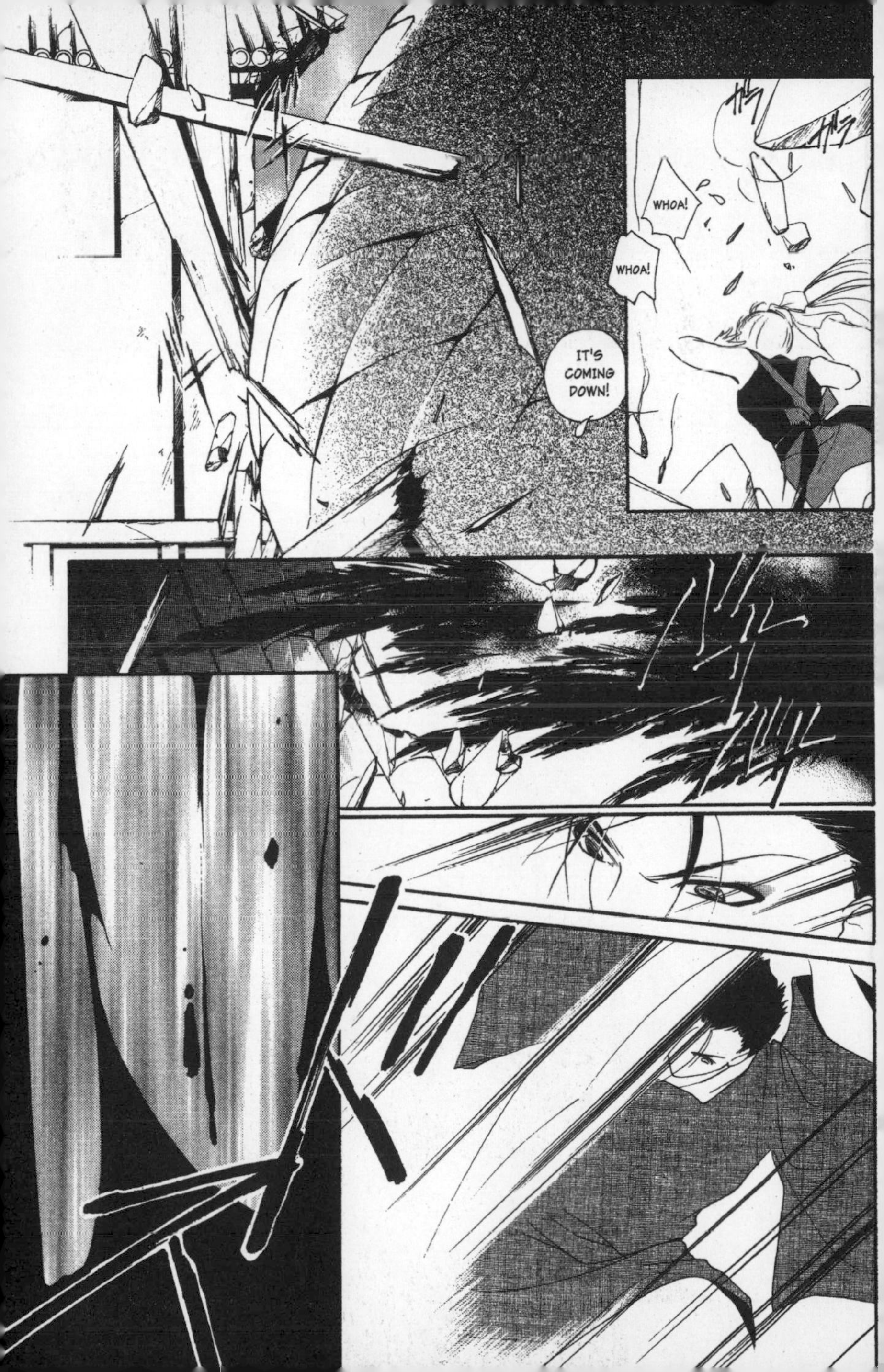
WHOA!
WHOA!
IT'S COMING DOWN!

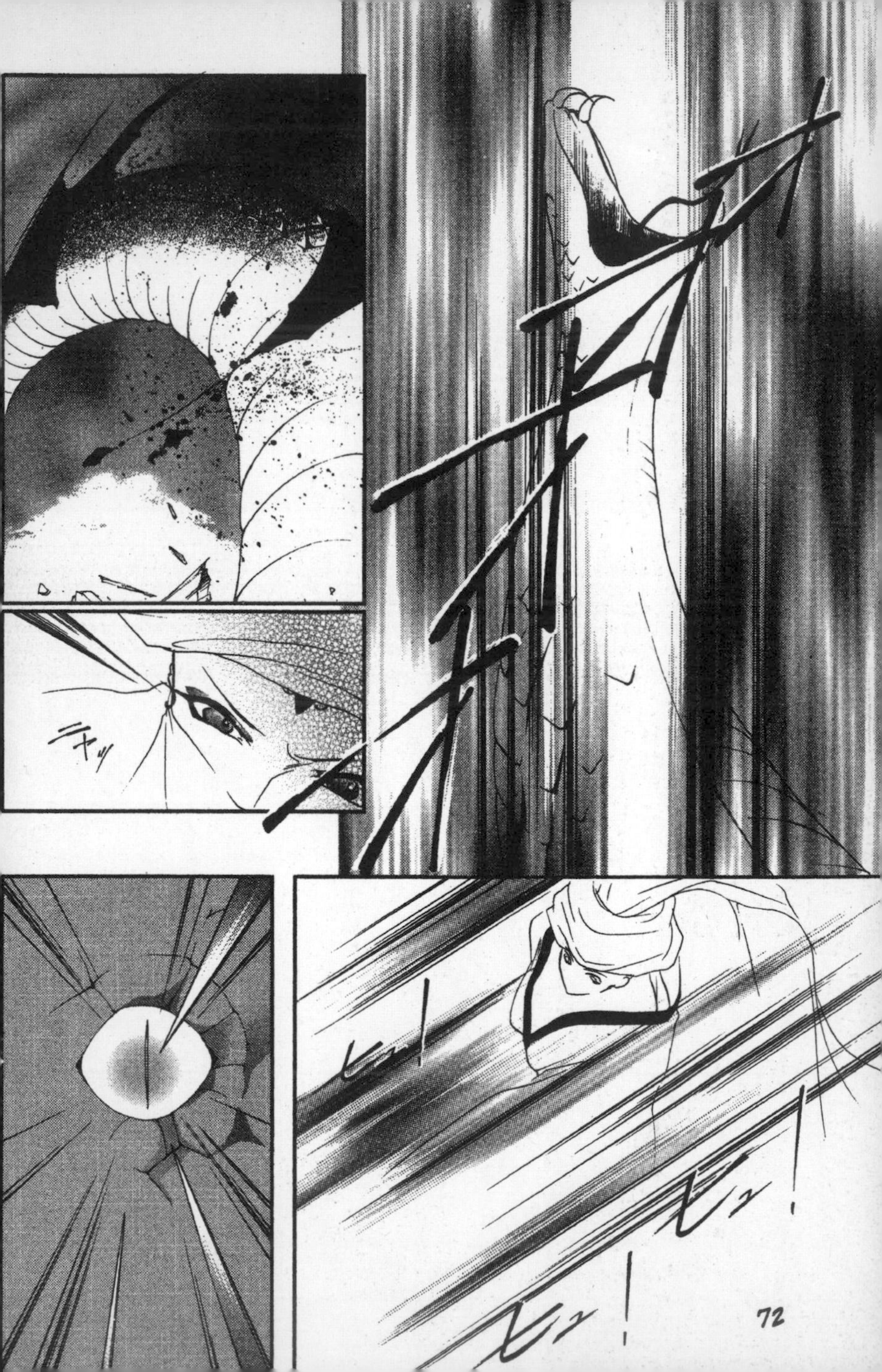
ニヤッ
ヒュ!
ヒュ!
ヒュ!

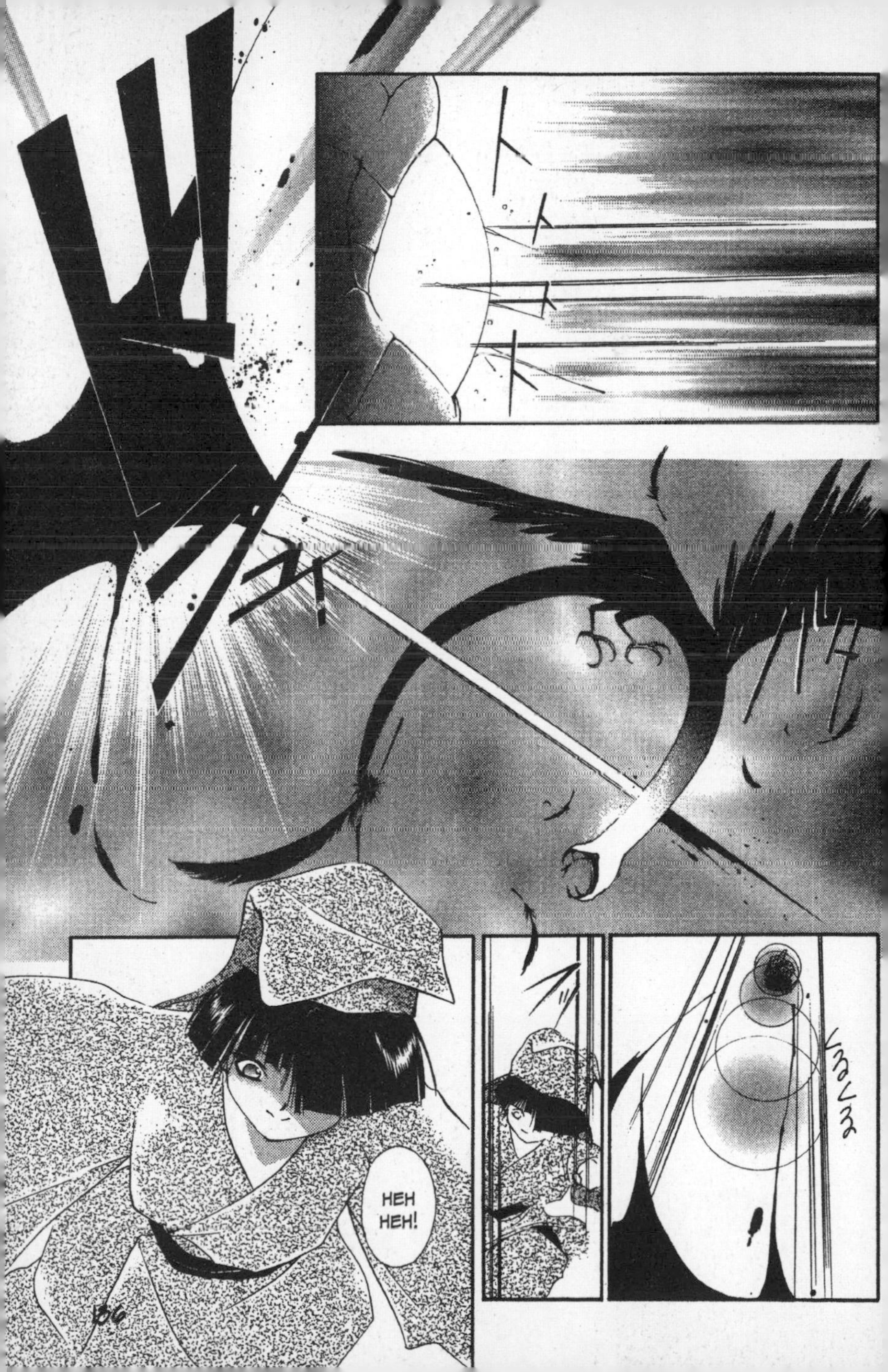
HEH HEH!

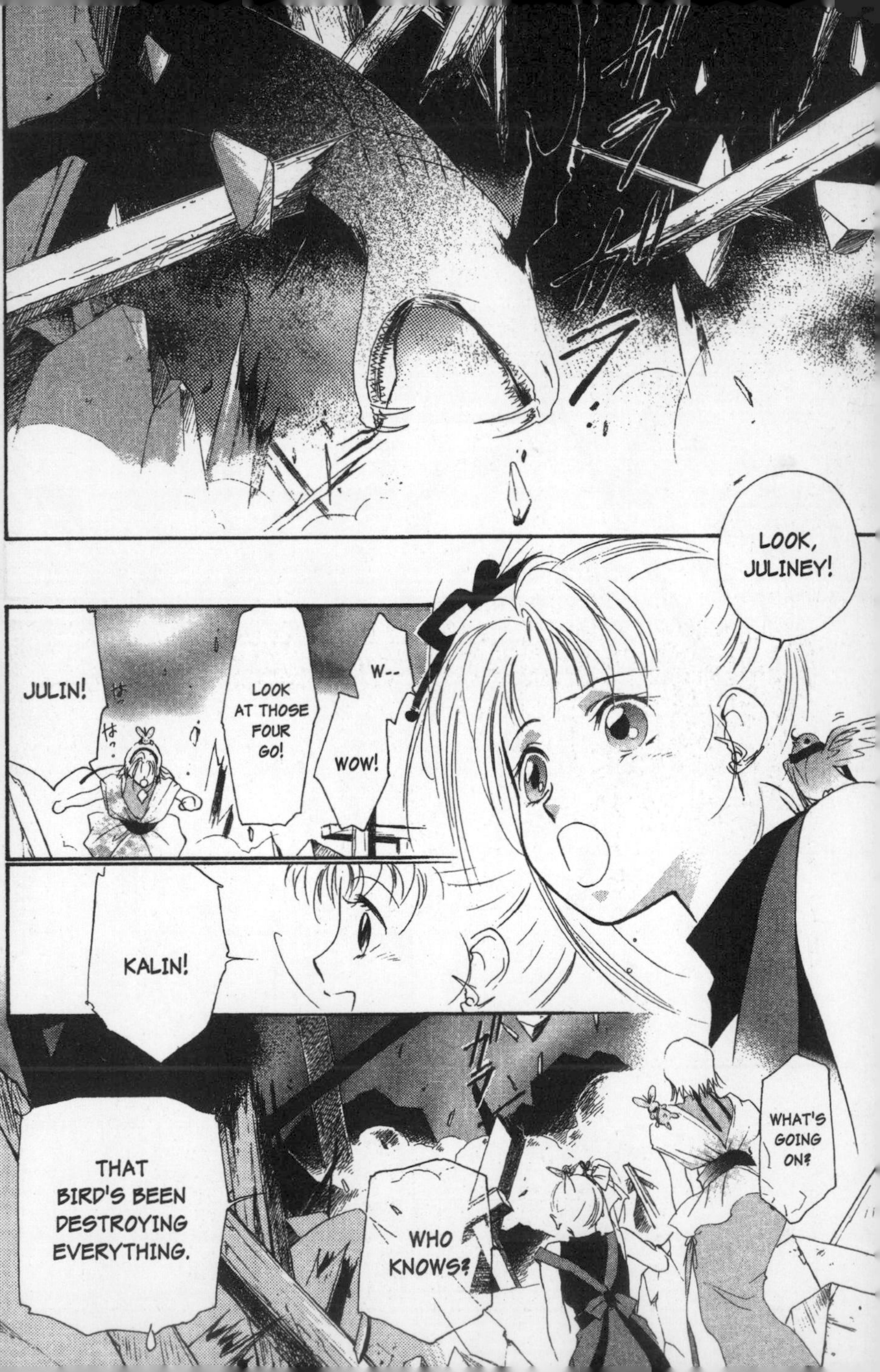
LOOK, JULINEY!
W--
WOW!
LOOK AT THOSE FOUR GO!
JULIN!
KALIN!
WHAT'S GOING ON?
WHO KNOWS?
THAT BIRD'S BEEN DESTROYING EVERYTHING.

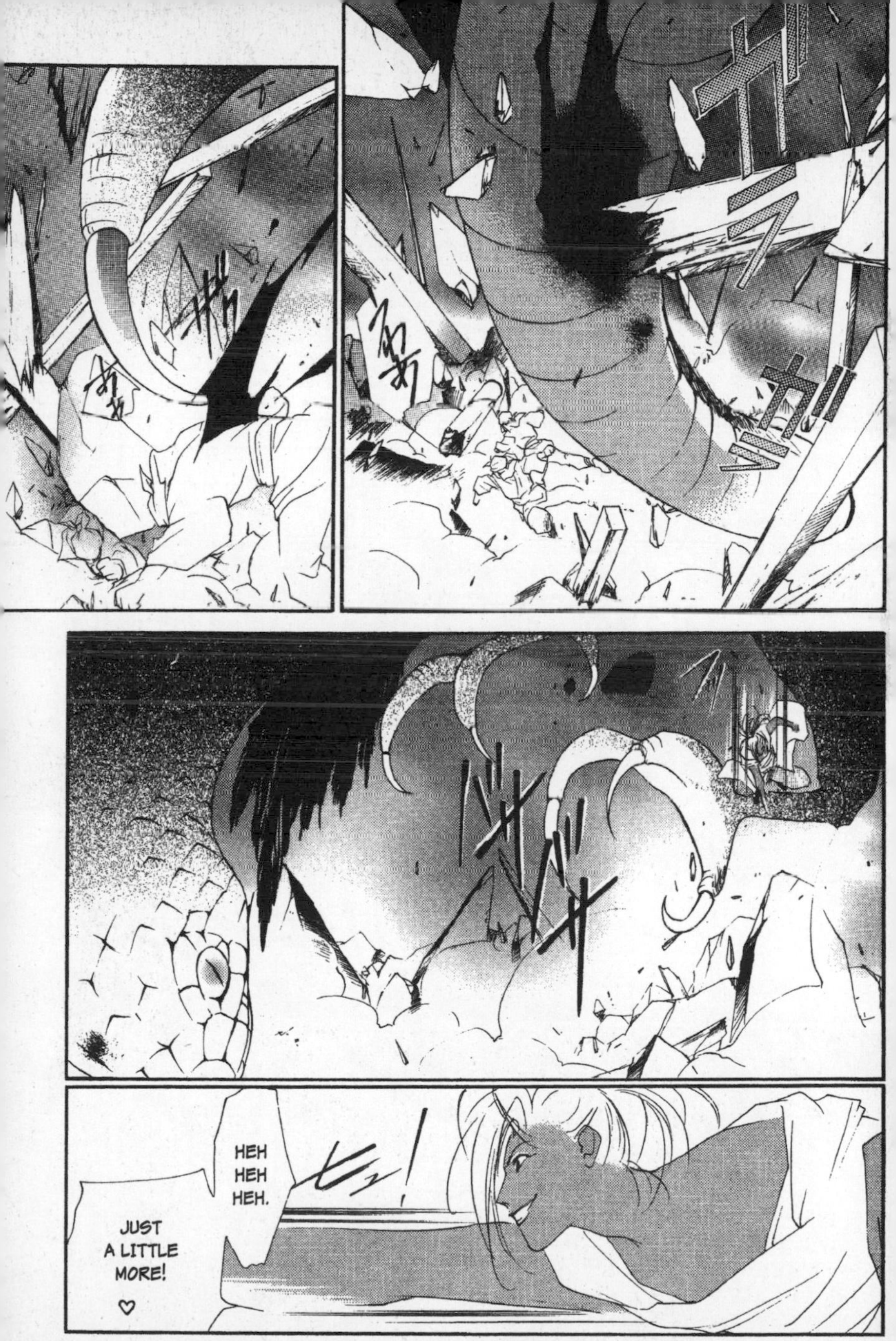
HEH HEH HEH.
JUST A LITTLE MORE! ♡

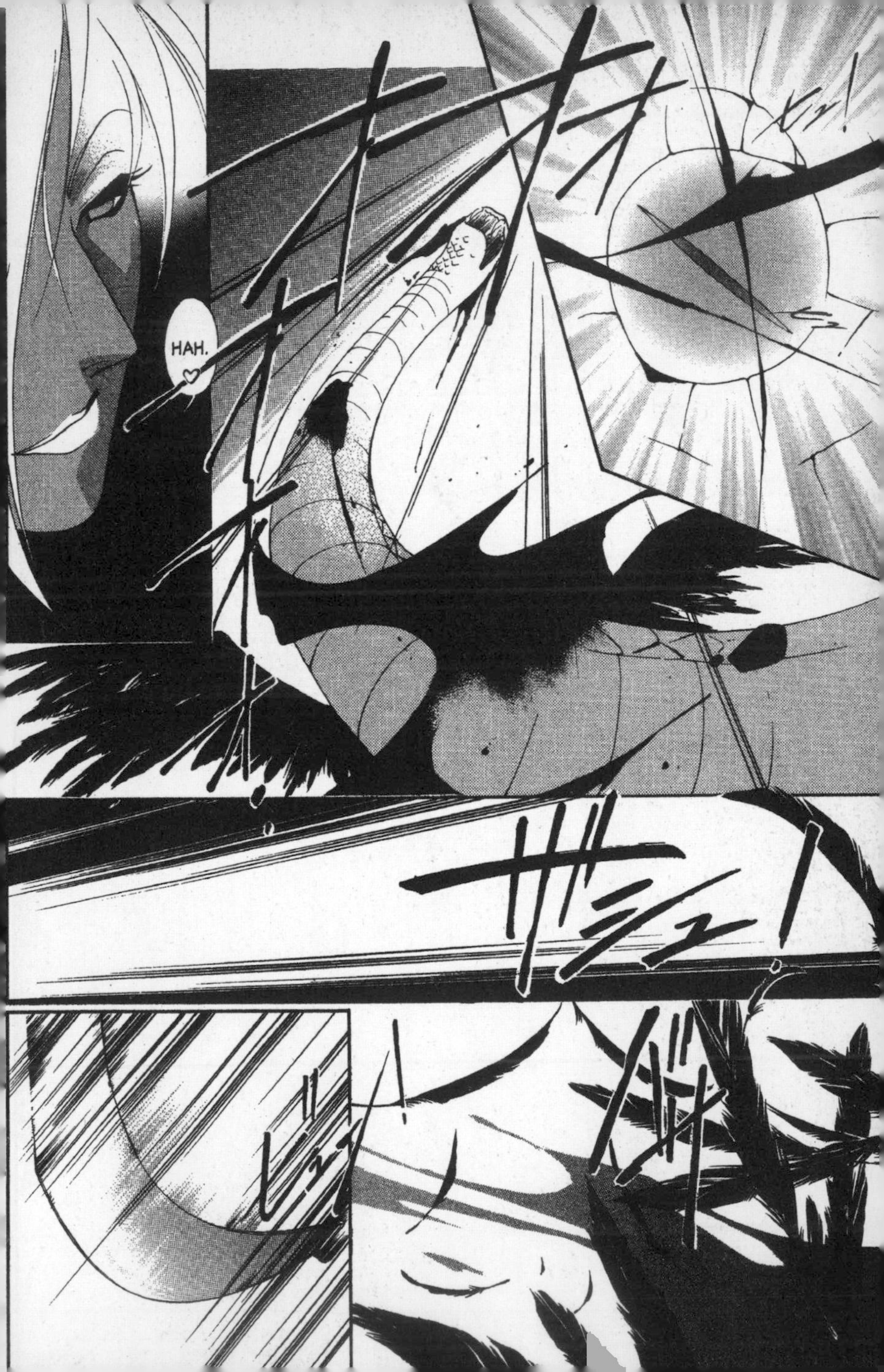
HAH. ♡

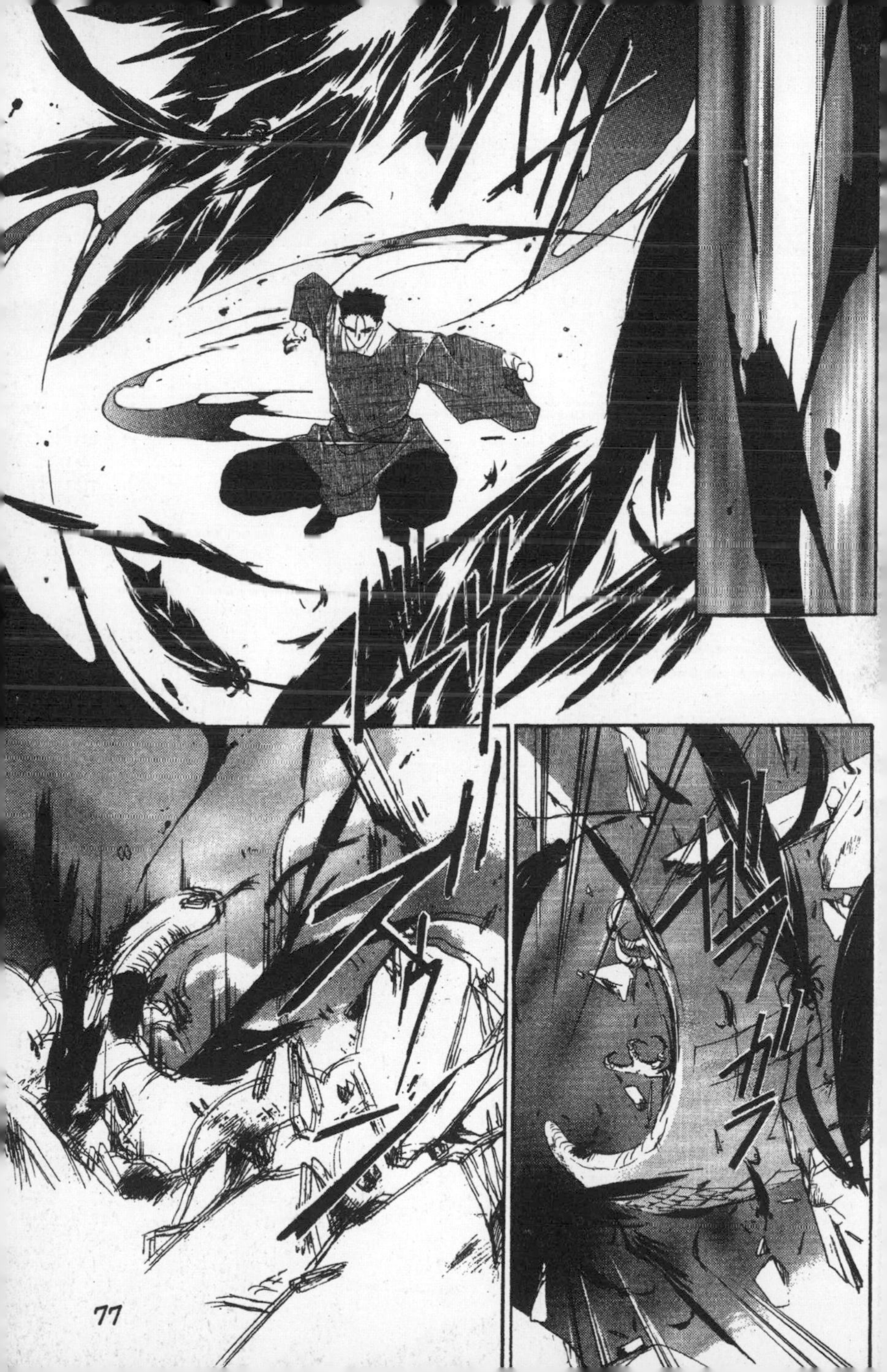
ガラ

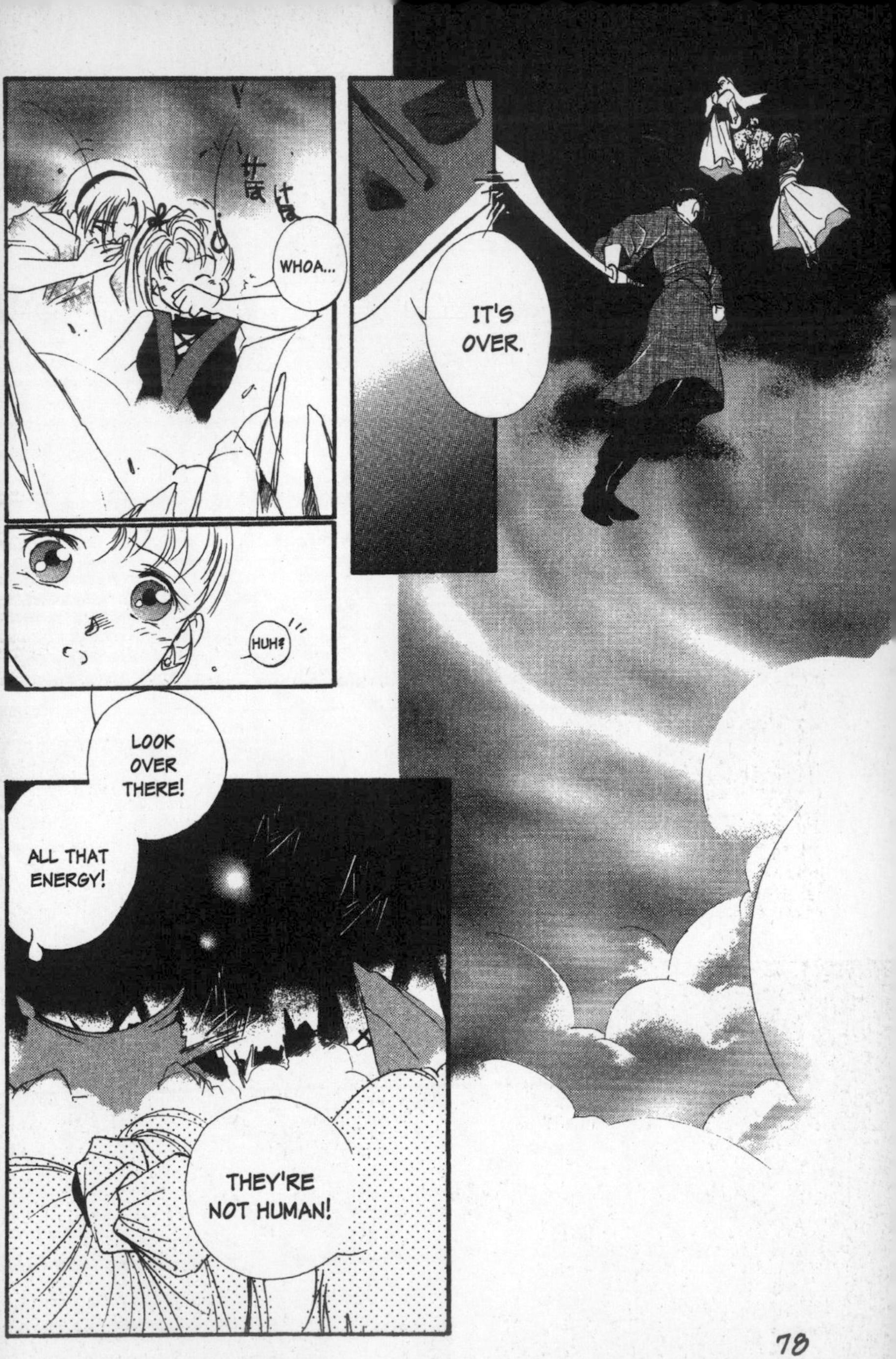
IT'S OVER.
WHOA...
HUH?
LOOK OVER THERE!
ALL THAT ENERGY!
THEY'RE NOT HUMAN!

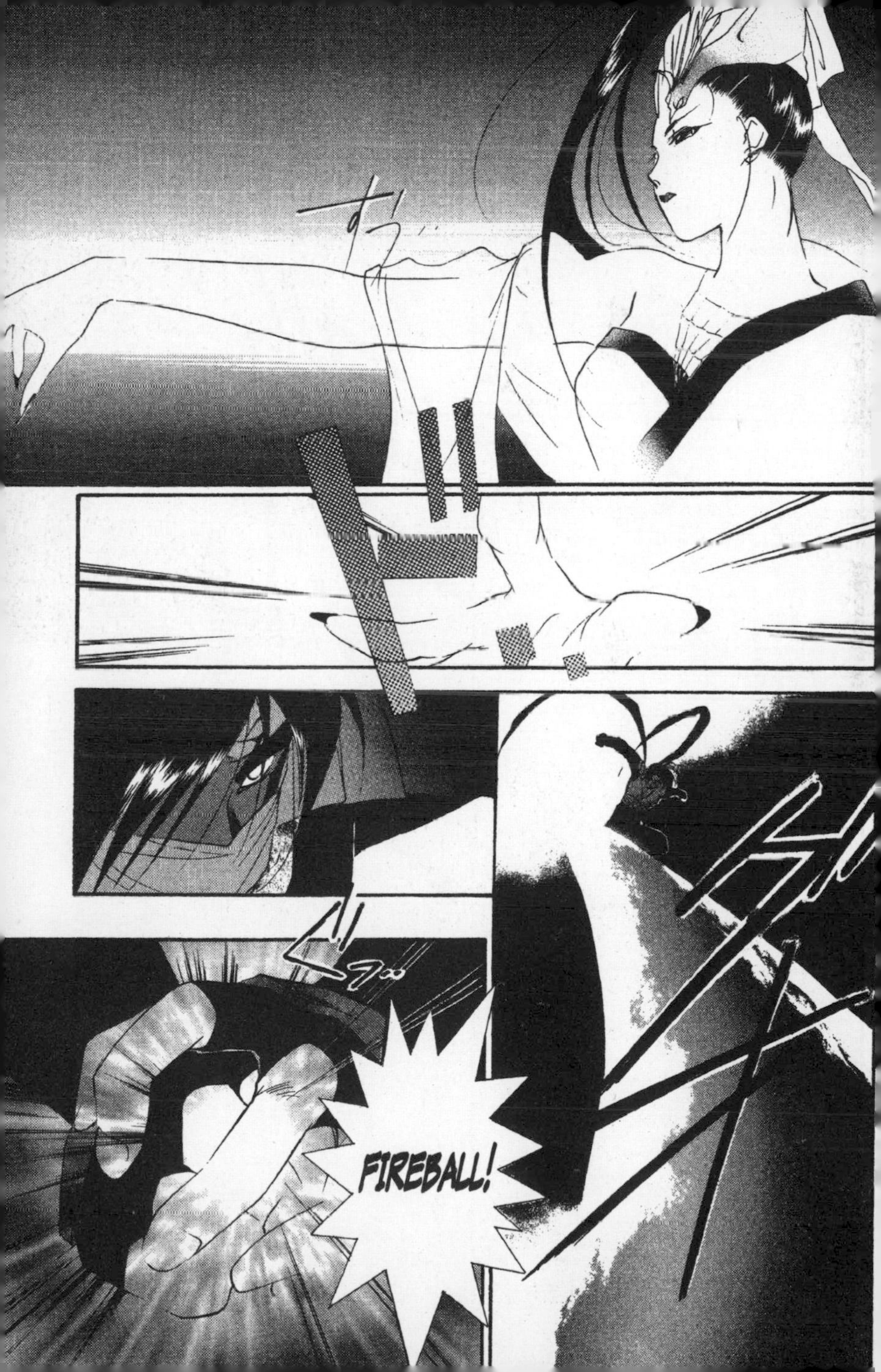
FIREBALL!

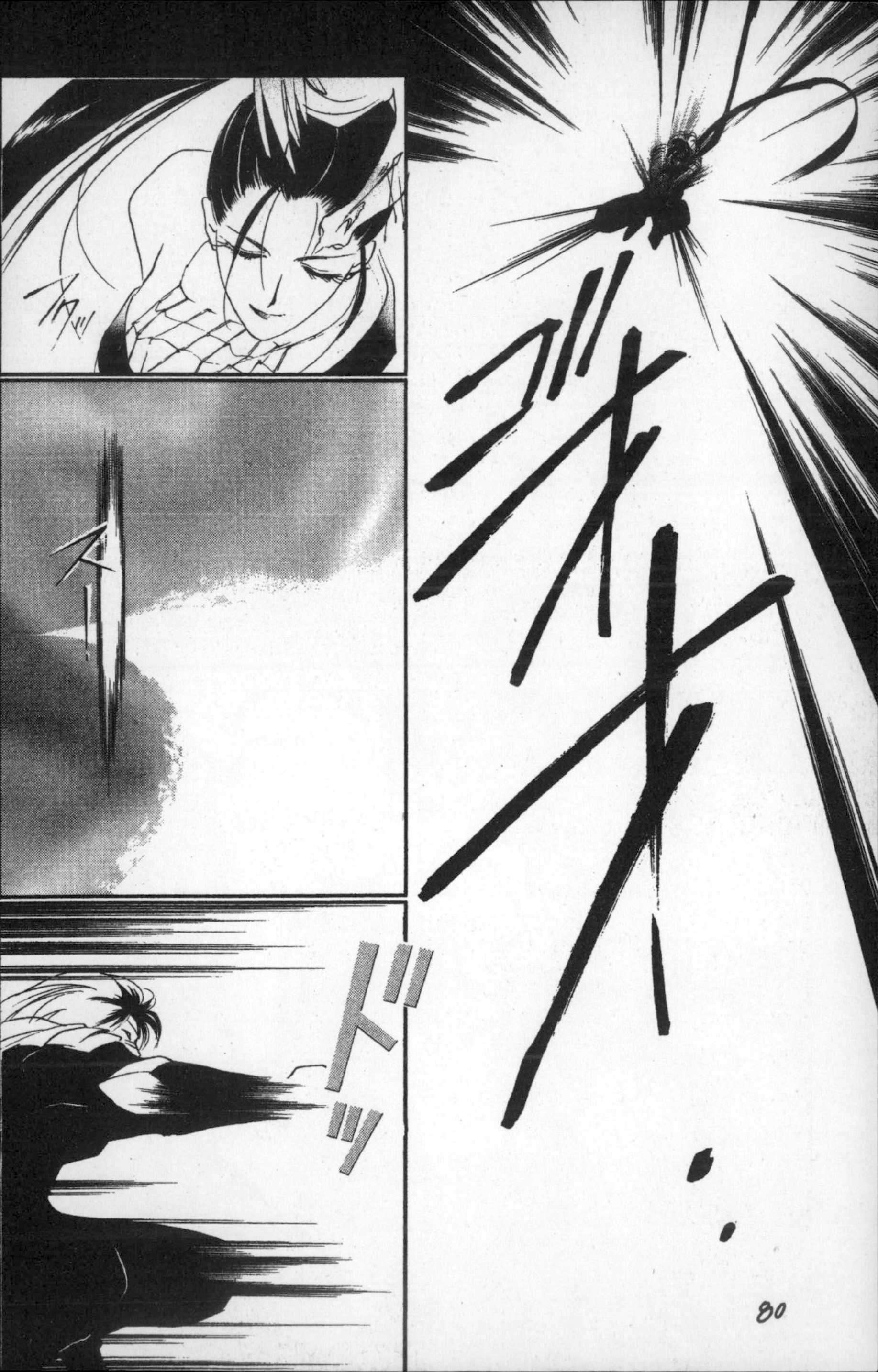
ゴオオ!.
フワッ
スーー
ドッ

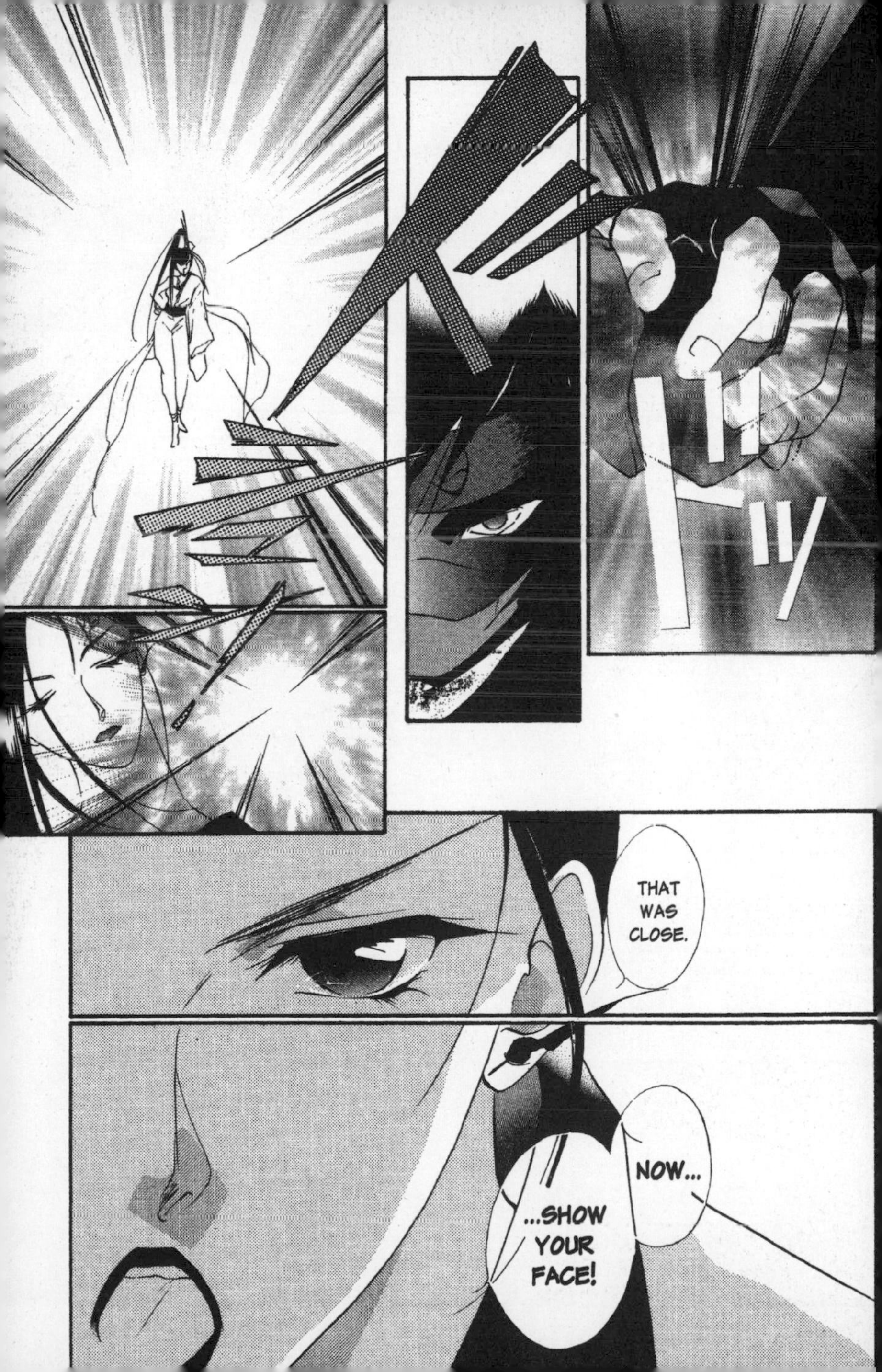
THAT WAS CLOSE.
NOW...
...SHOW YOUR FACE!

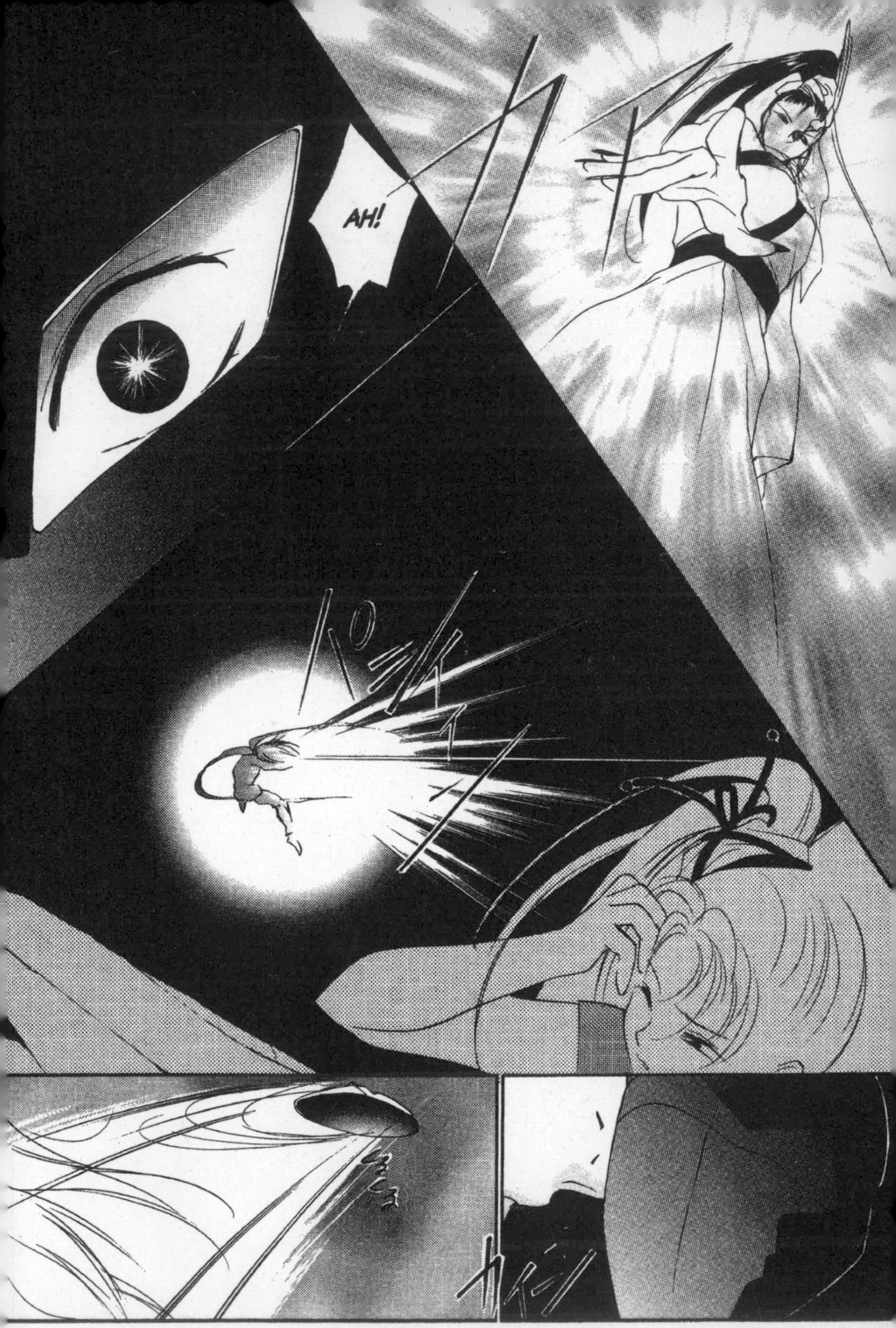
AH!

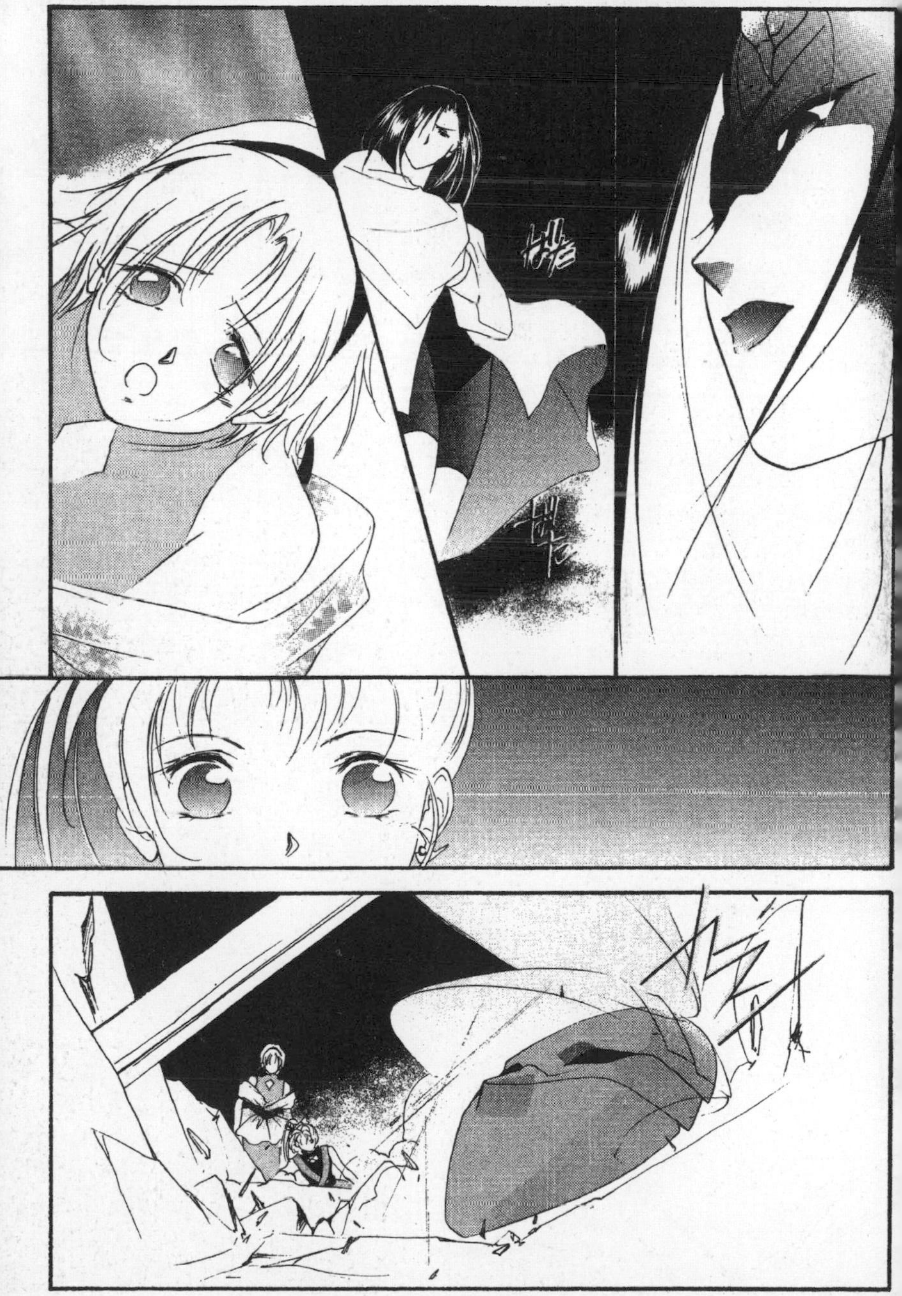

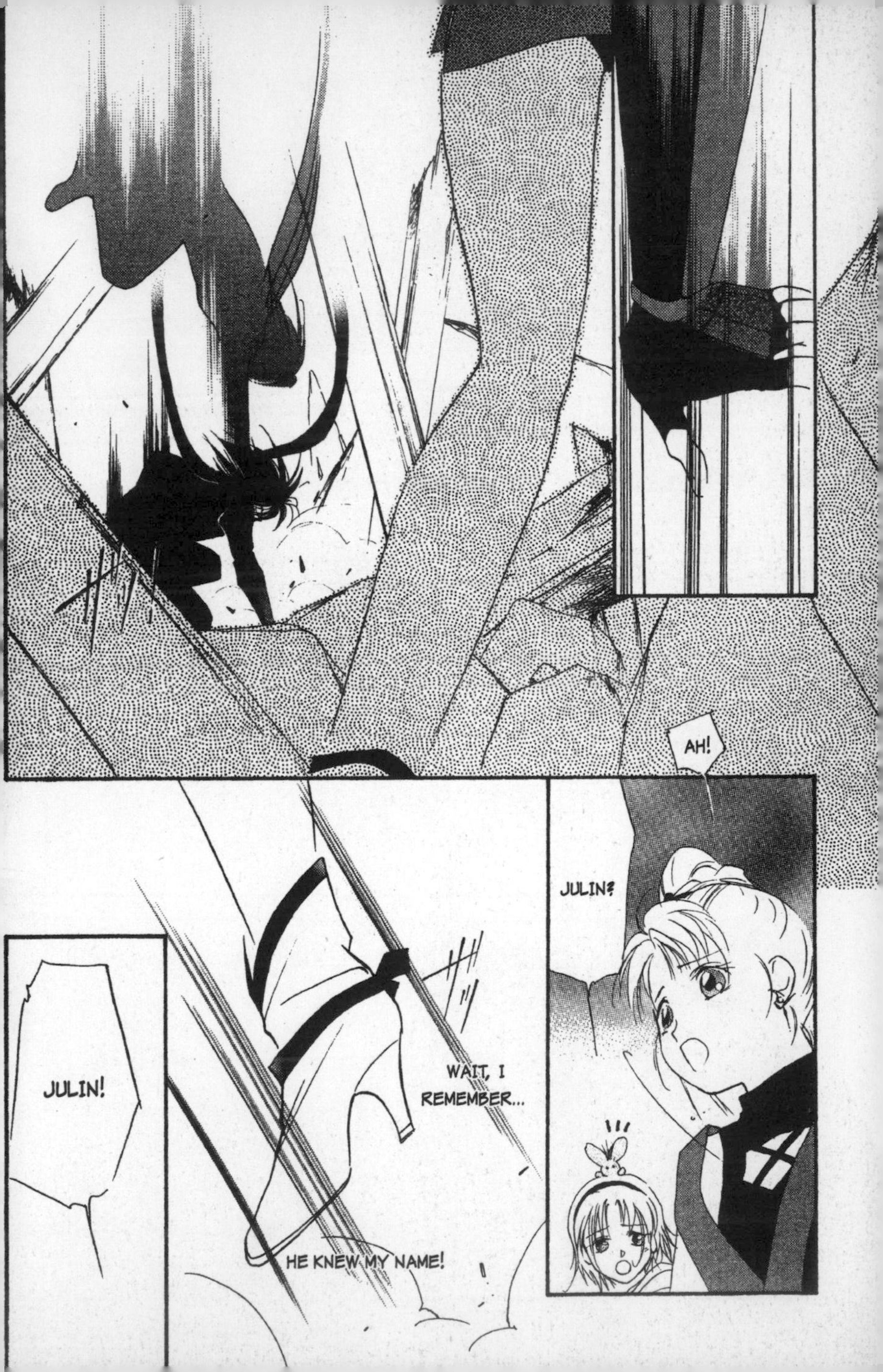
AH!
JULIN?
WAIT, I REMEMBER...
HE KNEW MY NAME!
JULIN!

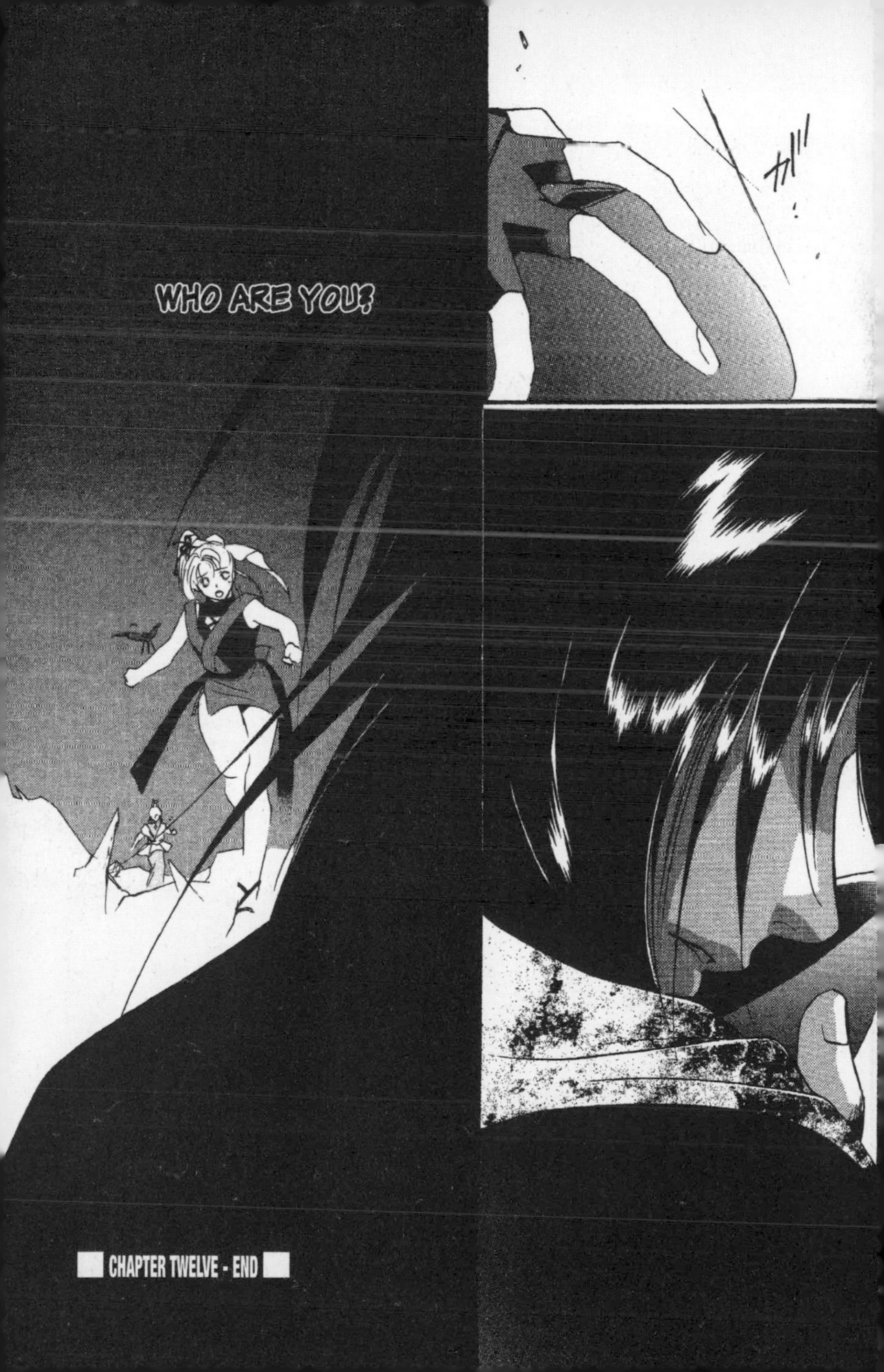
ガ
WHO ARE YOU!?
CHAPTER TWELVE - END

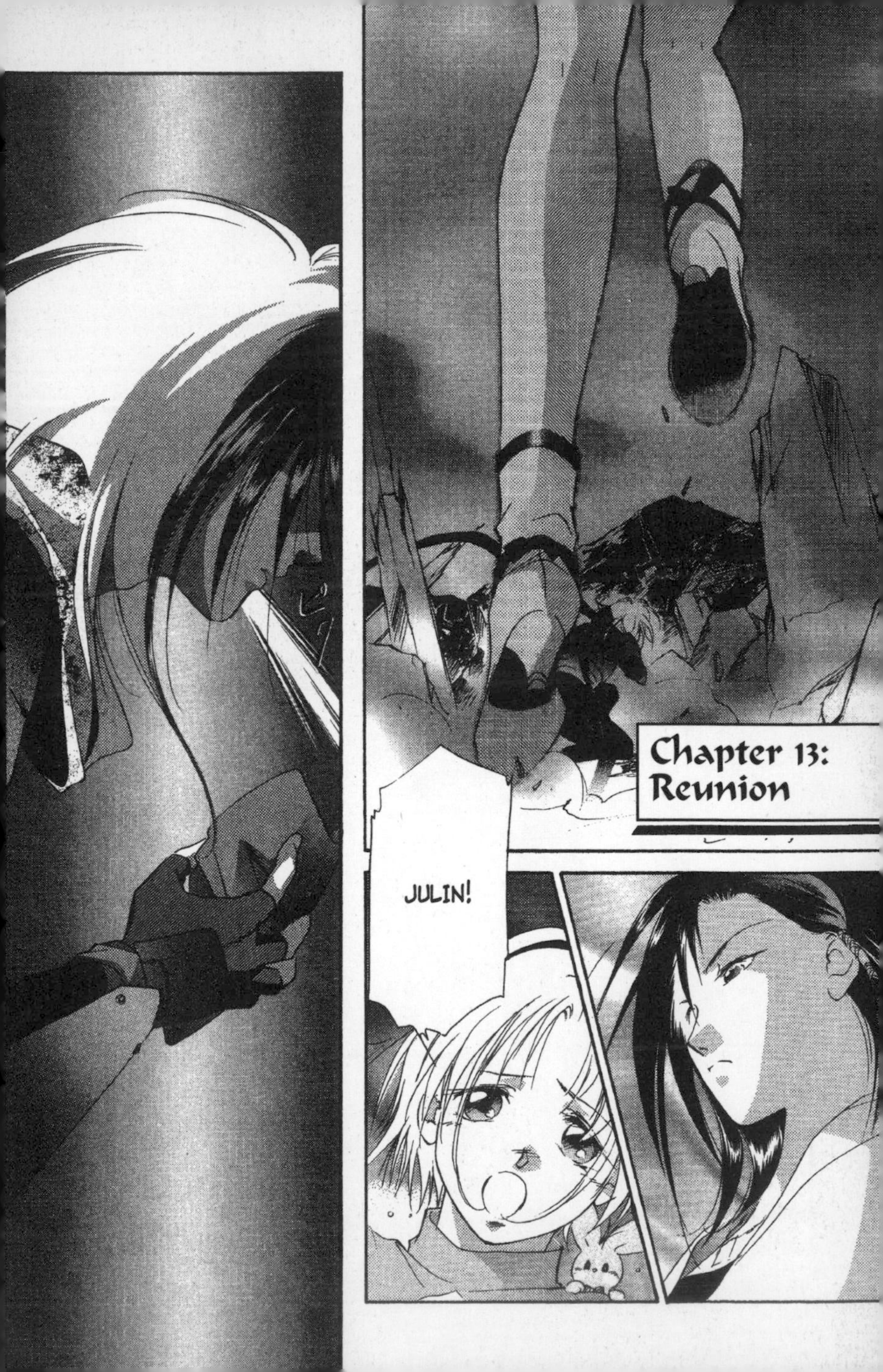
Chapter 13:
Reunion
JULIN!

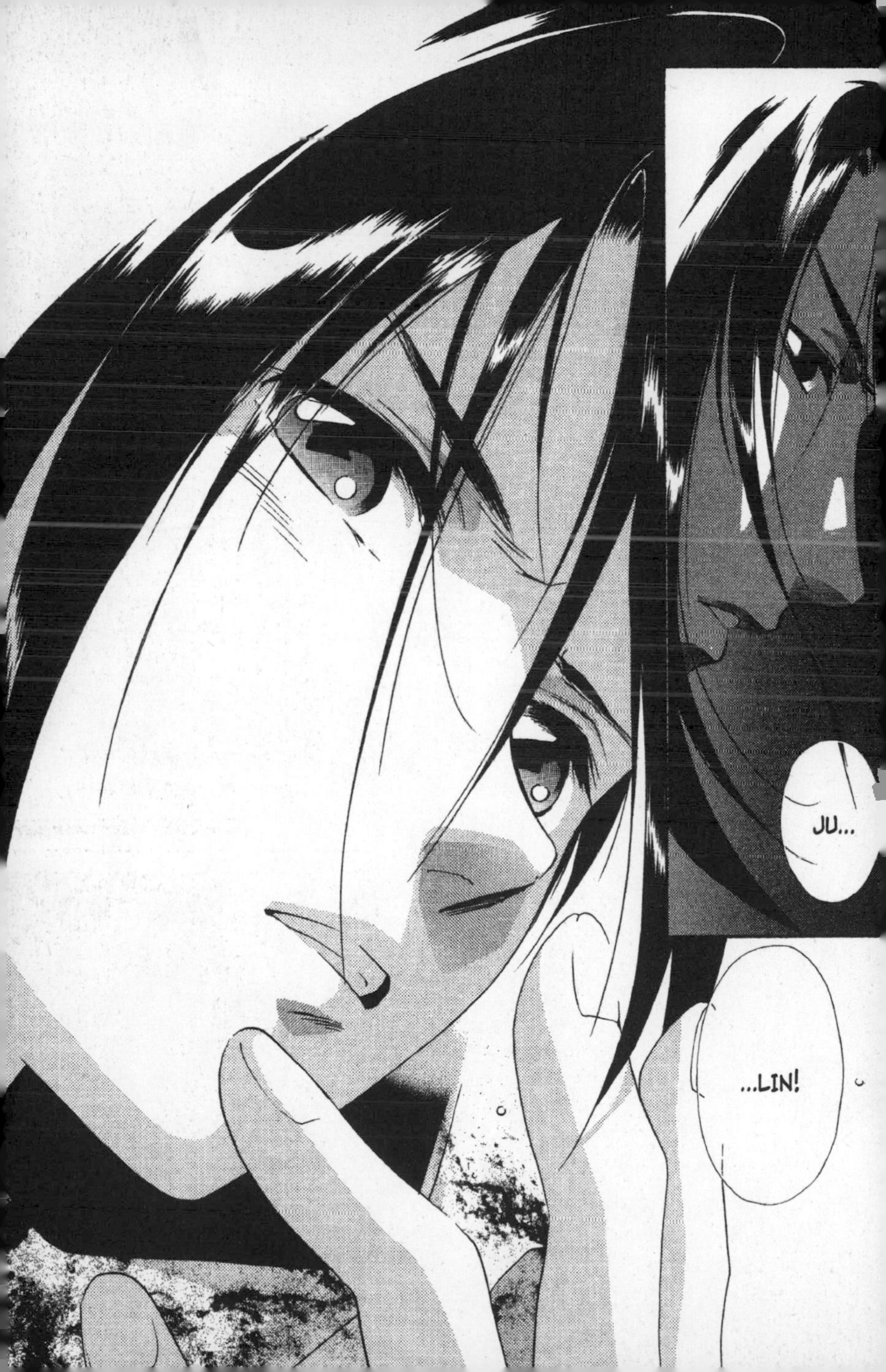
JU...
...LIN!

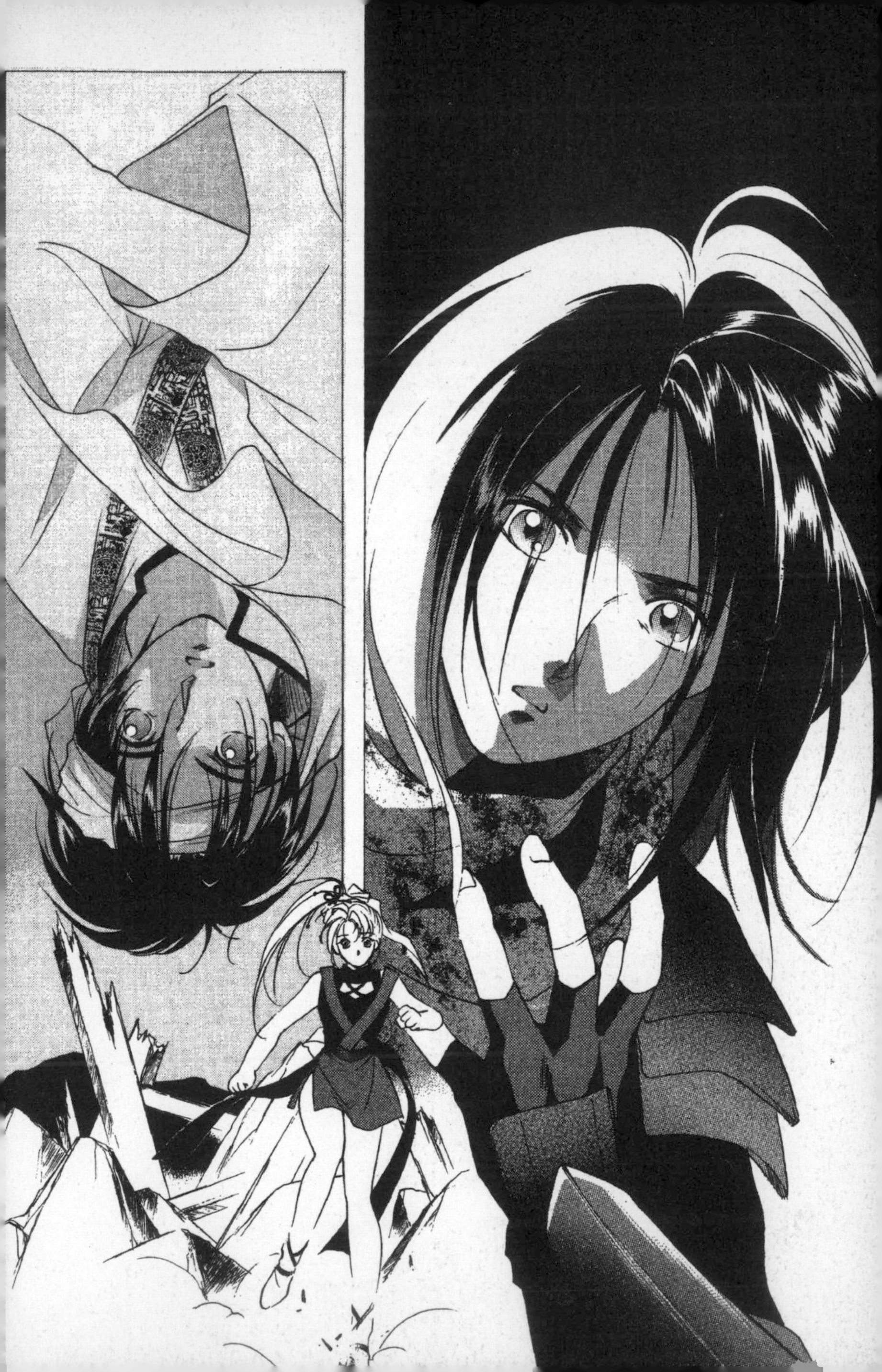

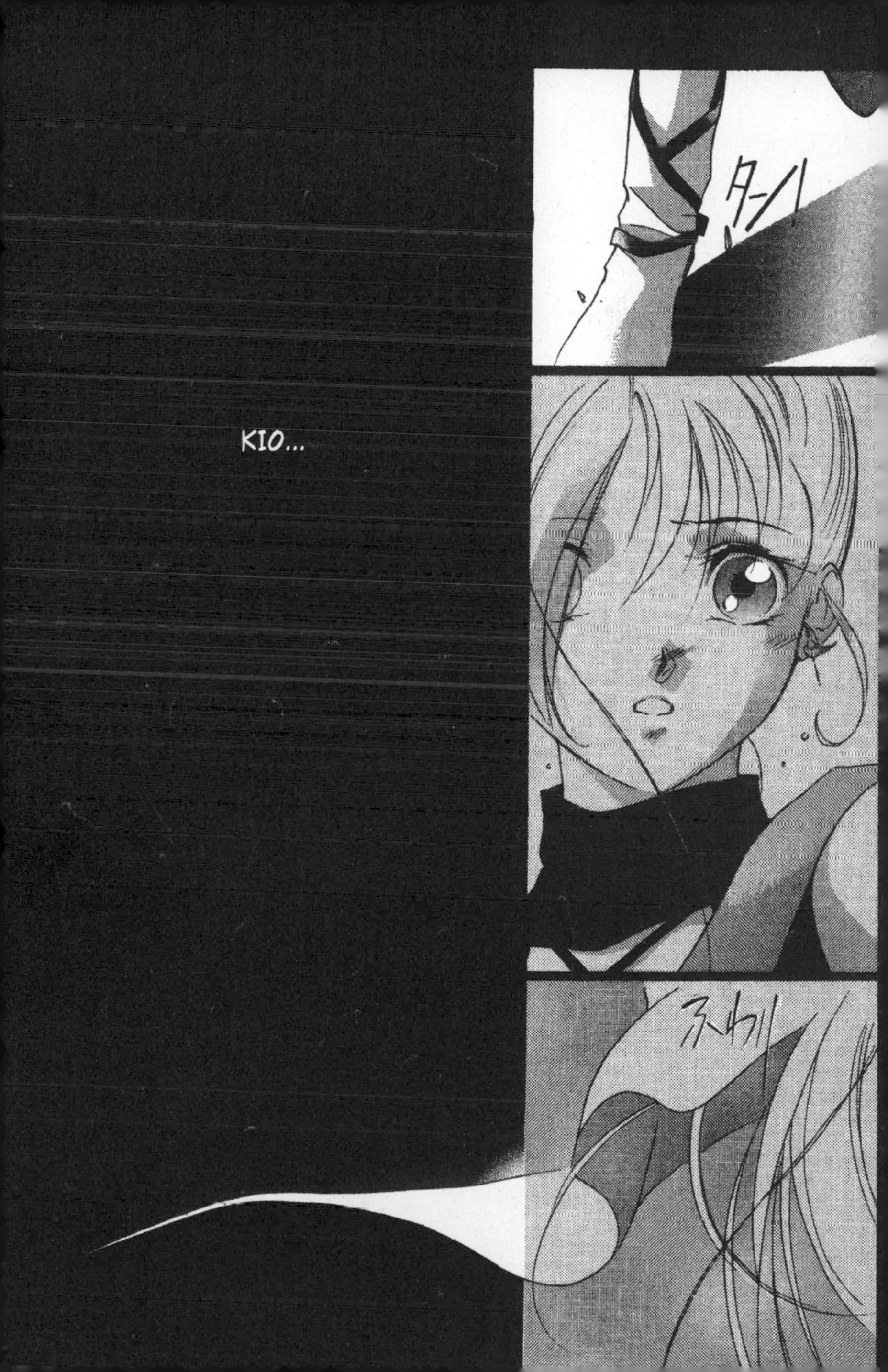
KIO...

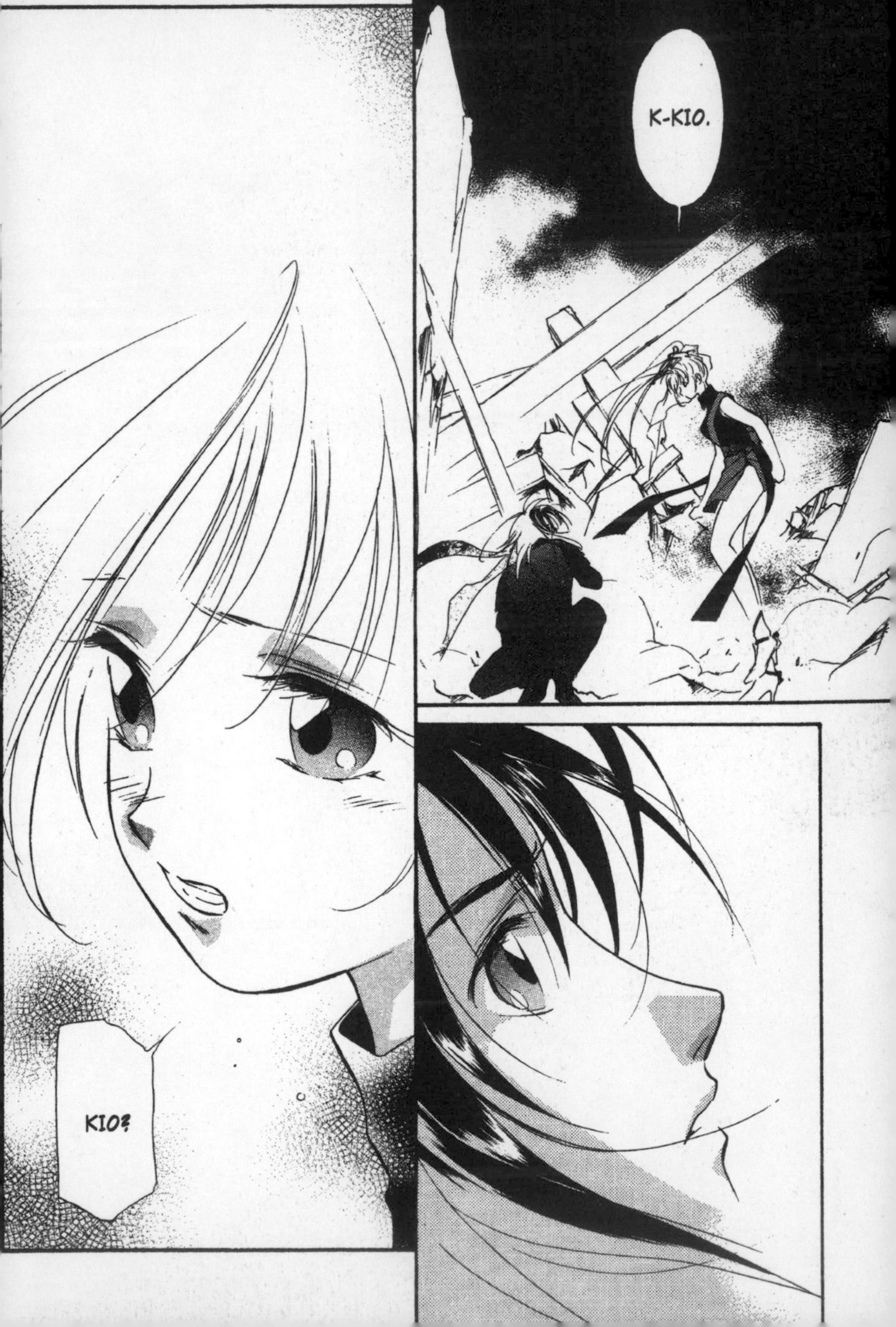
K-KIO.
KIO?

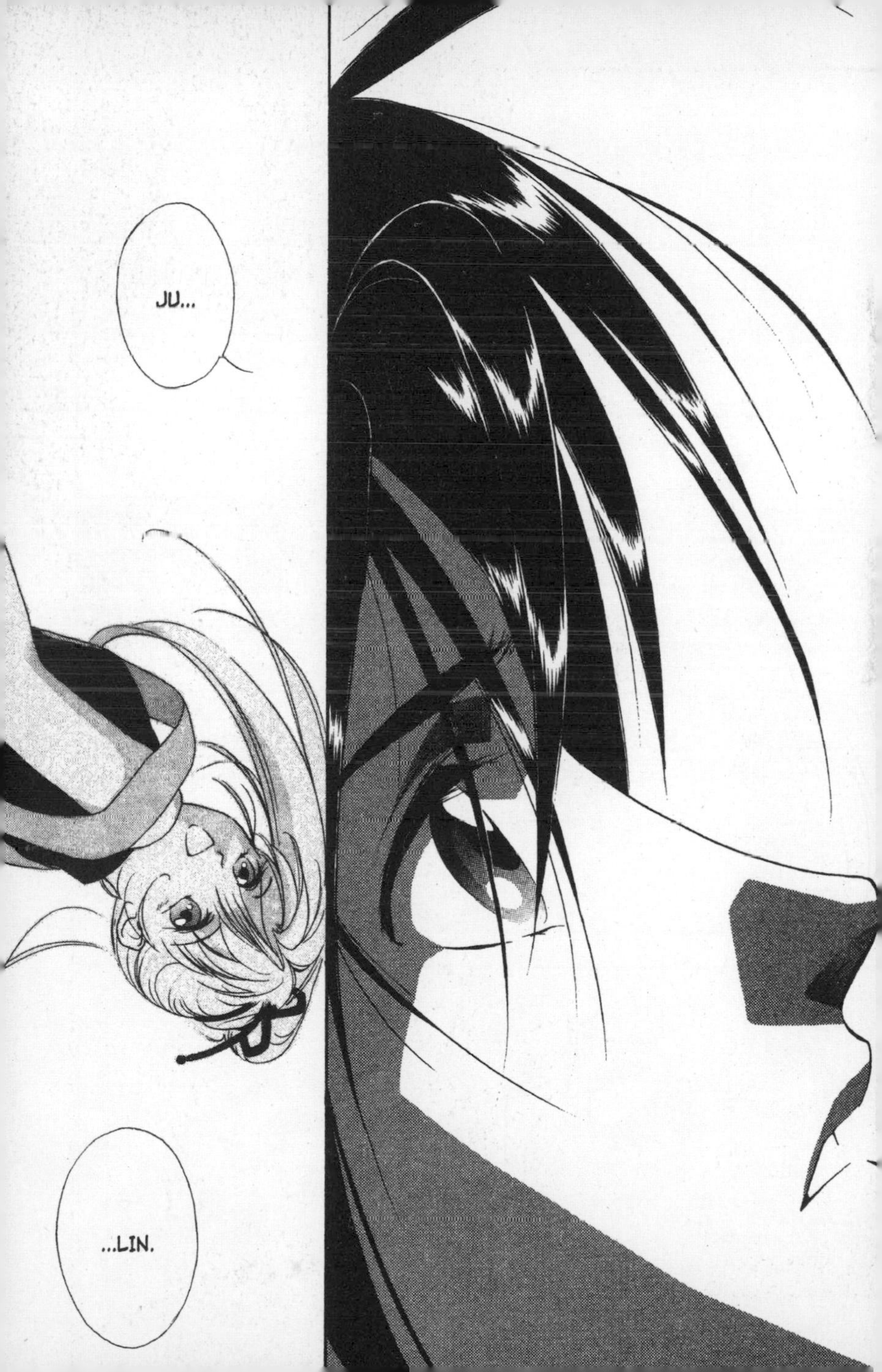
JU...
...LIN.

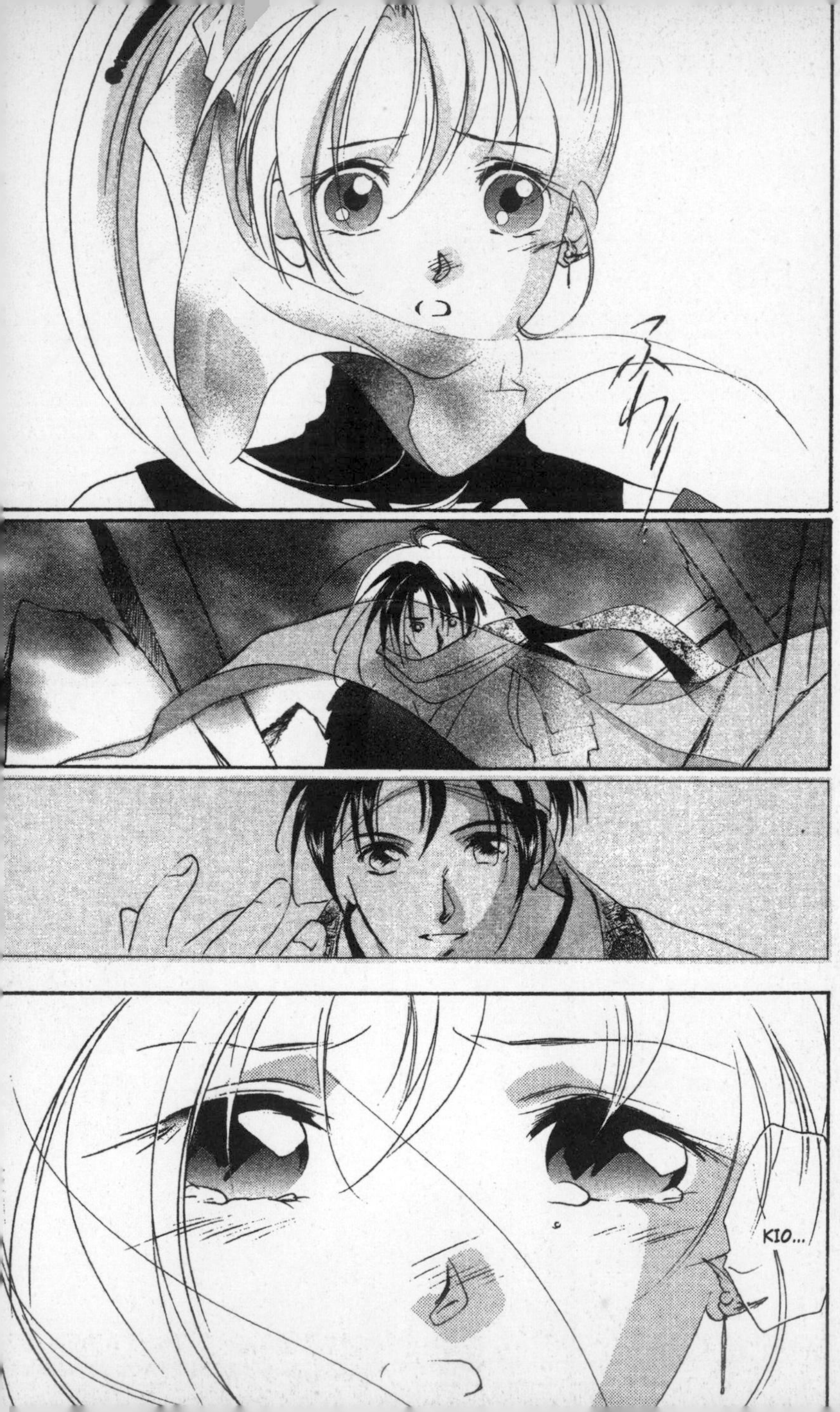
KIO...

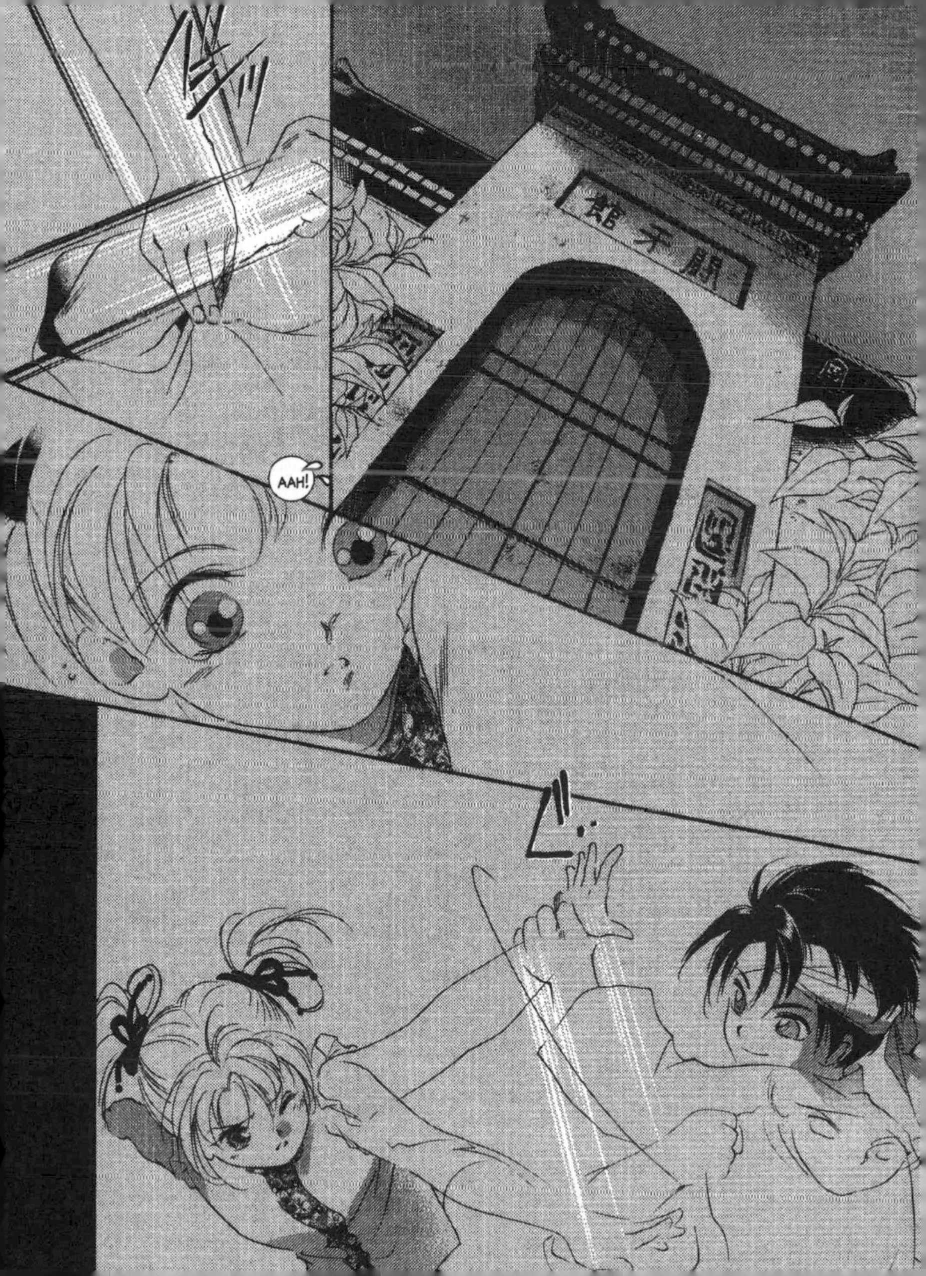
AAH!

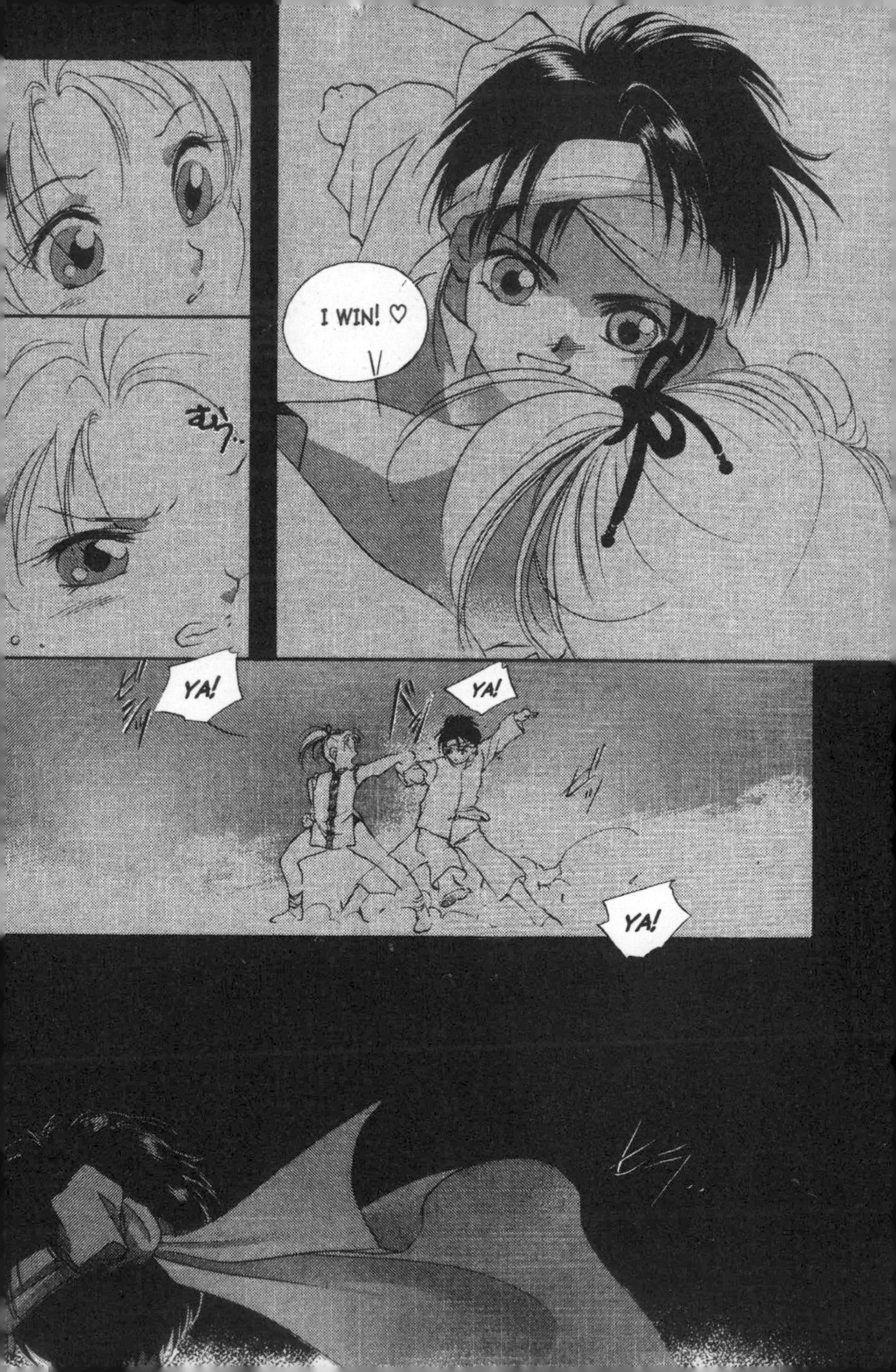

I WIN! ♡
YA!
YA!
YA!

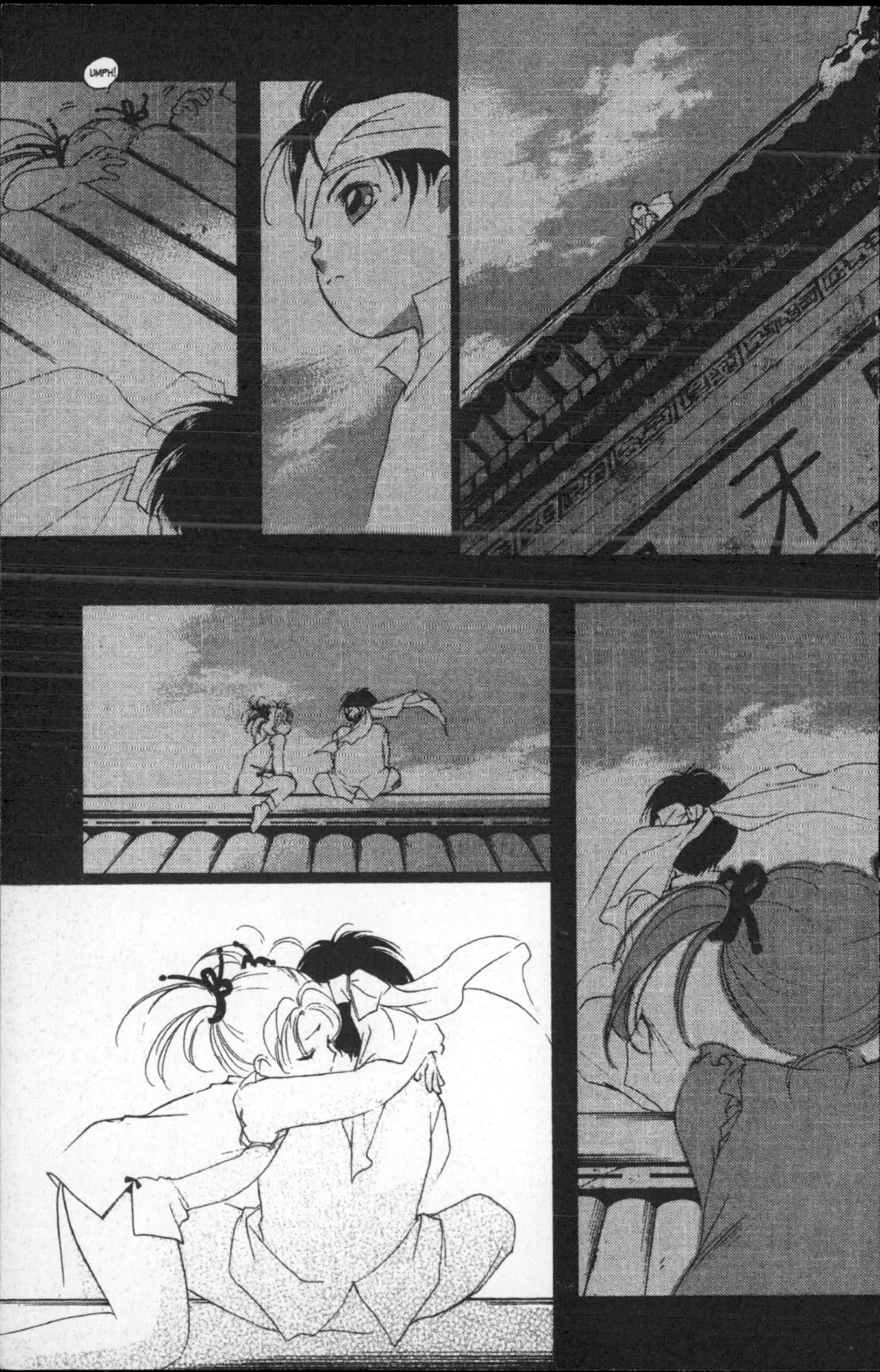
天
UMPH!

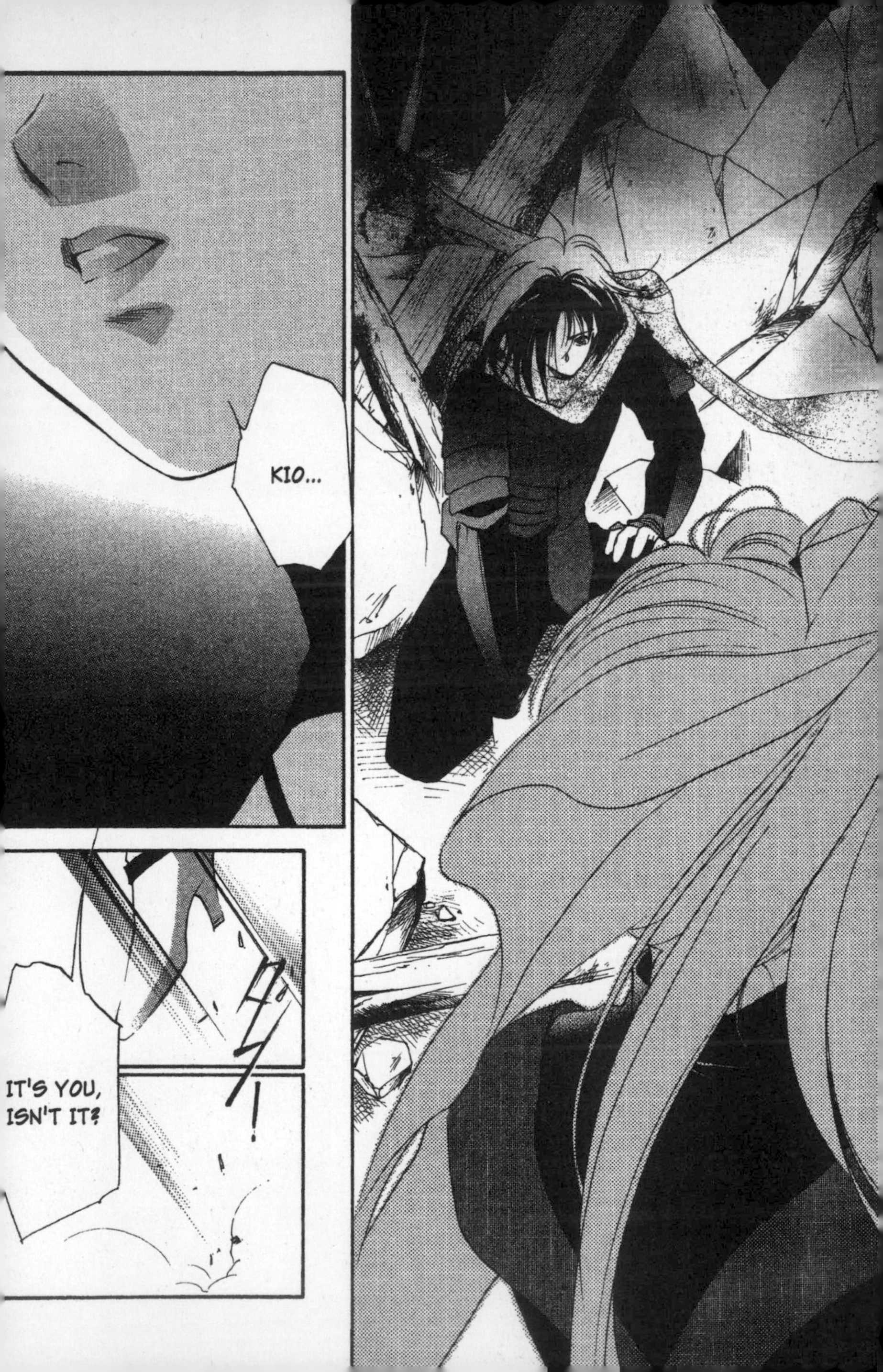
KIO...
IT'S YOU, ISN'T IT?

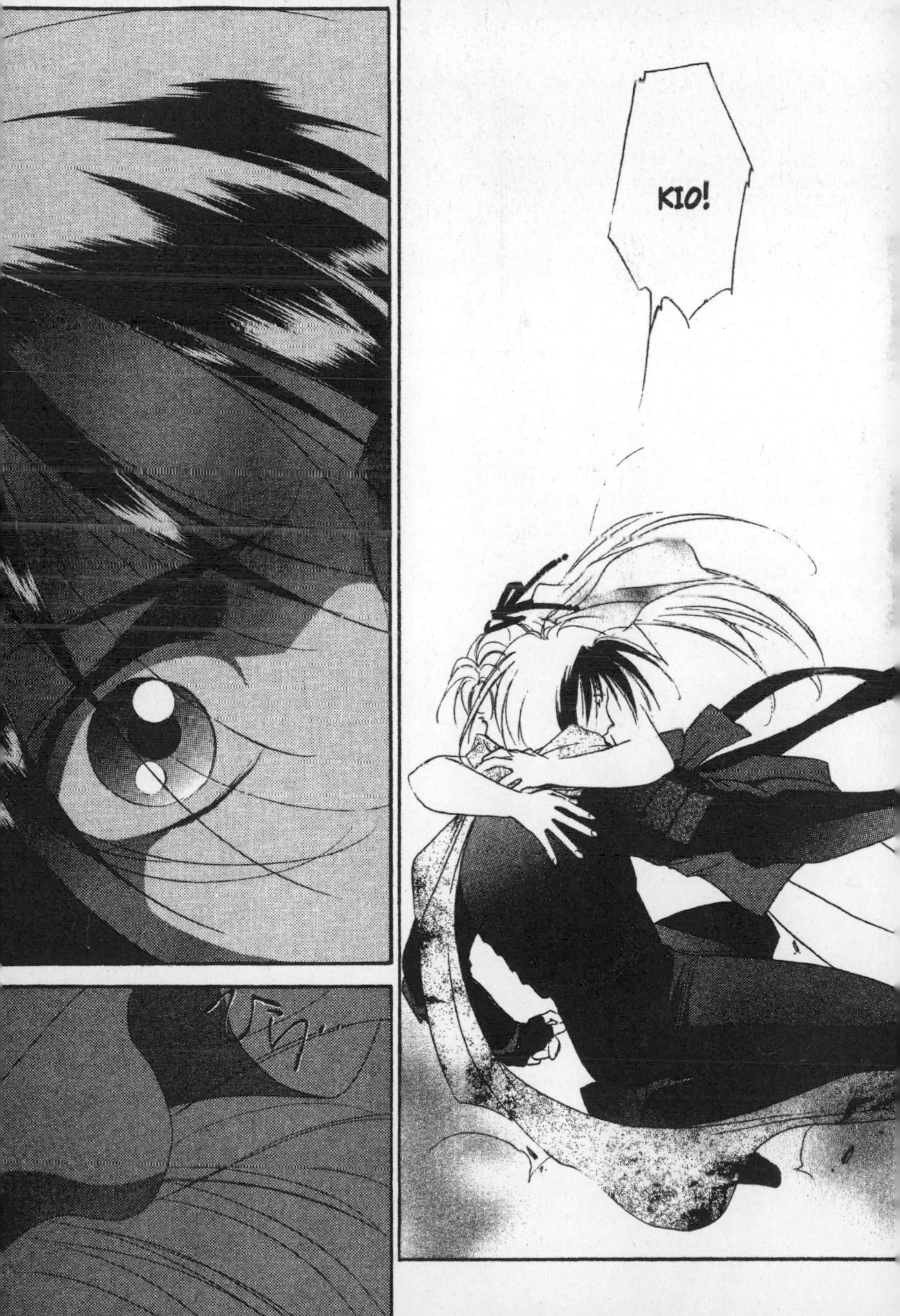
KIO!

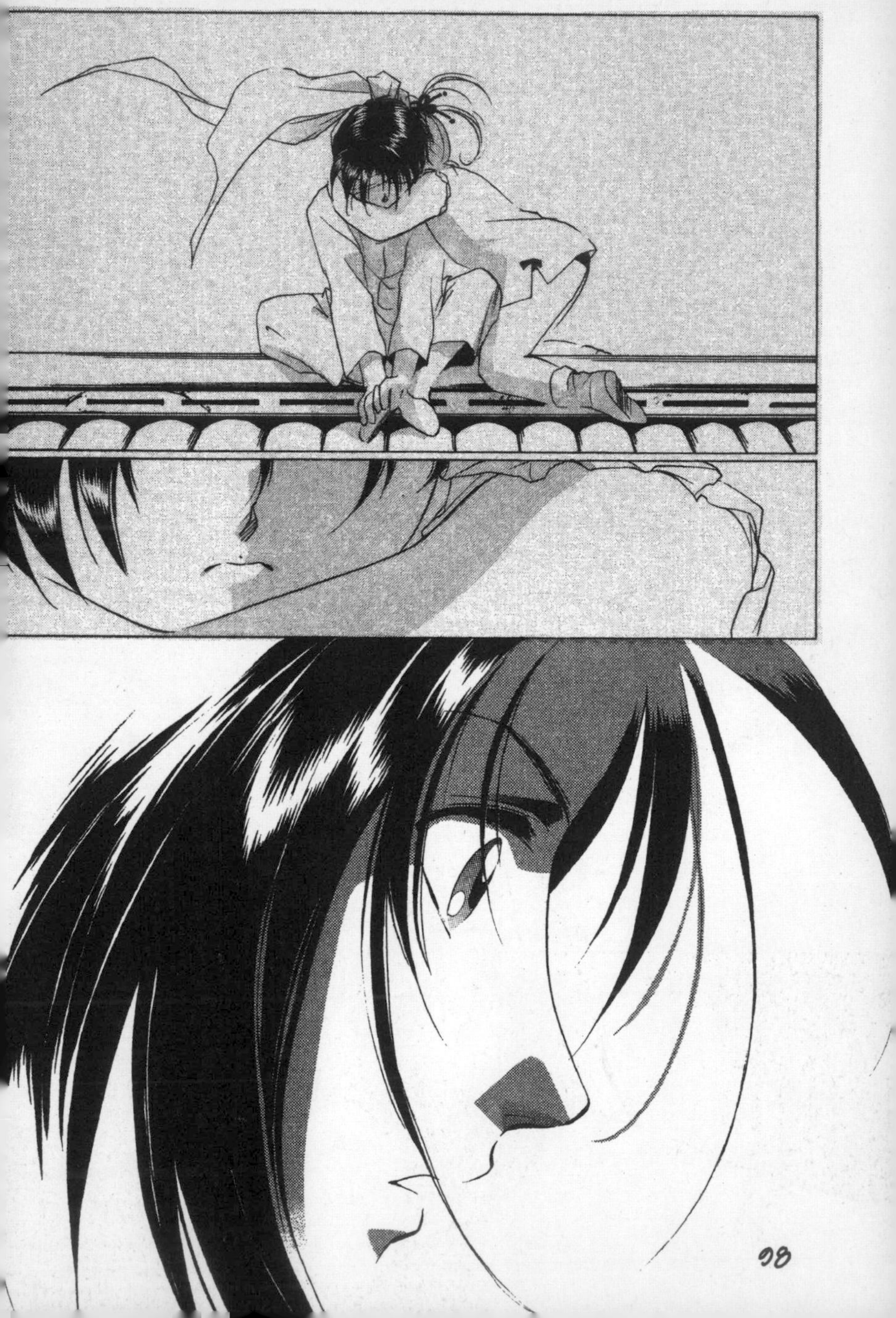

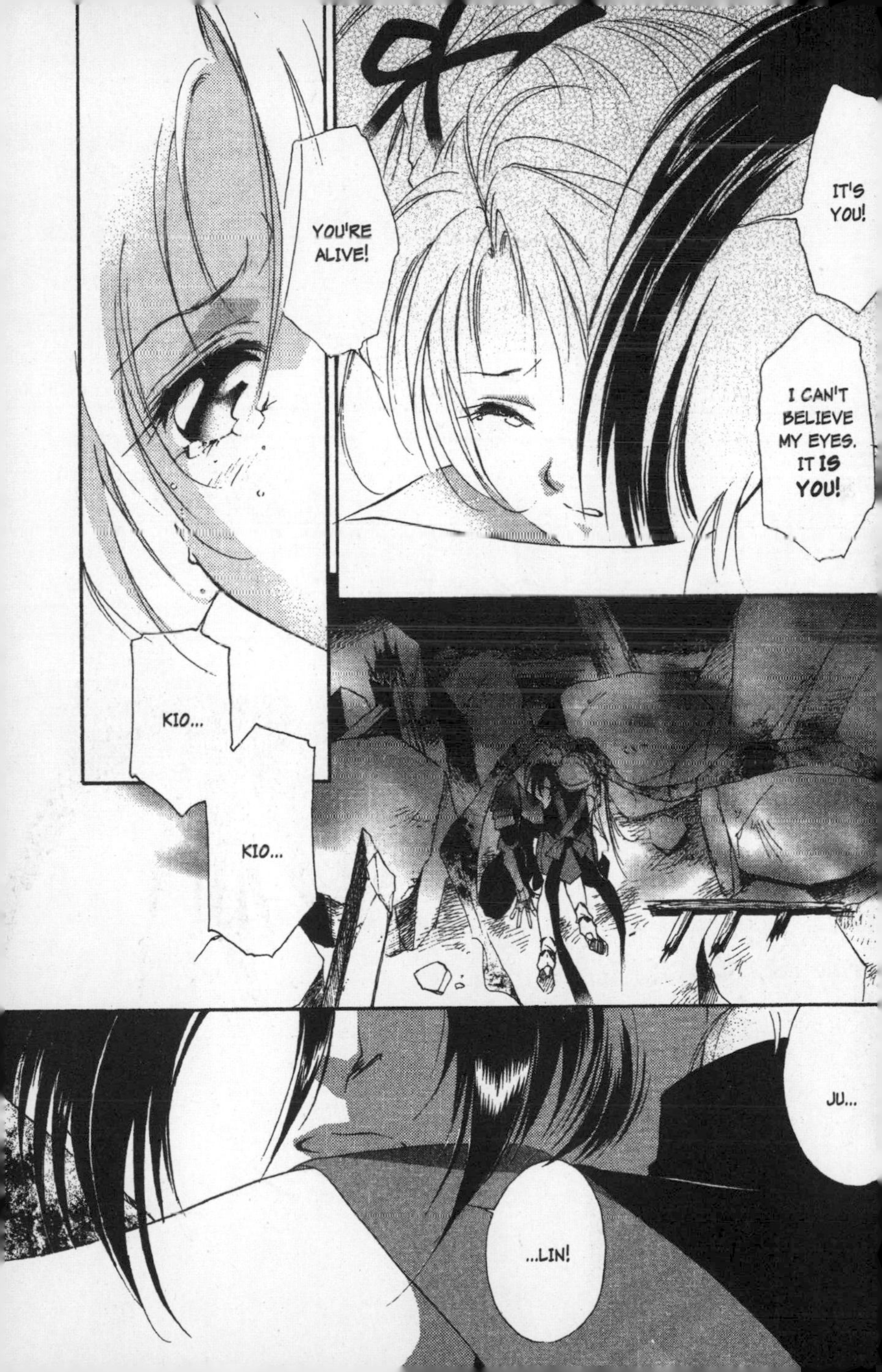
IT'S YOU!
YOU'RE ALIVE!
I CAN'T BELIEVE MY EYES. IT IS YOU!
KIO...
KIO...
JU...
...LIN!

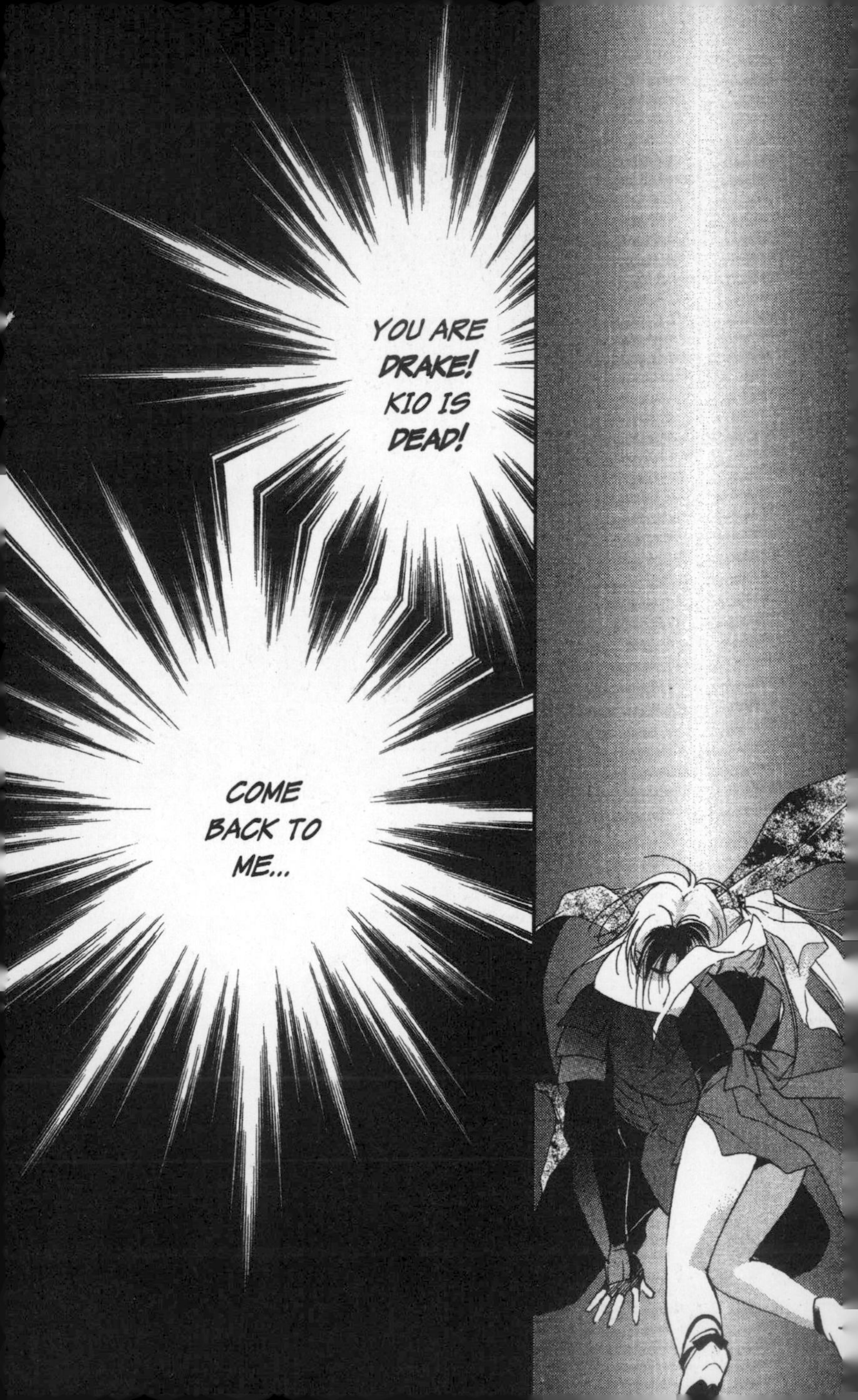
YOU ARE DRAKE! KIO IS DEAD!
COME BACK TO ME...

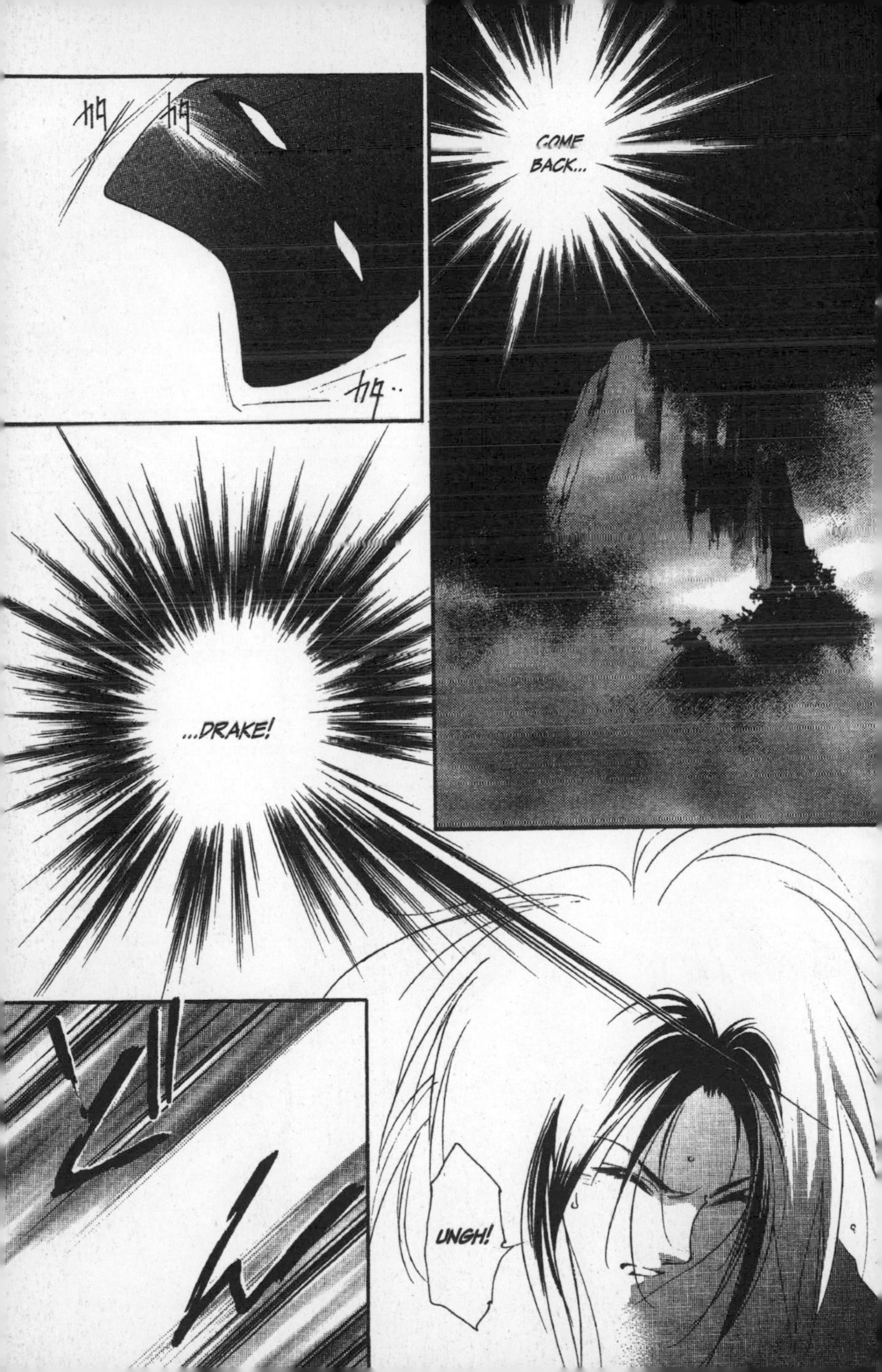
COME BACK...
...DRAKE!
UNGH!

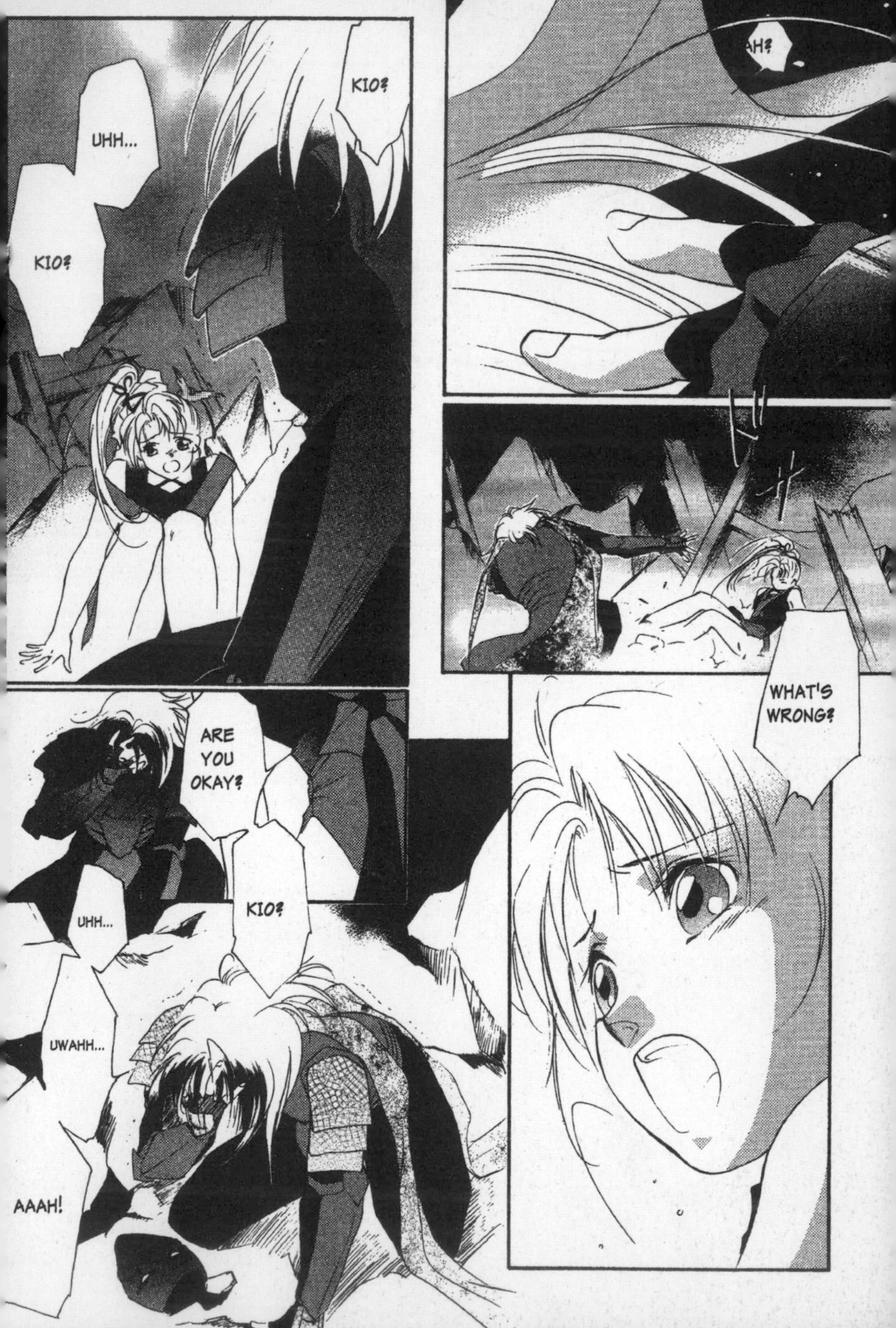
AH?
KIO?
UHH...
KIO?
WHAT'S WRONG?
ARE YOU OKAY?
KIO?
UHH...
UWAHH...
AAAH!

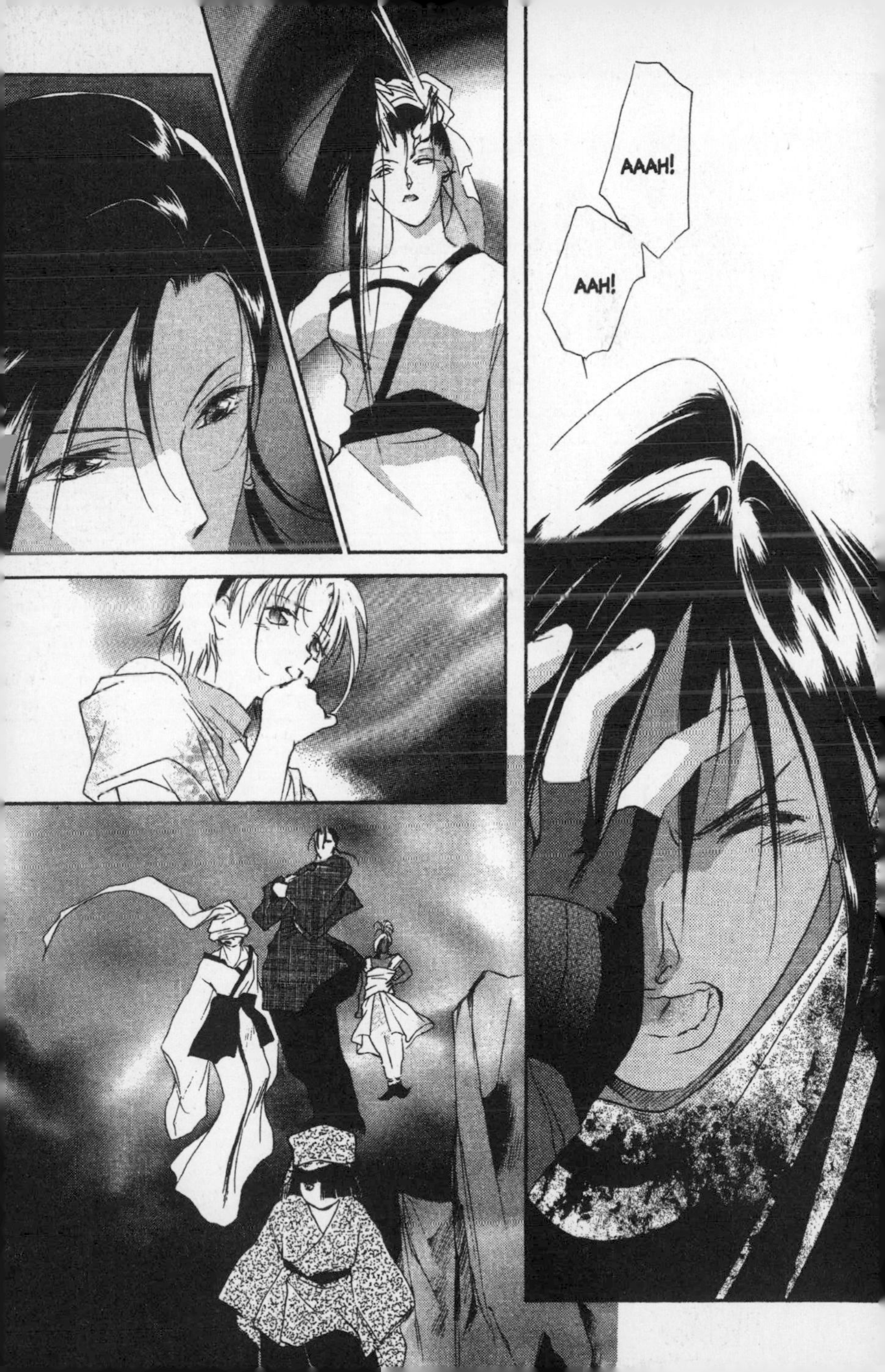
AAAH!
AAH!

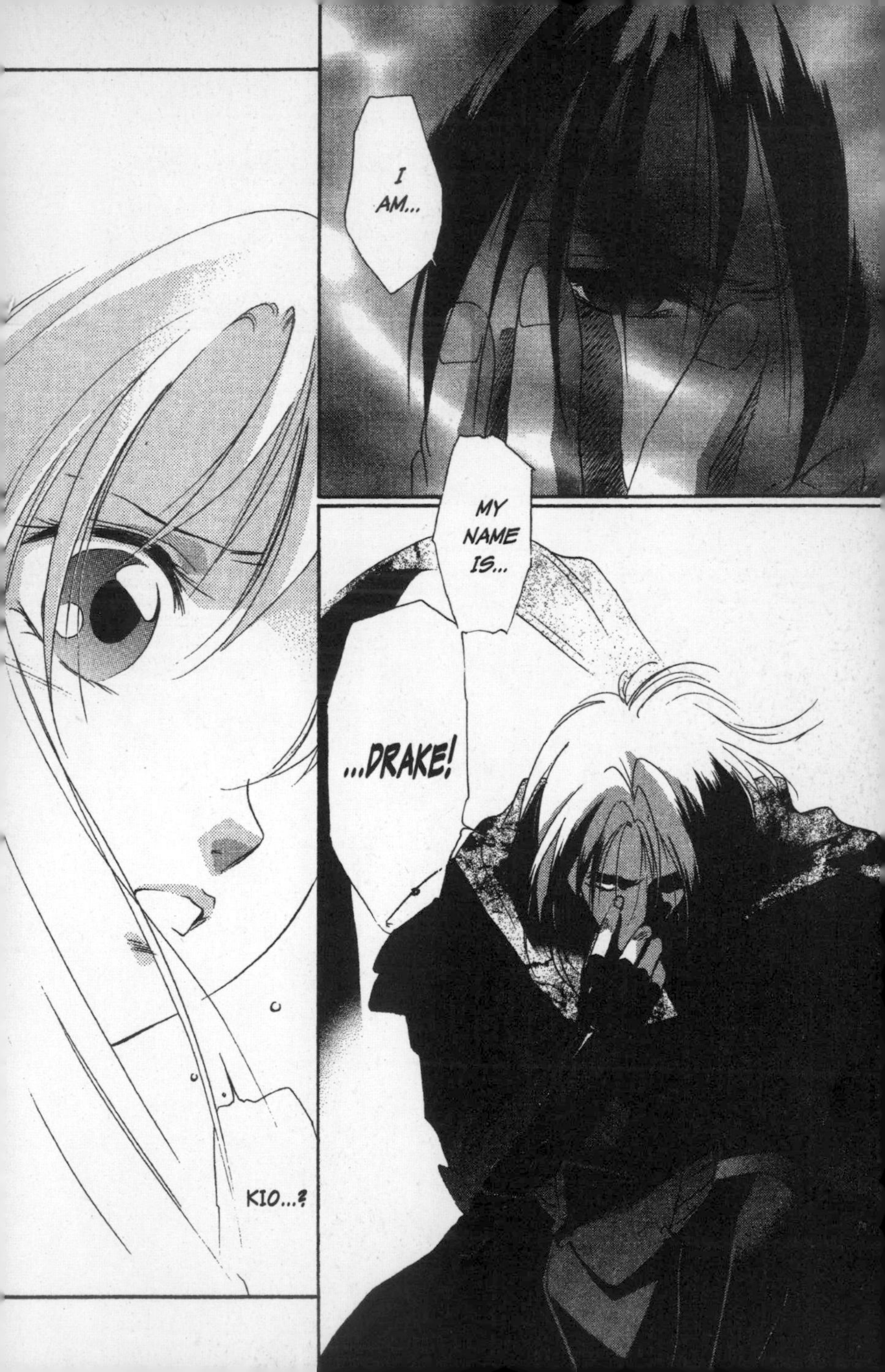
I AM...
MY NAME IS...
...DRAKE!
KIO...?

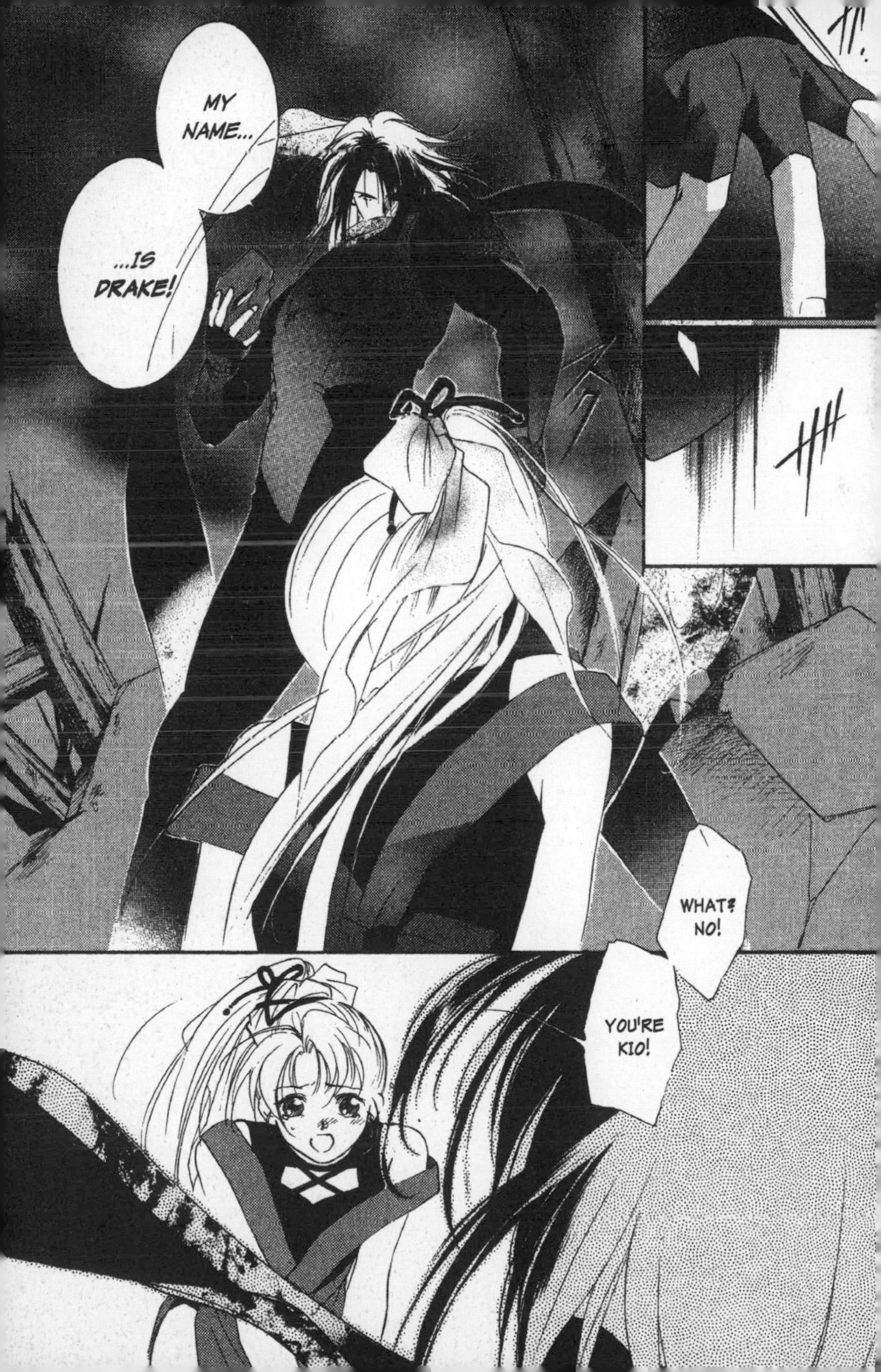
MY NAME...
...IS DRAKE!
WHAT? NO!
YOU'RE KIO!

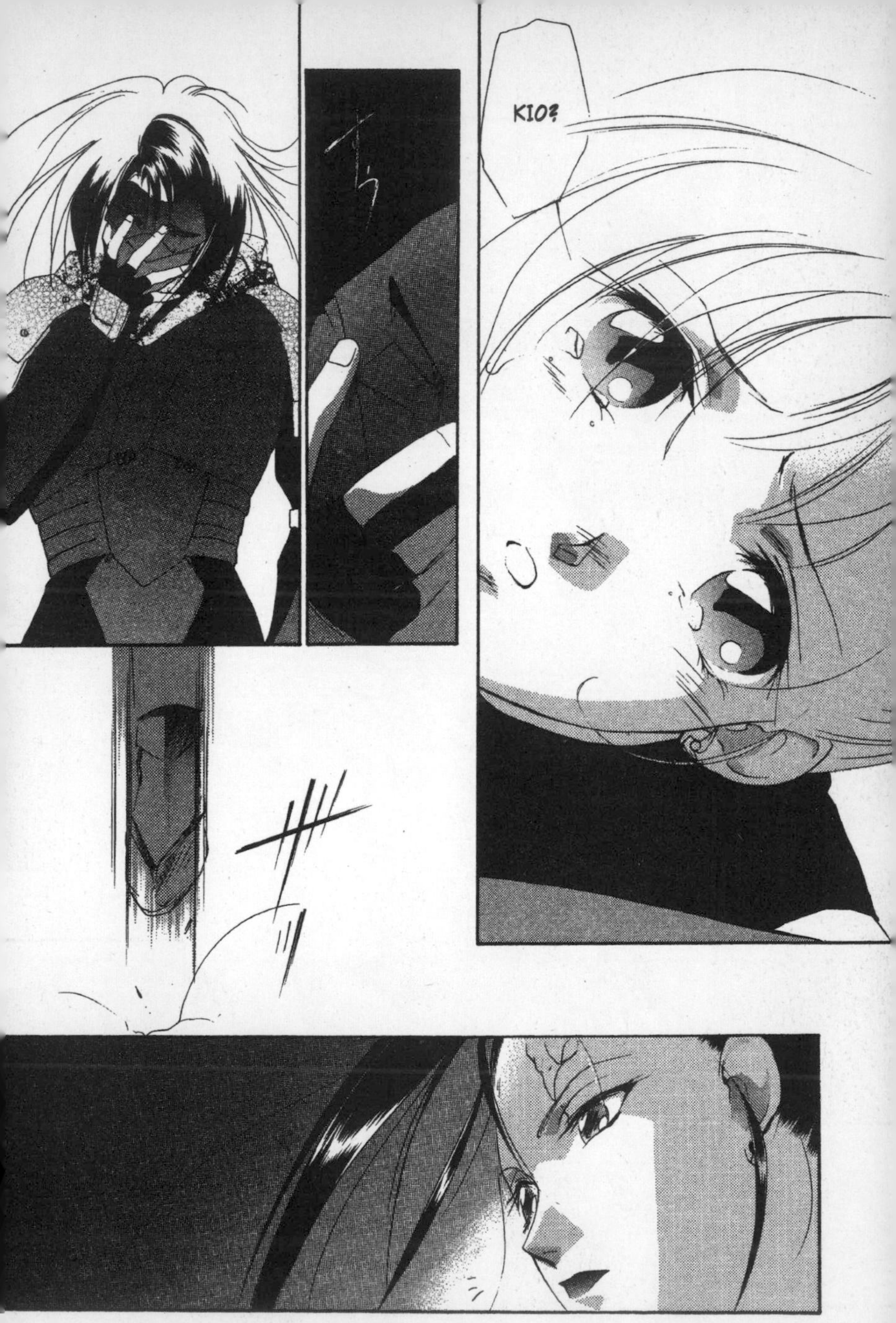
KIO?

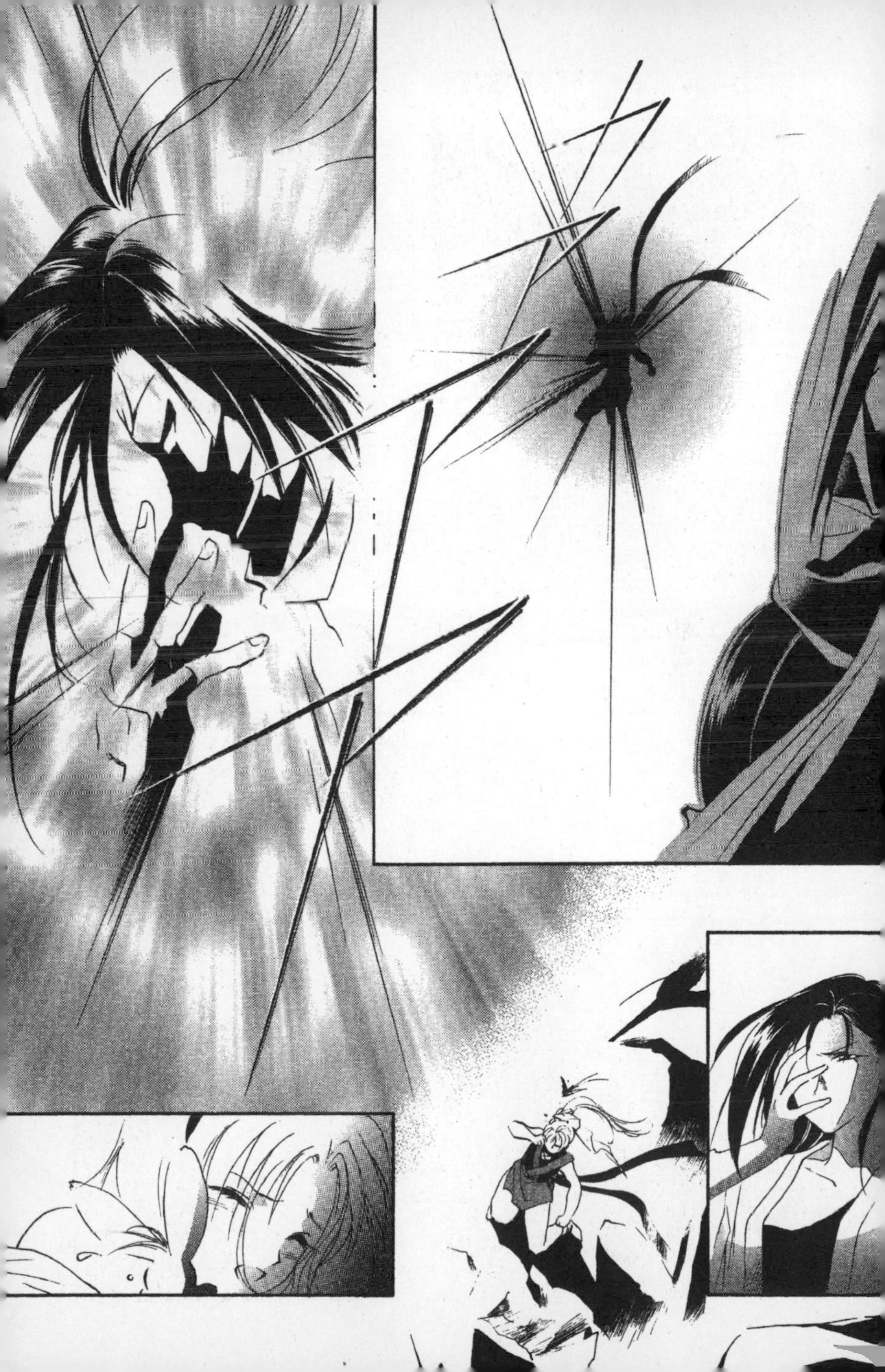

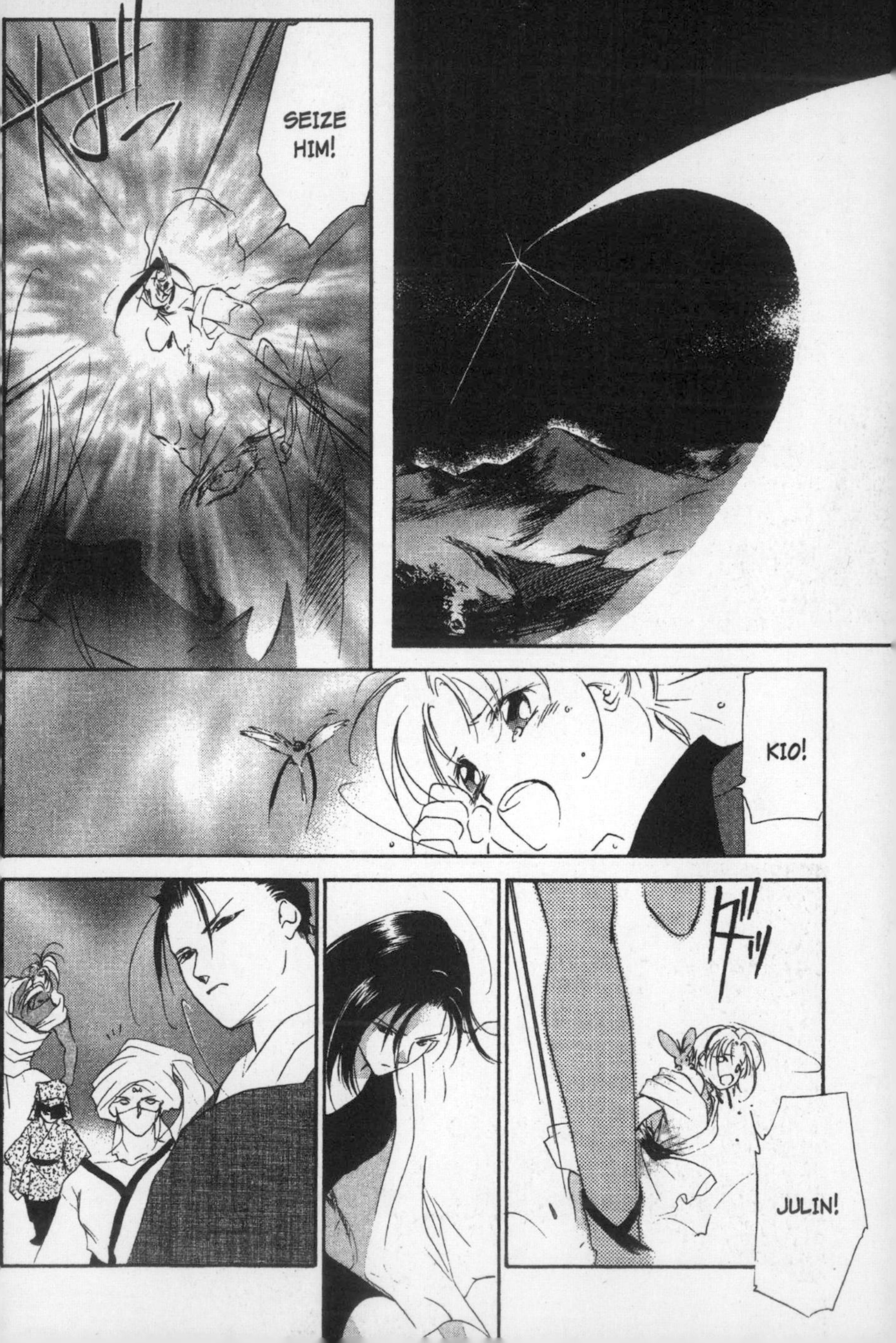
SEIZE HIM!
KIO!
JULIN!

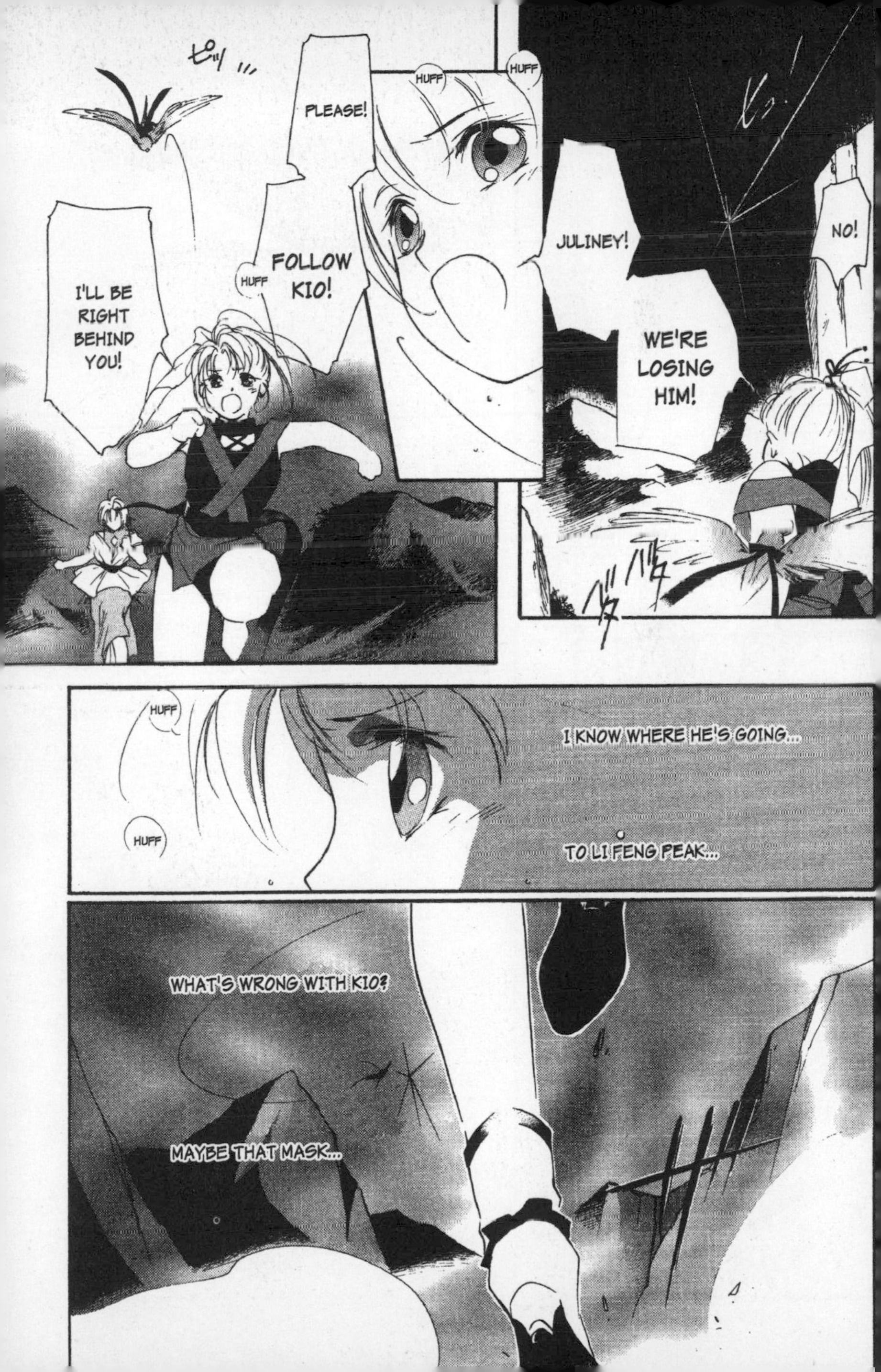
NO!
JULINEY!
WE'RE LOSING HIM!
HUFF
HUFF
PLEASE!
FOLLOW KIO!
HUFF
I'LL BE RIGHT BEHIND YOU!
HUFF
I KNOW WHERE HE'S GOING...
HUFF
TO LI FENG PEAK...
WHAT'S WRONG WITH KIO?
MAYBE THAT MASK...

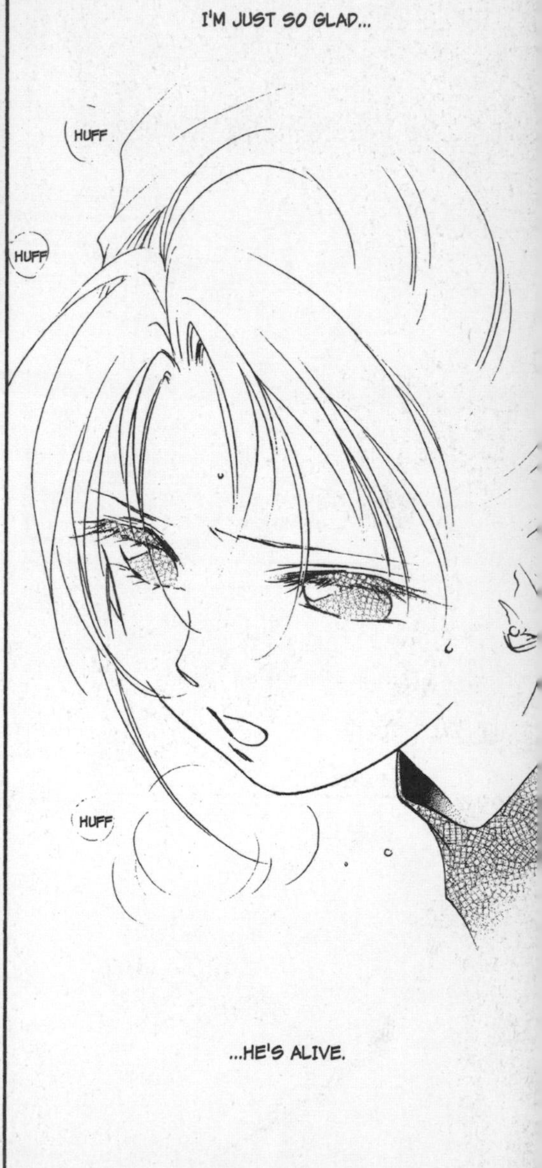
I'M JUST SO GLAD...
HUFF
HUFF
HUFF
...HE'S ALIVE.

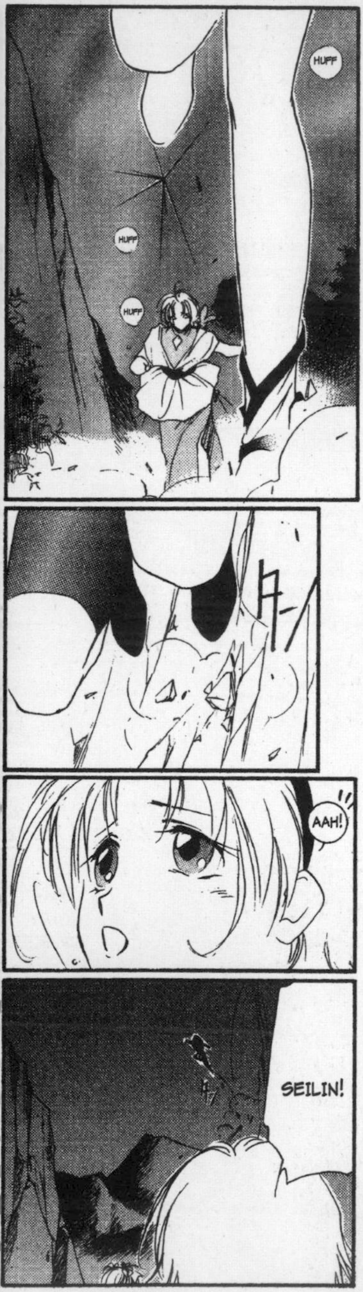
HUFF
HUFF
HUFF
AAH!
SEILIN!

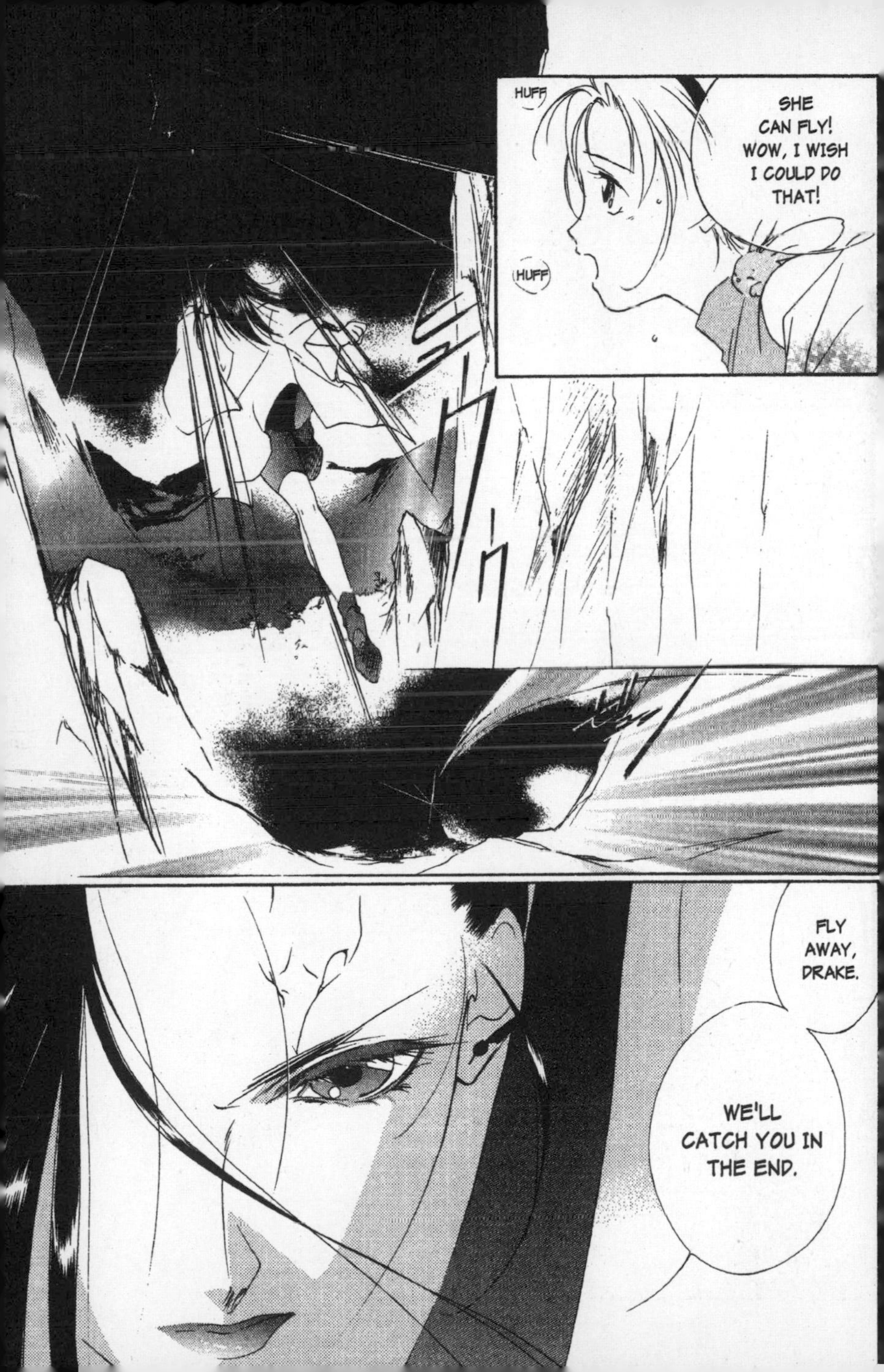
SHE CAN FLY! WOW, I WISH I COULD DO THAT!
HUFF
HUFF
FLY AWAY, DRAKE.
WE'LL CATCH YOU IN THE END.

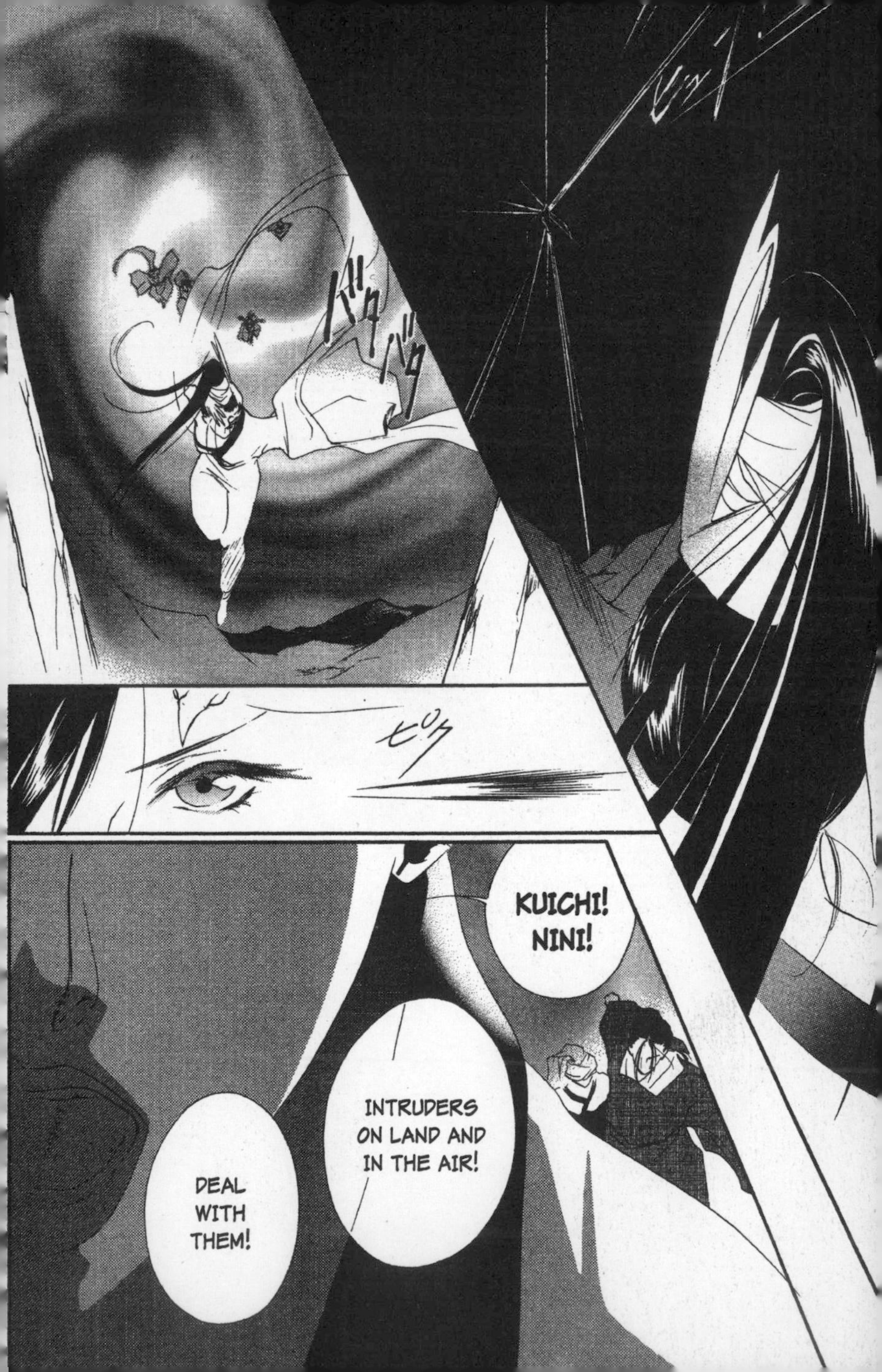
KUICHI! NINI!
INTRUDERS ON LAND AND IN THE AIR!
DEAL WITH THEM!

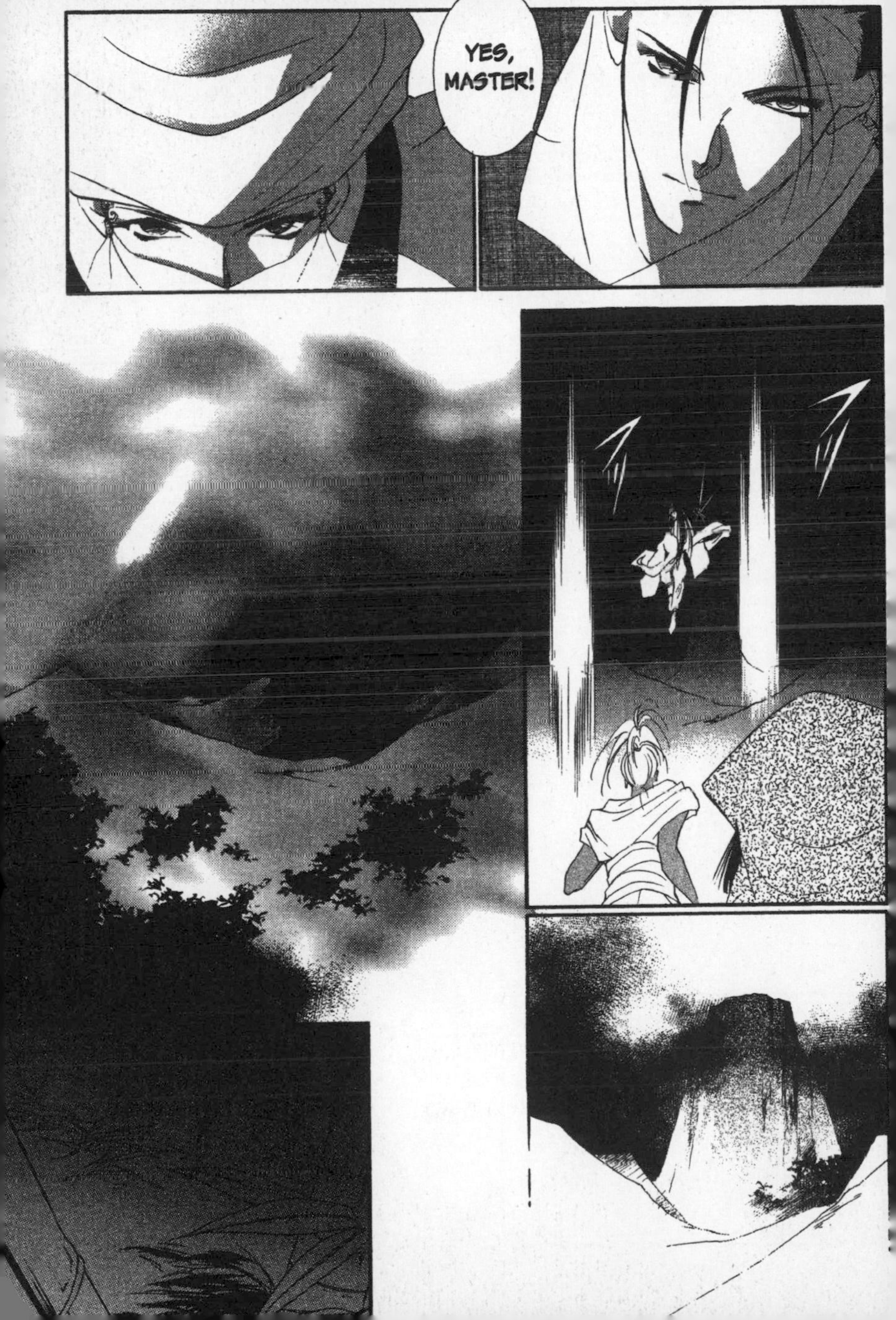
YES, MASTER!

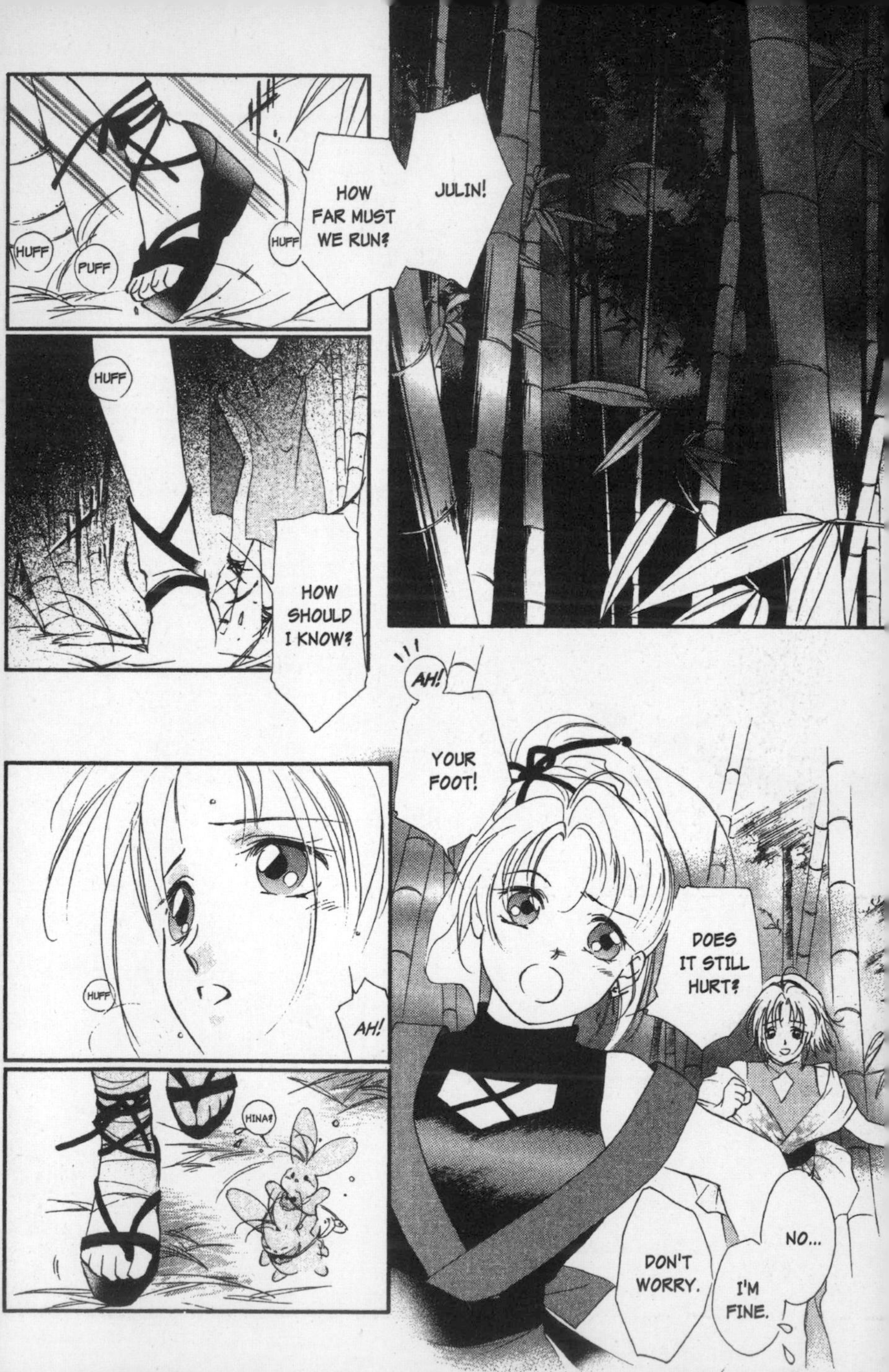
HUFF
PUFF
HUFF
JULIN!
HOW FAR MUST WE RUN?
HUFF
HOW SHOULD I KNOW?
AH!
YOUR FOOT!
DOES IT STILL HURT?
NO...
I'M FINE.
DON'T WORRY.
HUFF
AH!
HINA?

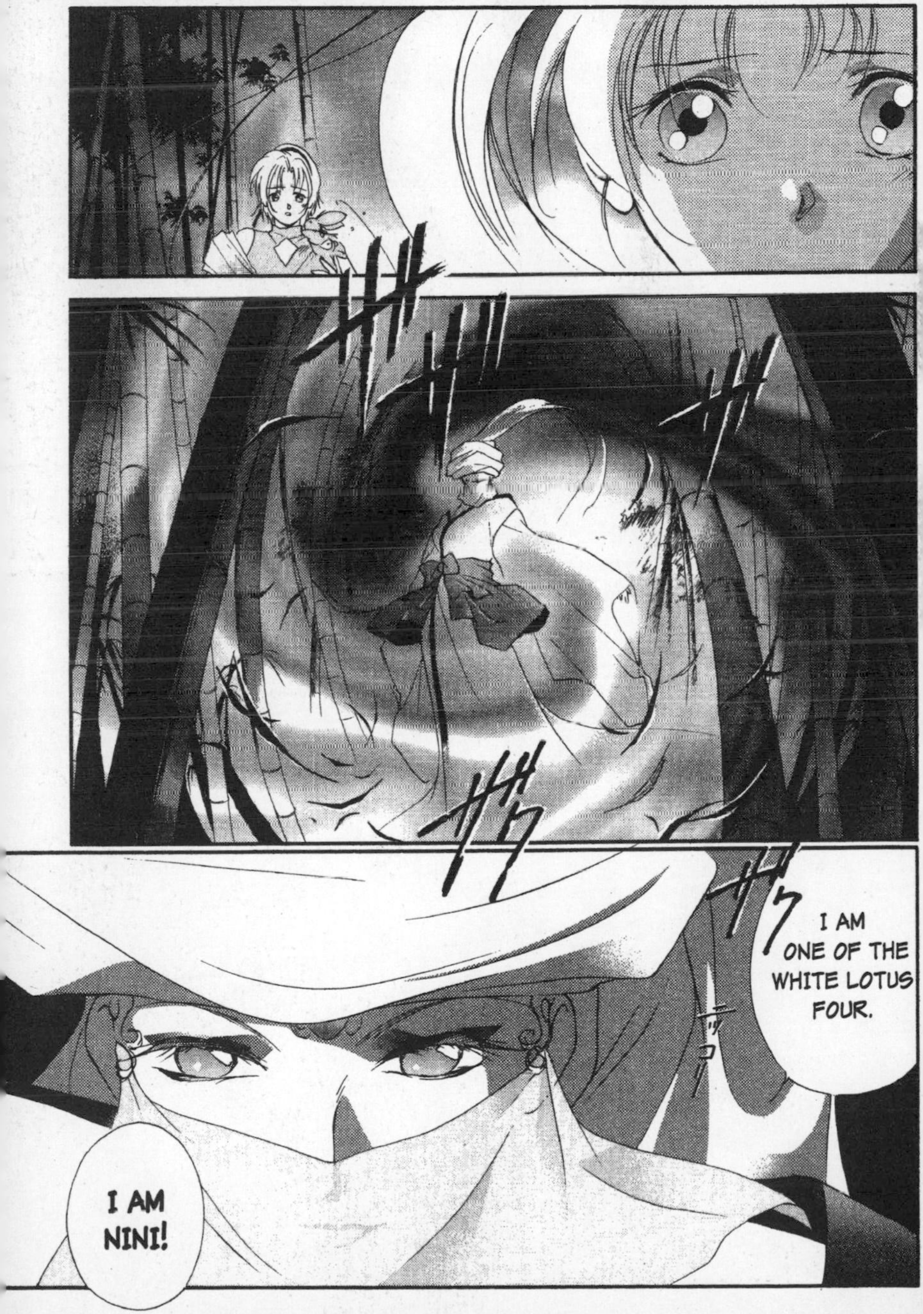
I AM ONE OF THE WHITE LOTUS FOUR.
I AM NINI!

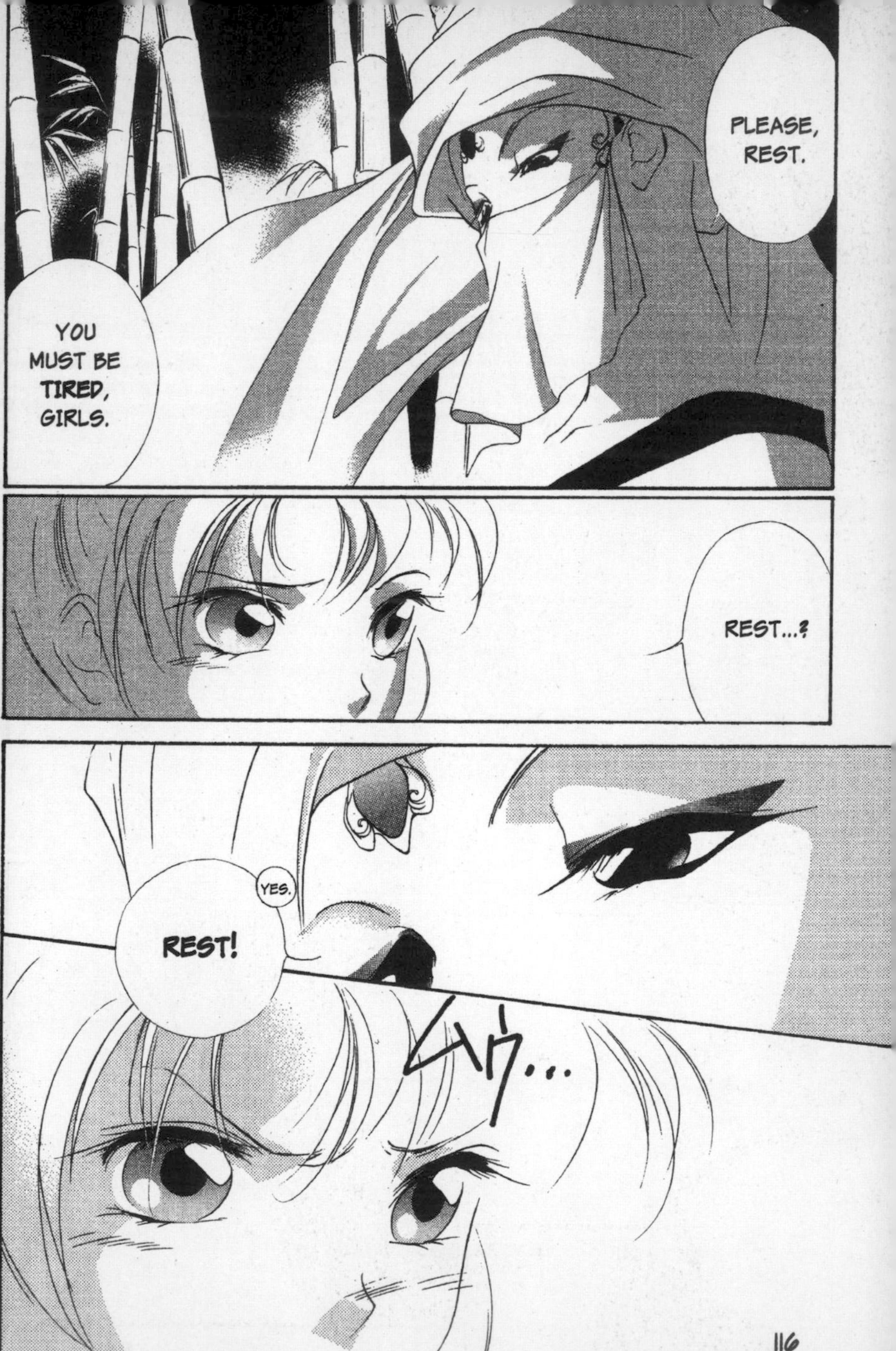
PLEASE, REST.
YOU MUST BE TIRED, GIRLS.
REST...?
YES.
REST!
ムッ...

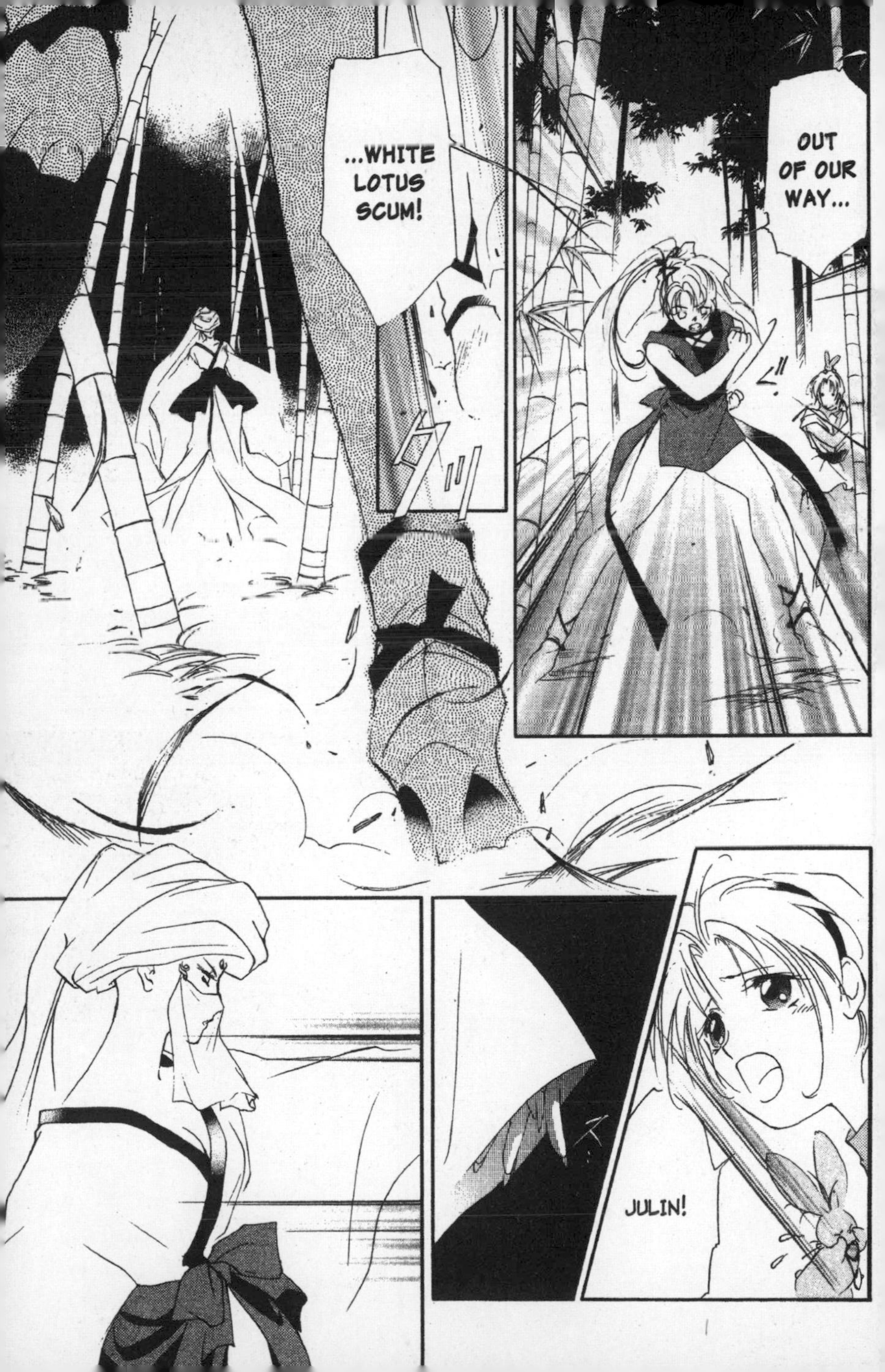
OUT OF OUR WAY...
...WHITE LOTUS SCUM!
JULIN!

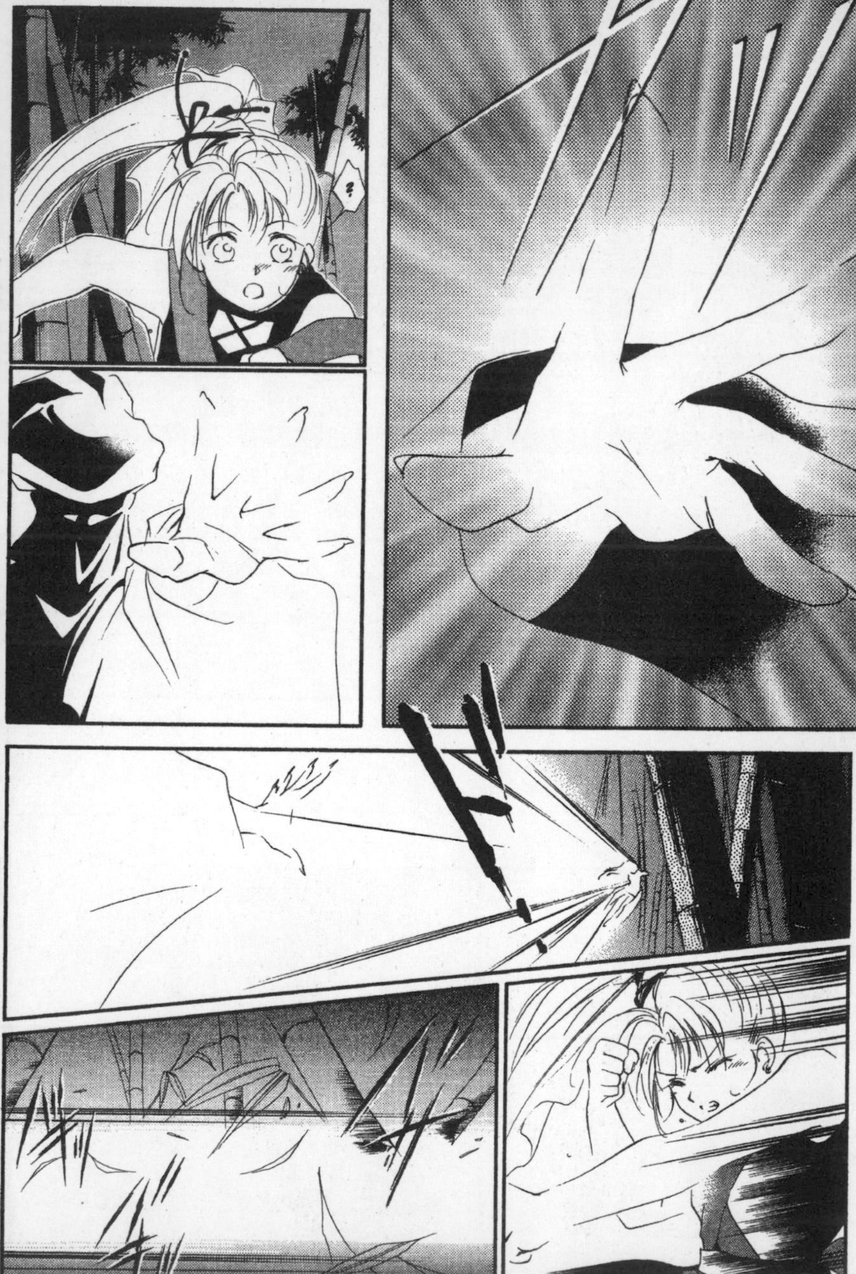
?

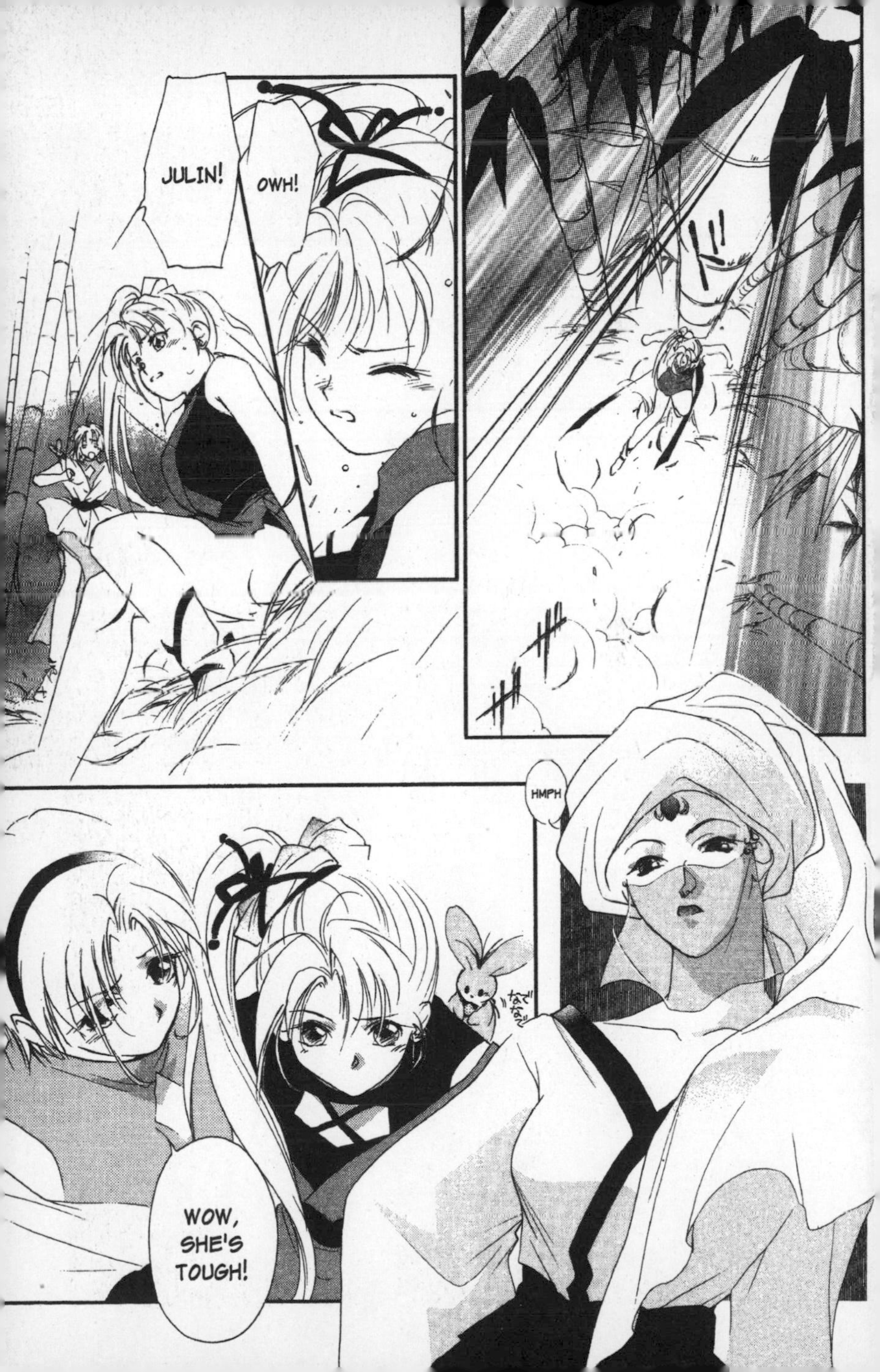
OWH!
JULIN!
HMPH
なで なで
WOW, SHE'S TOUGH!

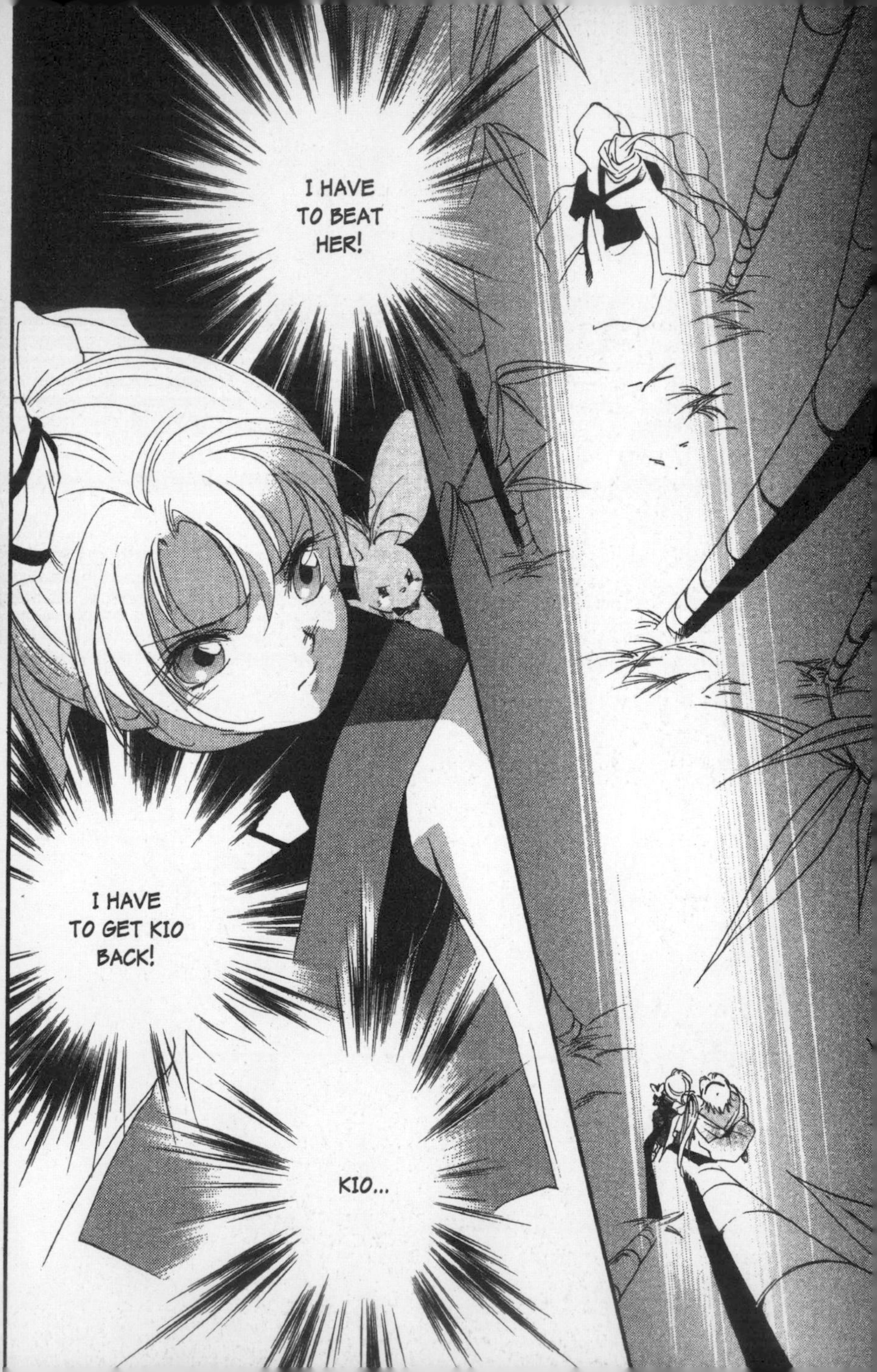
I HAVE TO BEAT HER!
I HAVE TO GET KIO BACK!
KIO...

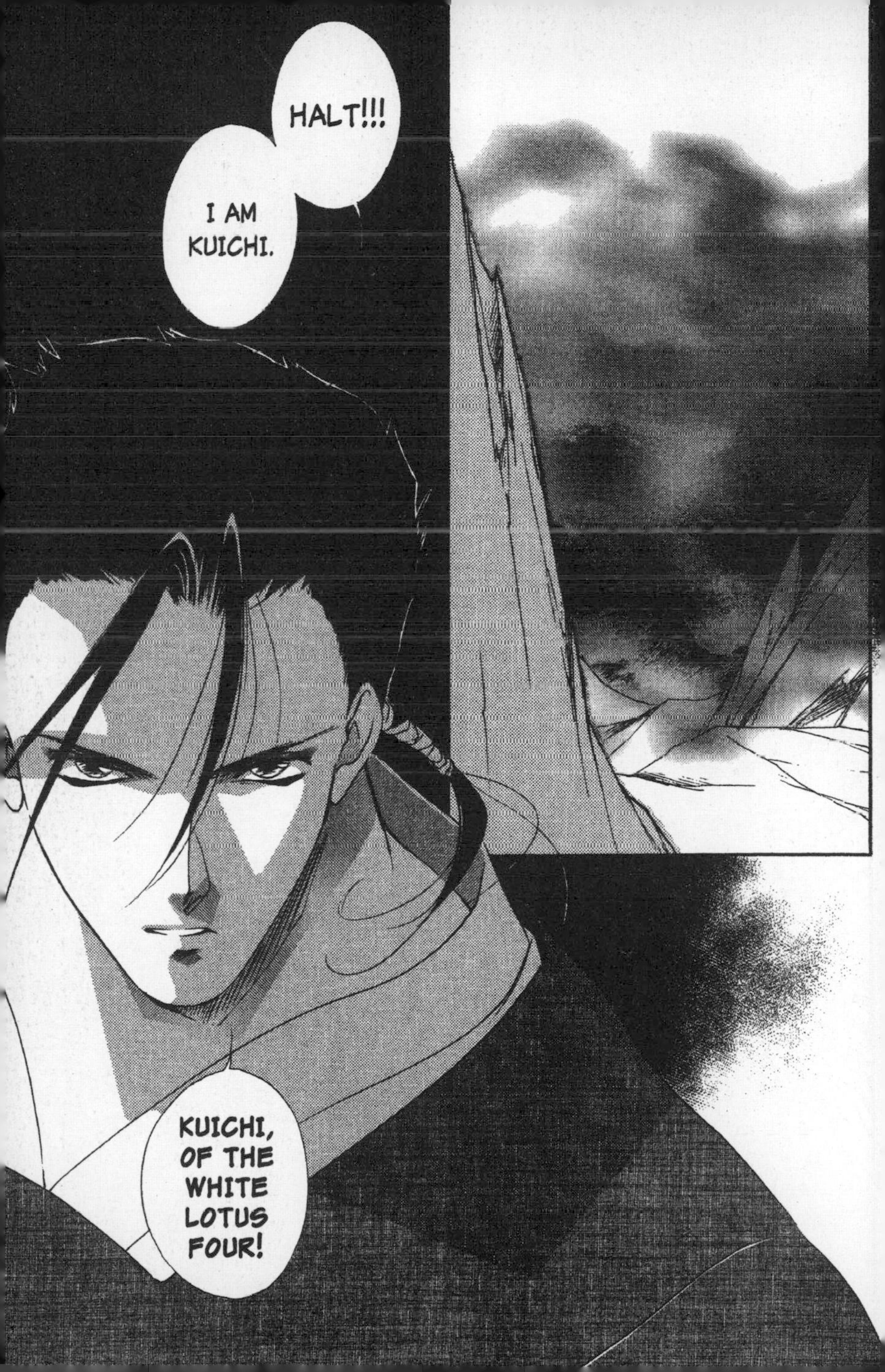
HALT!!!
I AM KUICHI.
KUICHI, OF THE WHITE LOTUS FOUR!

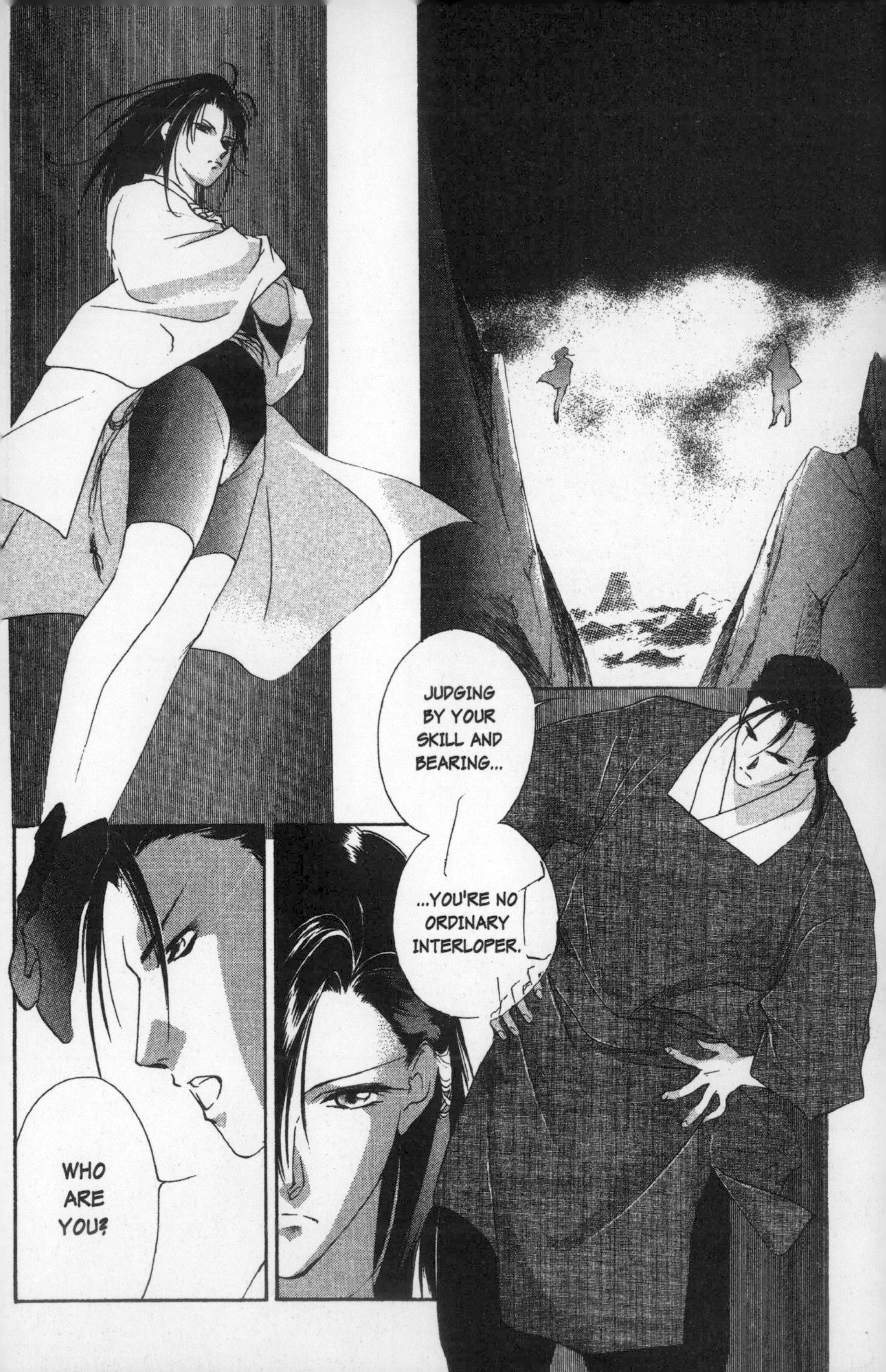
JUDGING BY YOUR SKILL AND BEARING...
...YOU'RE NO ORDINARY INTERLOPER.
WHO ARE YOU?

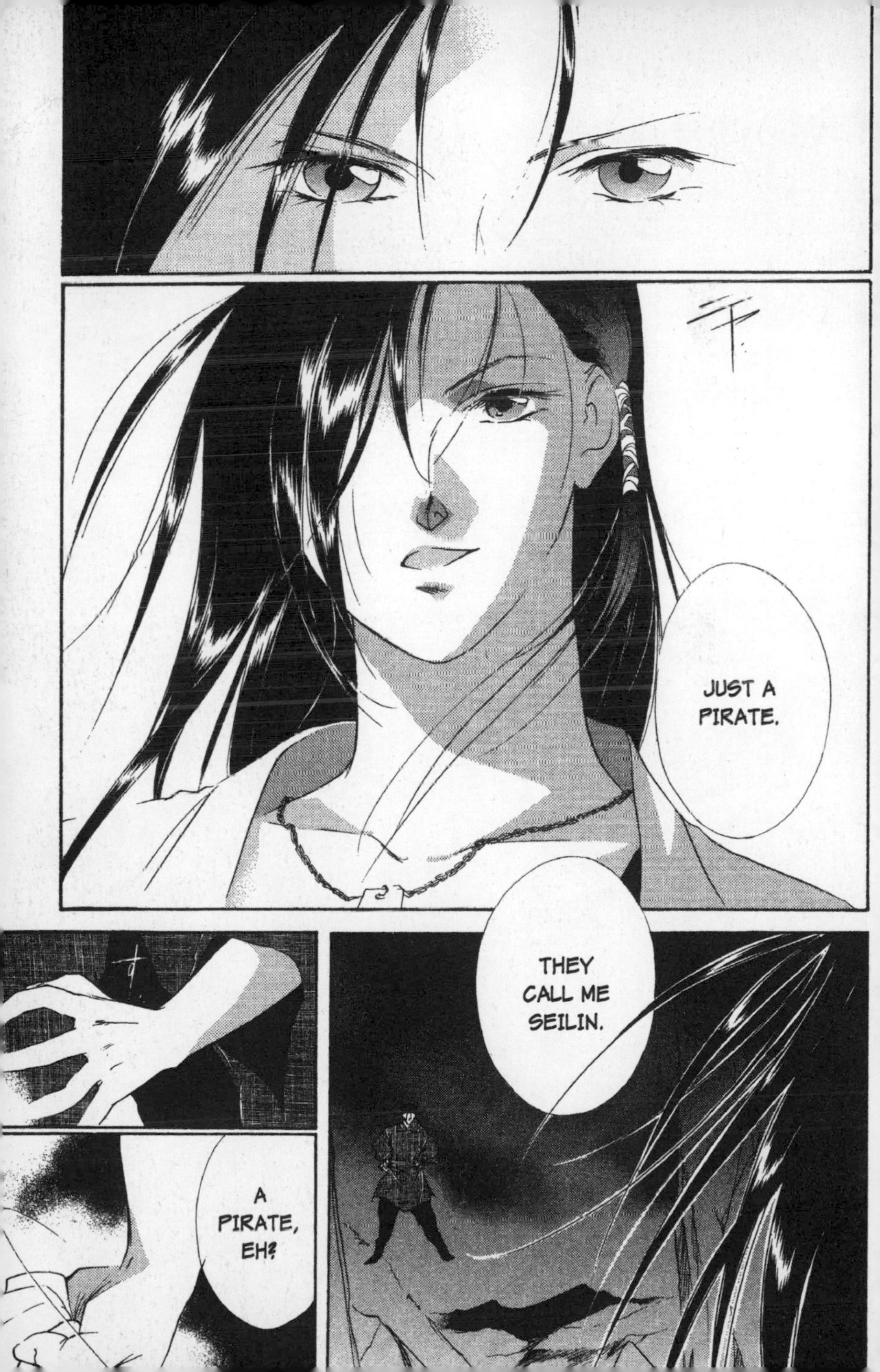
JUST A PIRATE.
THEY CALL ME SEILIN.
A PIRATE, EH?

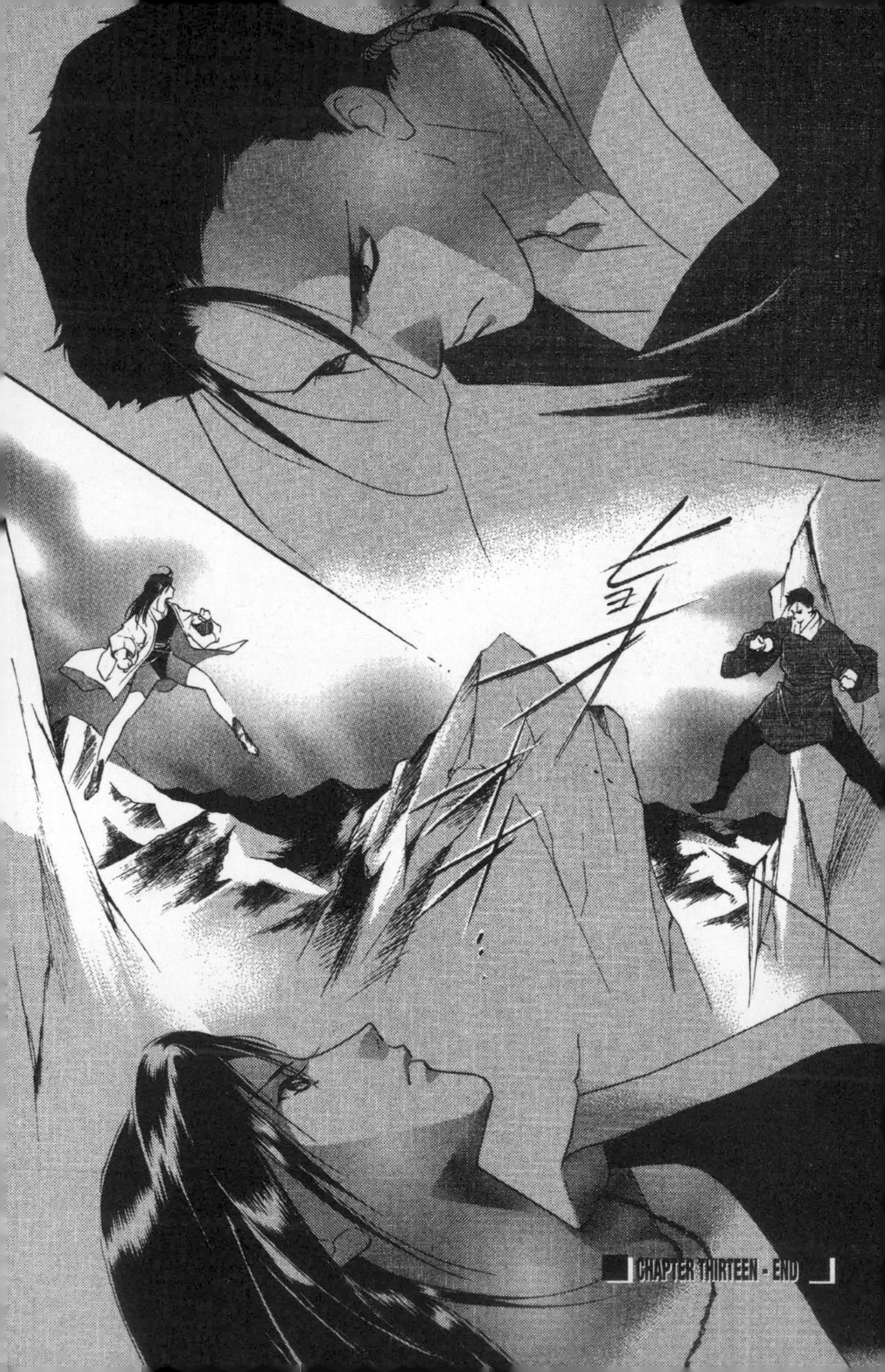
CHAPTER THIRTEEN - END

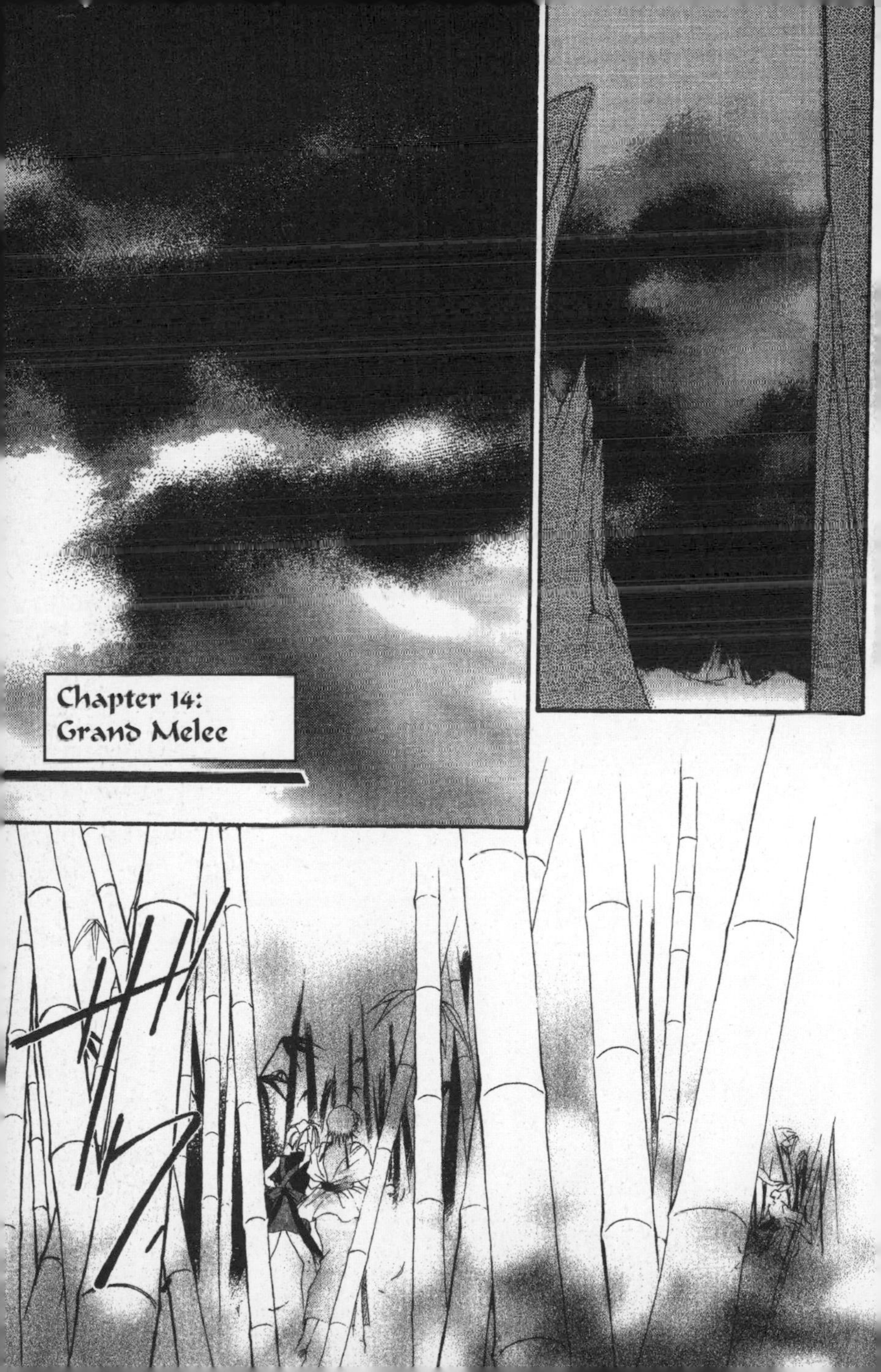
Chapter 14:
Grand Melee

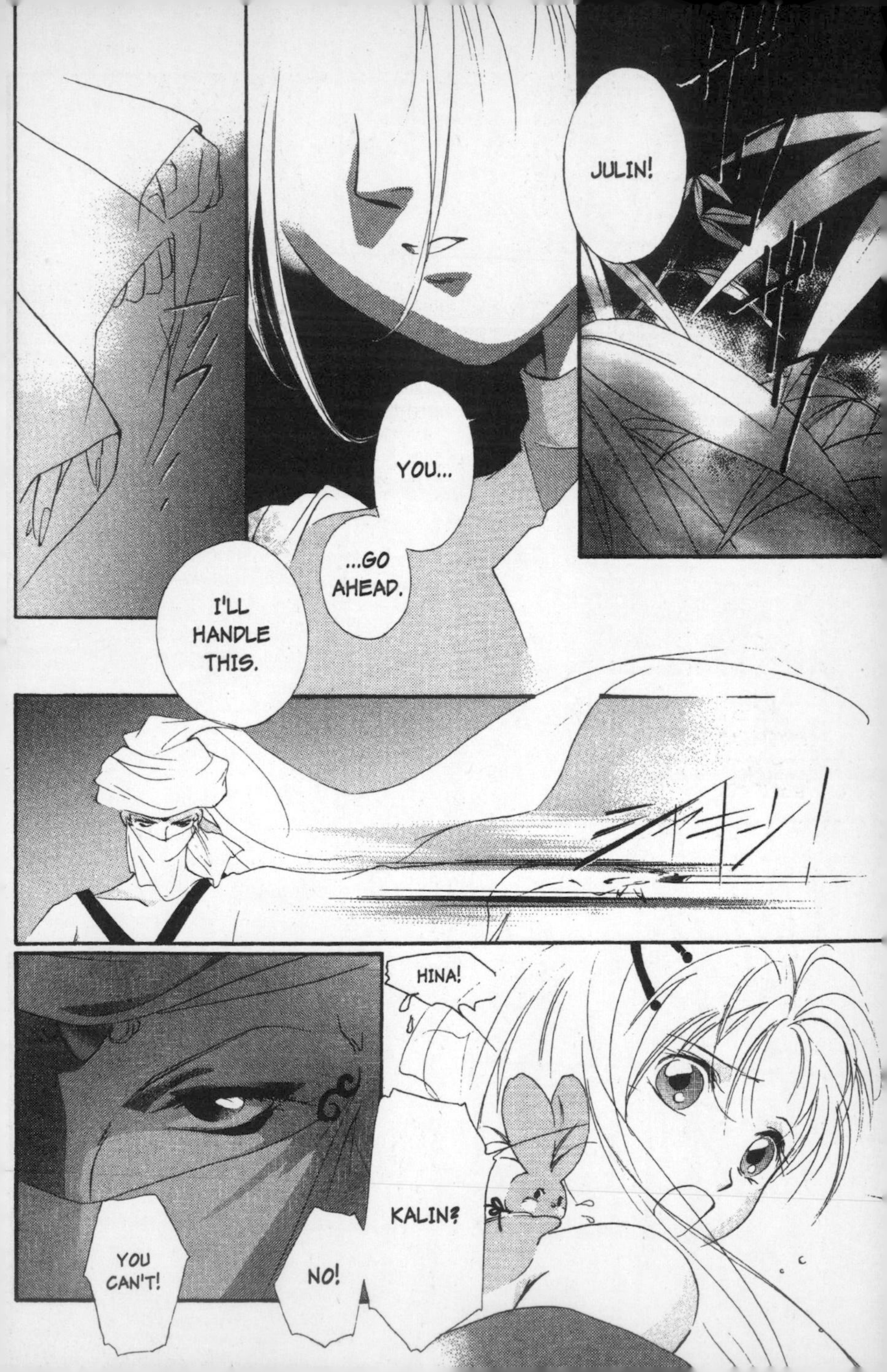
JULIN!
YOU...
...GO AHEAD.
I'LL HANDLE THIS.
HINA!
KALIN?
NO!
YOU CAN'T!

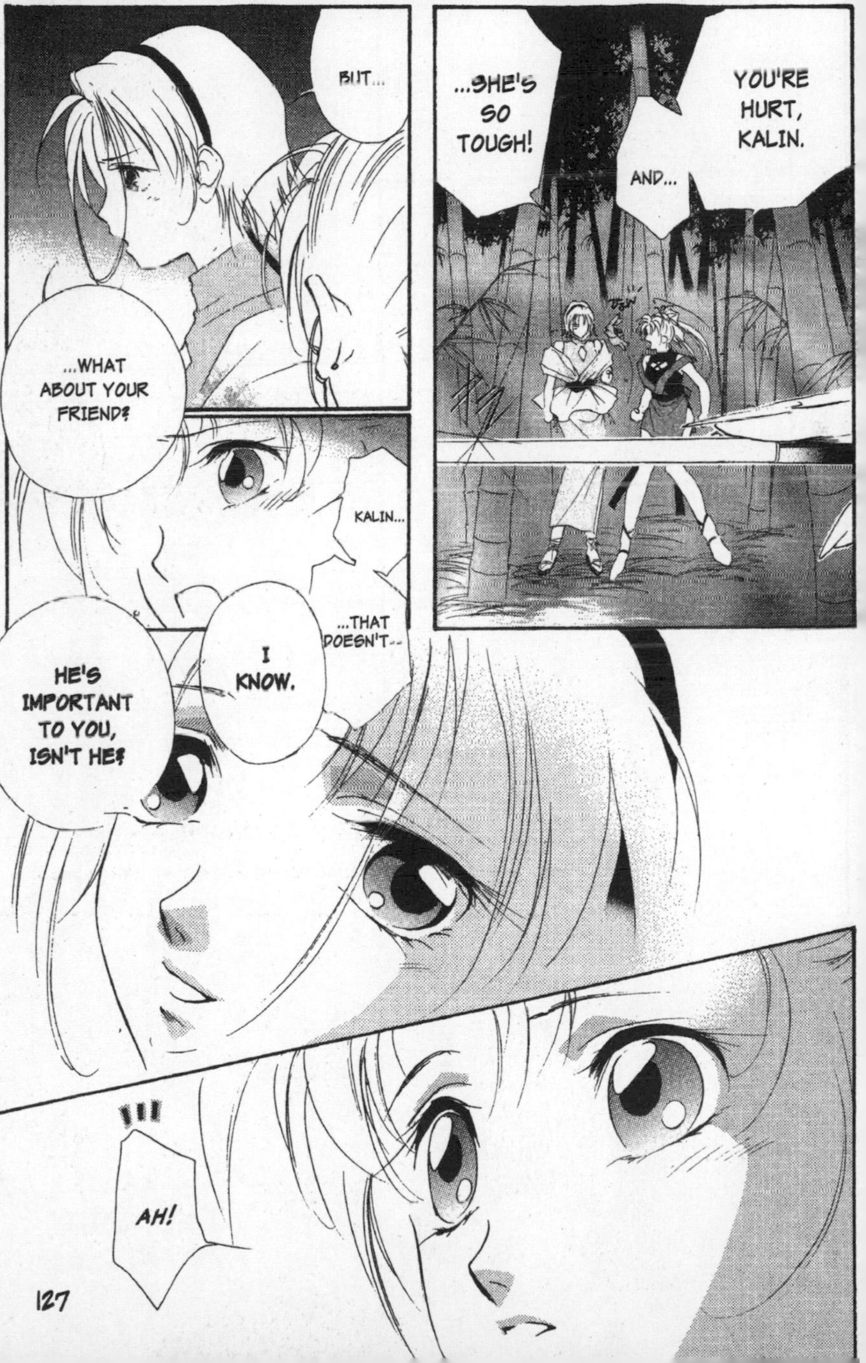
YOU'RE HURT, KALIN.
AND...
...SHE'S SO TOUGH!
BUT...
...WHAT ABOUT YOUR FRIEND?
KALIN...
...THAT DOESN'T--
I KNOW.
HE'S IMPORTANT TO YOU, ISN'T HE?
!!!
AH!

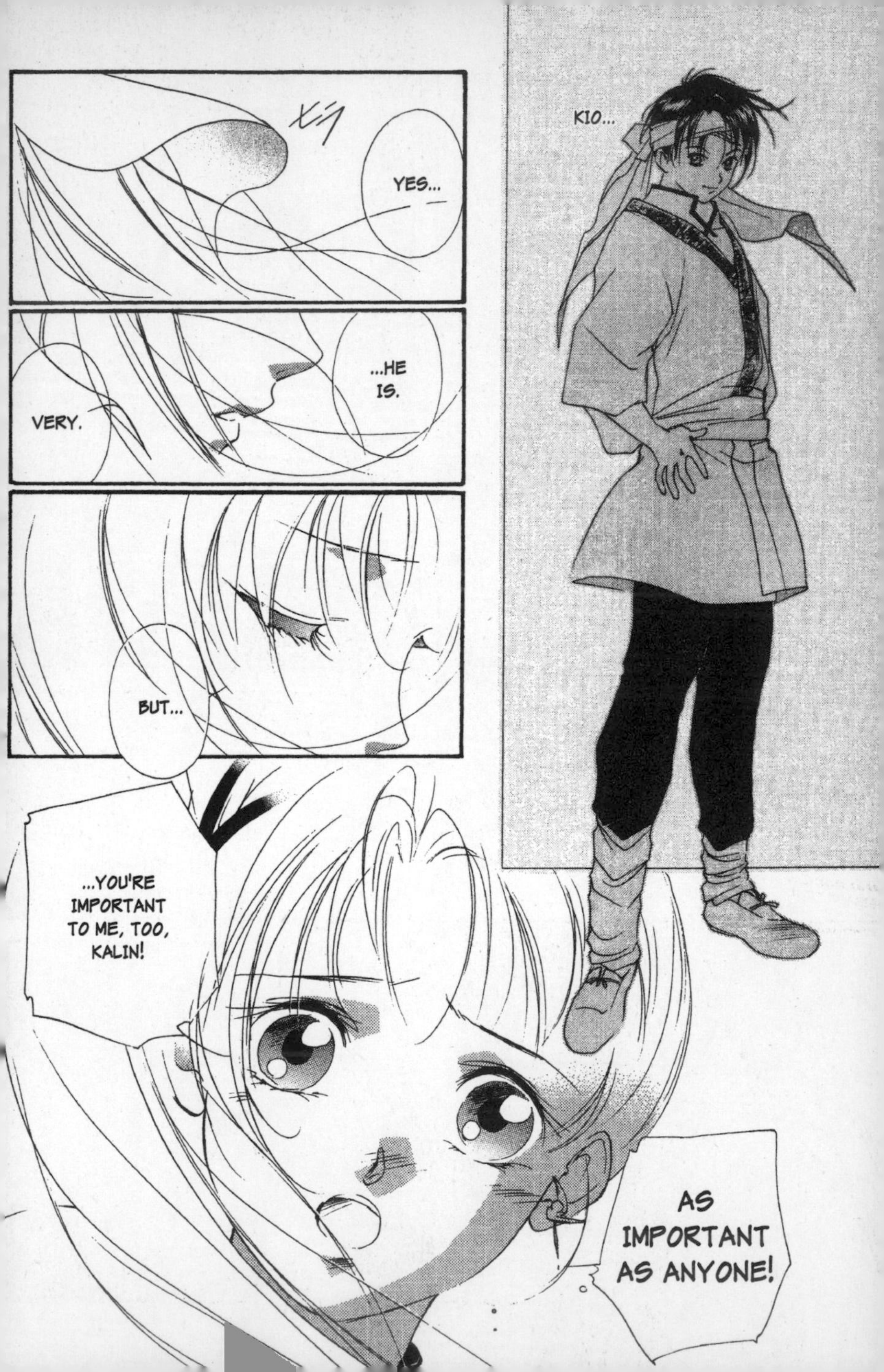
KIO...
YES...
...HE IS.
VERY.
BUT...
...YOU'RE IMPORTANT TO ME, TOO, KALIN!
AS IMPORTANT AS ANYONE!

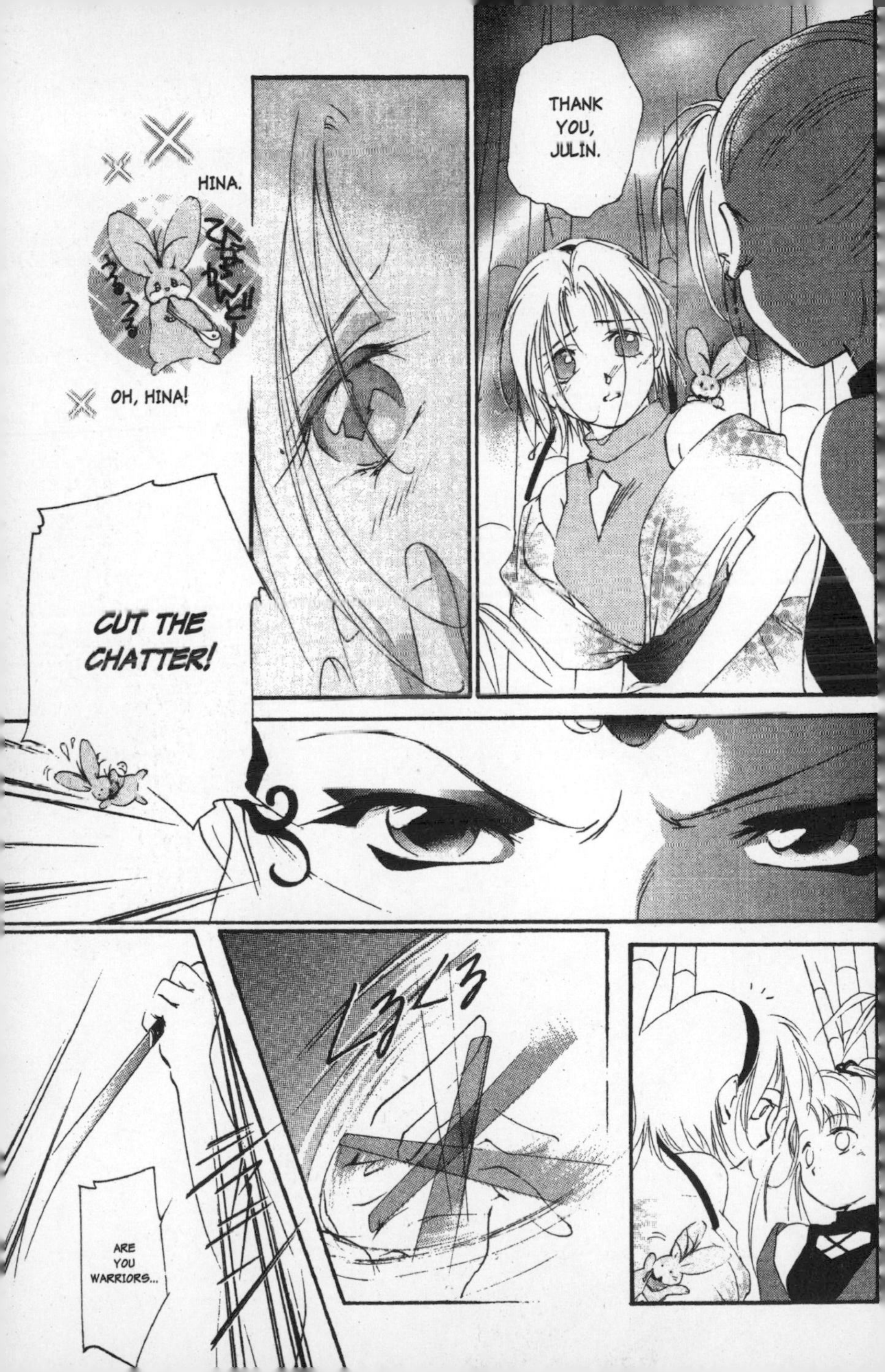
THANK YOU, JULIN.
HINA.
OH, HINA!
CUT THE CHATTER!
ARE YOU WARRIORS...

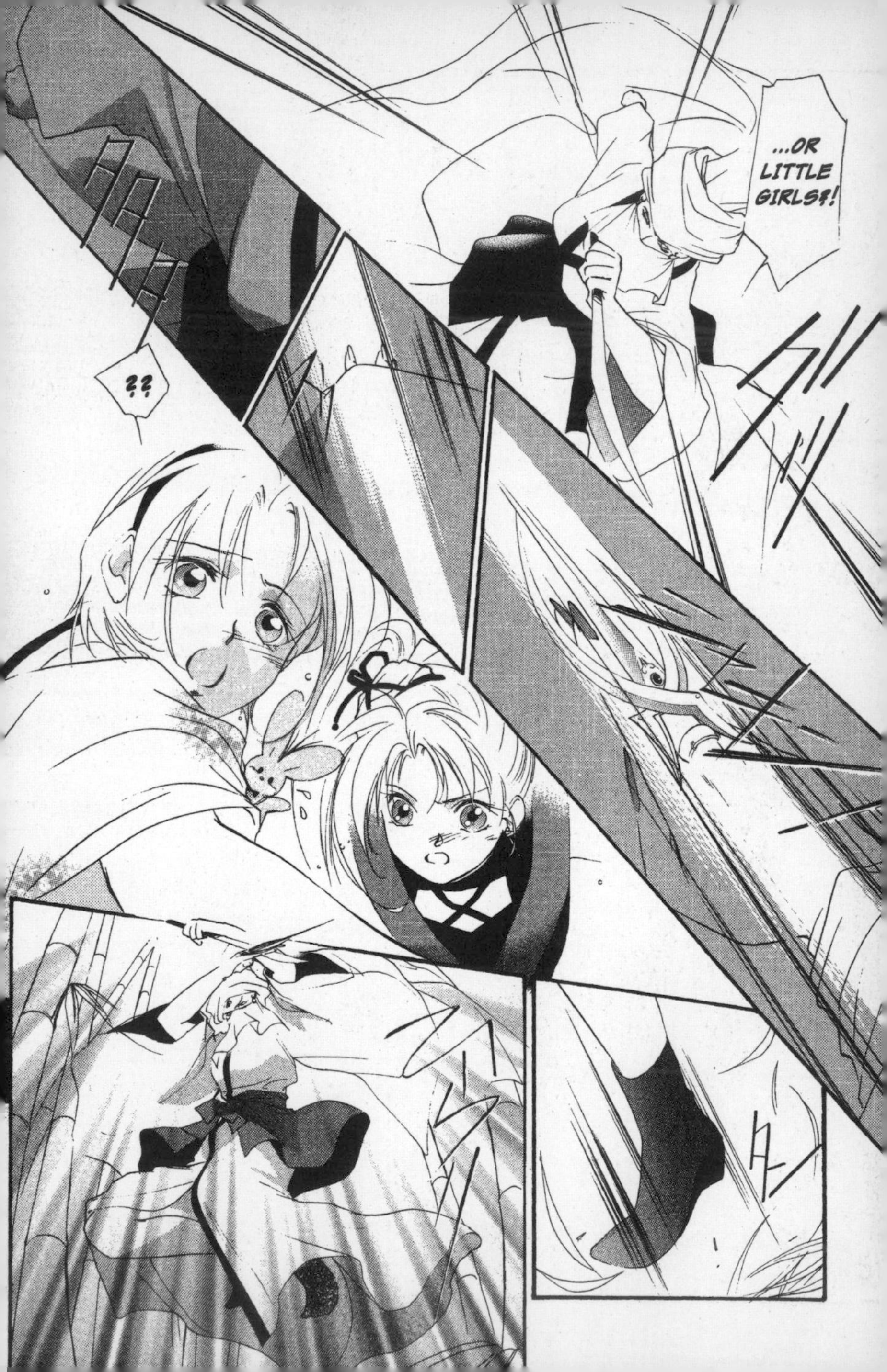
...OR LITTLE GIRLS?!
??

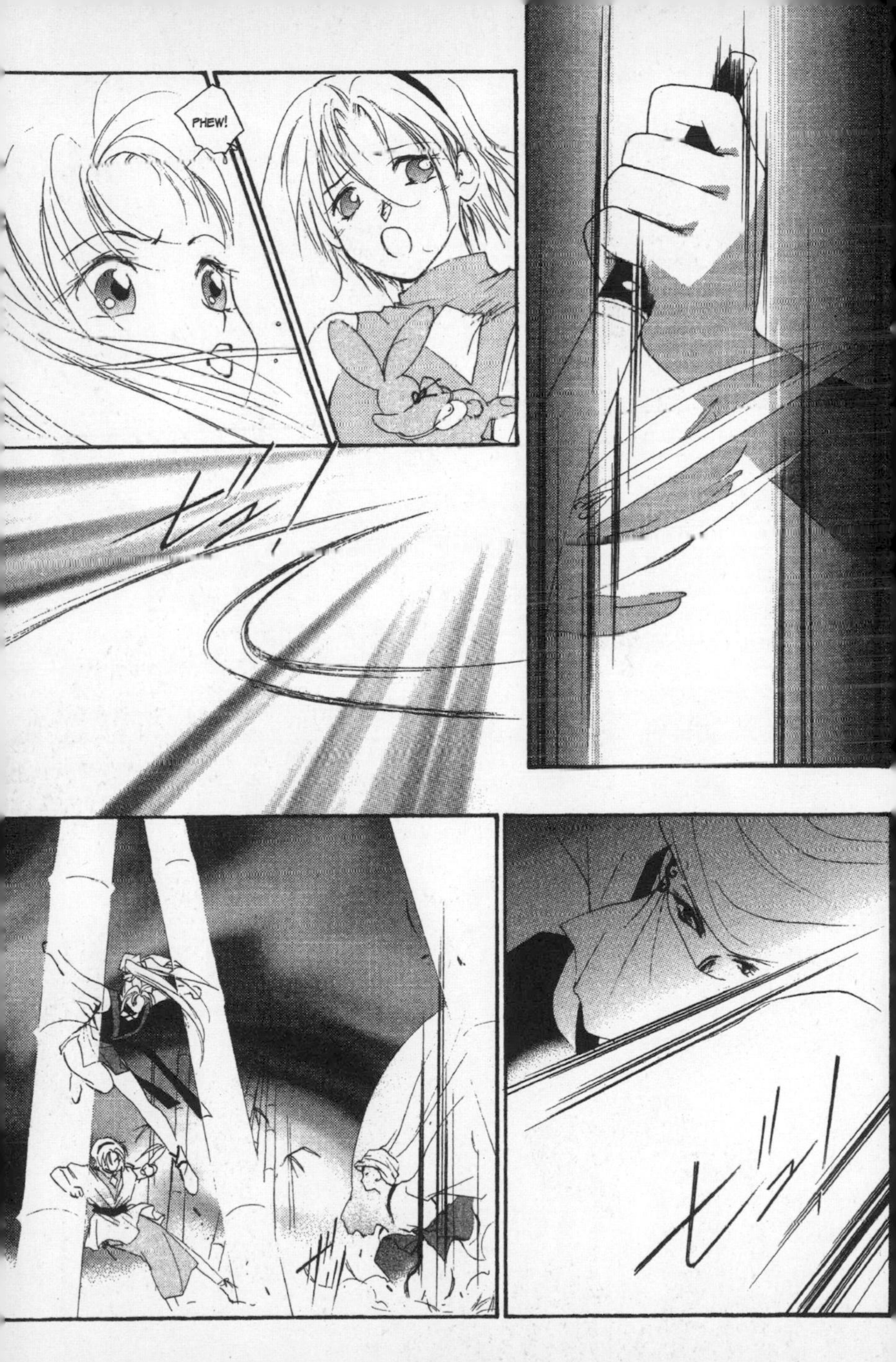
PHEW!

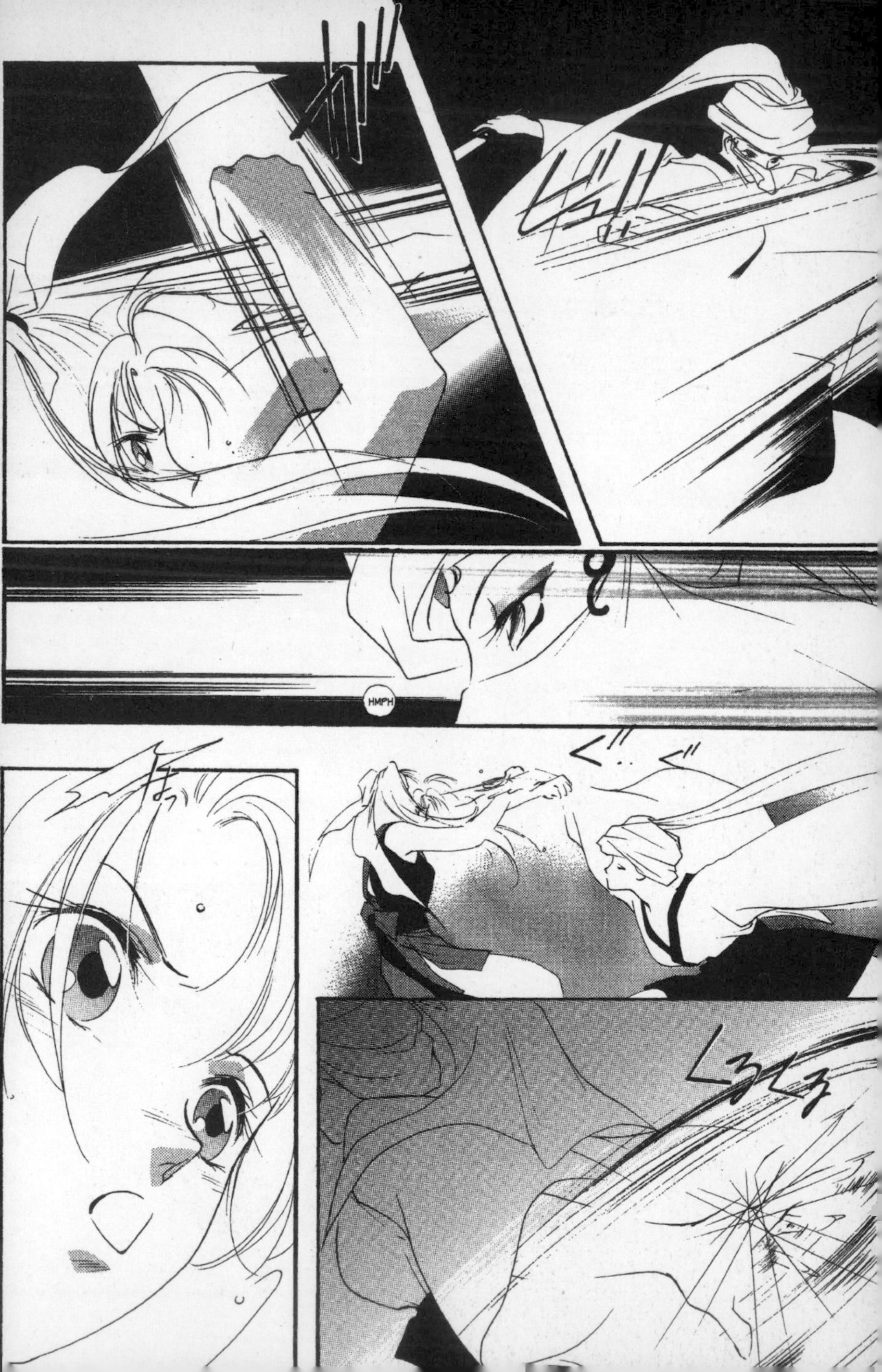
HMPH

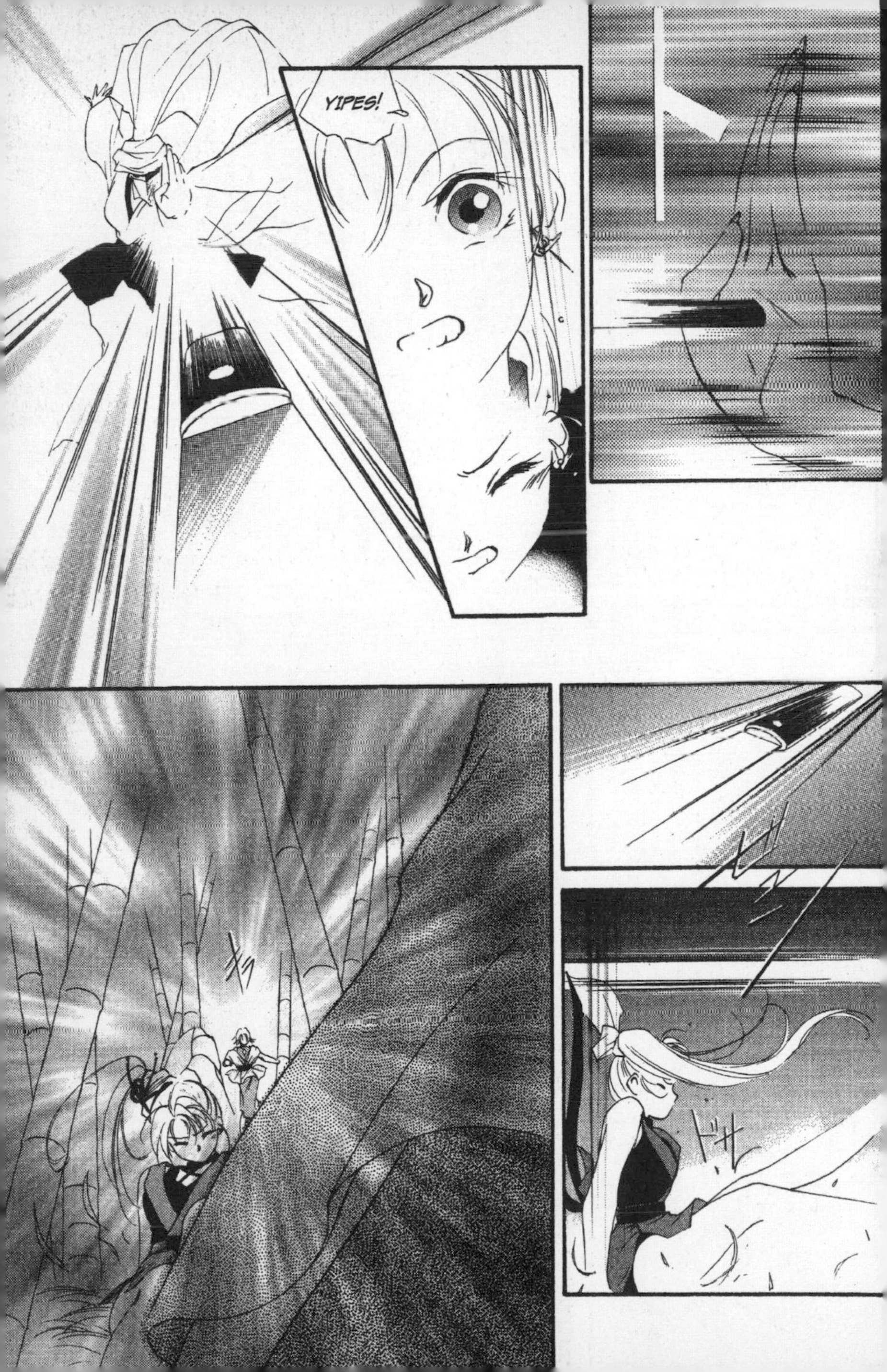
YIPES!

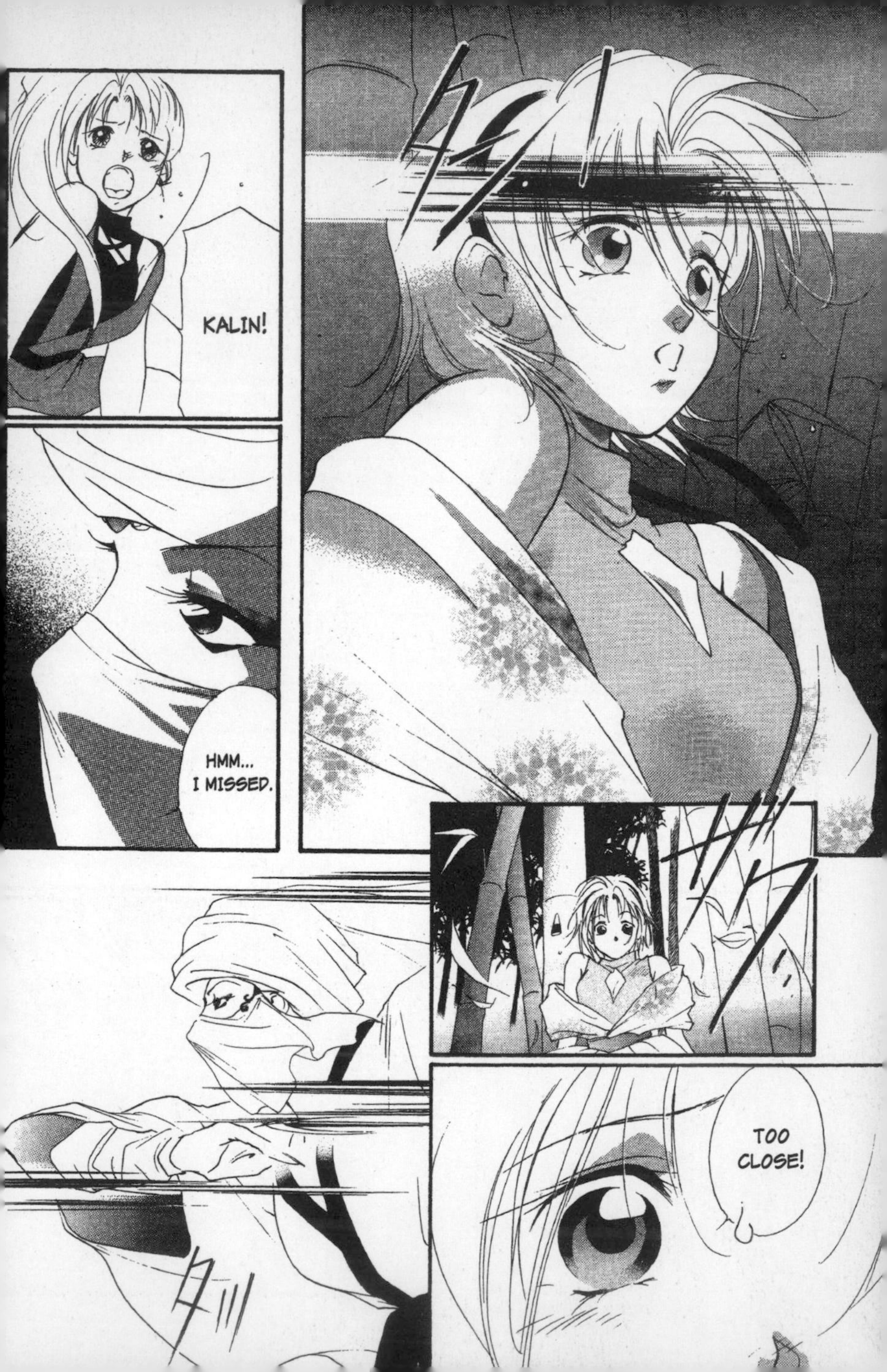
KALIN!
HMM... I MISSED.
TOO CLOSE!

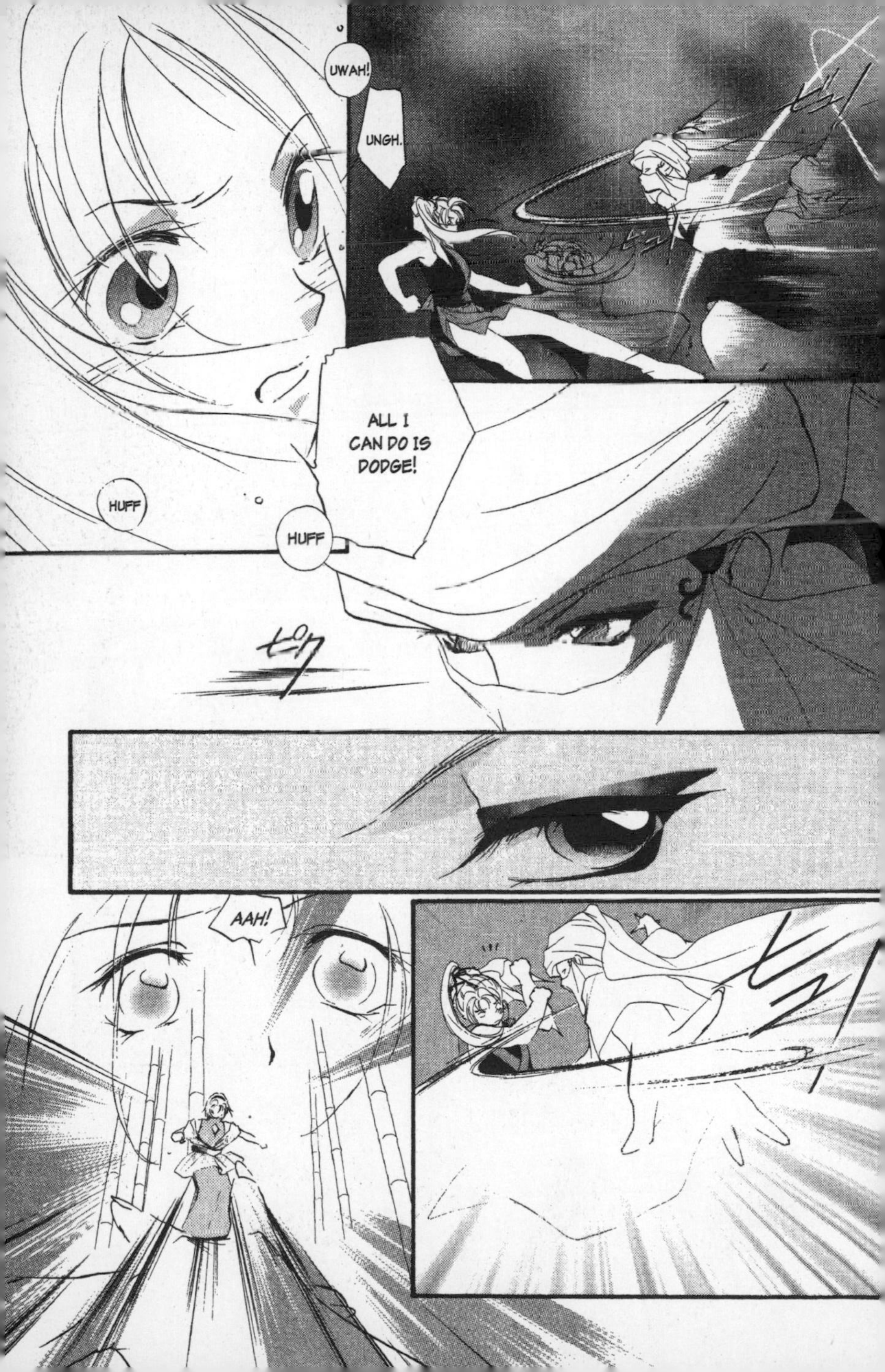
UWAH!
UNGH.
ALL I CAN DO IS DODGE!
HUFF
HUFF
AAH!

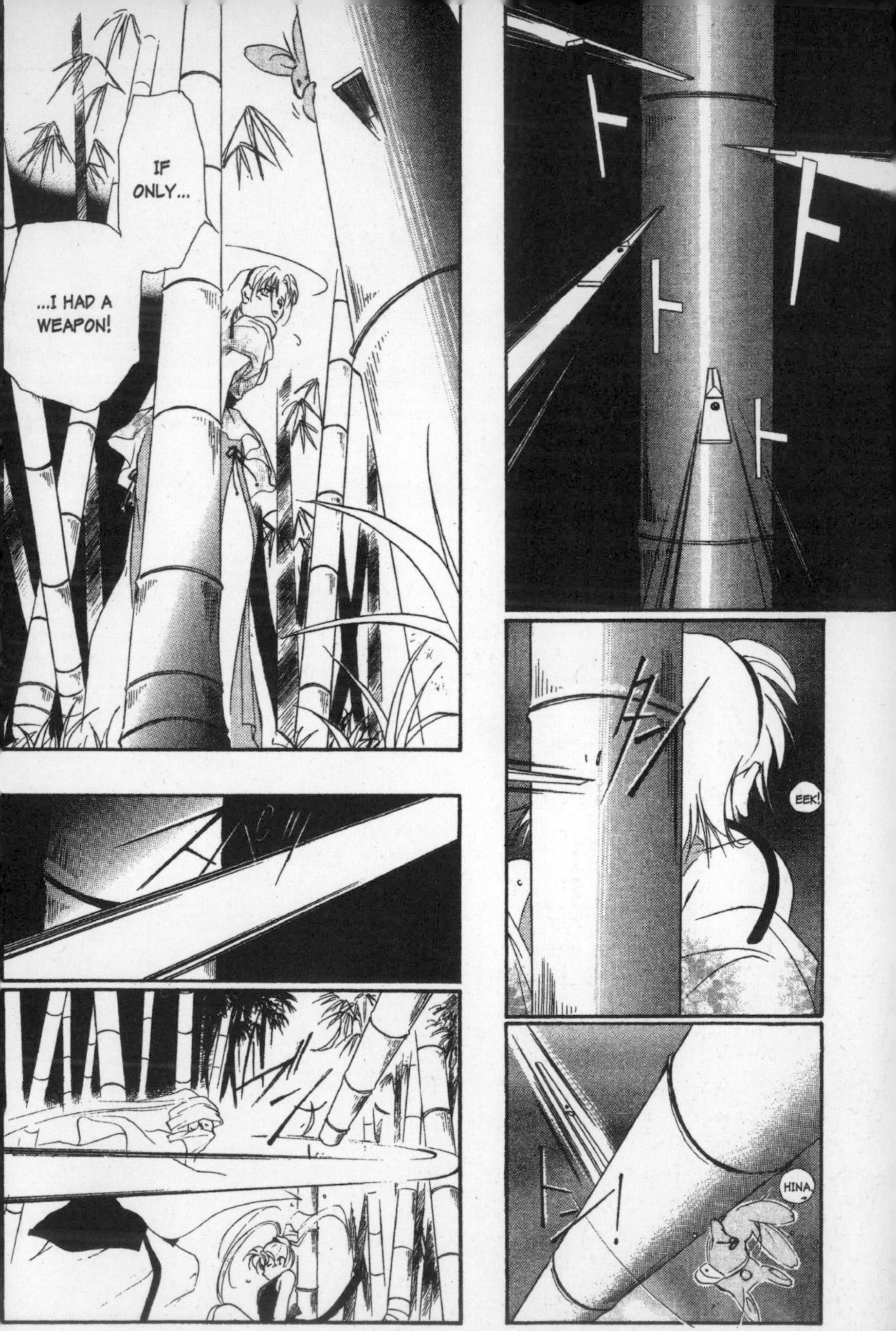
IF ONLY...
...I HAD A WEAPON!
EEK!
HINA.

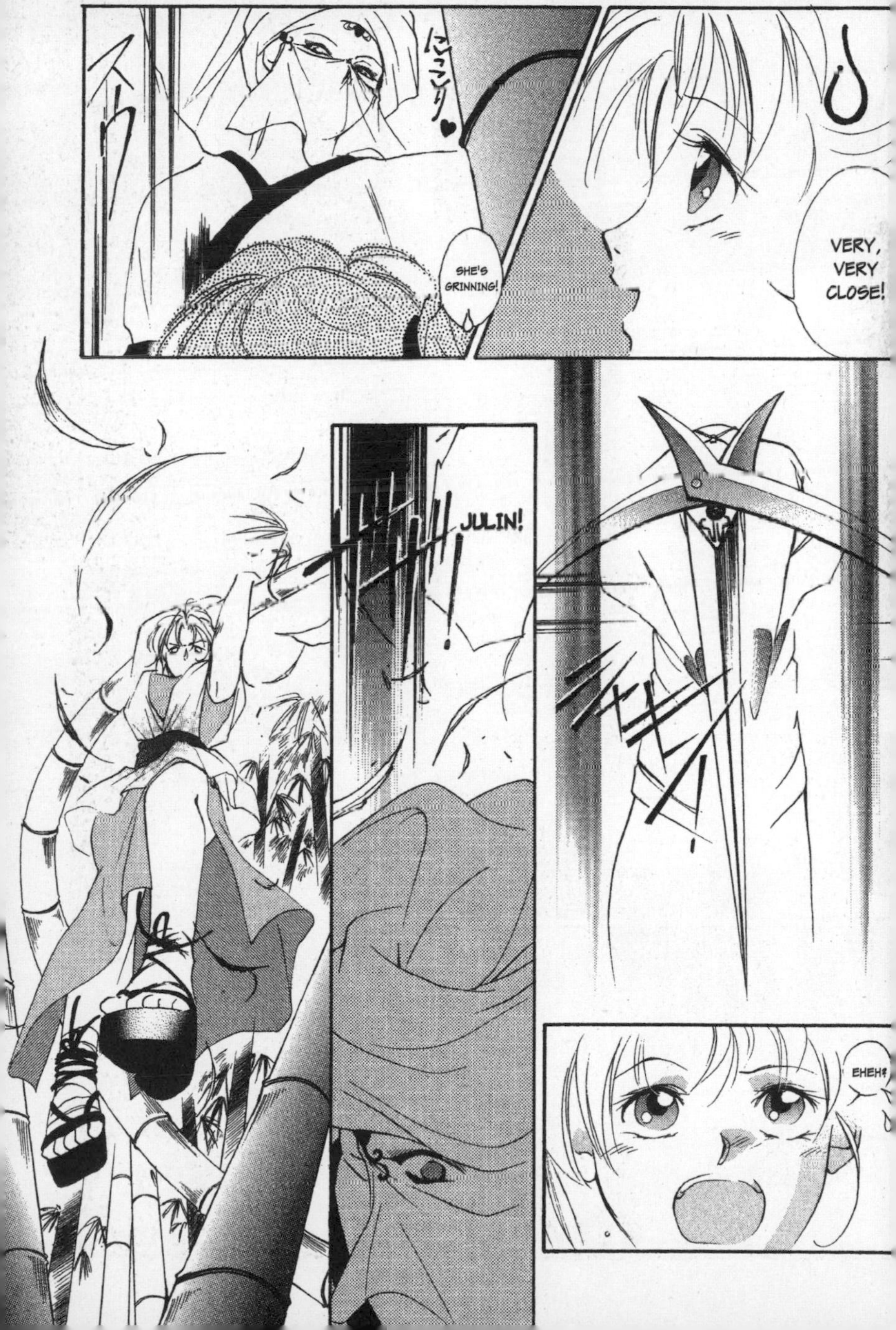
VERY, VERY CLOSE!
にっこり♥
SHE'S GRINNING!
EHEH?
JULIN!

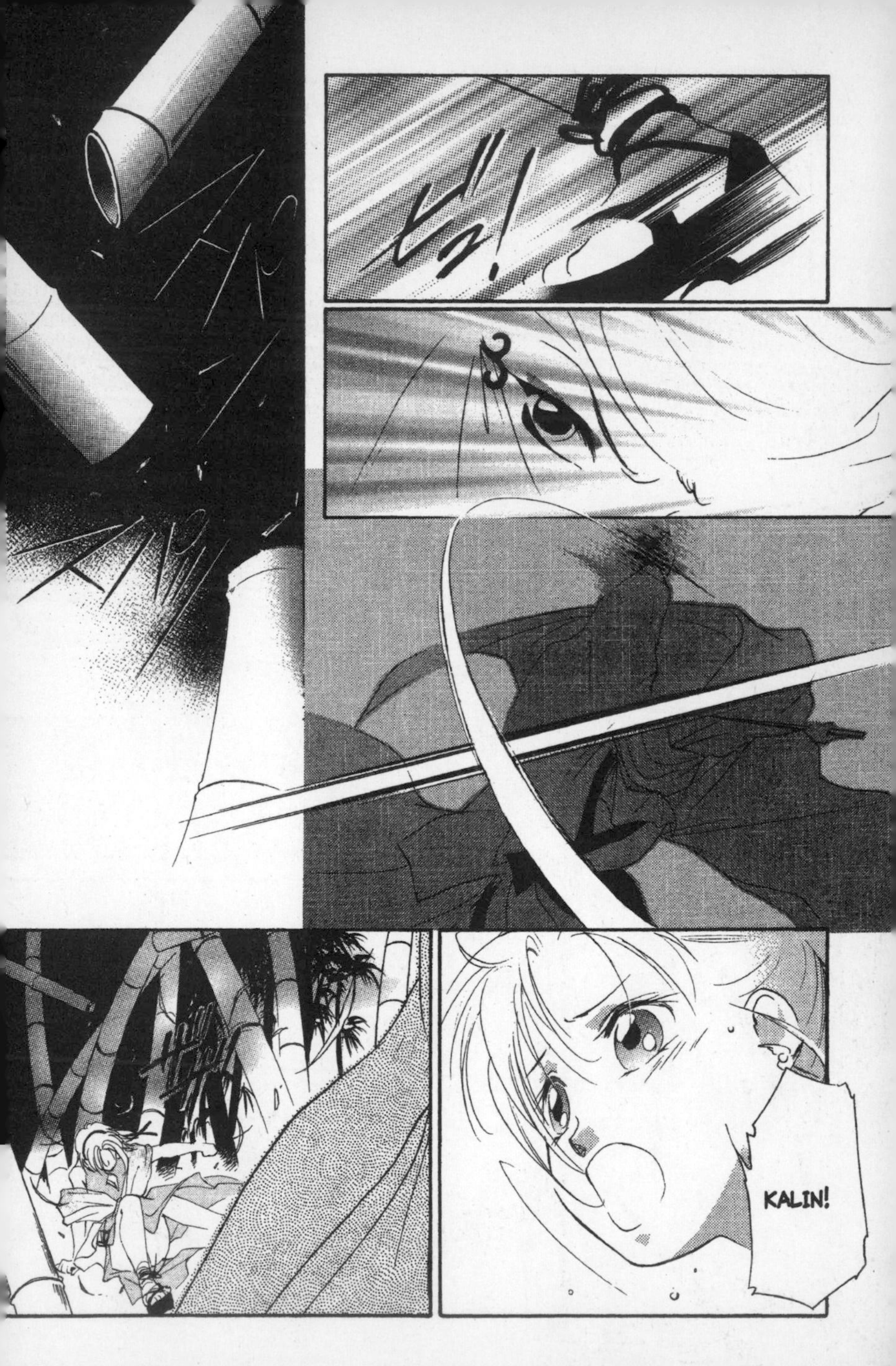
KALIN!

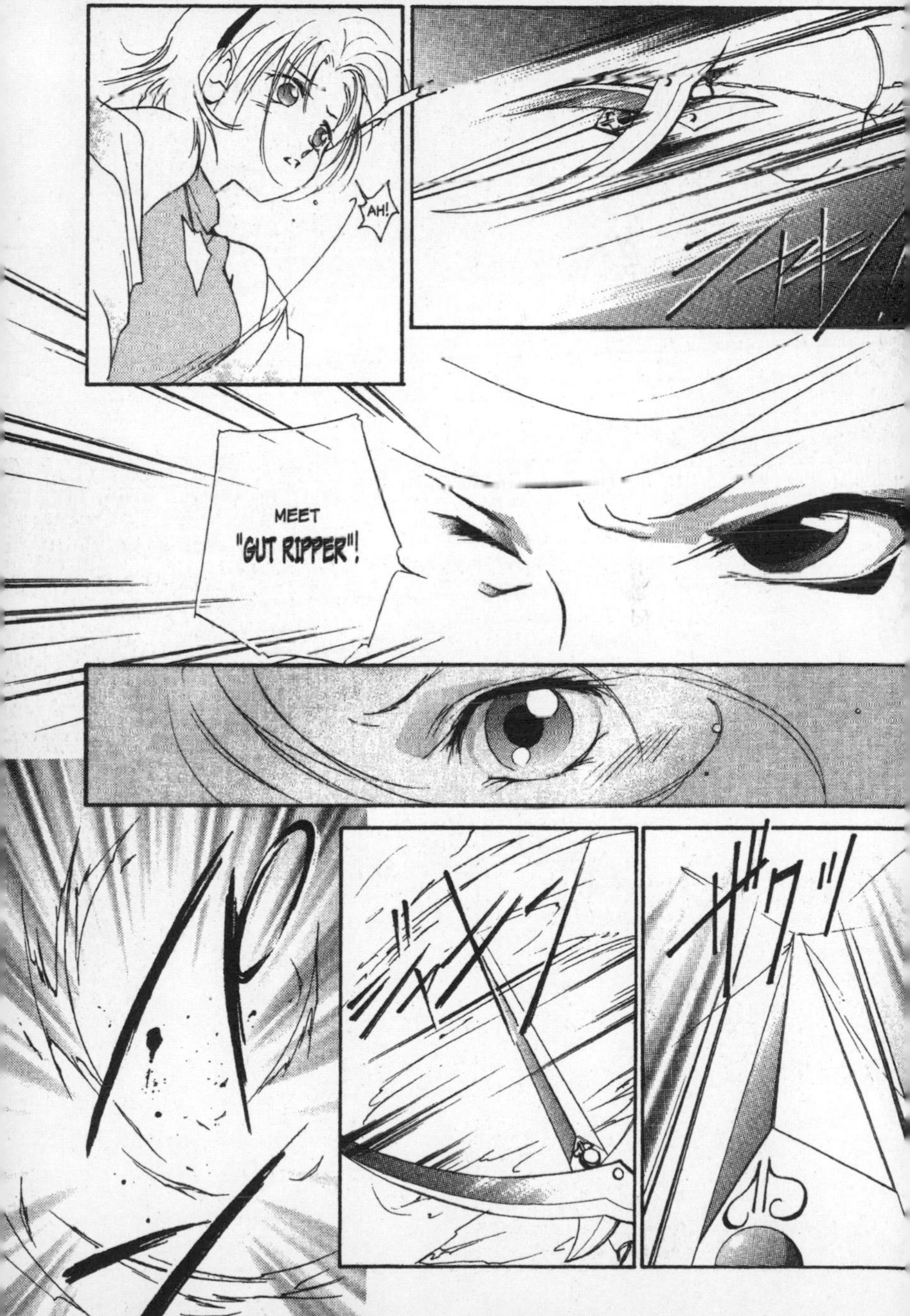
AH!
MEET "GUT RIPPER"!

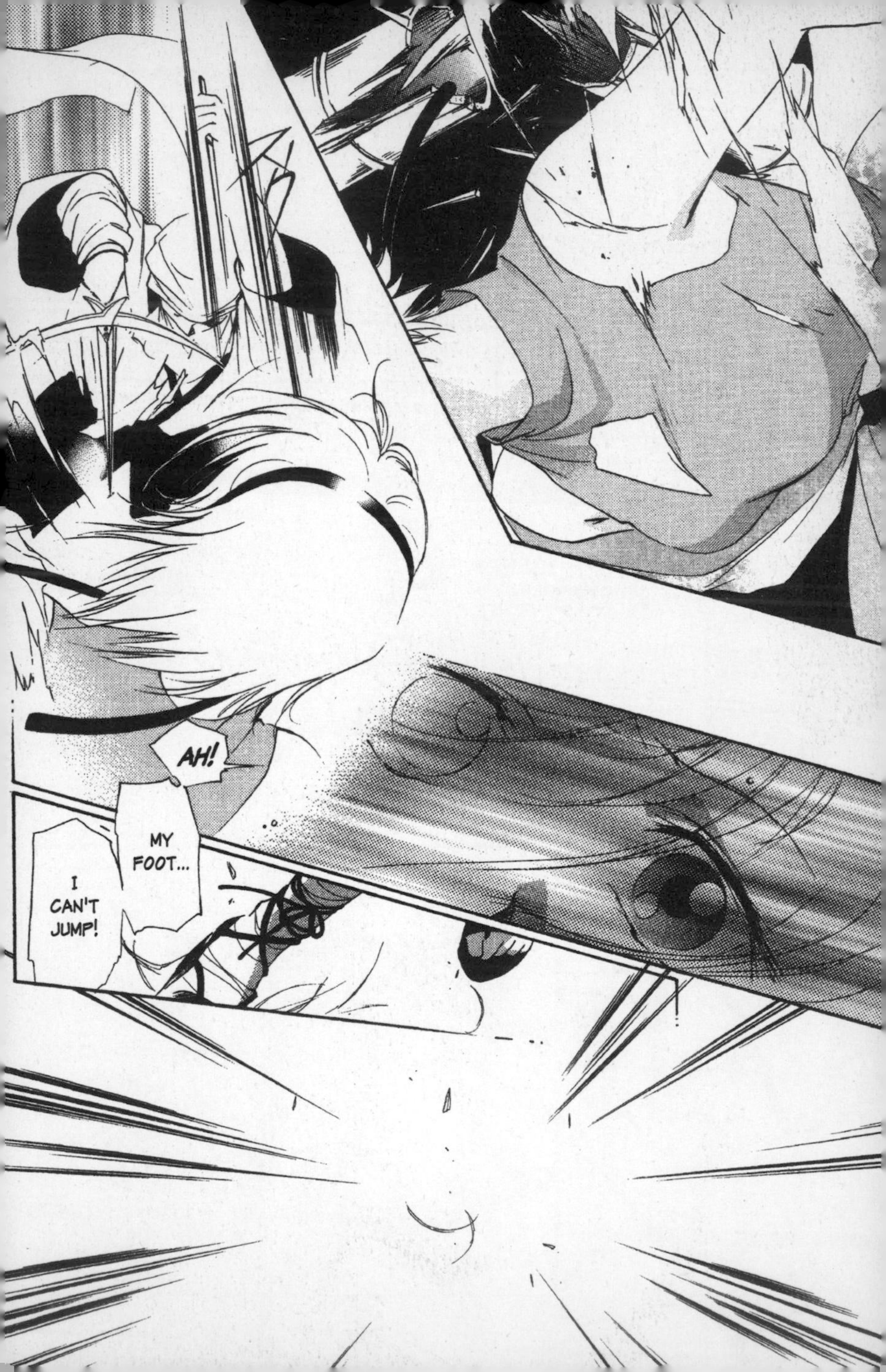
AH!
MY FOOT...
I CAN'T JUMP!

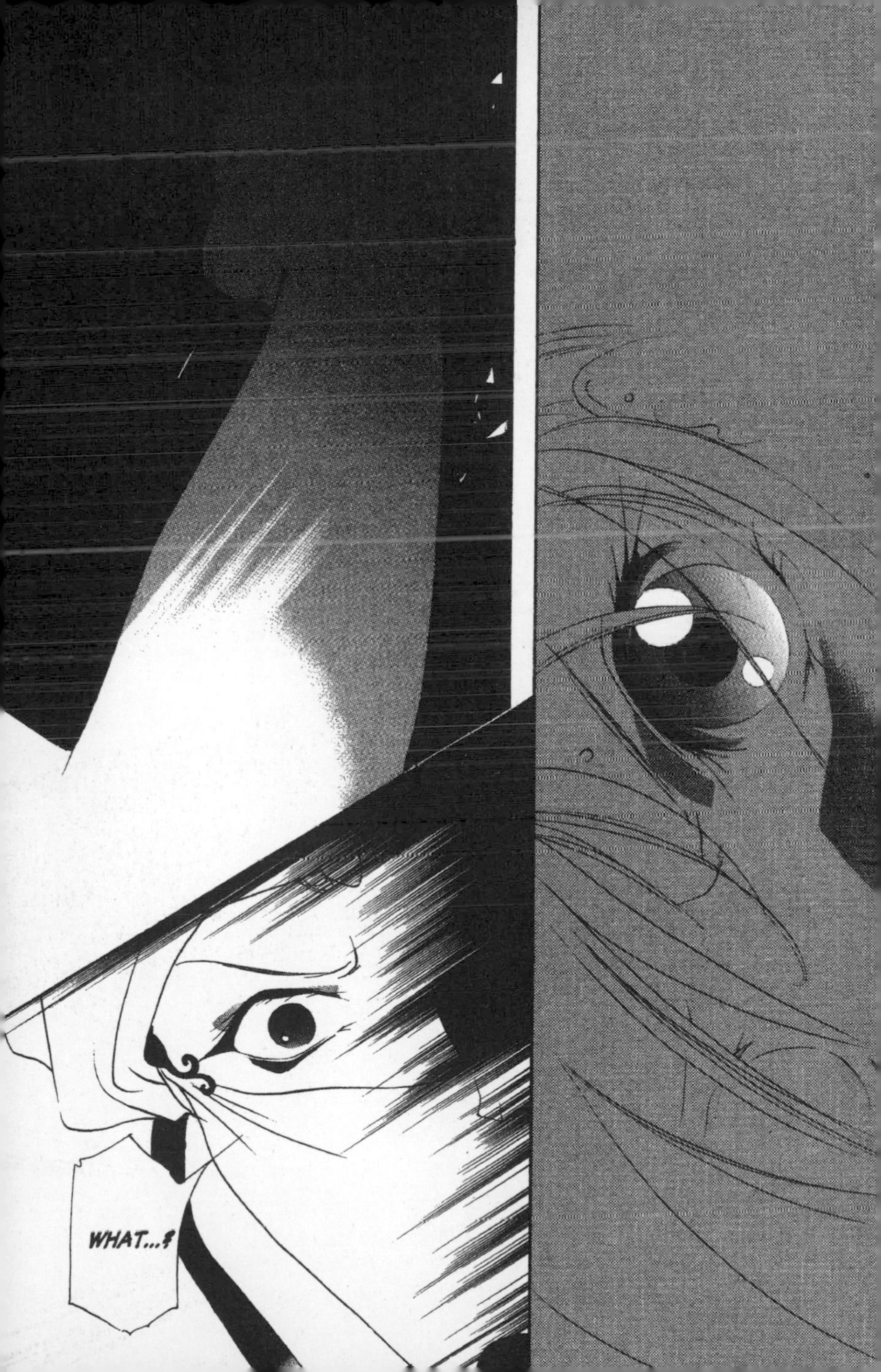
WHAT...?

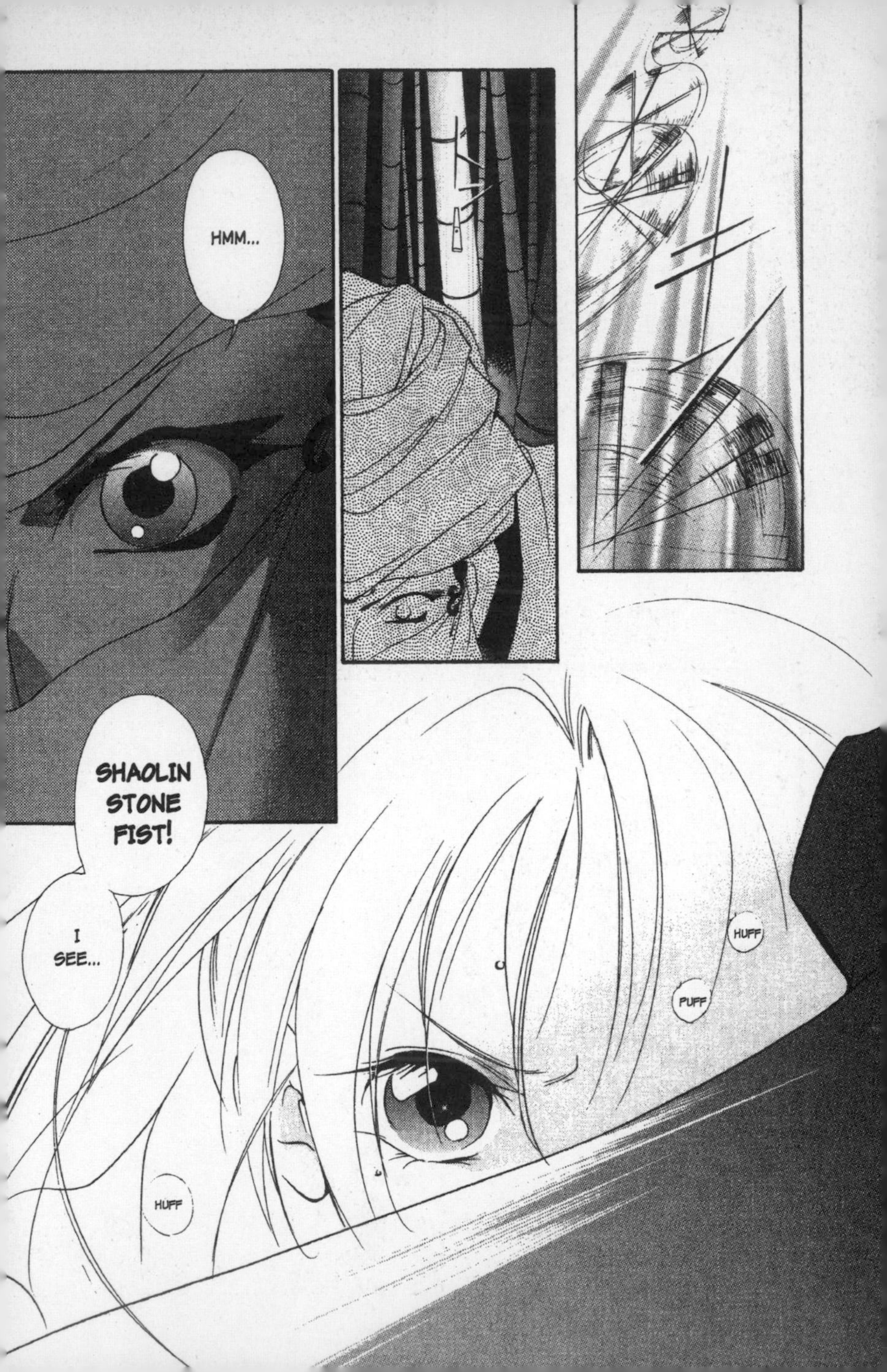
HMM...
SHAOLIN STONE FIST!
I SEE...
HUFF
PUFF
HUFF

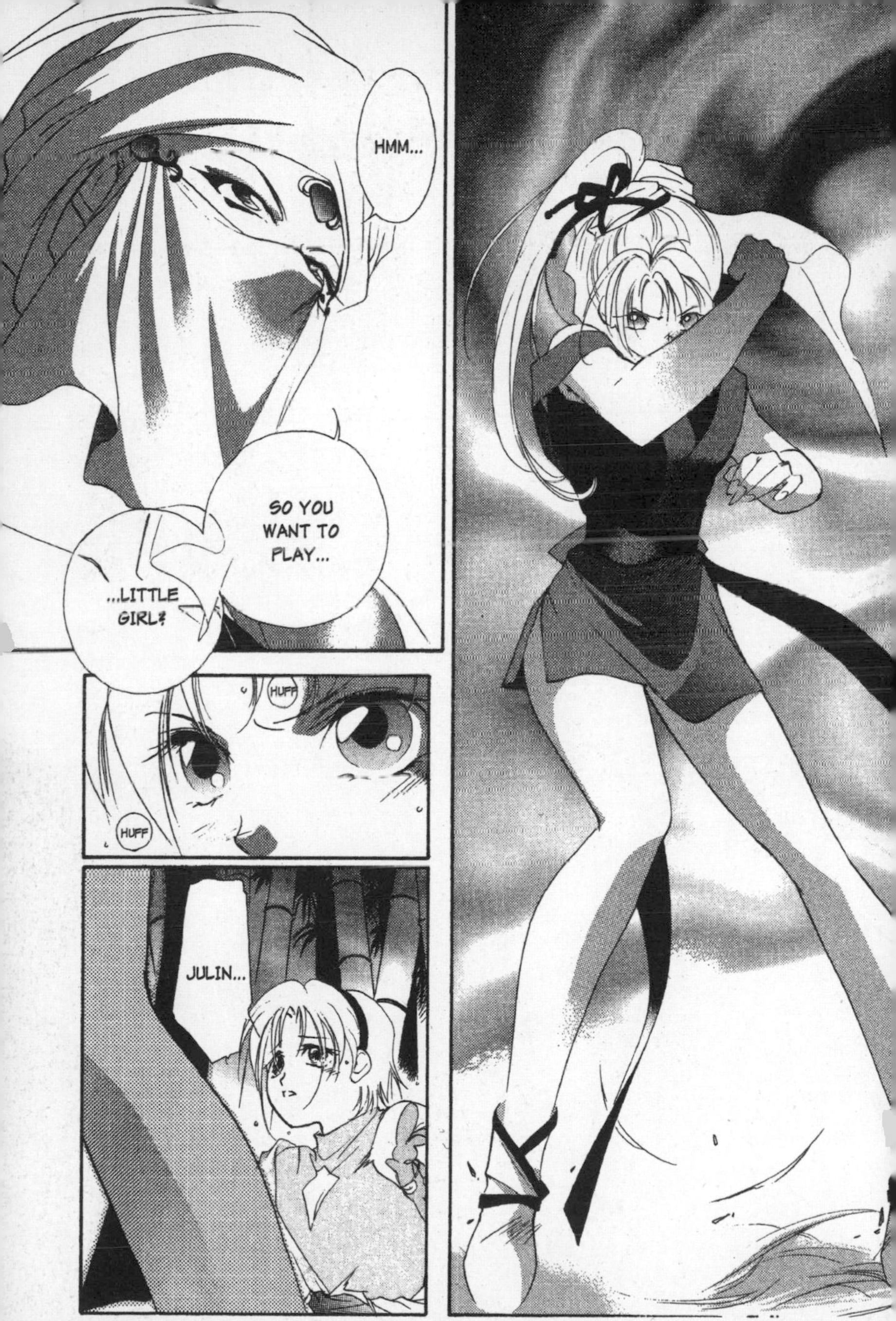
HMM...
SO YOU WANT TO PLAY...
...LITTLE GIRL?
HUFF
HUFF
JULIN...

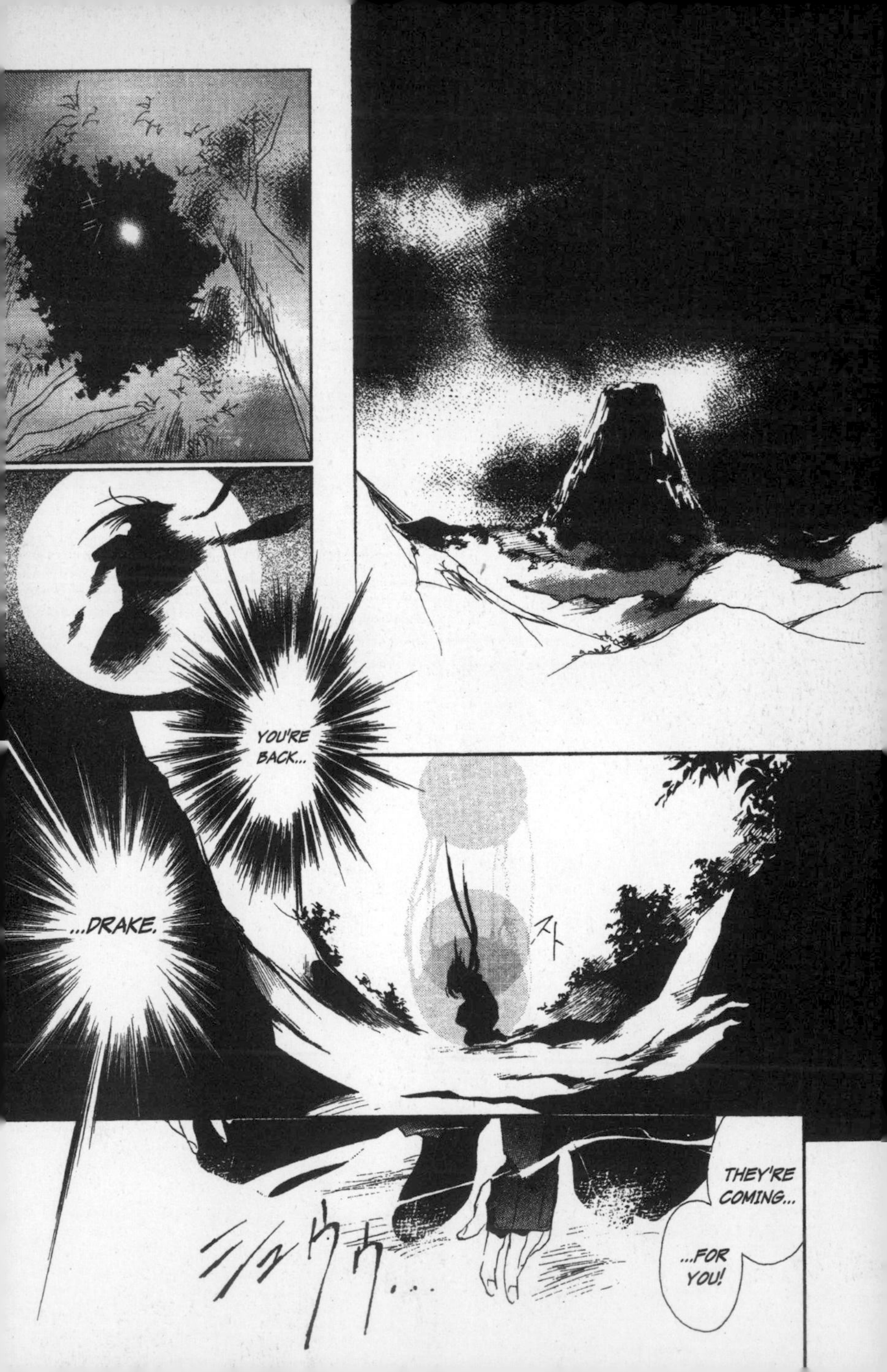
YOU'RE BACK...
...DRAKE.
スト
THEY'RE COMING...
...FOR YOU!

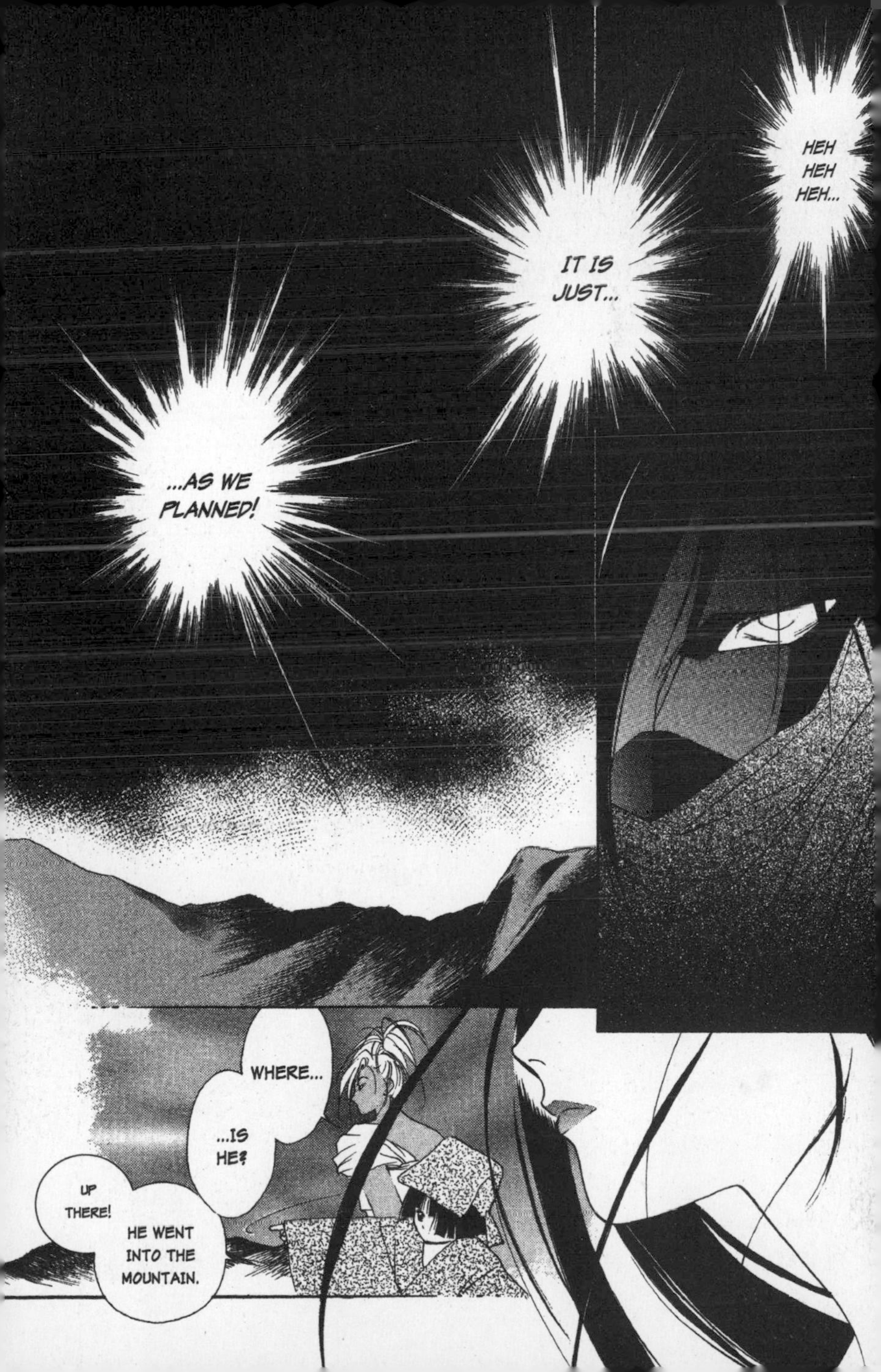
HEH HEH HEH...
IT IS JUST...
...AS WE PLANNED!
WHERE...
...IS HE?
UP THERE!
HE WENT INTO THE MOUNTAIN.

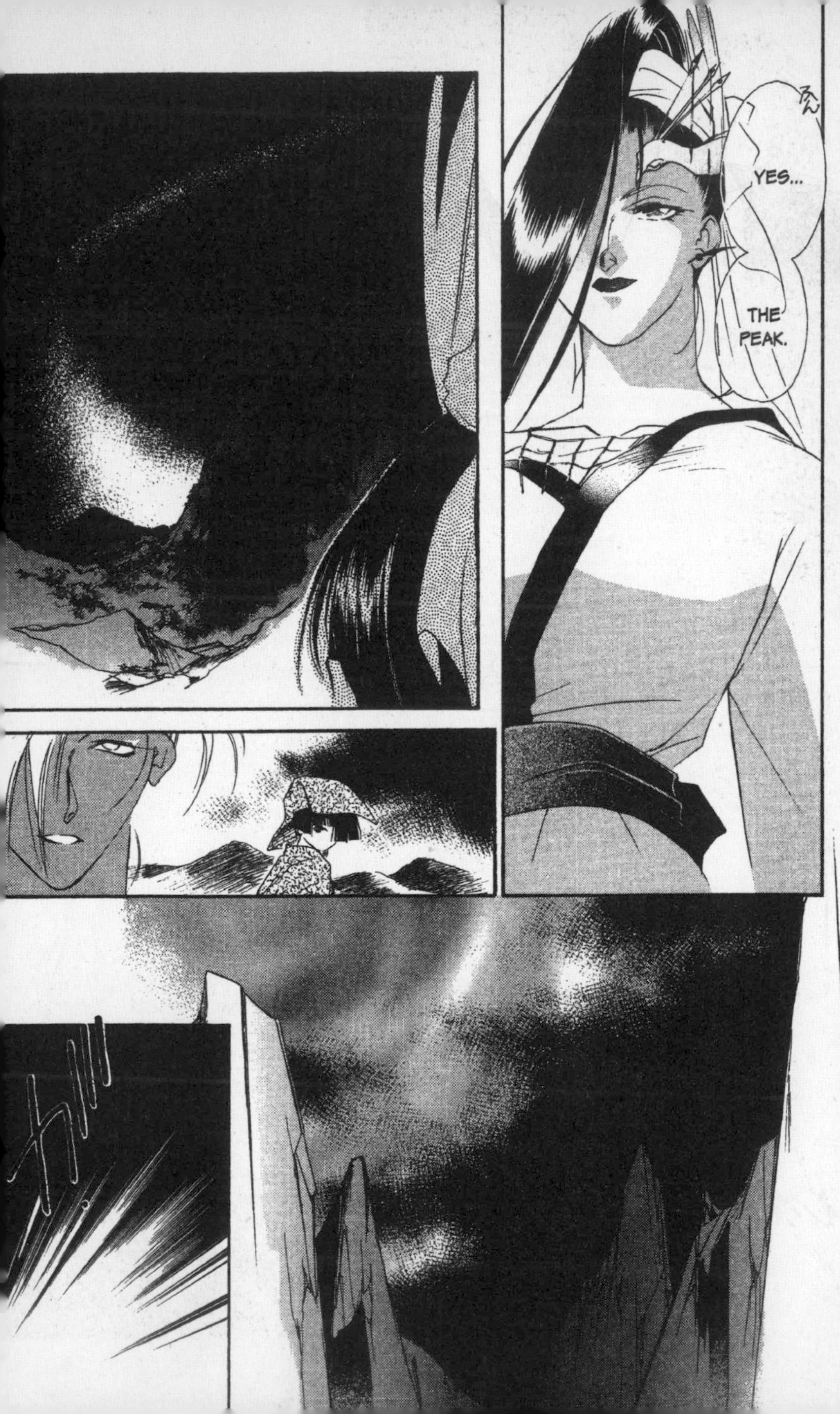
YES...
THE PEAK.

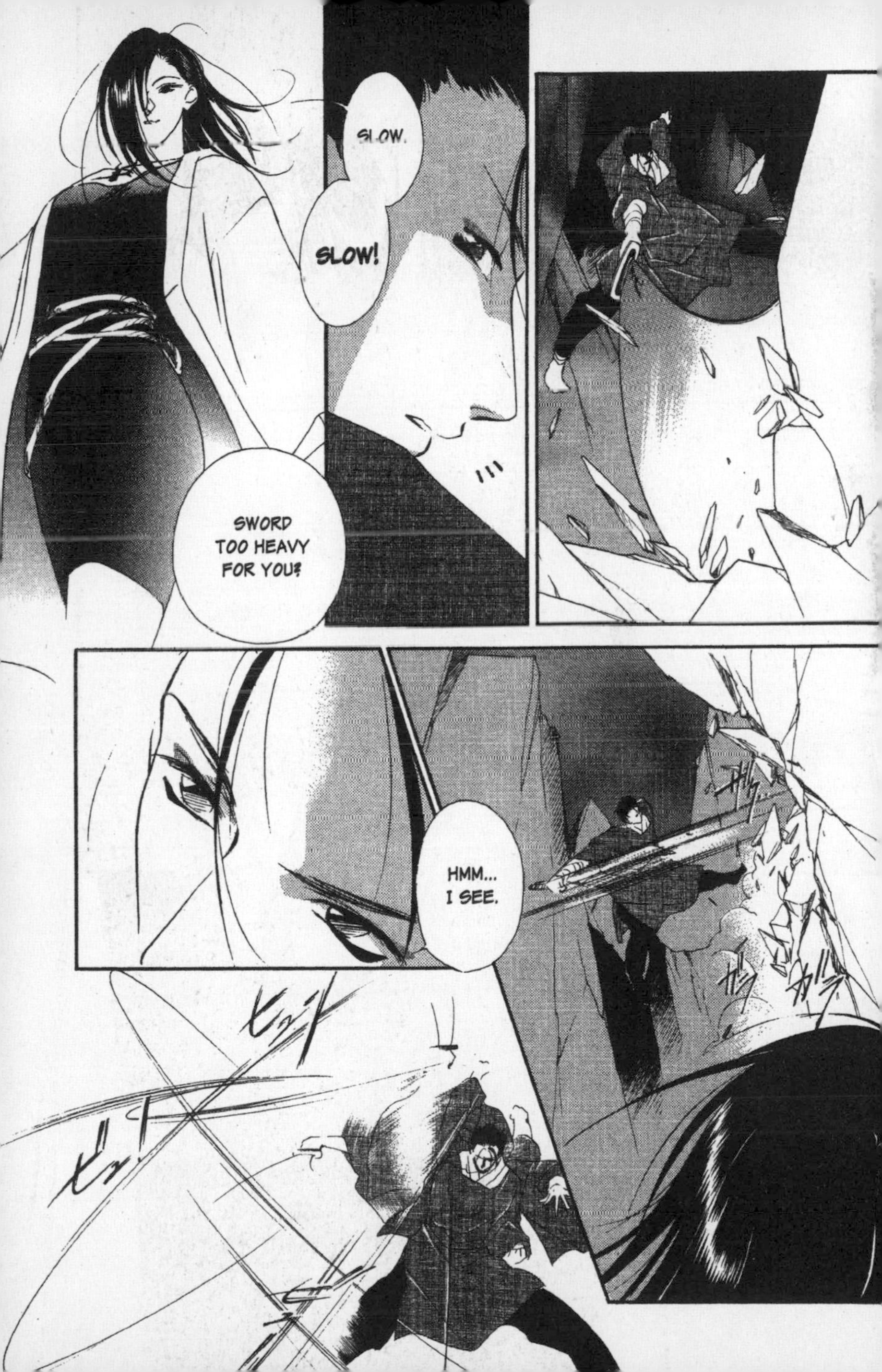
SLOW.
SLOW!
SWORD TOO HEAVY FOR YOU?
HMM... I SEE.

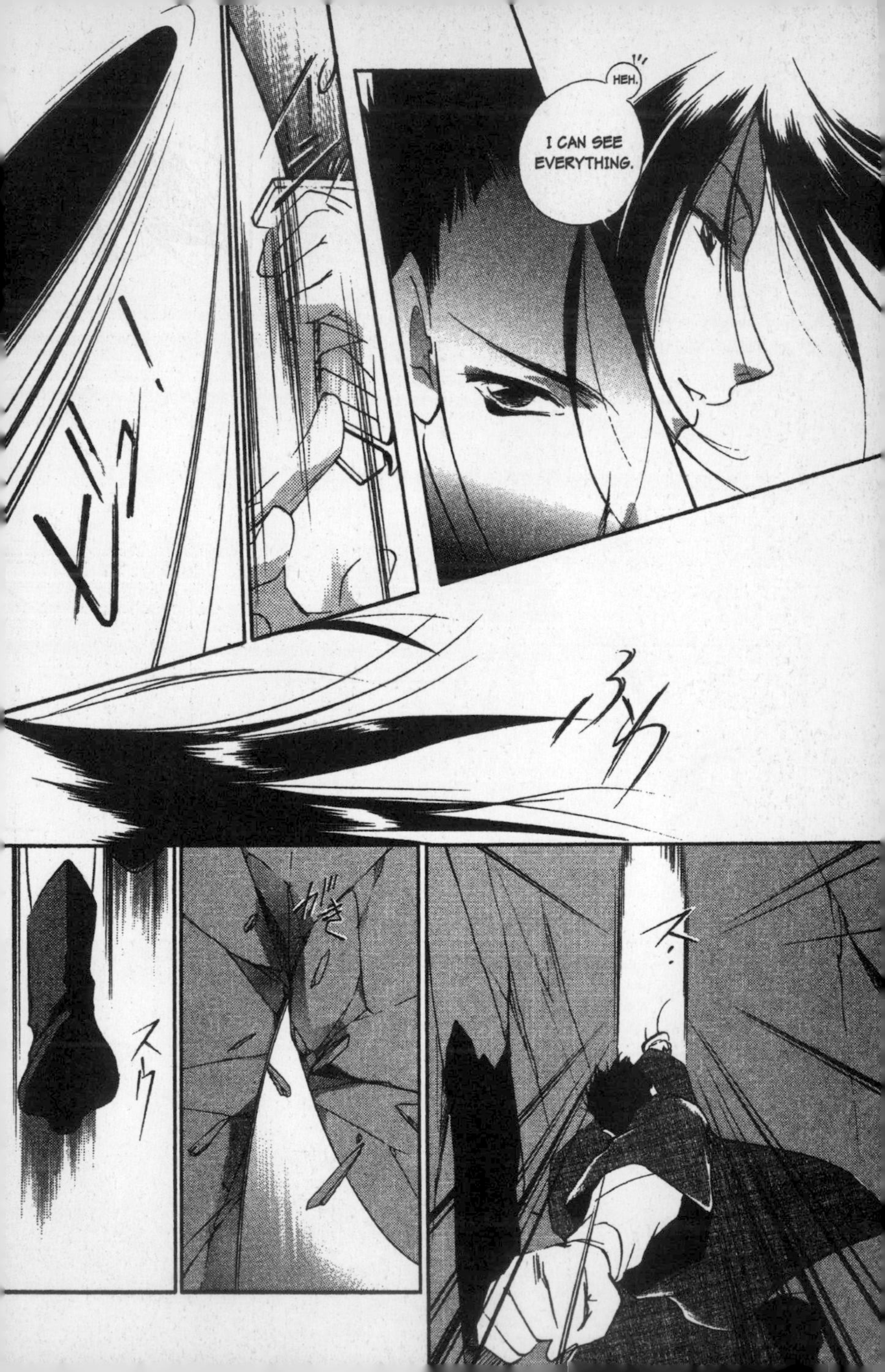
HEH.
I CAN SEE EVERYTHING.
ドン
ふわ
ガキ
ス
スウ

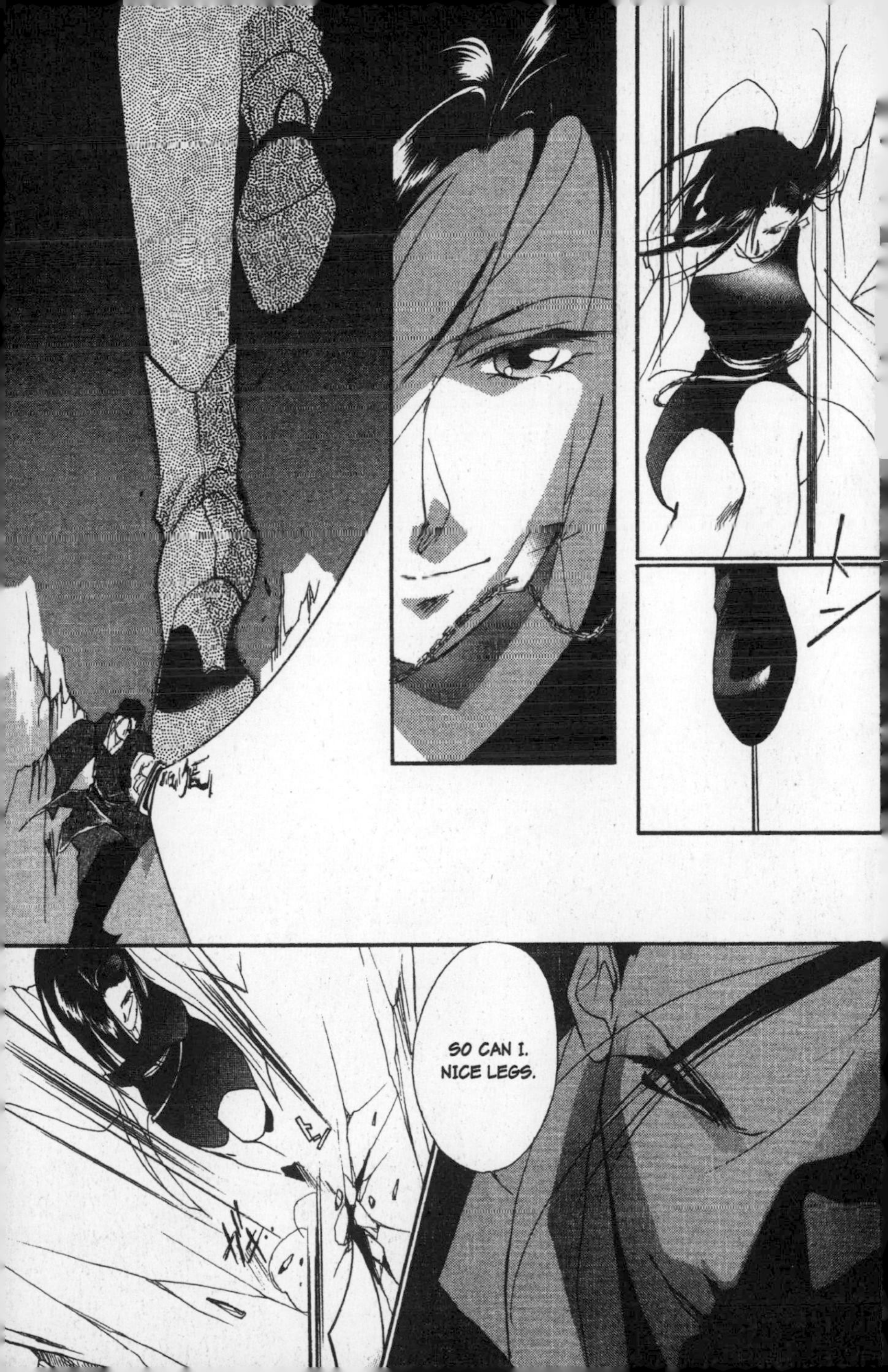
SO CAN I. NICE LEGS.

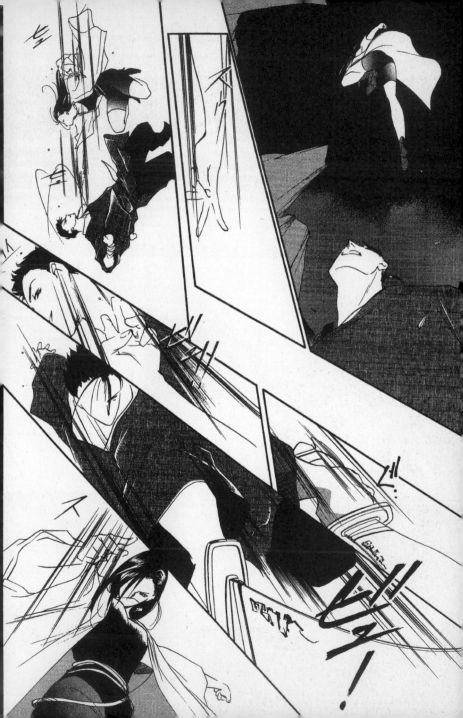

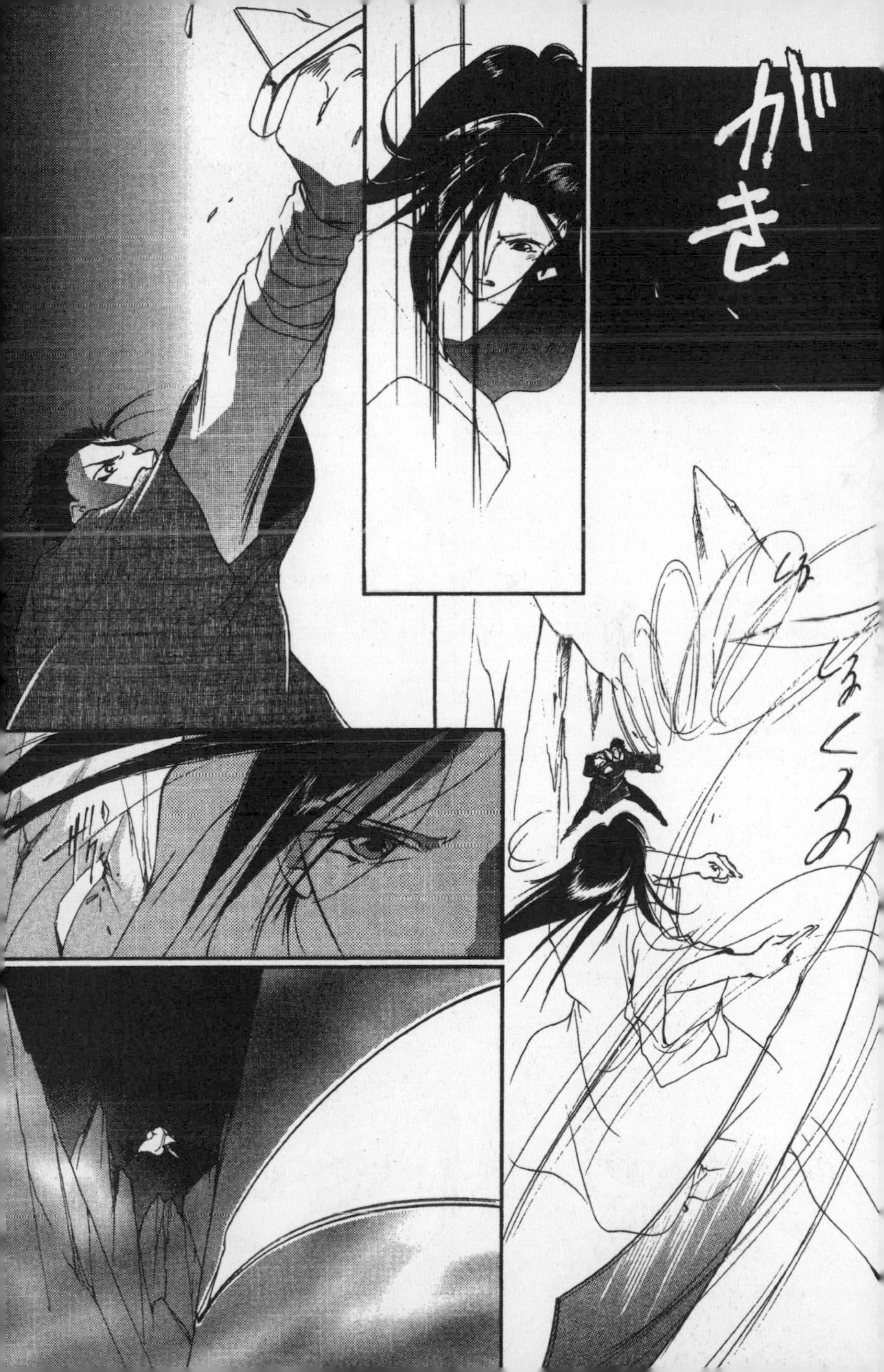
がき

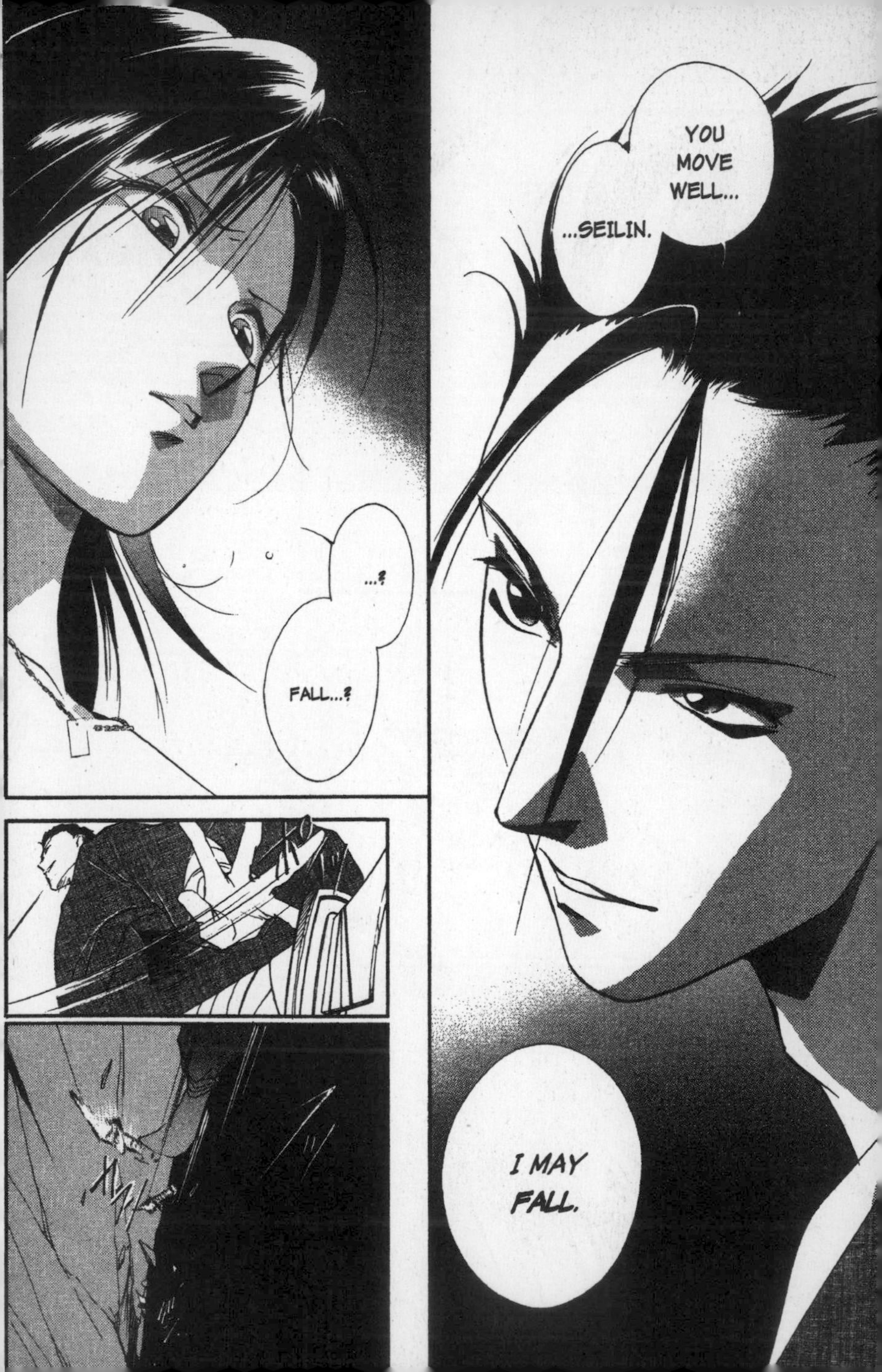
YOU MOVE WELL...
...SEILIN.
I MAY FALL.
...?
FALL...?

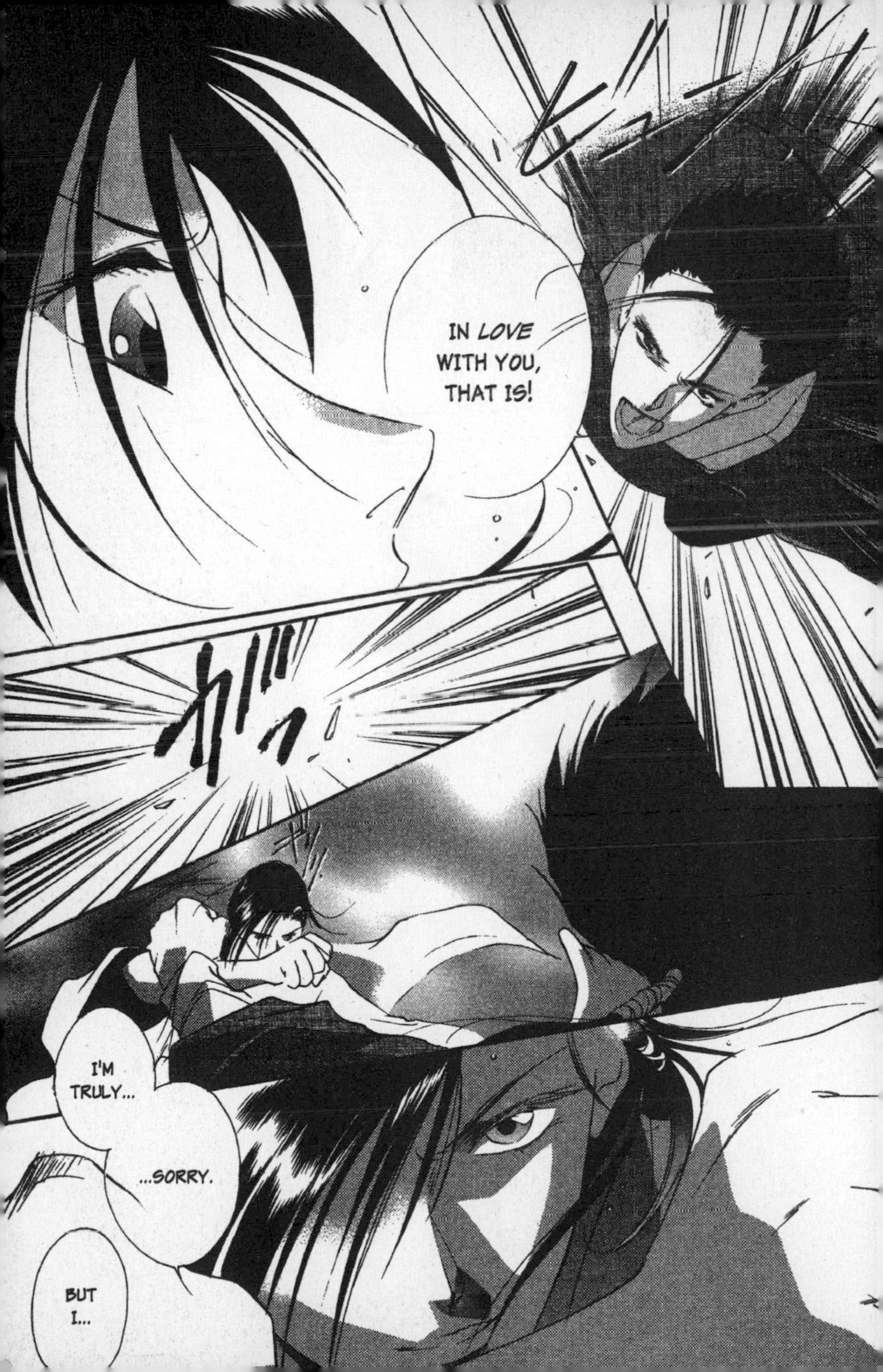
IN *LOVE* WITH YOU, THAT IS!
I'M TRULY...
...SORRY.
BUT I...

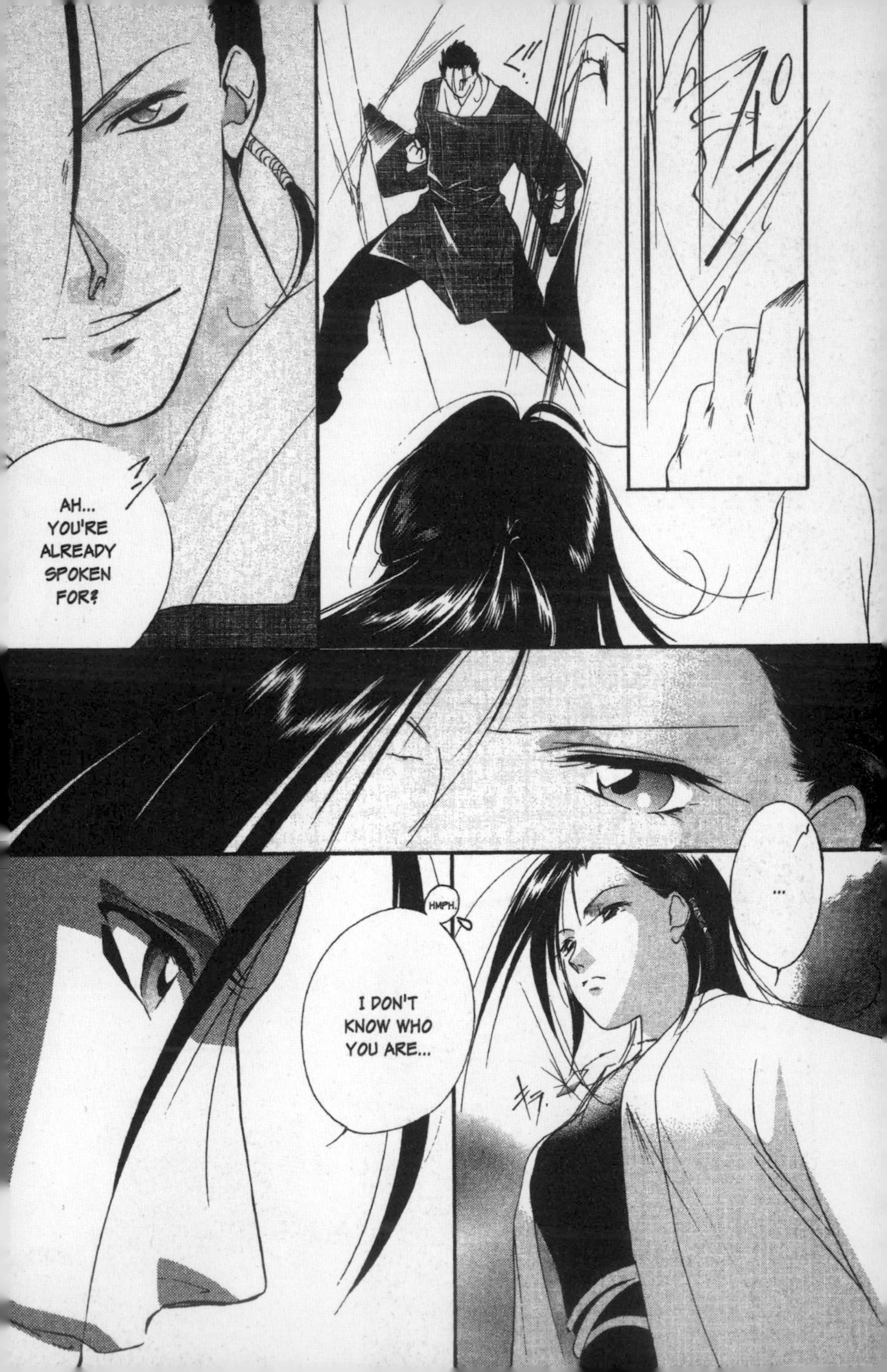
AH... YOU'RE ALREADY SPOKEN FOR?
...
HMPH.
I DON'T KNOW WHO YOU ARE...

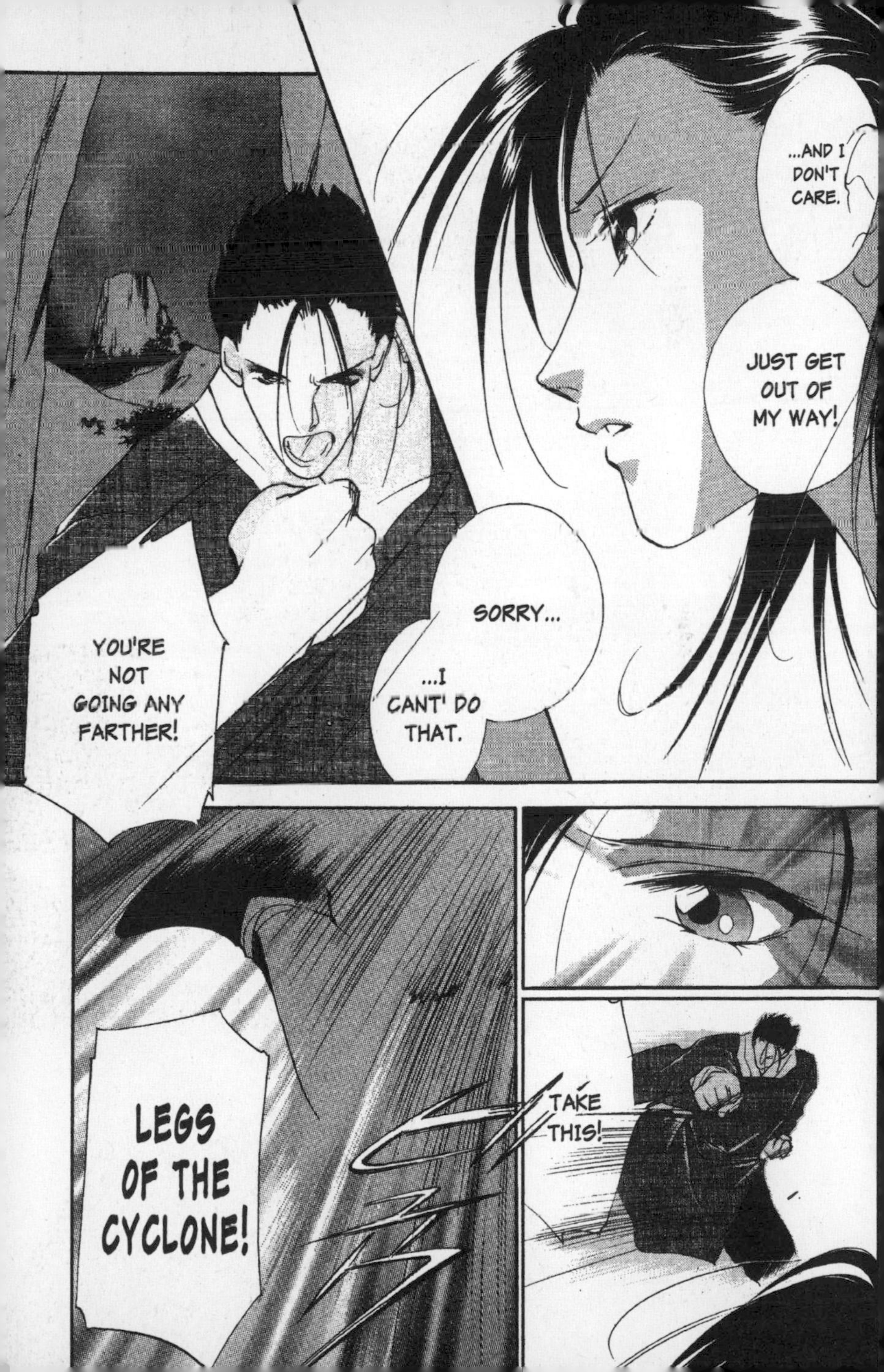
...AND I DON'T CARE.
JUST GET OUT OF MY WAY!
SORRY...
...I CANT' DO THAT.
YOU'RE NOT GOING ANY FARTHER!
TAKE THIS!
LEGS OF THE CYCLONE!

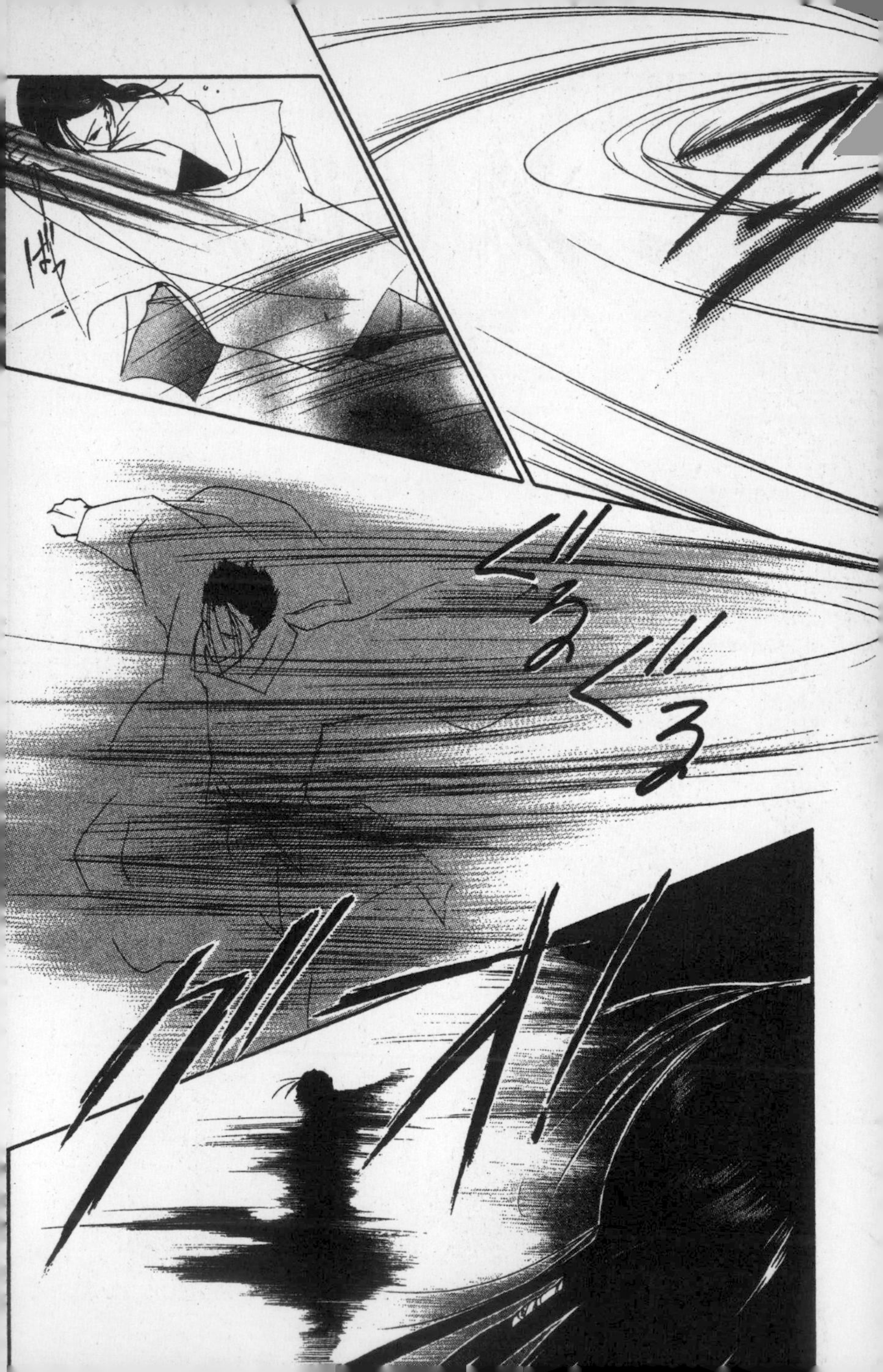
ぐるぐる

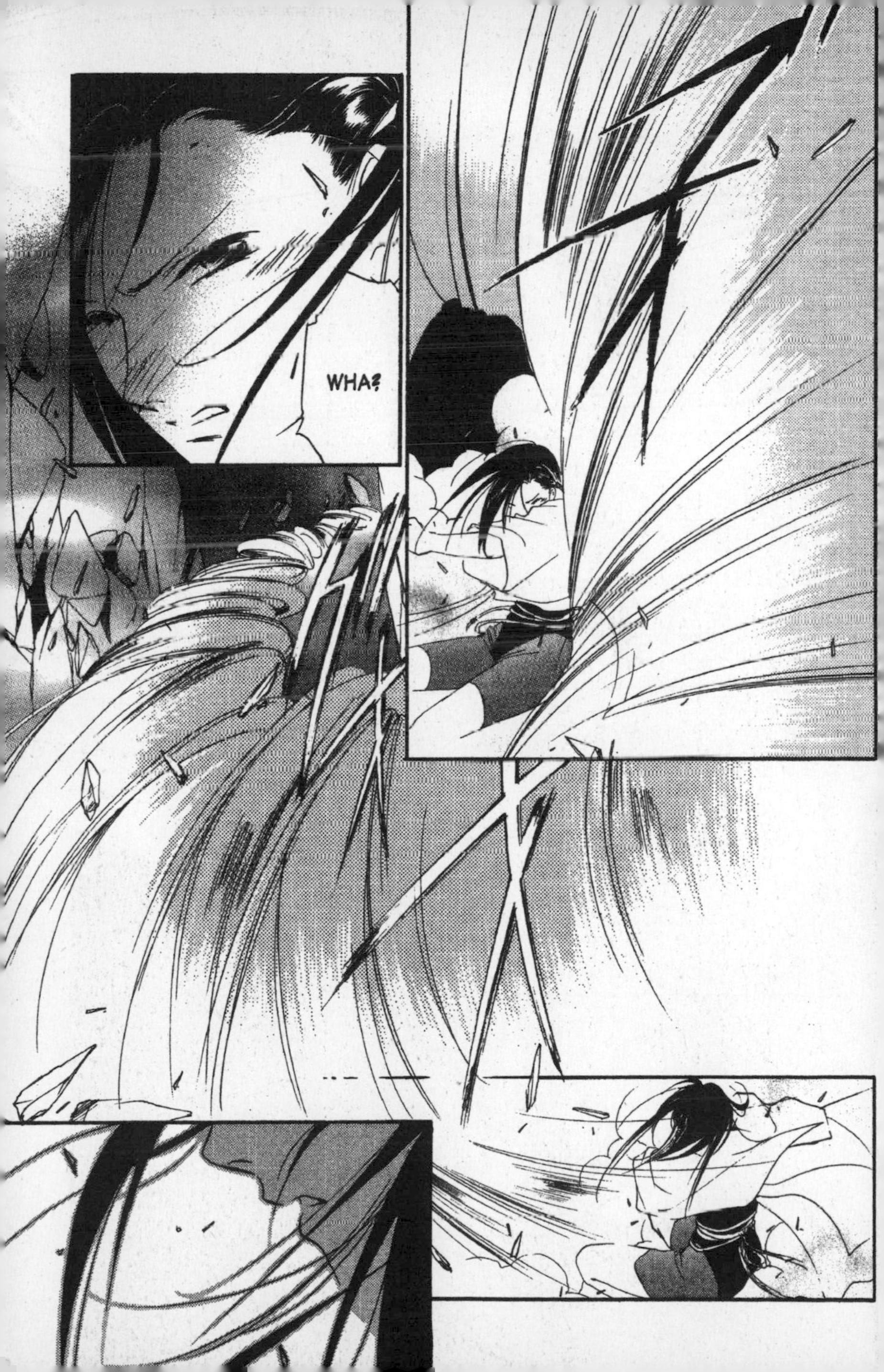
WHA?

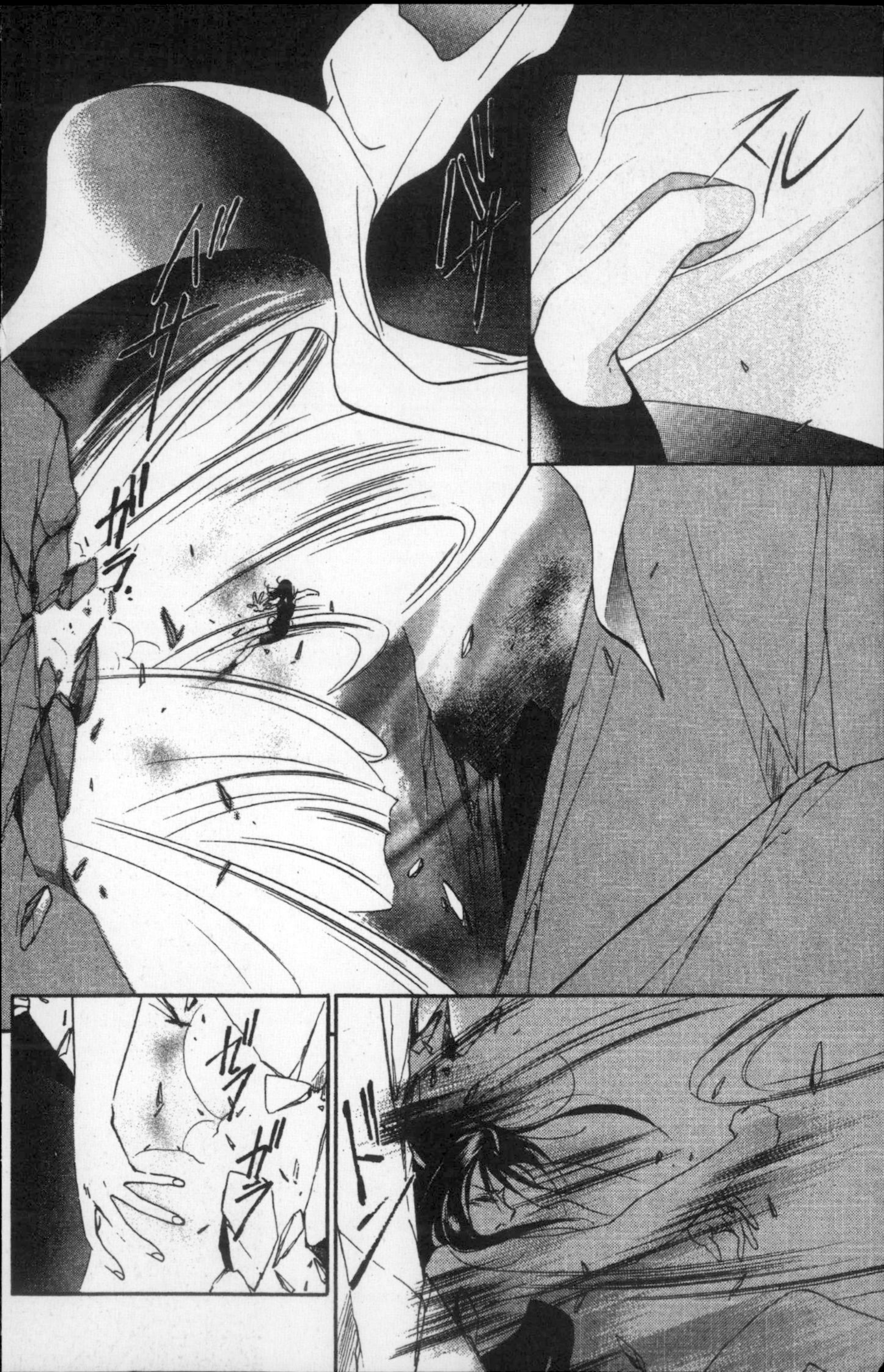
スル
バサ
バサ
ガラ
ド
ガラ
ガラ

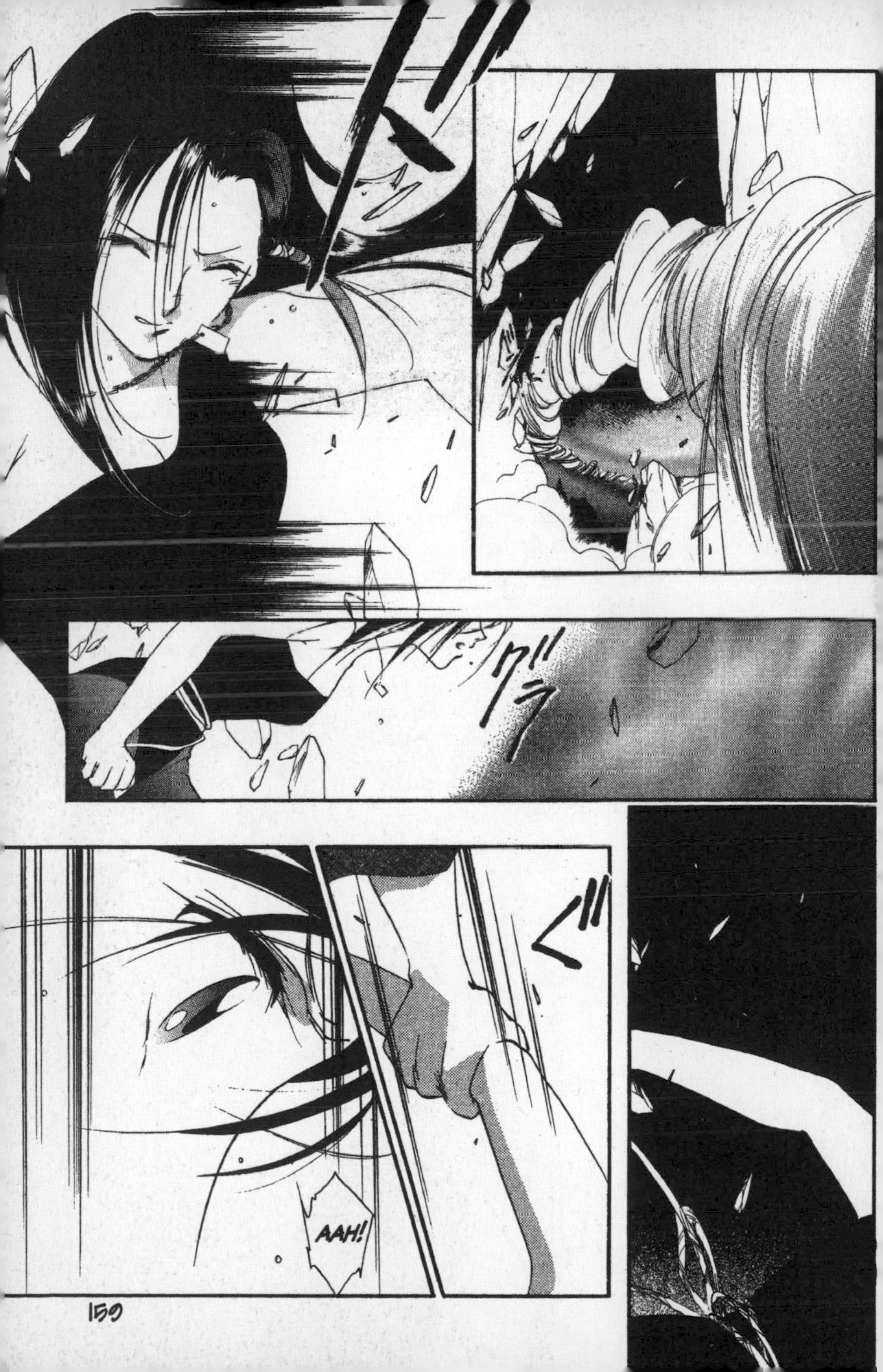
AAH!

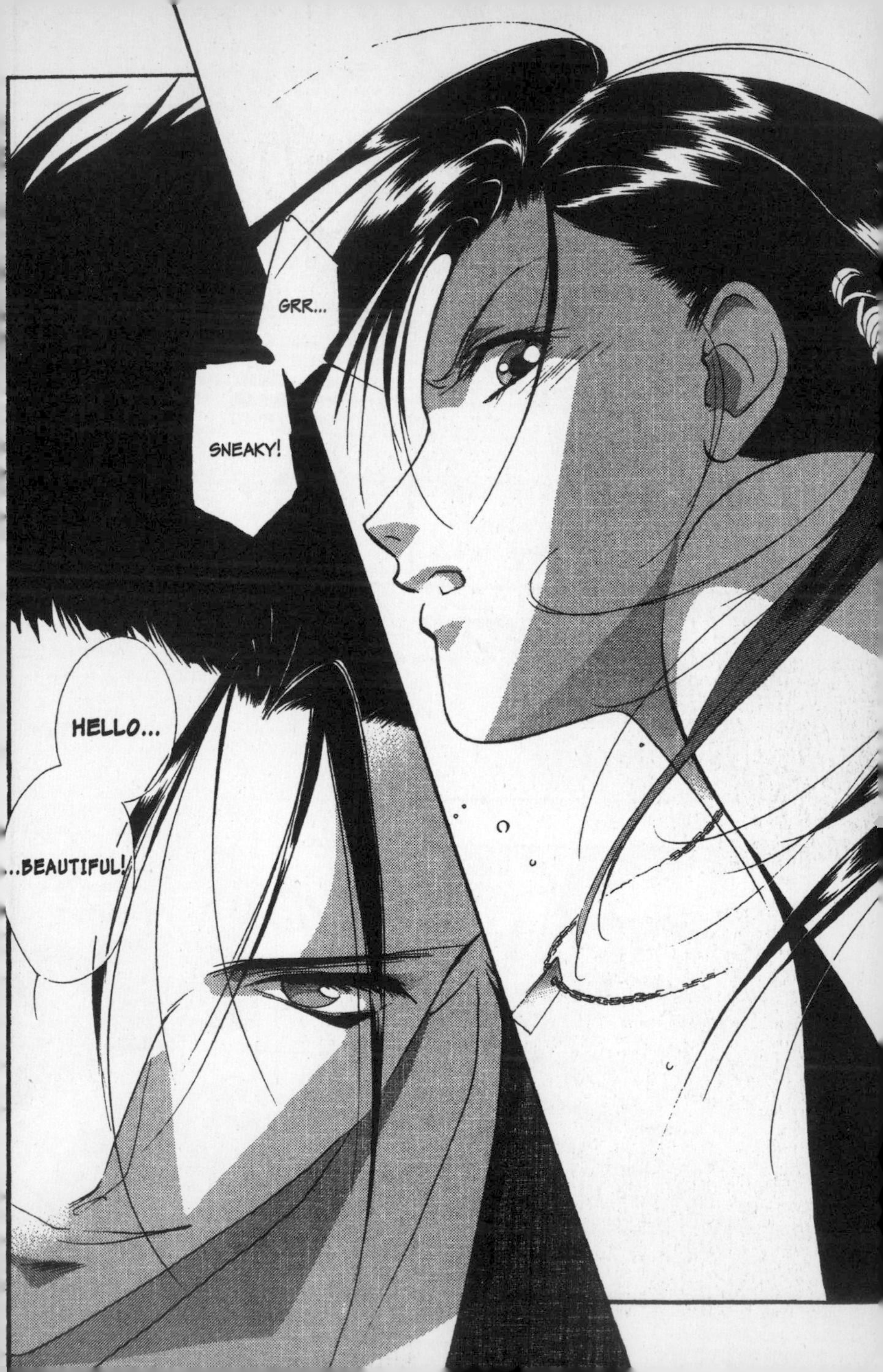
GRR...
SNEAKY!
HELLO...
...BEAUTIFUL!

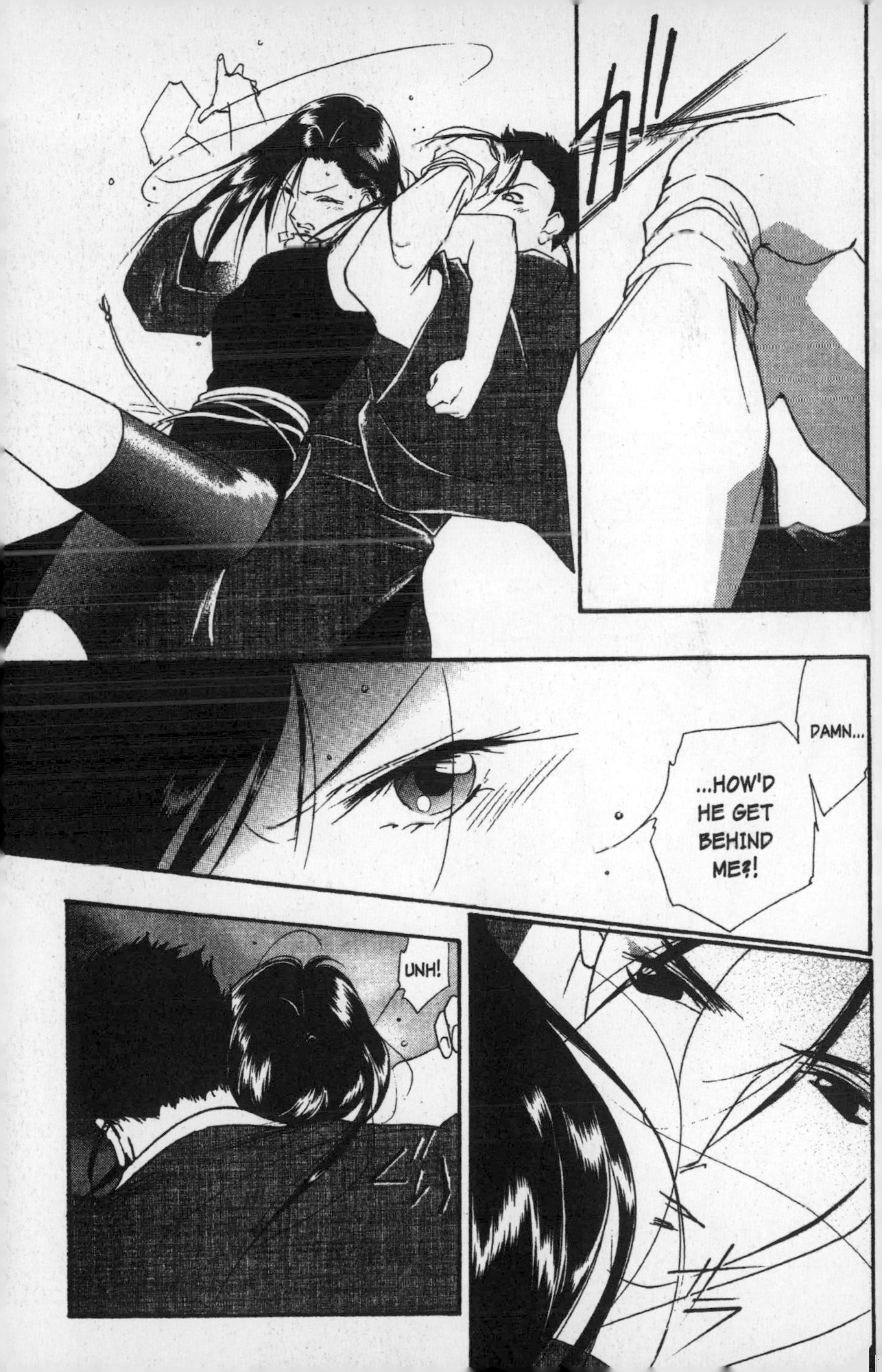
DAMN...
...HOW'D HE GET BEHIND ME?!
UNH!

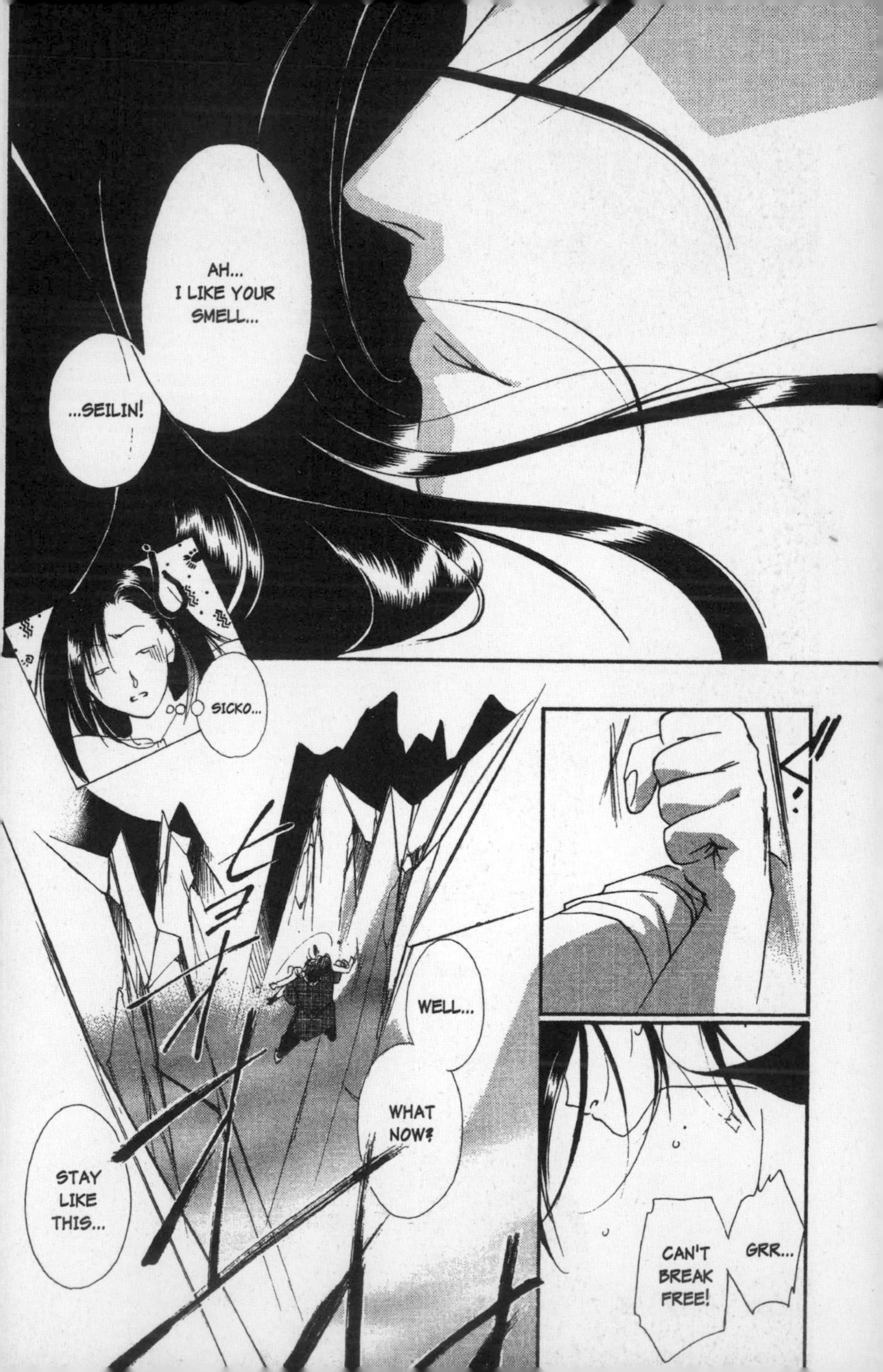
AH... I LIKE YOUR SMELL...
...SEILIN!
SICKO...
GRR...
CAN'T BREAK FREE!
WELL...
WHAT NOW?
STAY LIKE THIS...

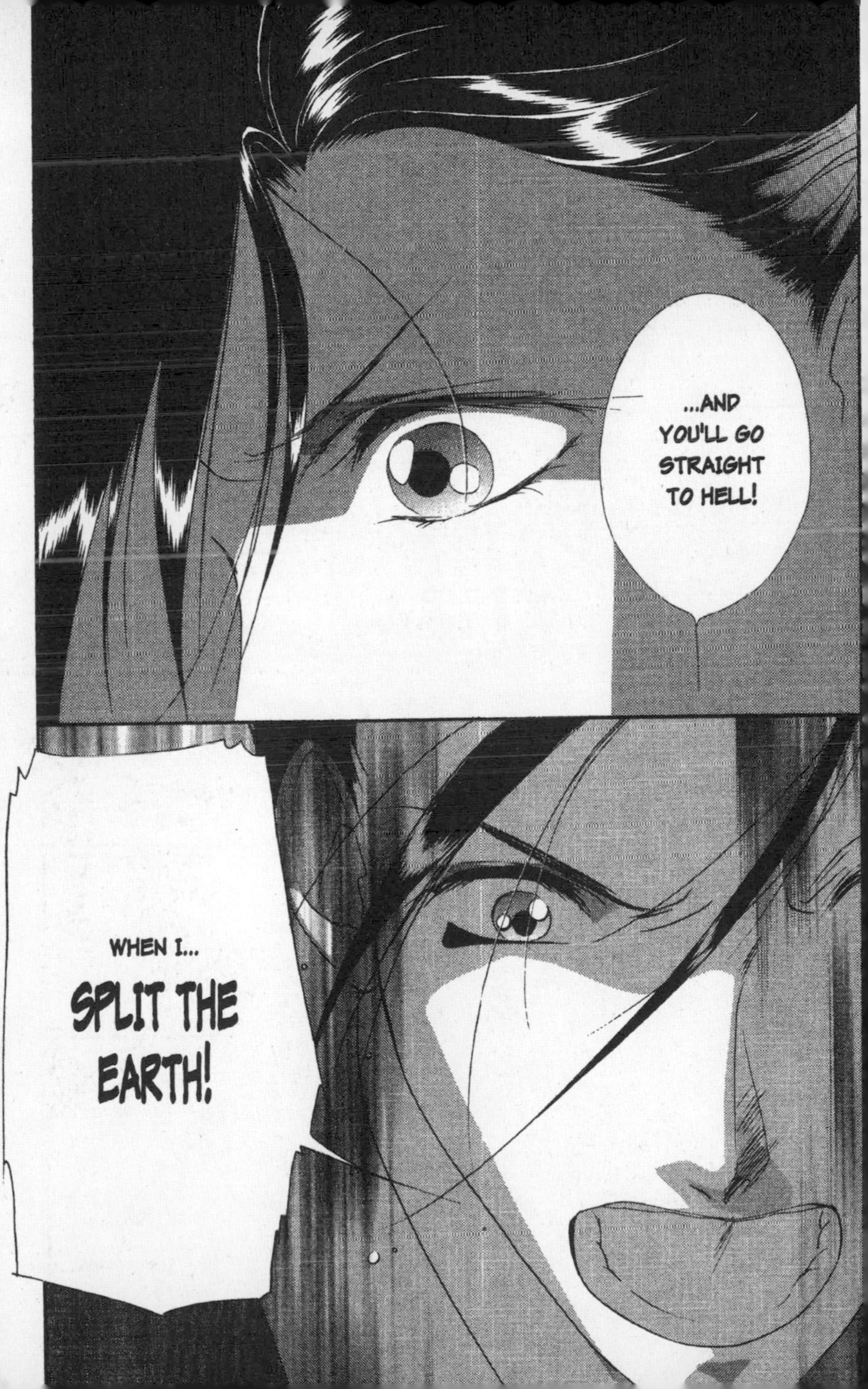
...AND YOU'LL GO STRAIGHT TO HELL!
WHEN I...
SPLIT THE EARTH!

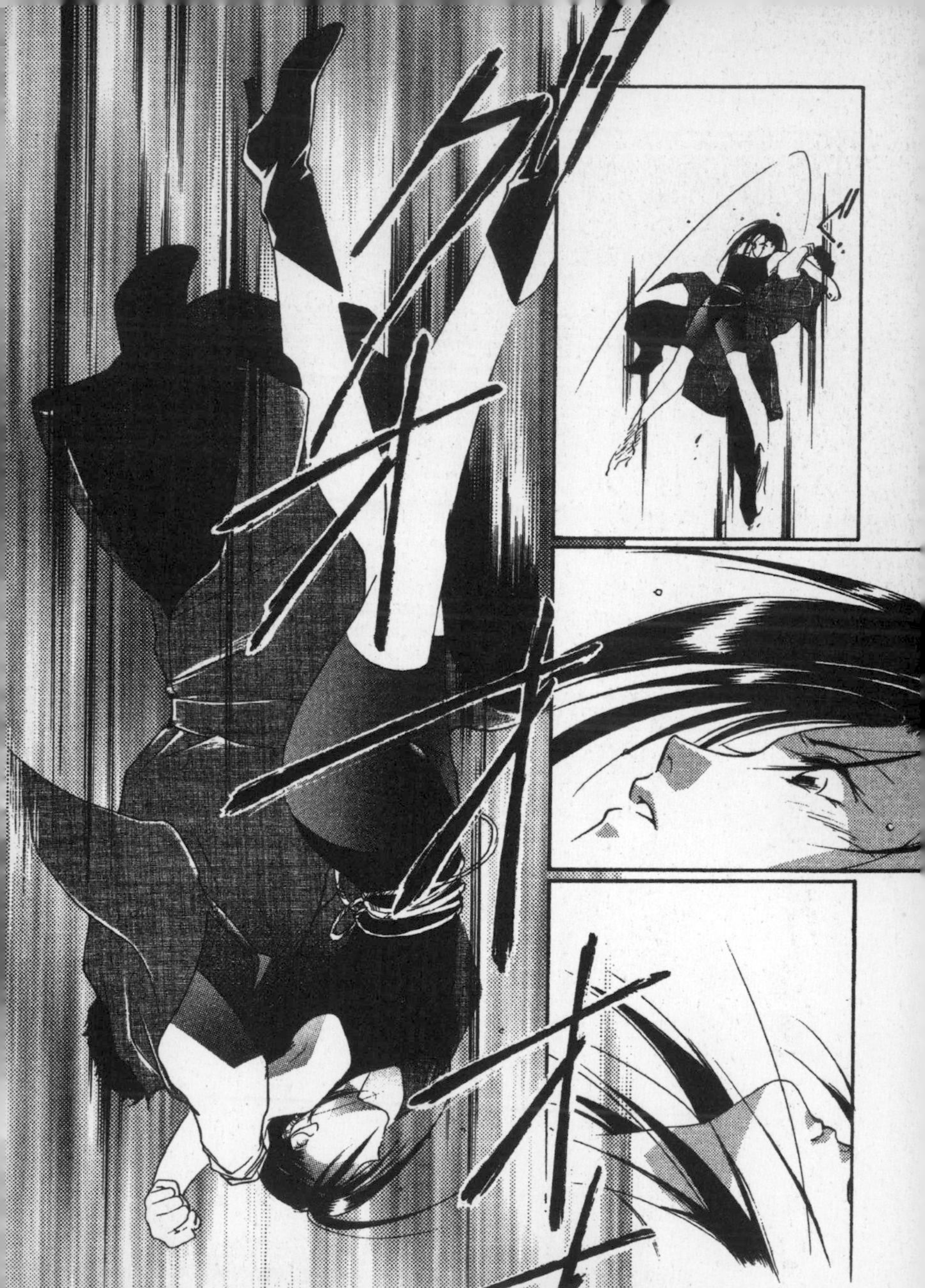
CHAPTER FOURTEEN - END

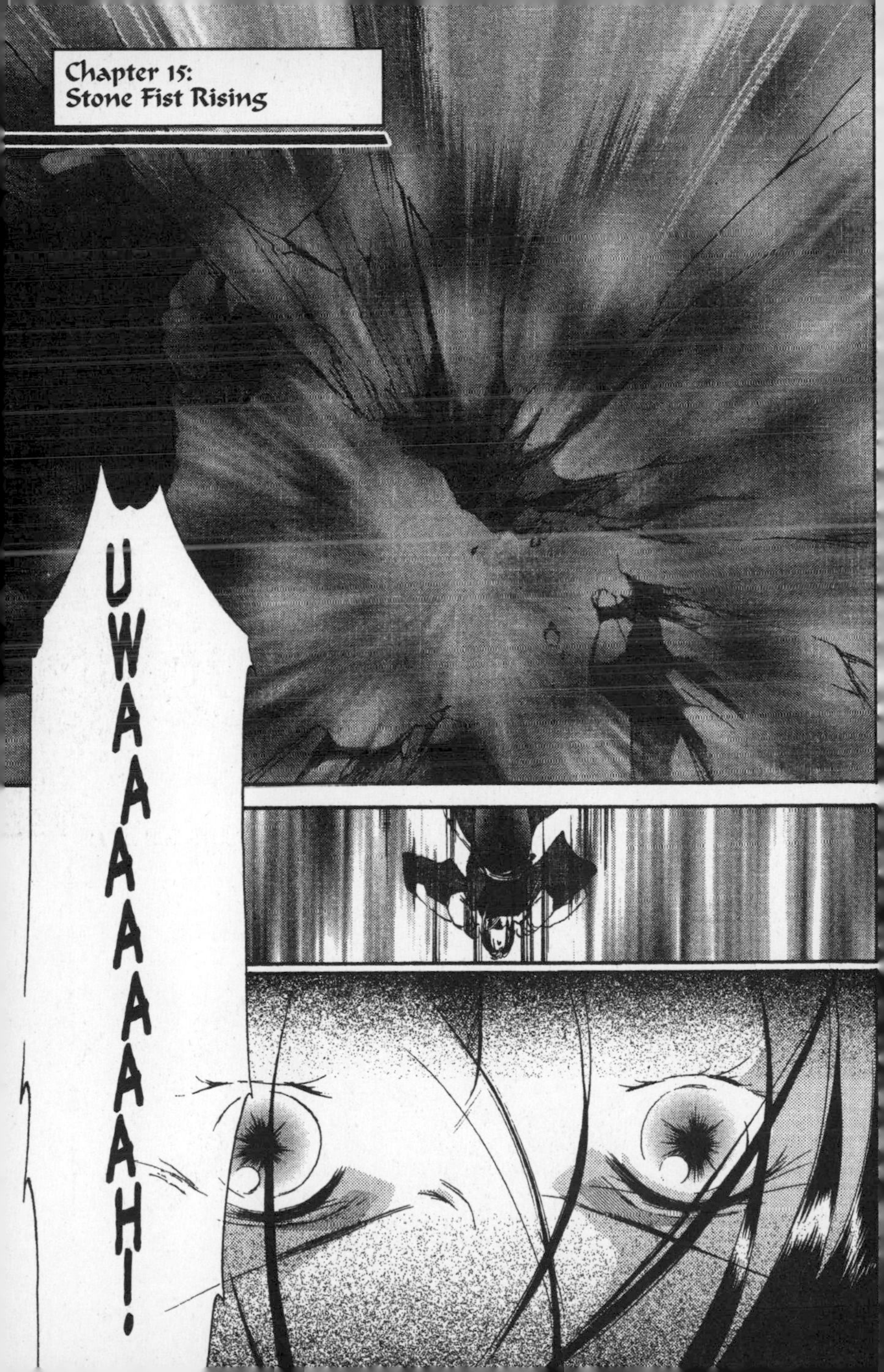
Chapter 15:
Stone Fist Rising
UWAAAAAAAH!

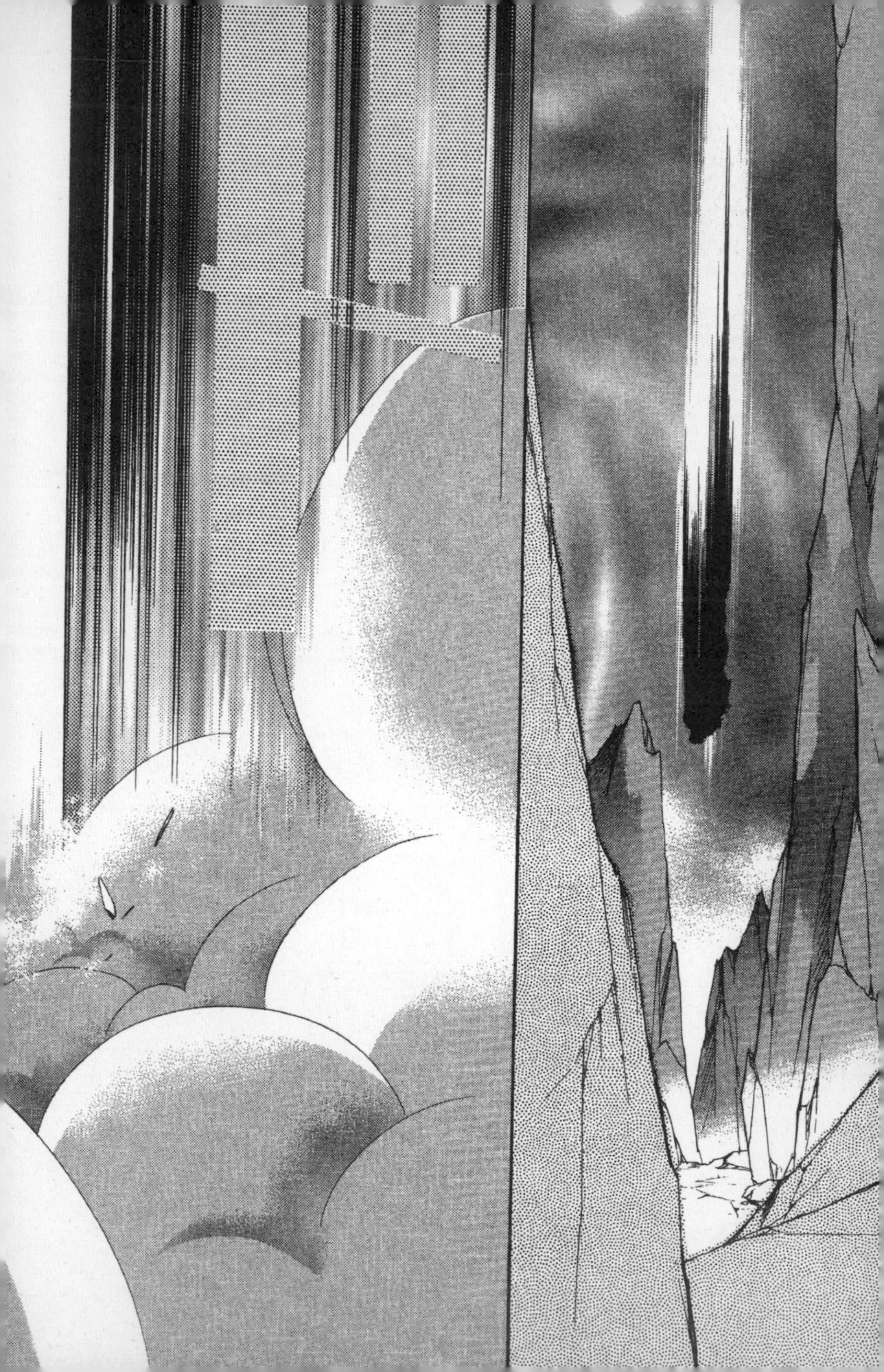

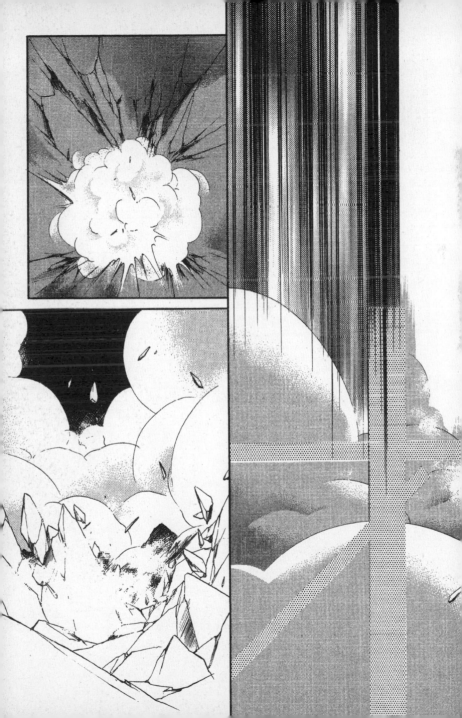

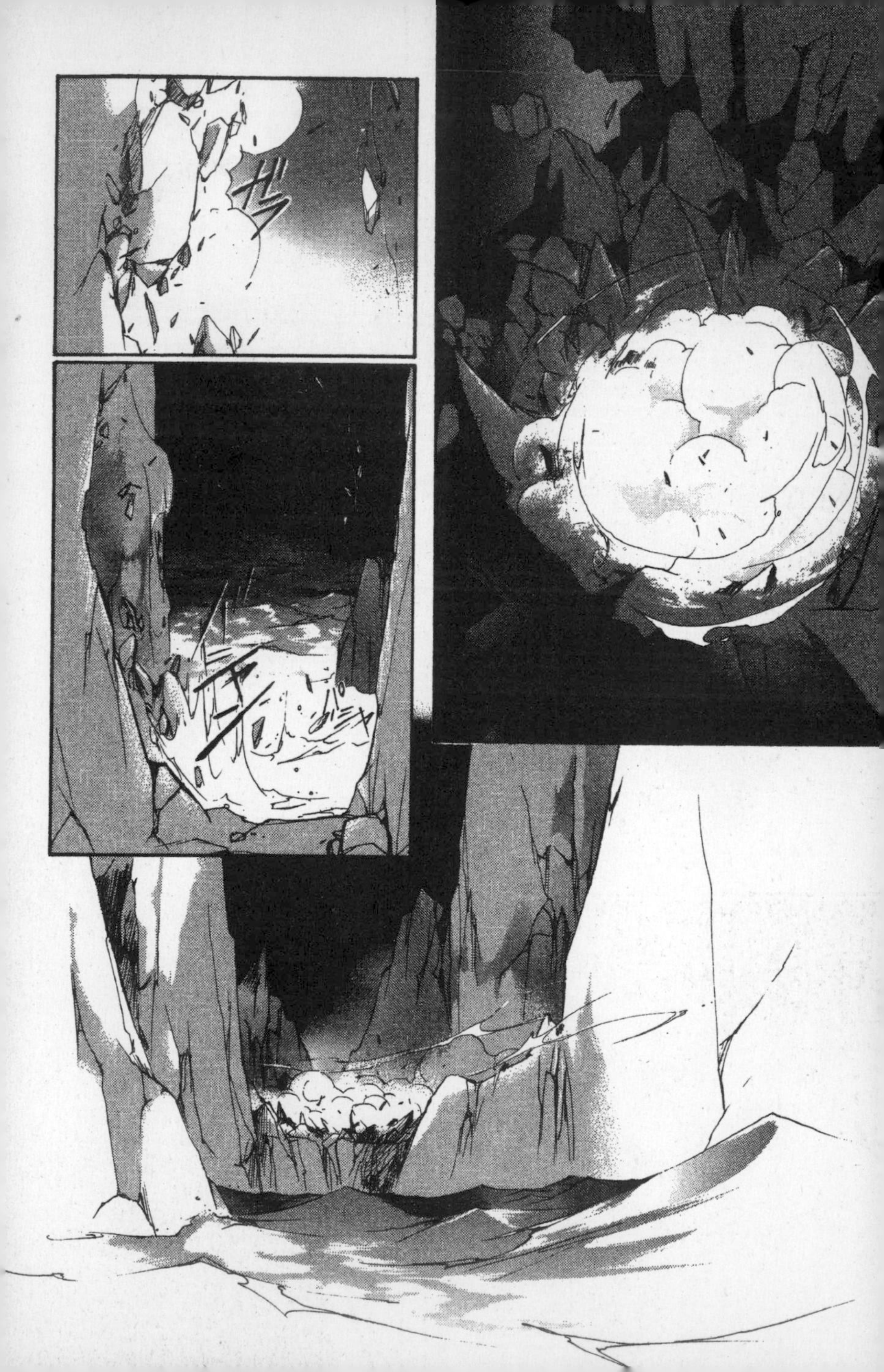
ガッ

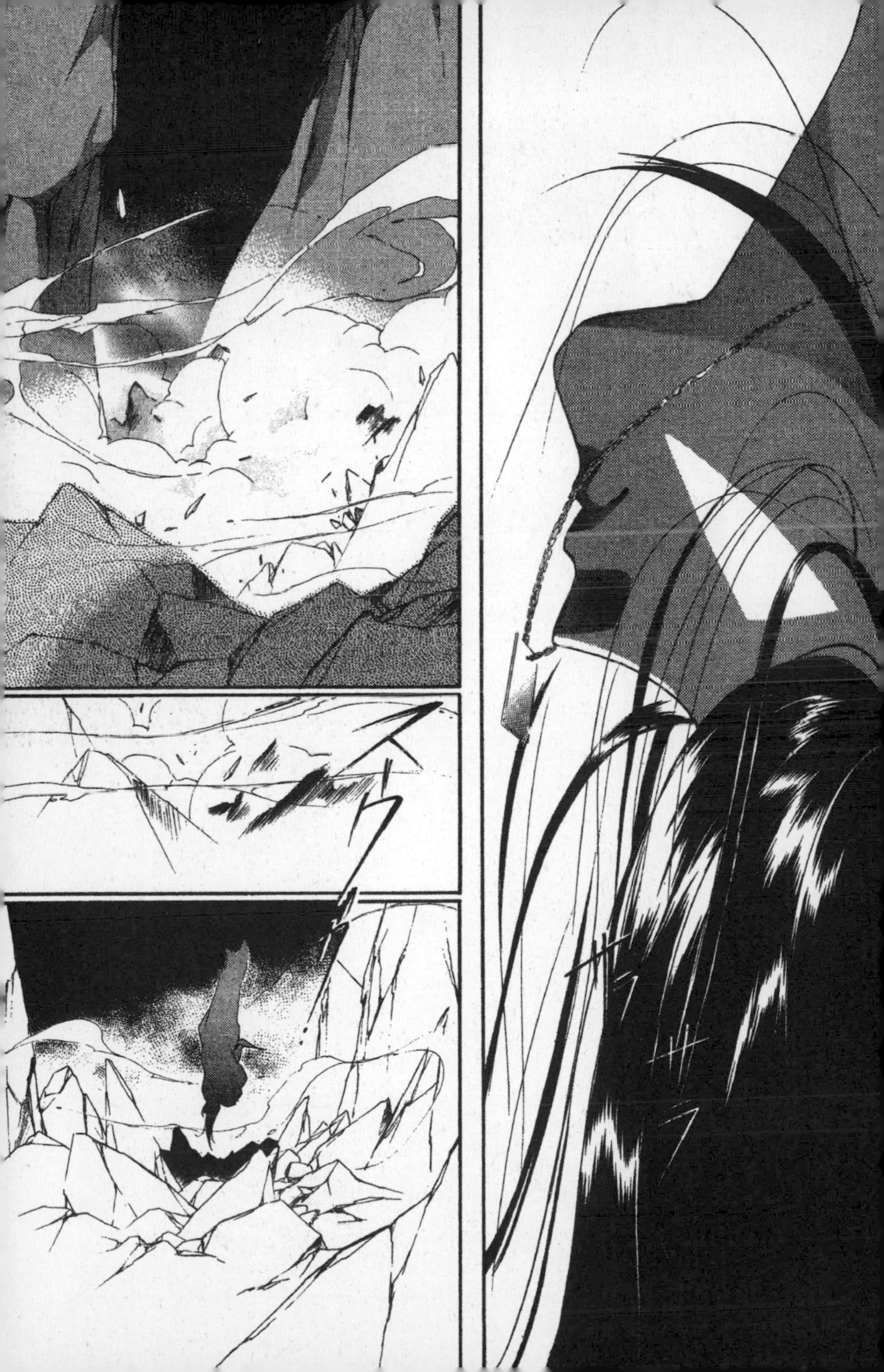

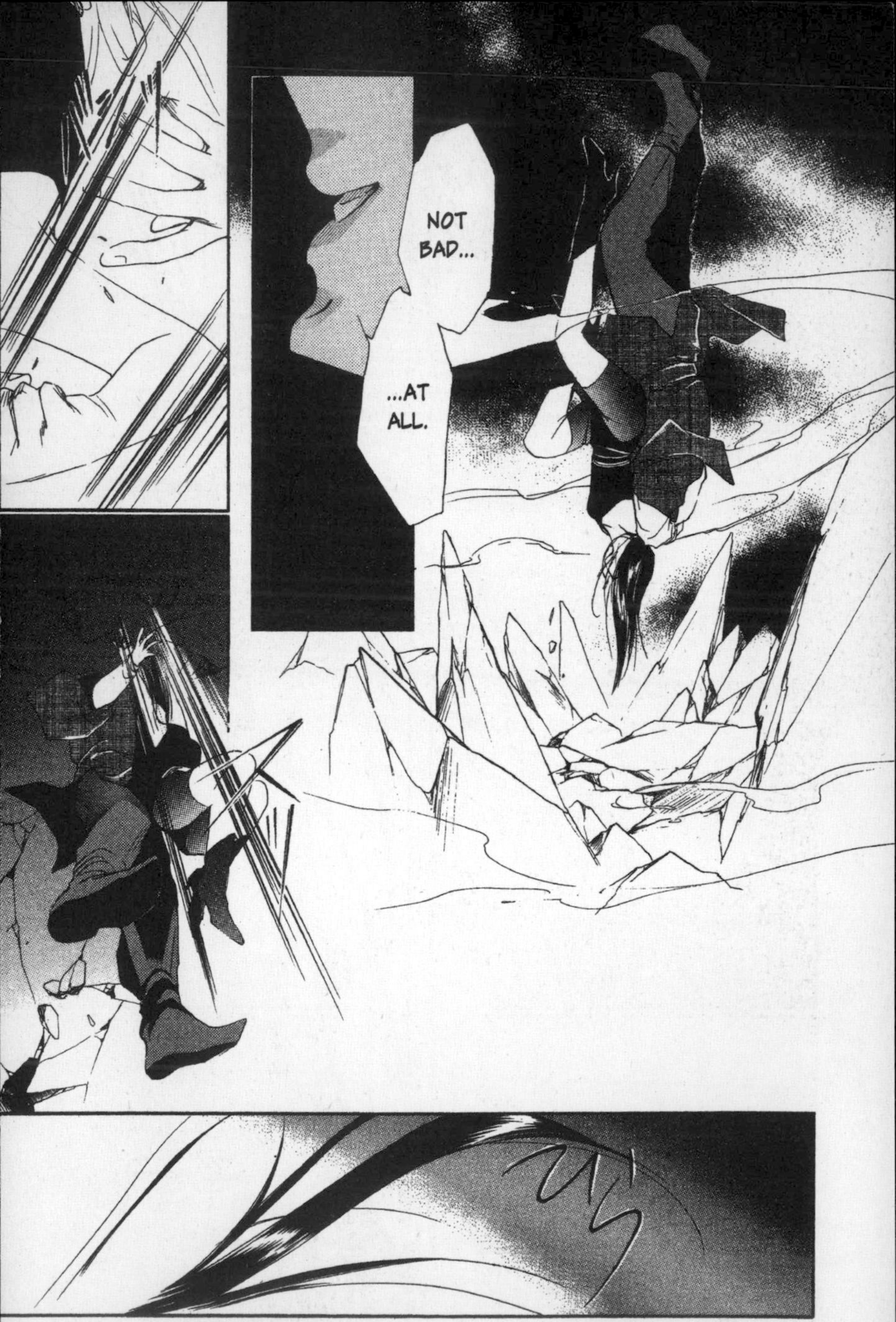
NOT BAD...
...AT ALL.

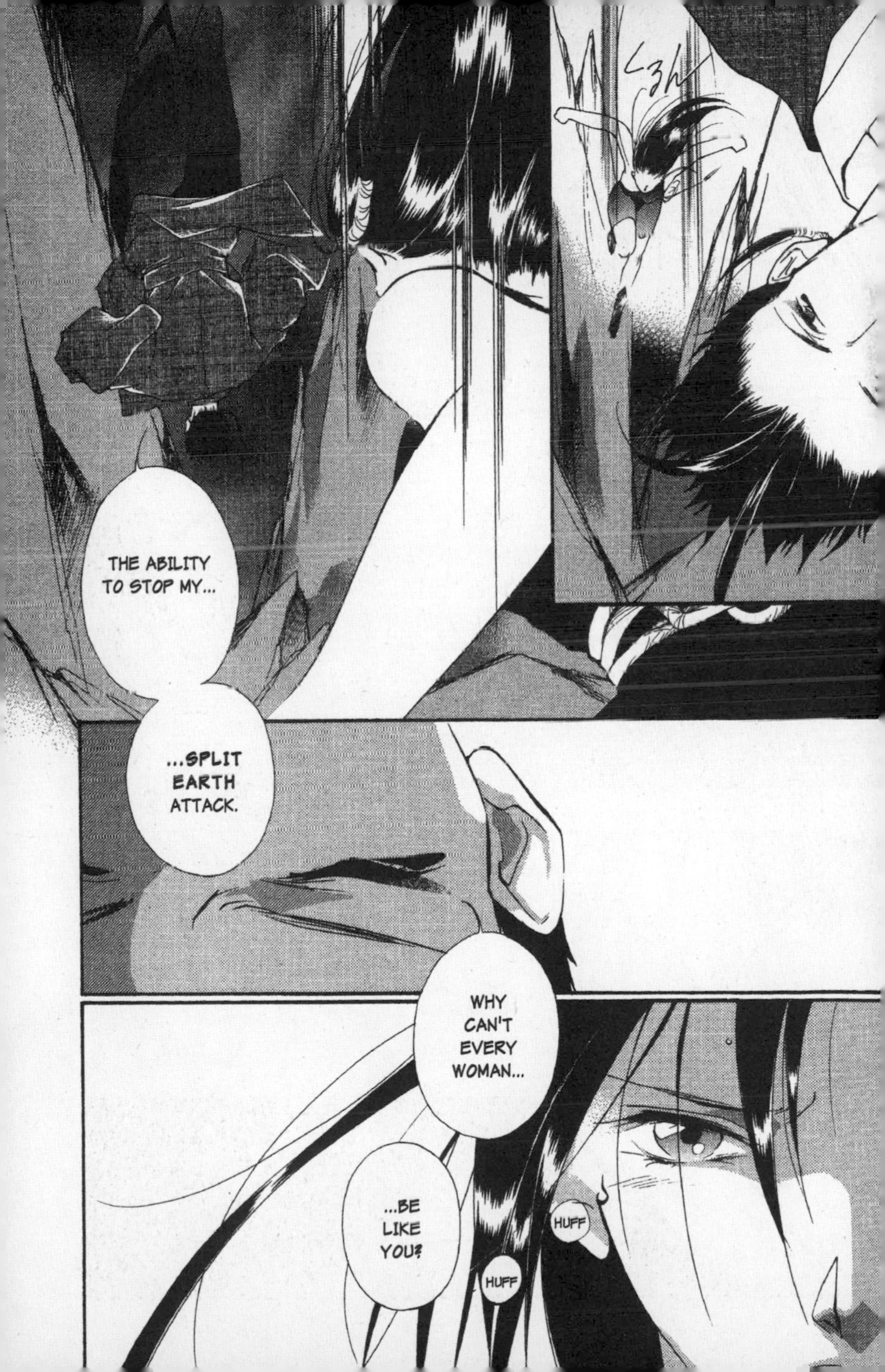
THE ABILITY TO STOP MY...
...SPLIT EARTH ATTACK.
WHY CAN'T EVERY WOMAN...
HUFF
HUFF
...BE LIKE YOU?

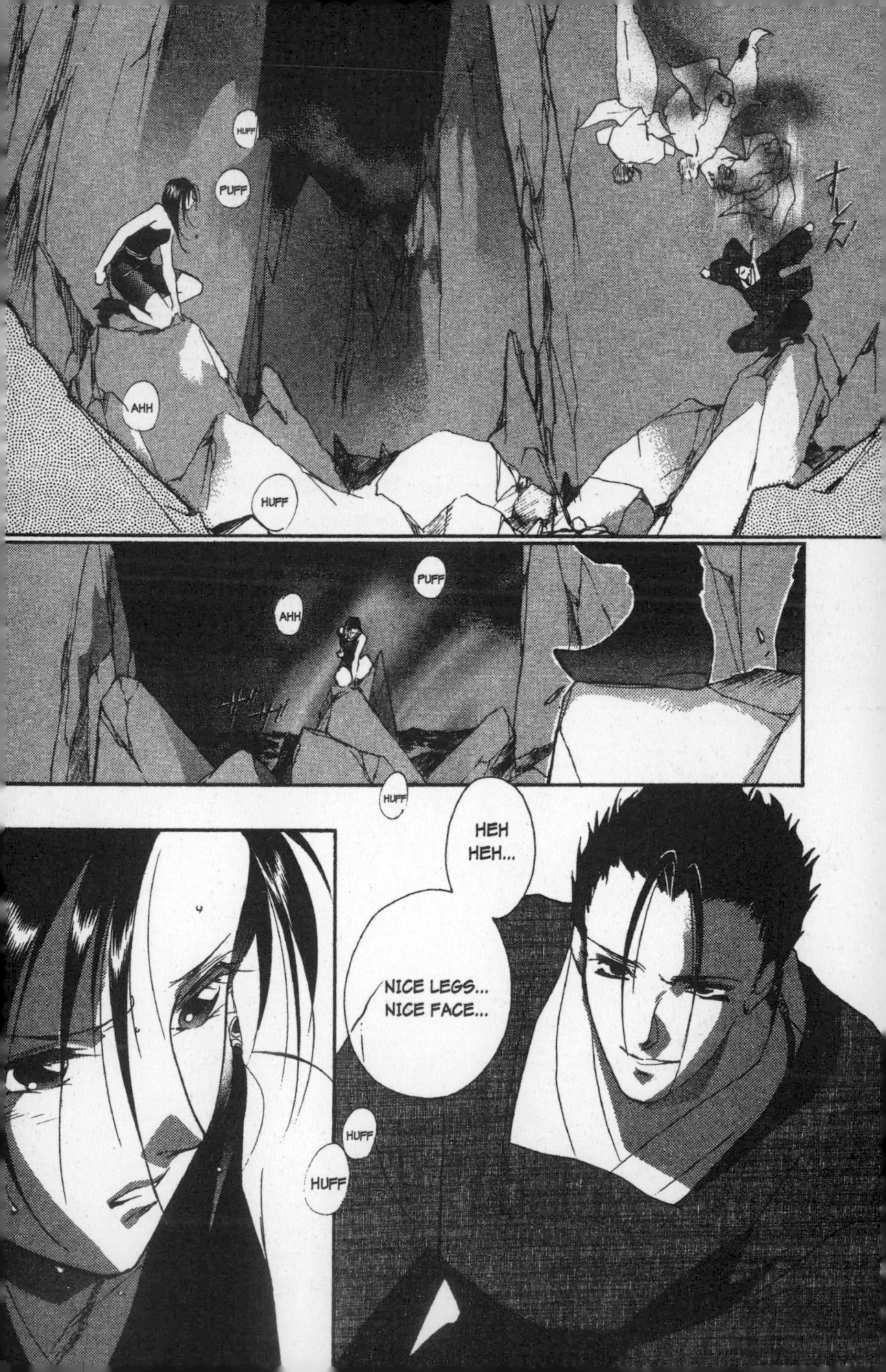
すとん
HUFF
PUFF
AHH
HUFF
PUFF
AHH
HUFF
HEH HEH...
NICE LEGS... NICE FACE...
HUFF
HUFF

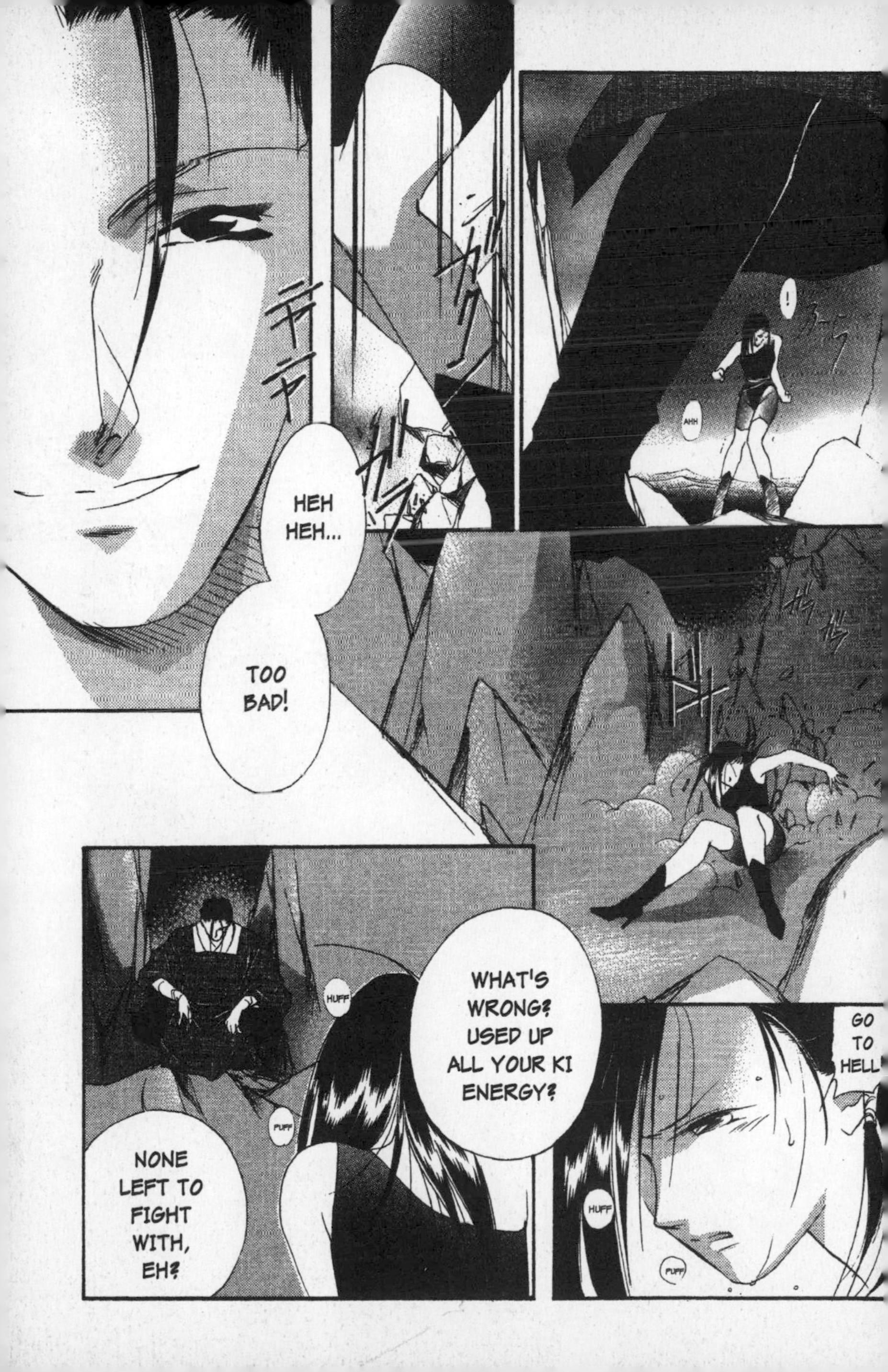
!
AHH
HEH HEH...
TOO BAD!
GO TO HELL
HUFF
PUFF
HUFF
WHAT'S WRONG? USED UP ALL YOUR KI ENERGY?
PUFF
NONE LEFT TO FIGHT WITH, EH?

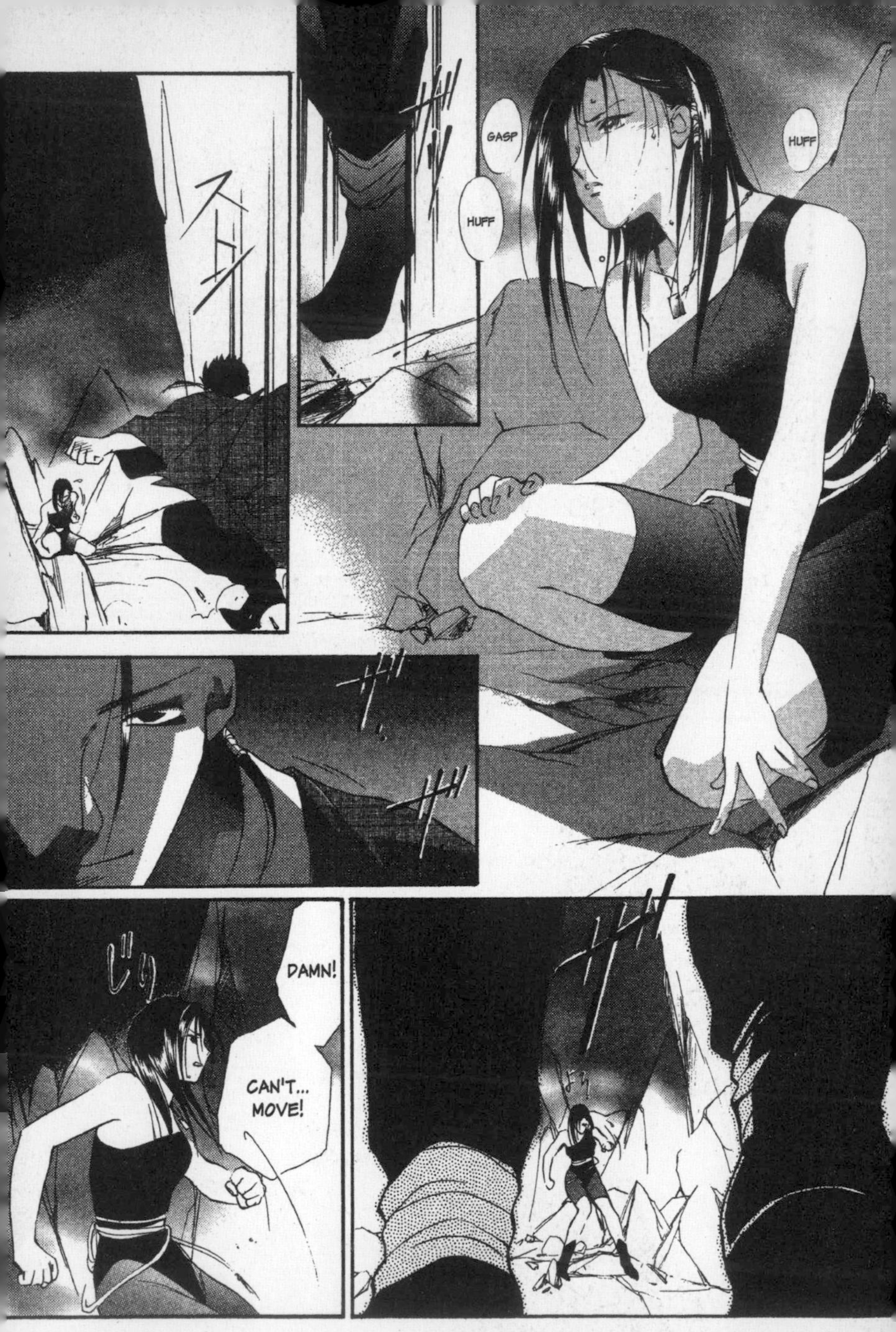
HUFF
GASP
HUFF
DAMN!
CAN'T... MOVE!

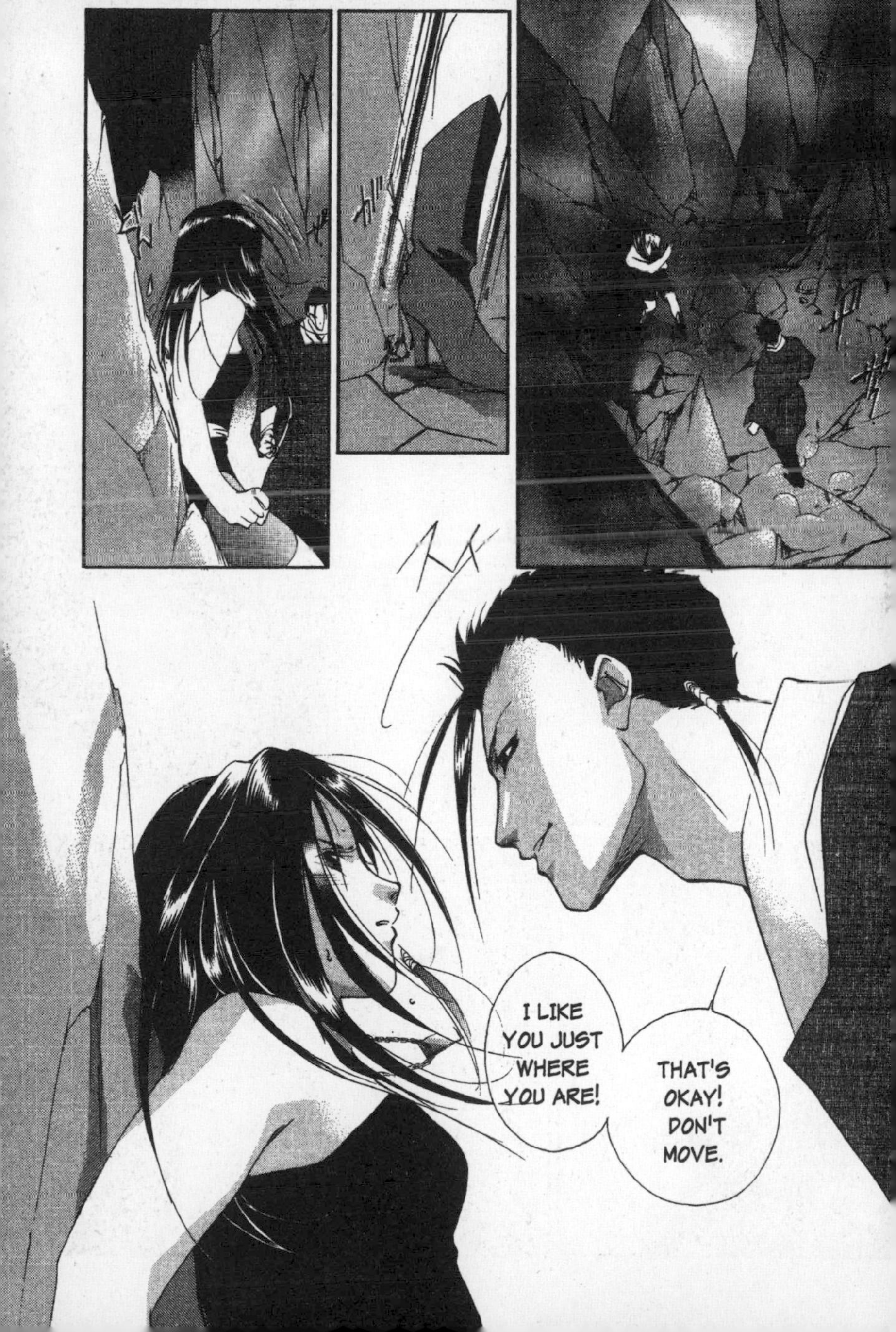
THAT'S OKAY! DON'T MOVE.
I LIKE YOU JUST WHERE YOU ARE!

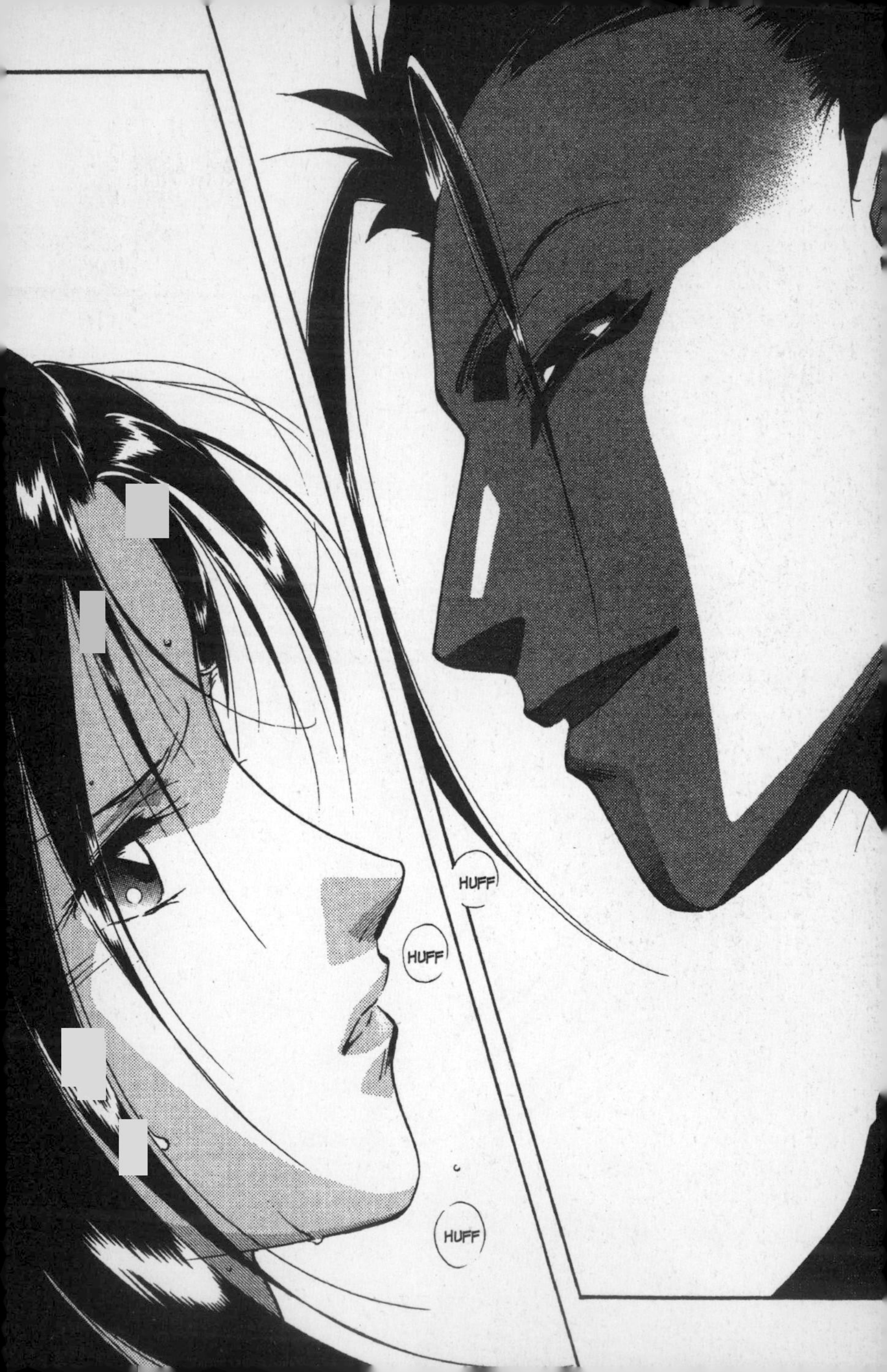
HUFF
HUFF
HUFF

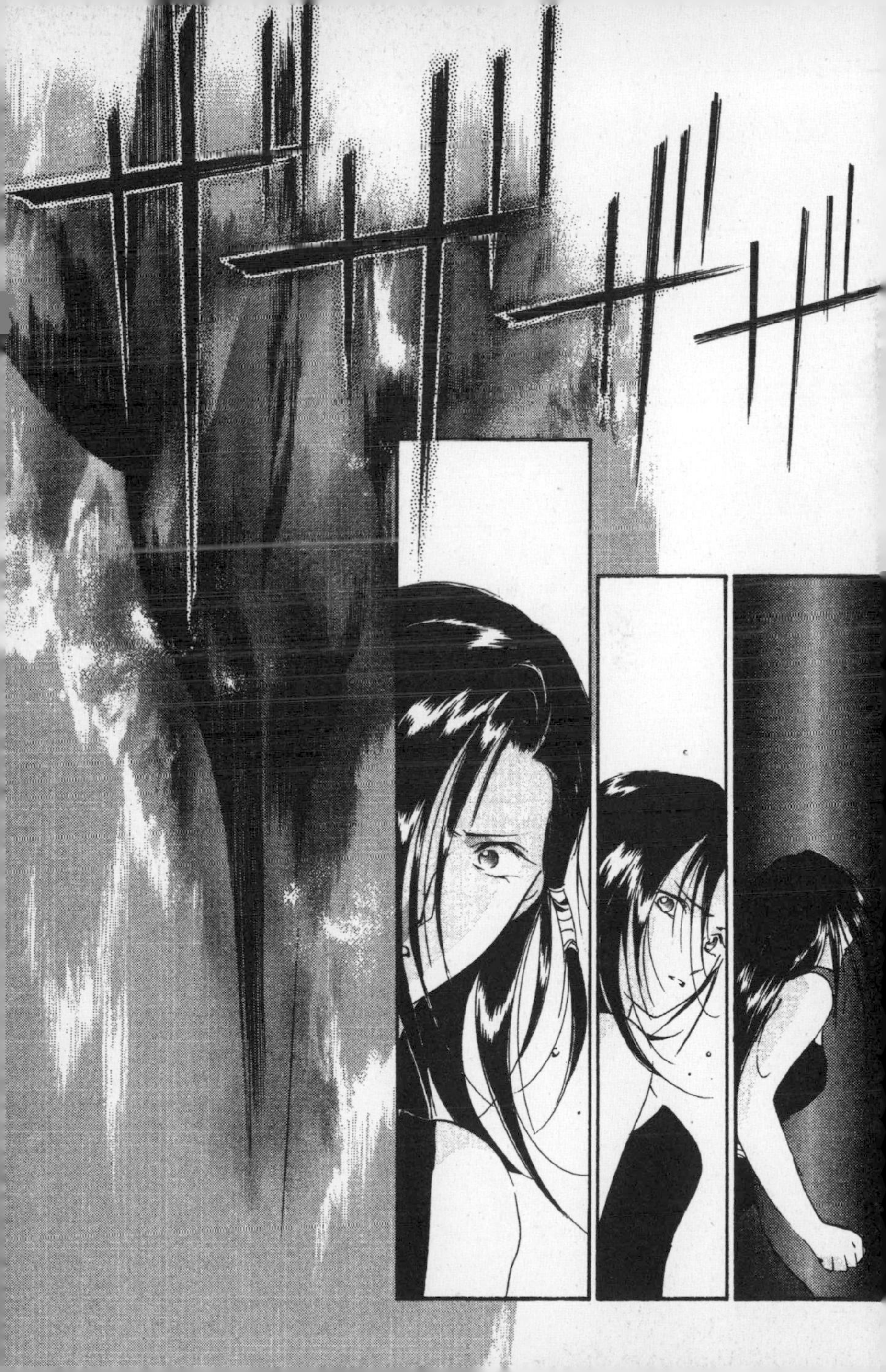

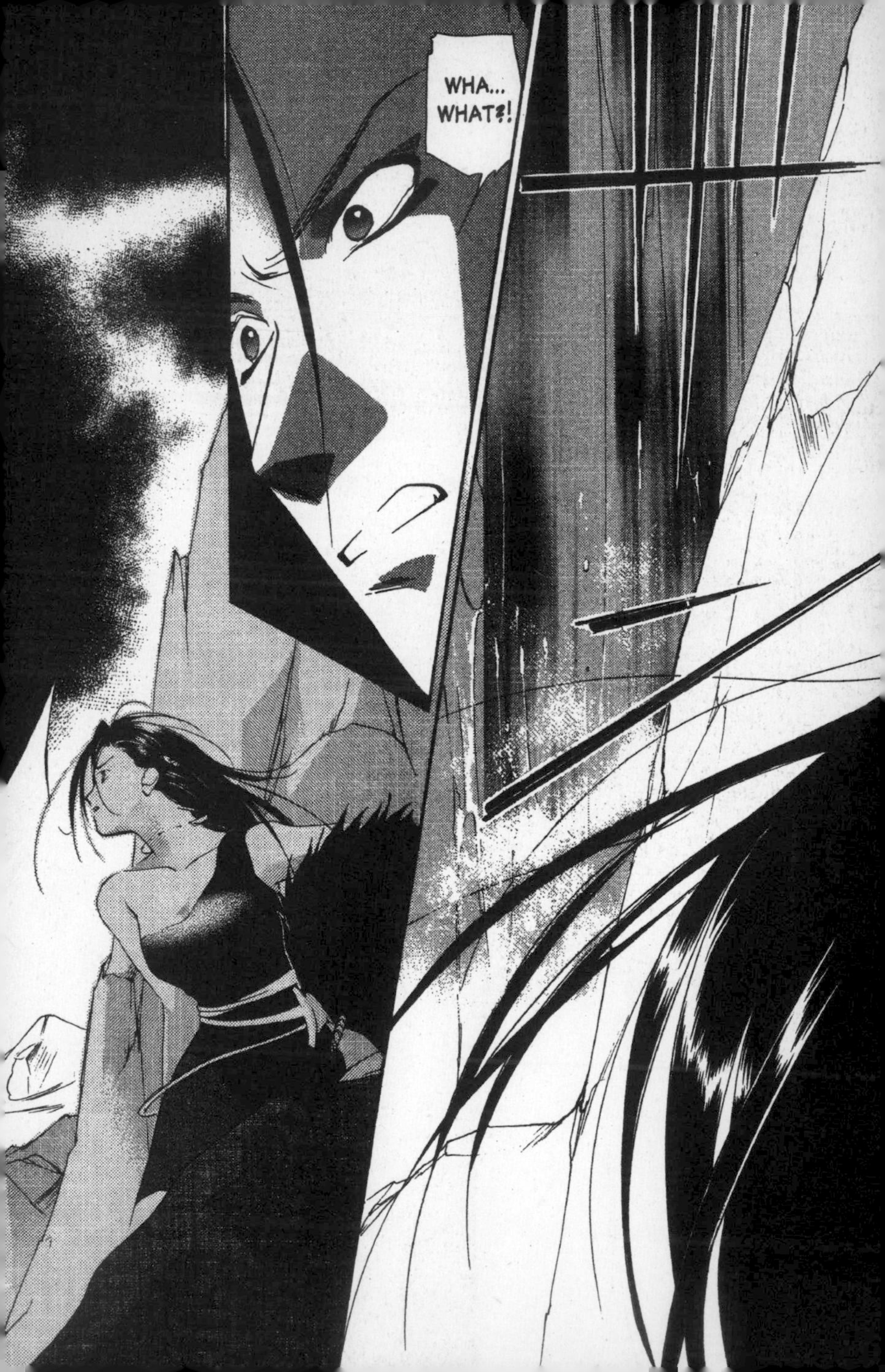
WHA... WHAT?!

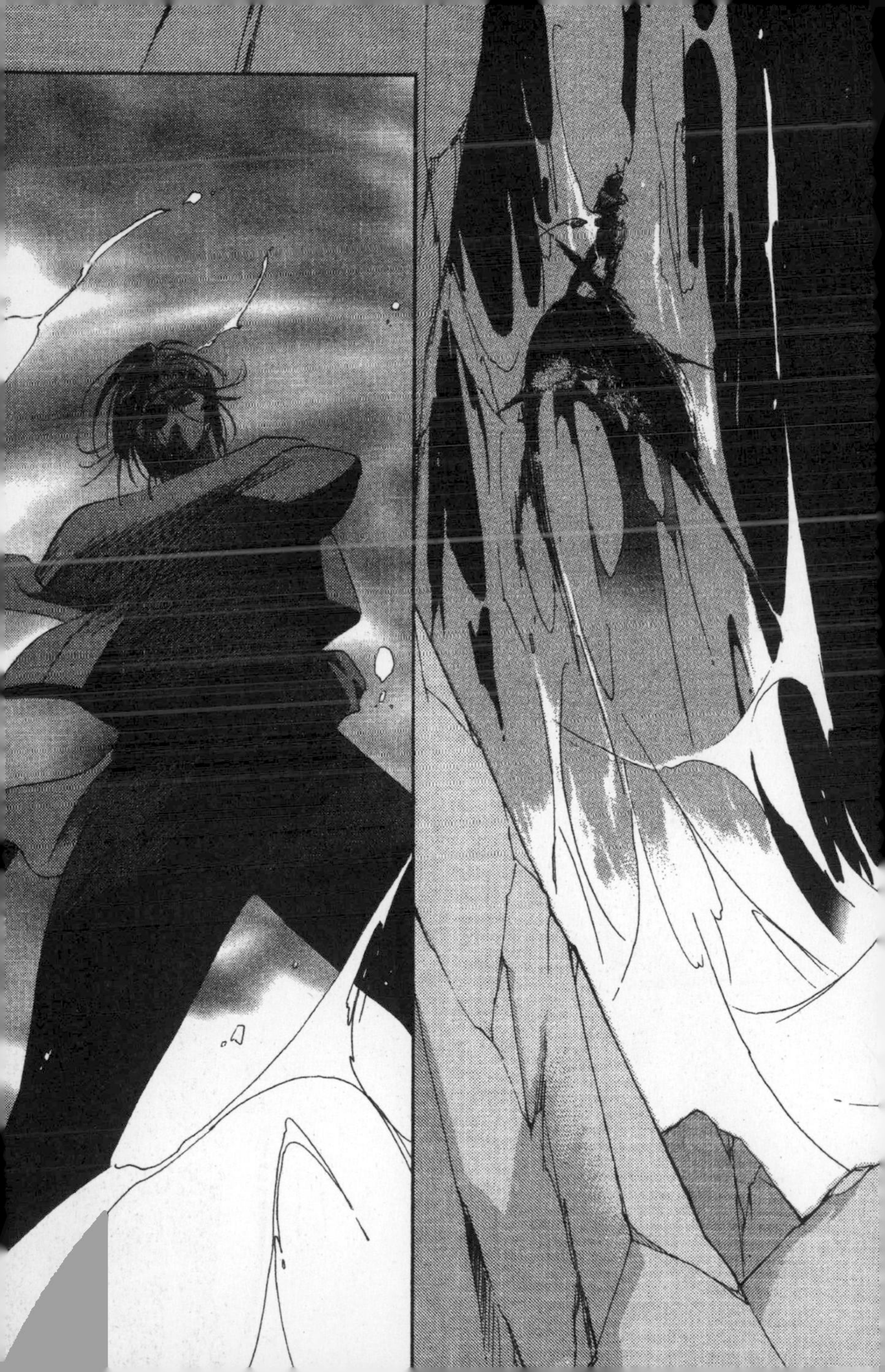

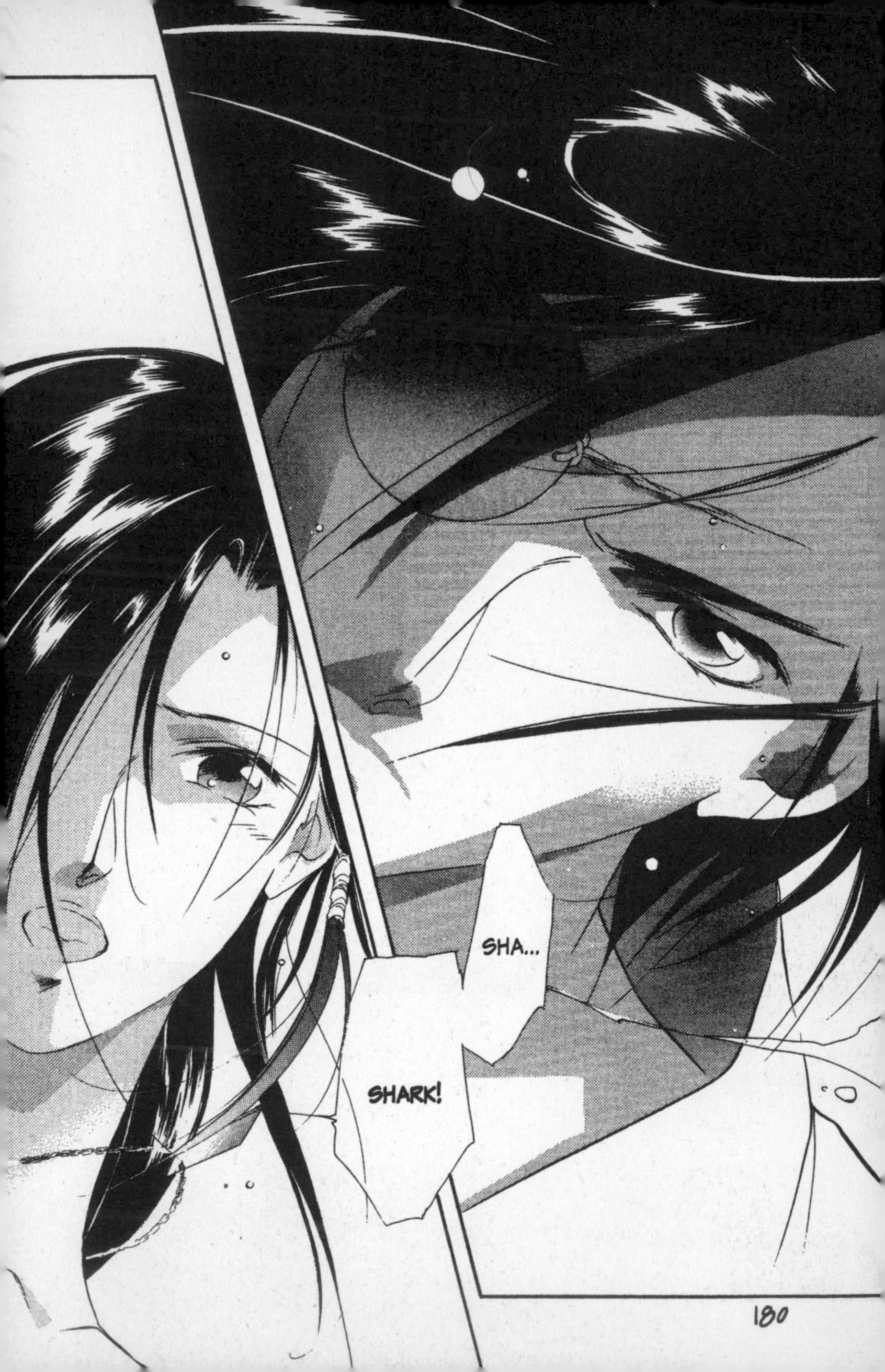
SHA...
SHARK!

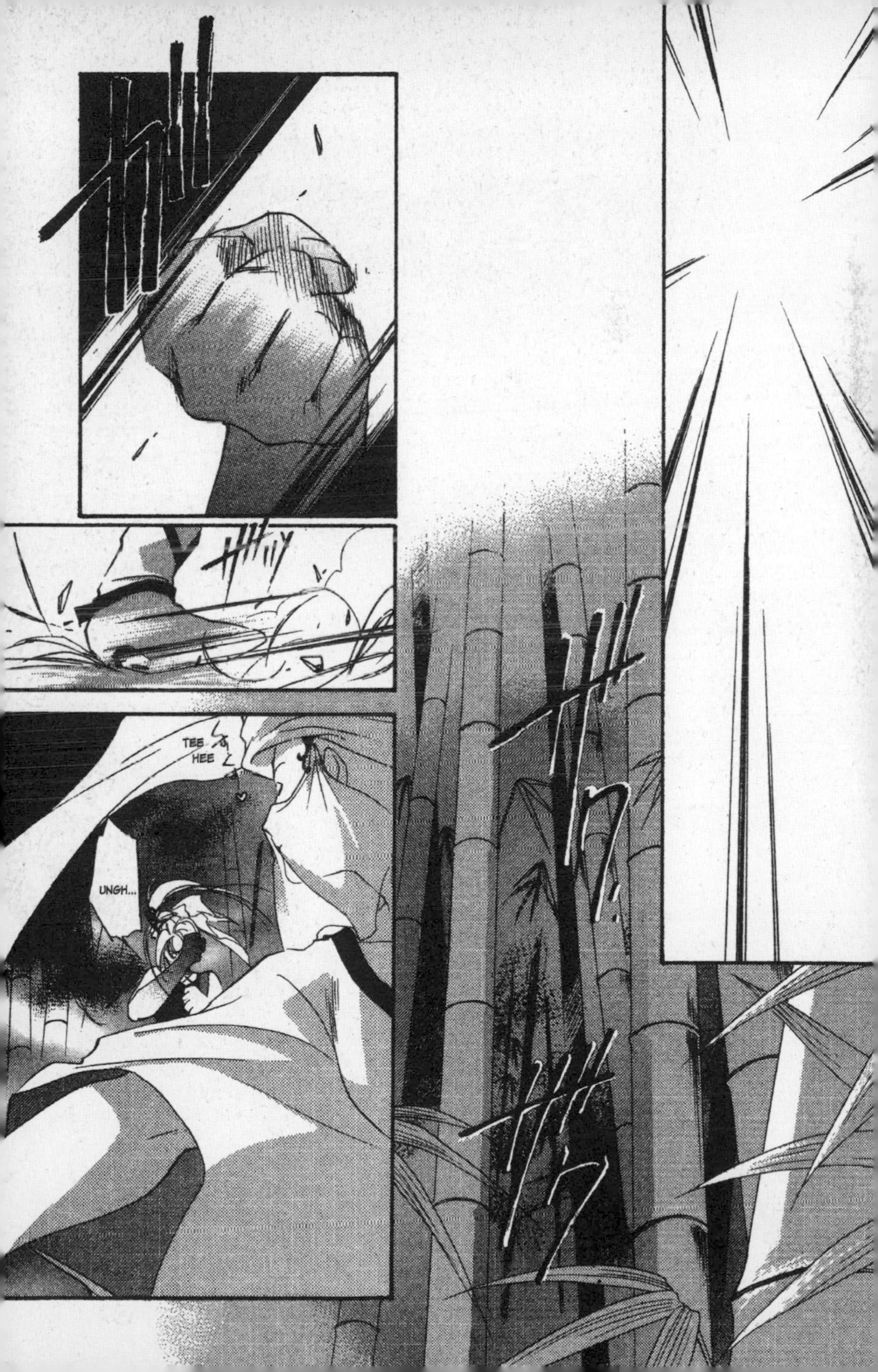
TEE HEE
UNGH...

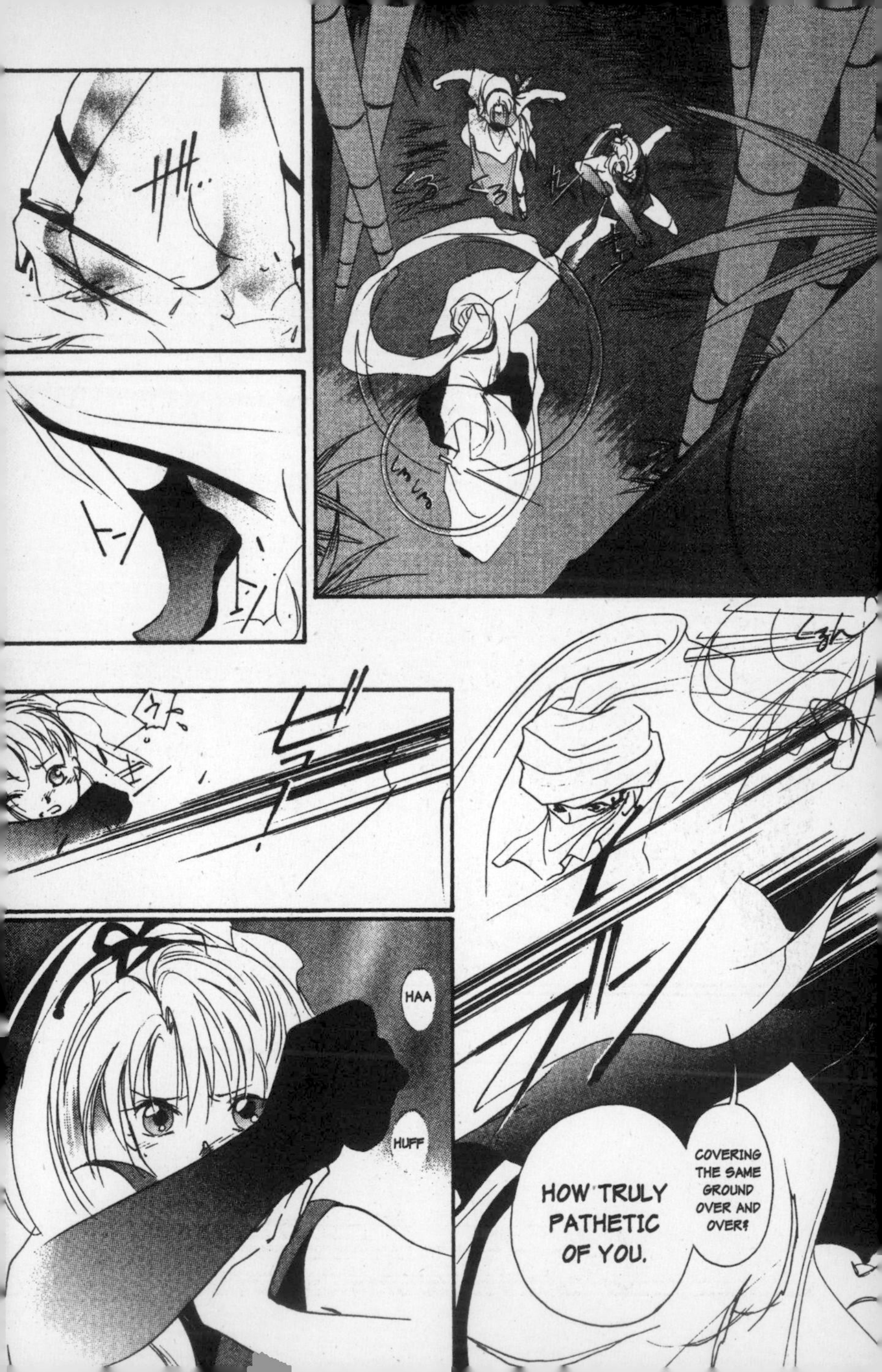
COVERING THE SAME GROUND OVER AND OVER?
HOW TRULY PATHETIC OF YOU.
HAA
HUFF

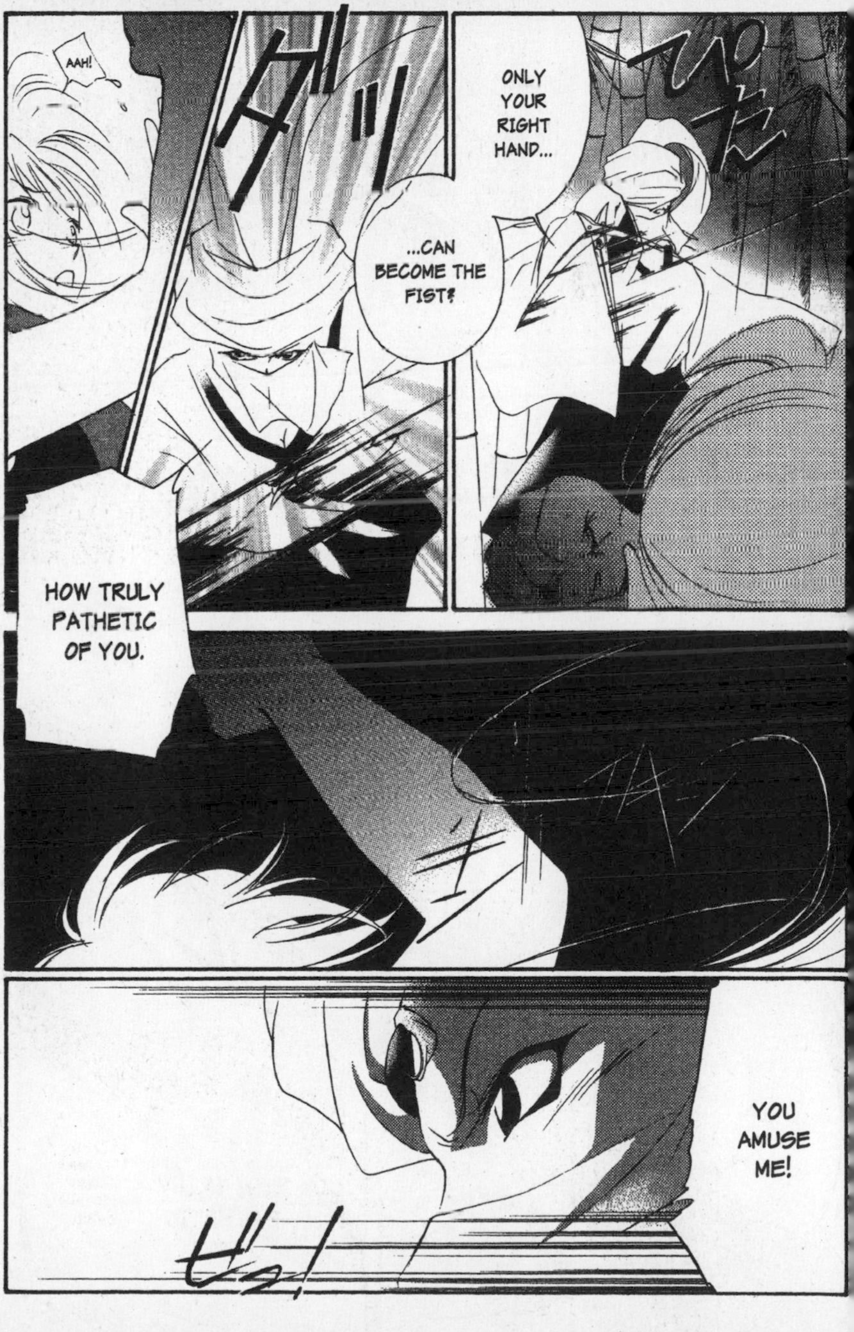
ONLY YOUR RIGHT HAND...
...CAN BECOME THE FIST?
AAH!
HOW TRULY PATHETIC OF YOU.
YOU AMUSE ME!

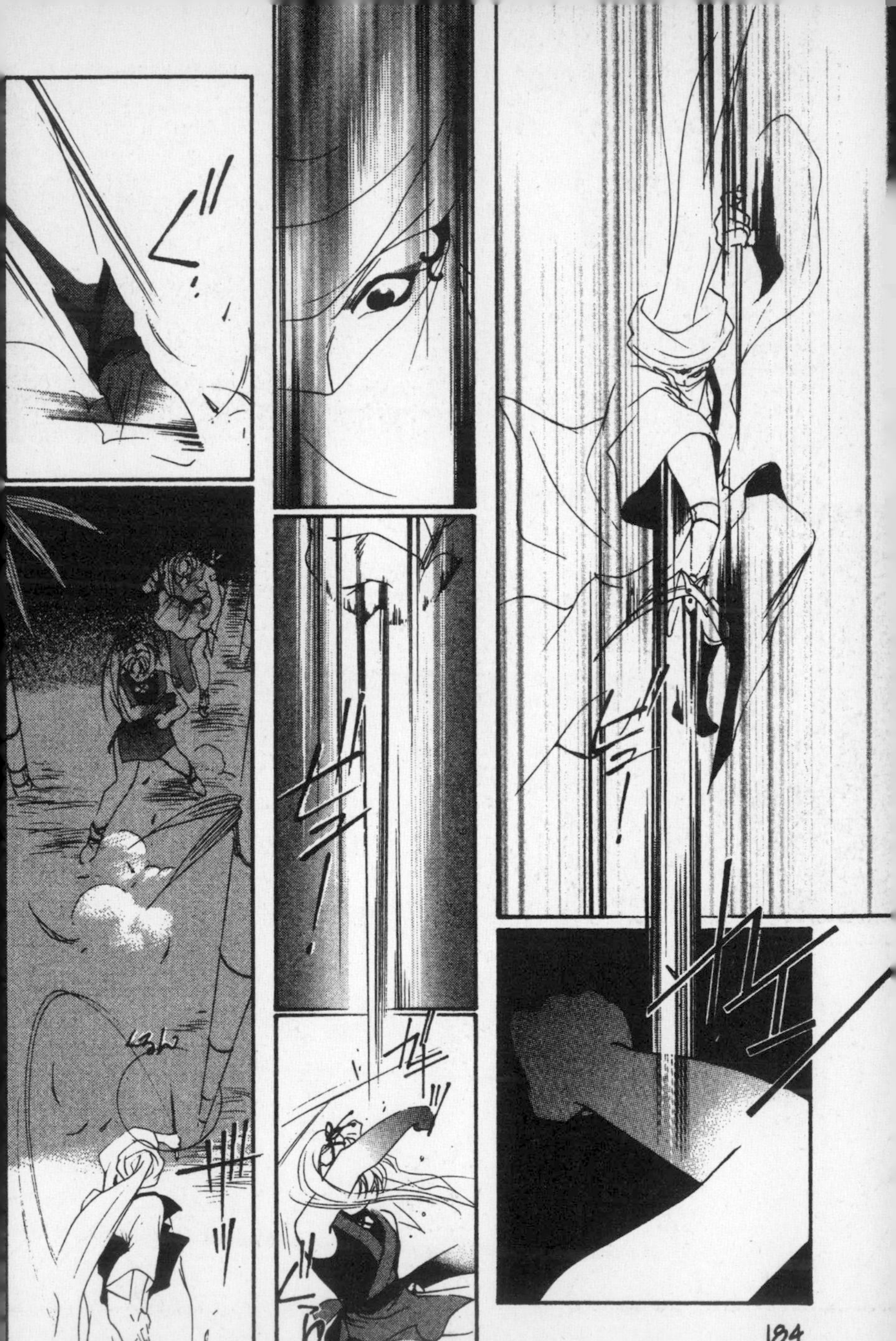
くるん

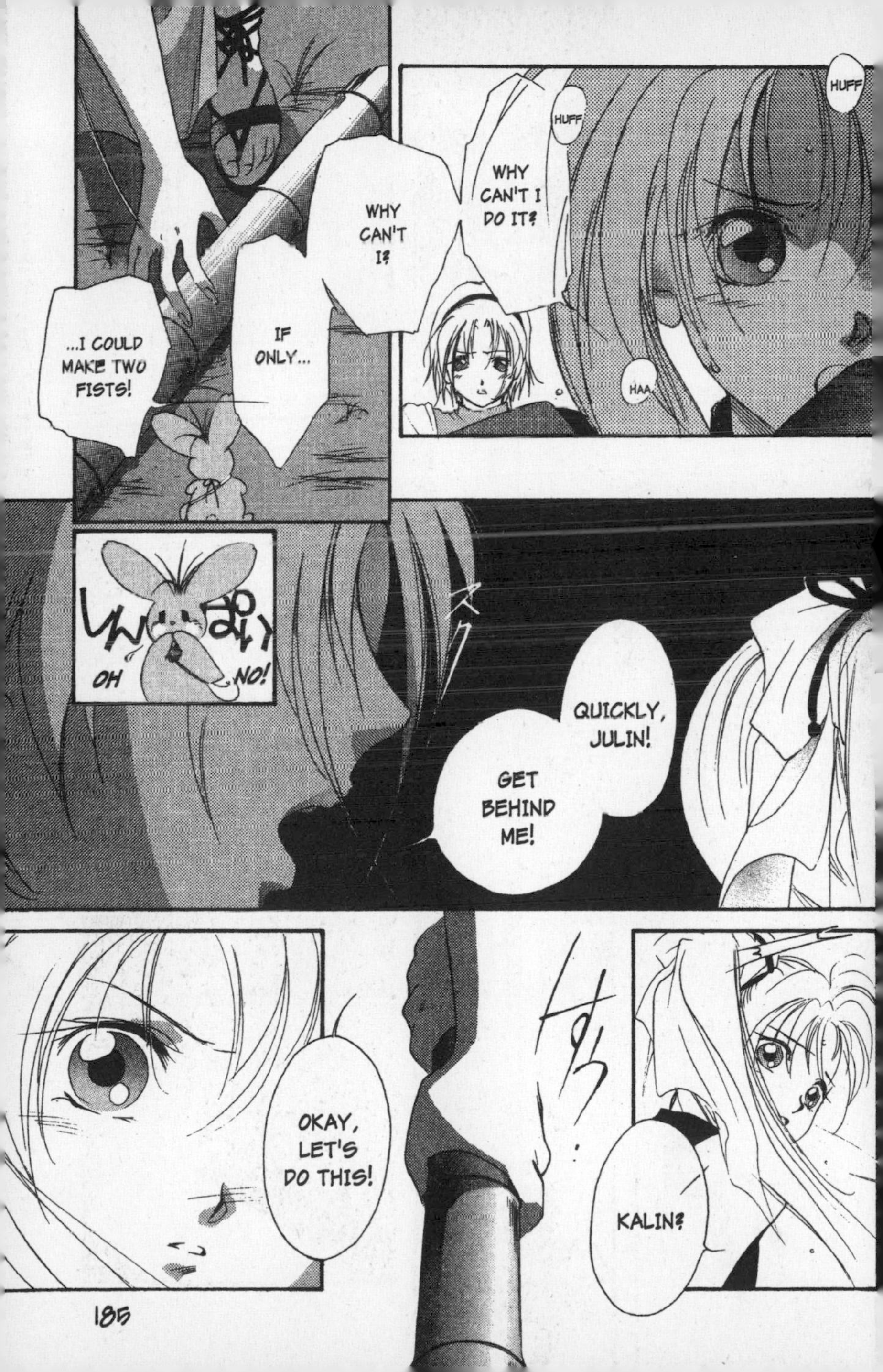
HUFF
HUFF
WHY CAN'T I DO IT?
WHY CAN'T I?
HAA
IF ONLY...
...I COULD MAKE TWO FISTS!
QUICKLY, JULIN!
GET BEHIND ME!
OH NO!
KALIN?
OKAY, LET'S DO THIS!

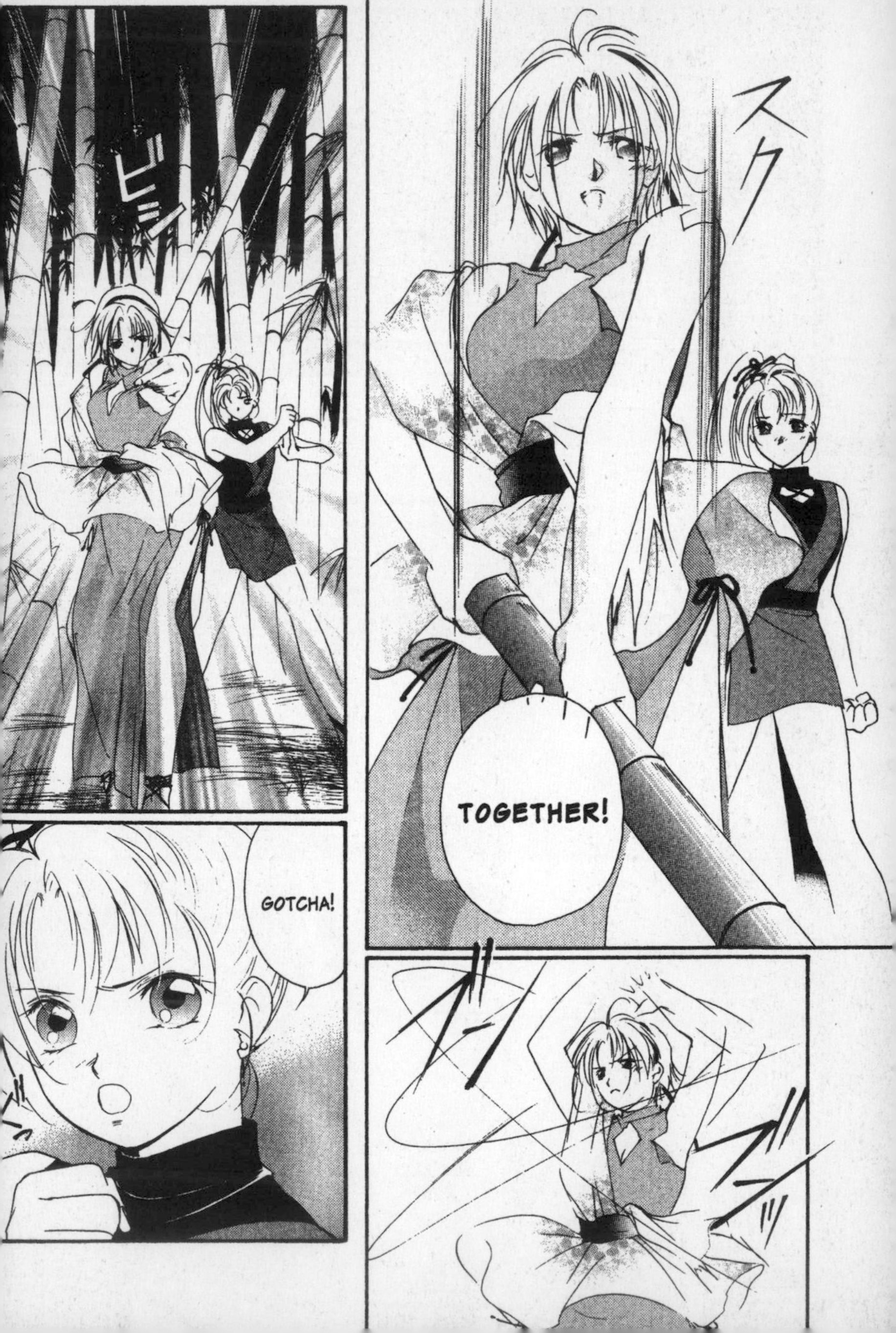
スク
TOGETHER!
ビシ
GOTCHA!

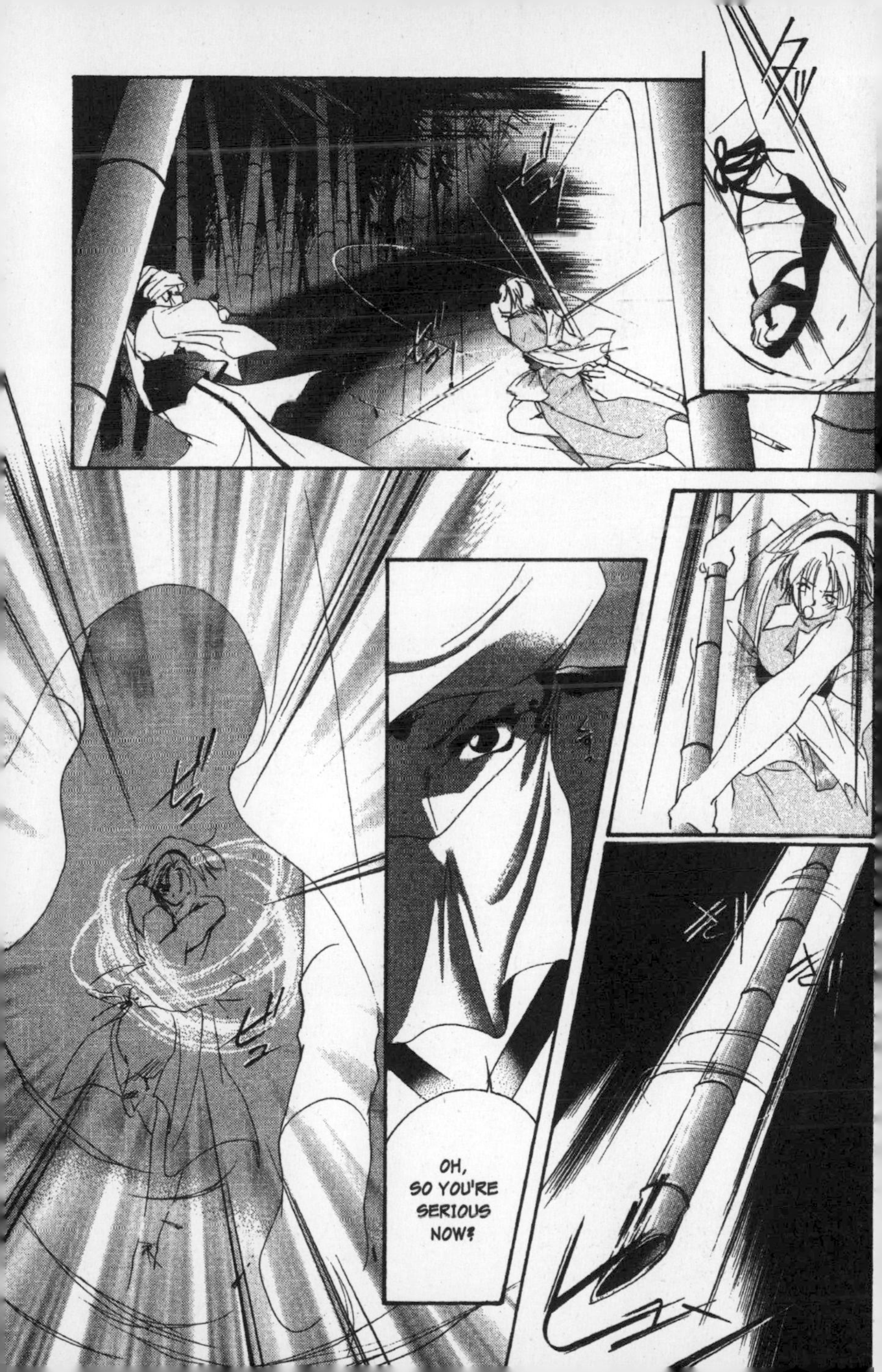
OH, SO YOU'RE SERIOUS NOW?

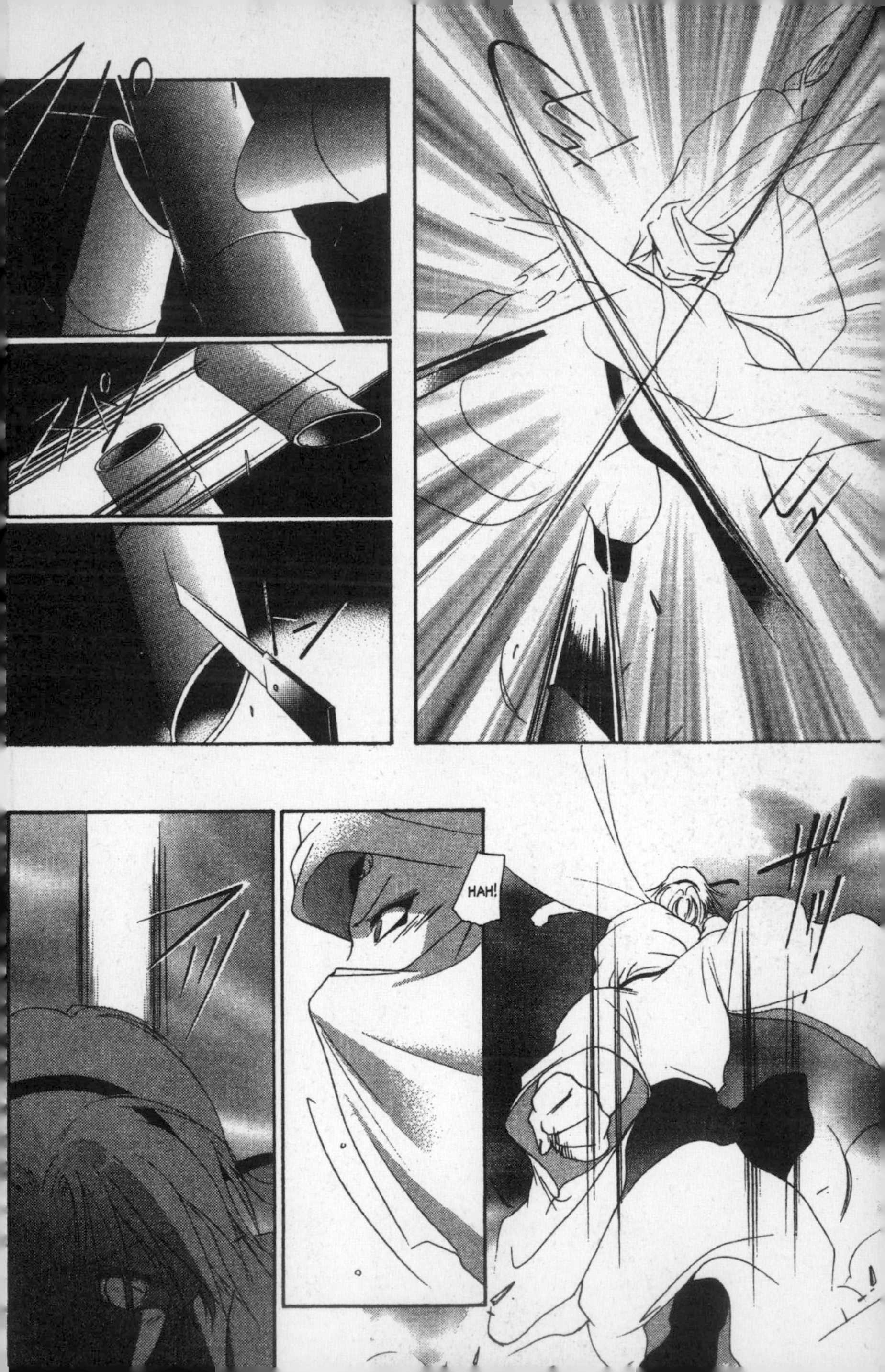
HAH!

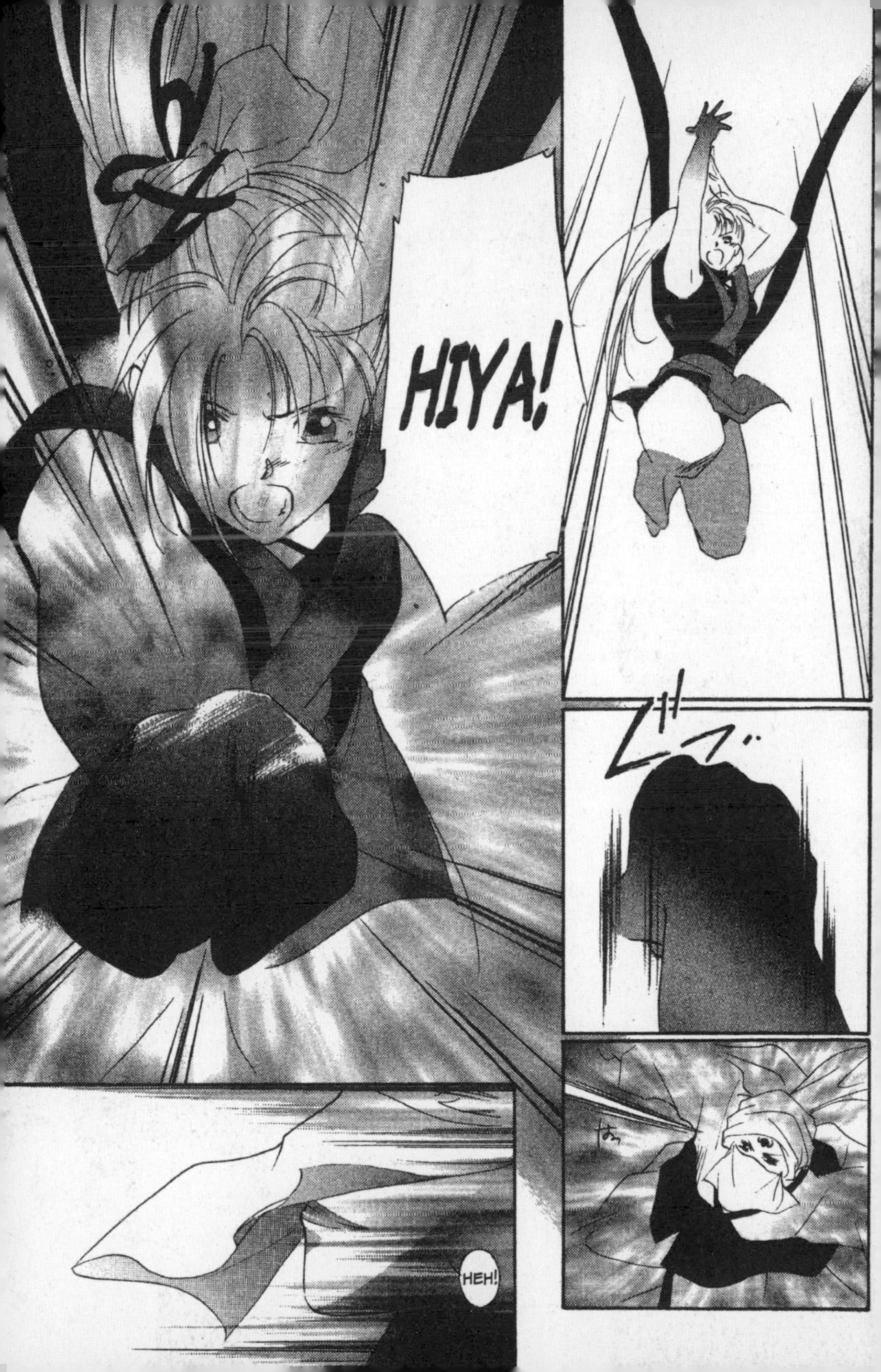
HIYA!
HEH!

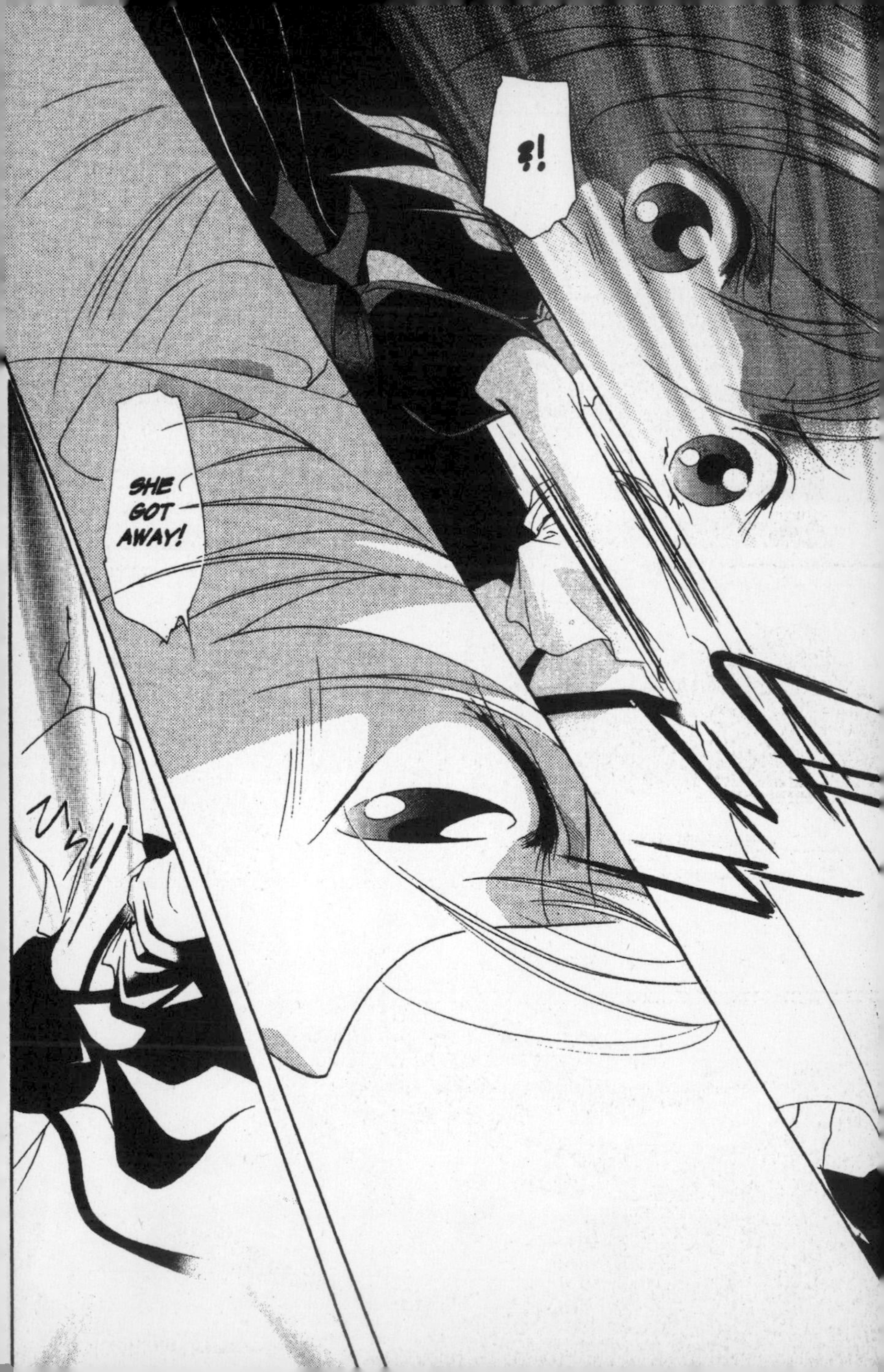
?!
SHE GOT AWAY!

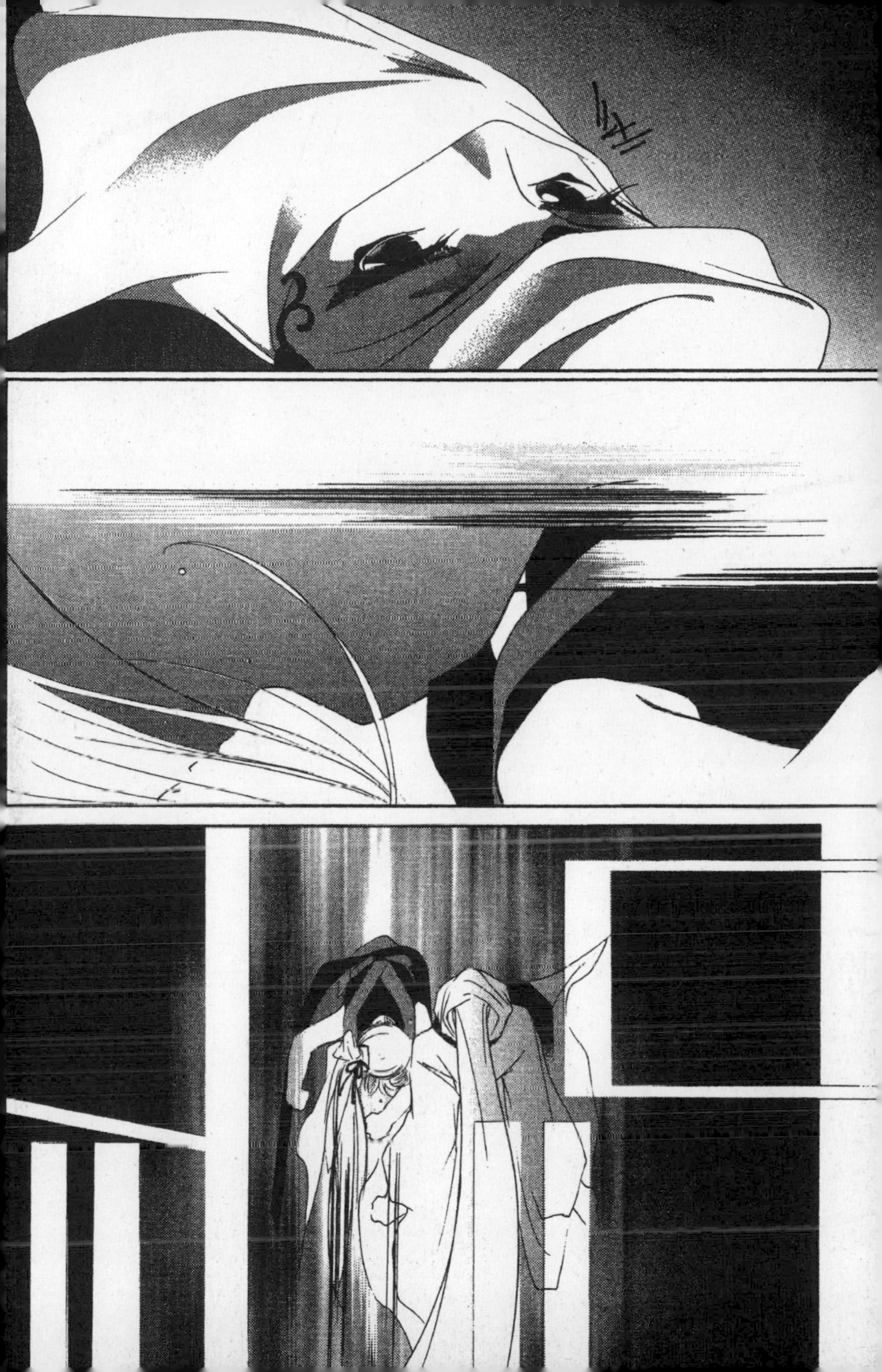

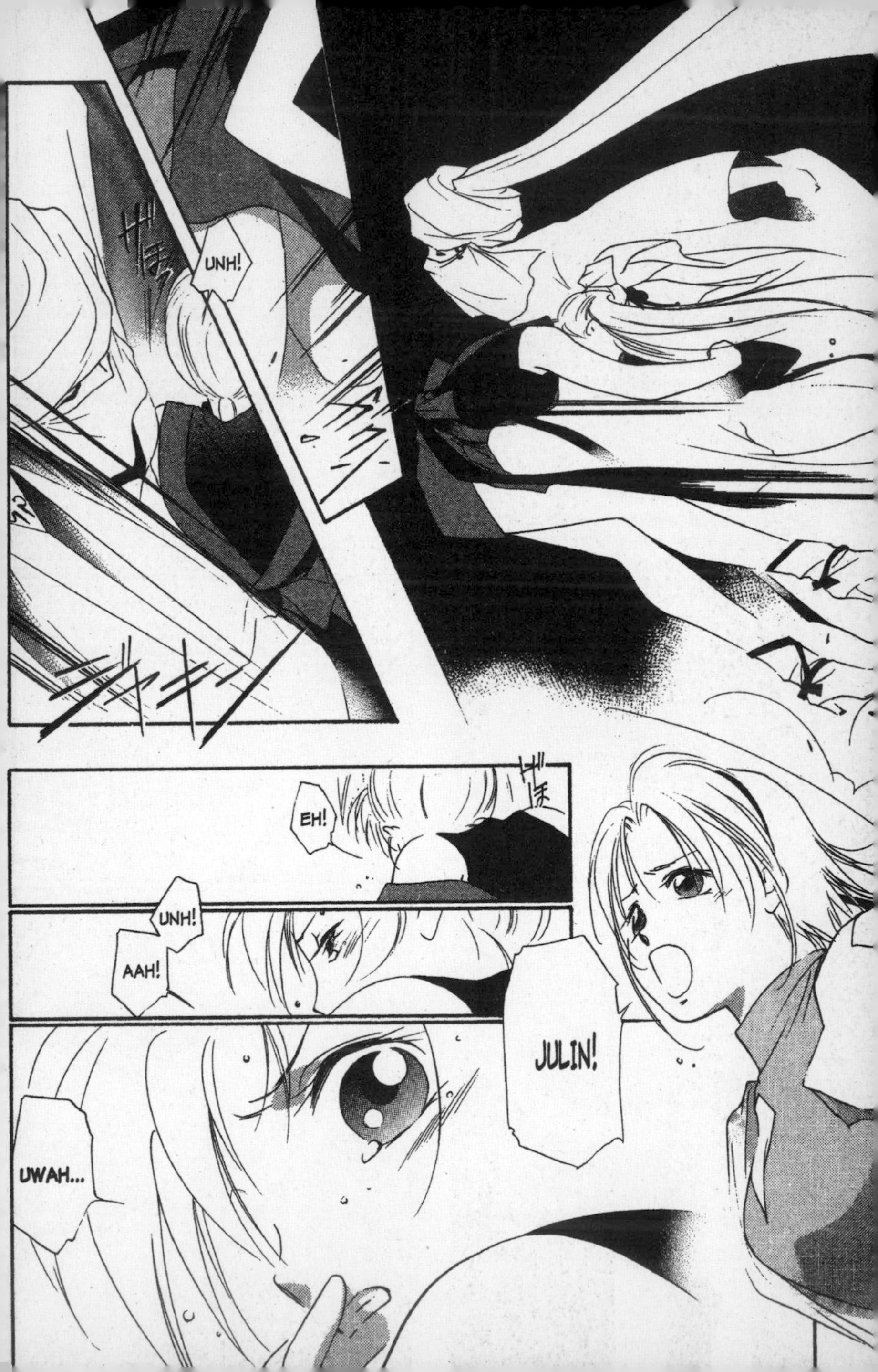
UNH!
JULIN!
EH!
UNH!
AAH!
UWAH...

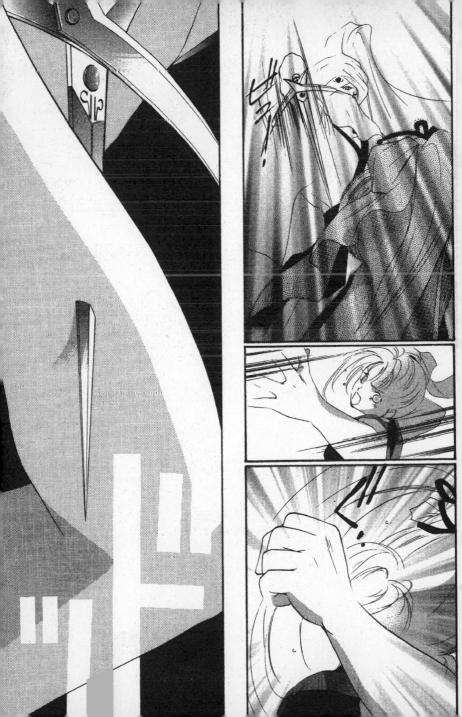

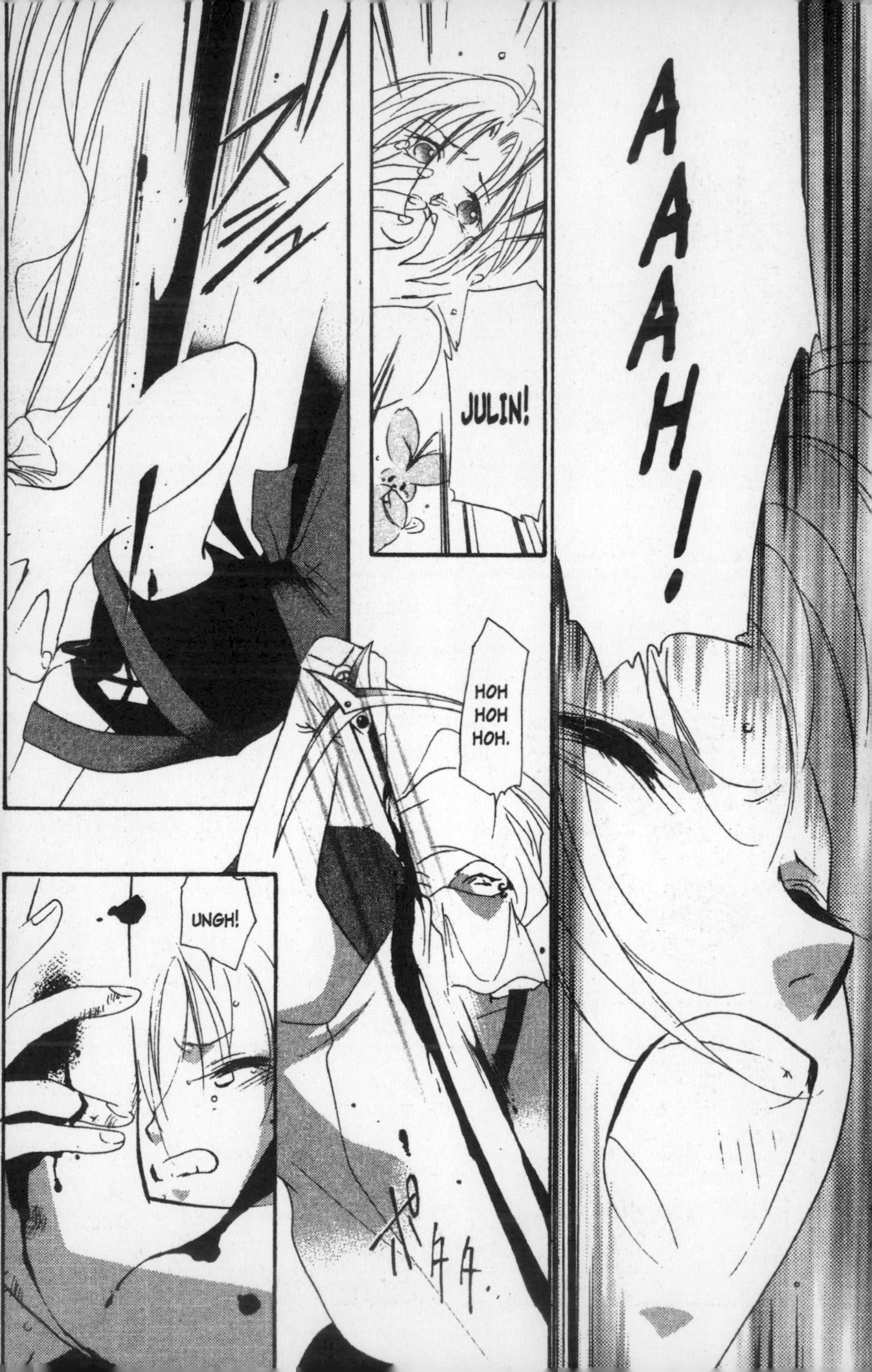
AAAH!
JULIN!
HOH HOH HOH.
UNGH!

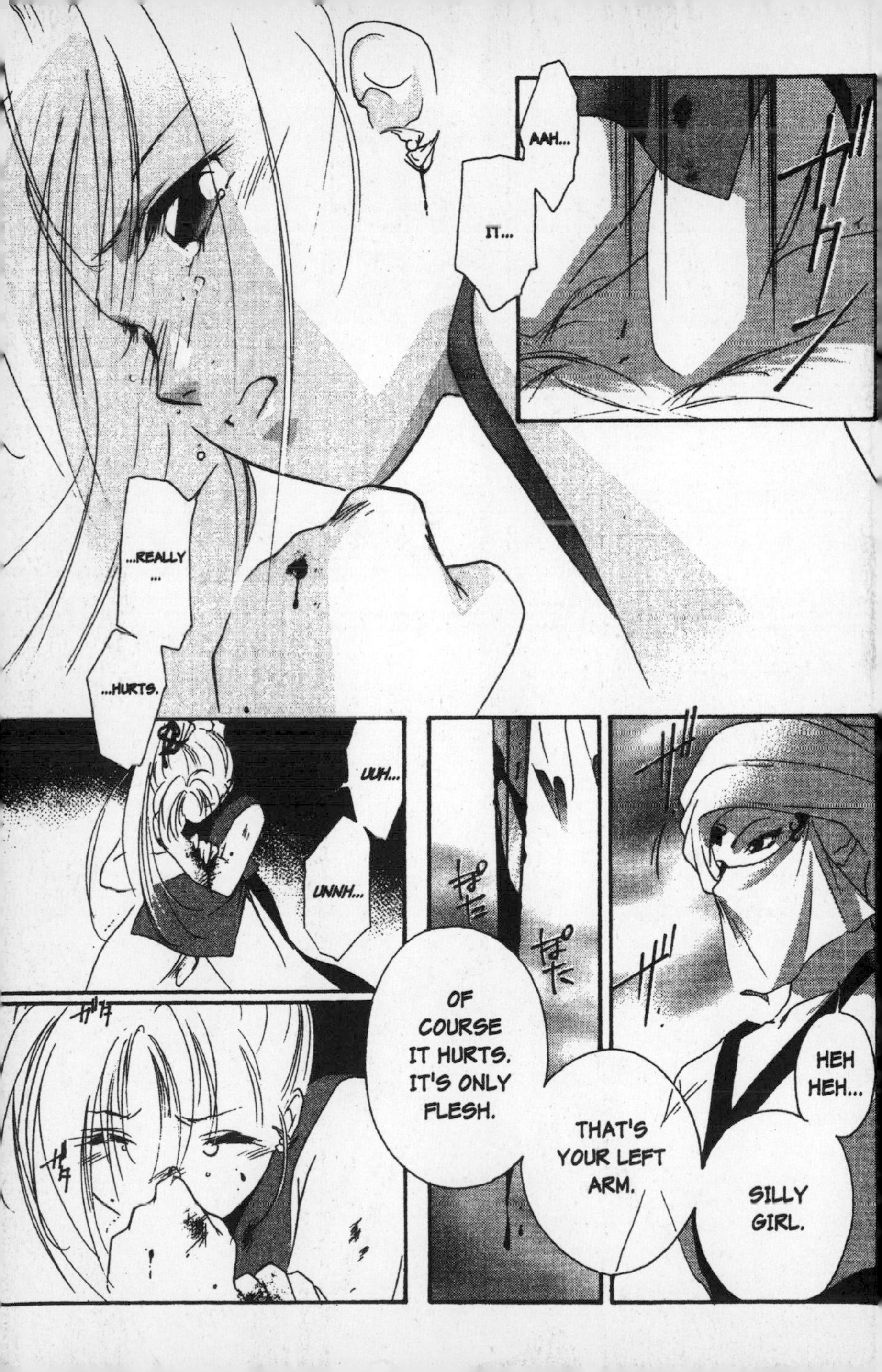
AAH...
IT...
...REALLY ...
...HURTS.
HEH HEH...
OF COURSE IT HURTS. IT'S ONLY FLESH.
THAT'S YOUR LEFT ARM.
SILLY GIRL.
UUH...
UNNH...

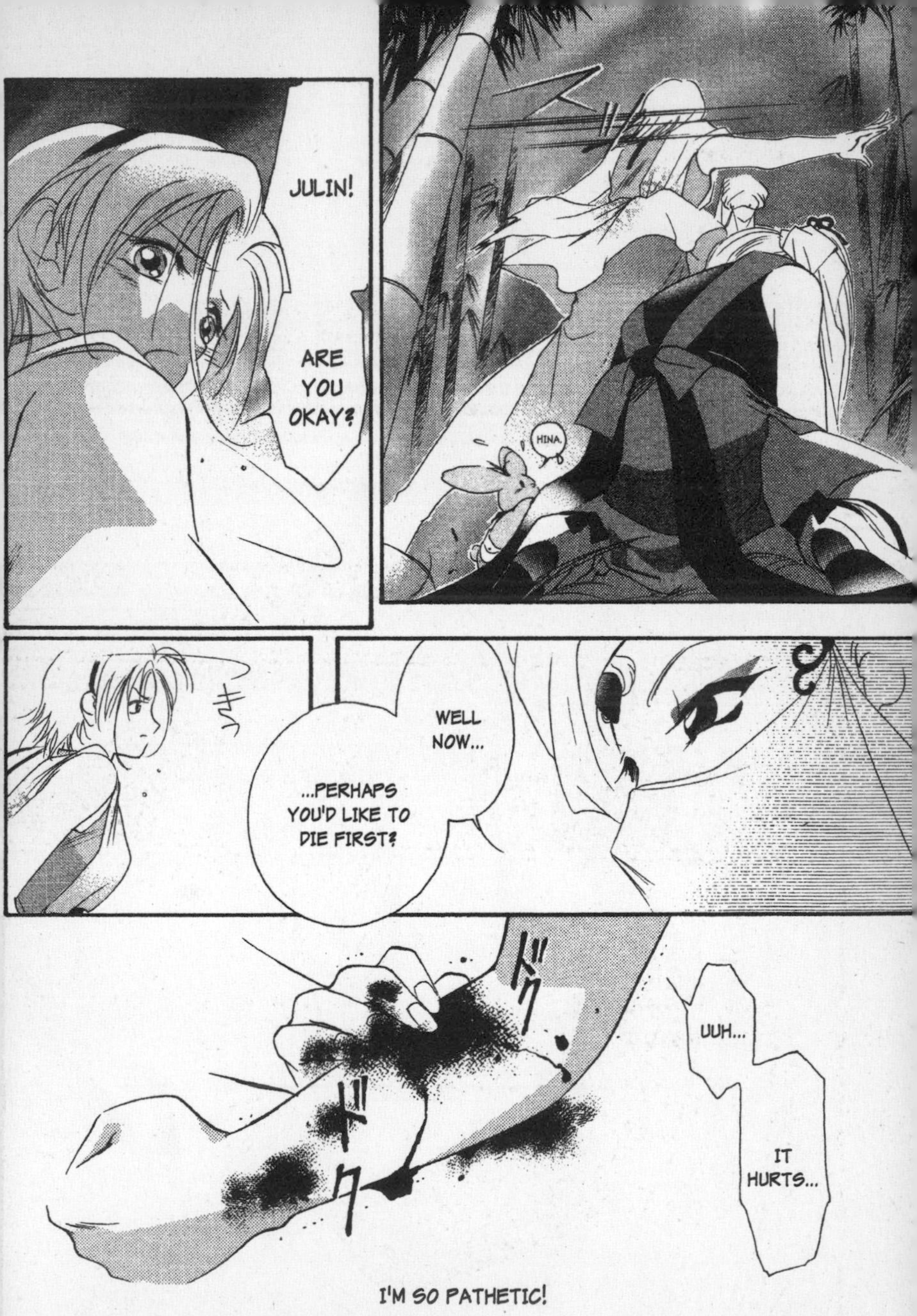
HINA.
JULIN!
ARE YOU OKAY?
WELL NOW...
...PERHAPS YOU'D LIKE TO DIE FIRST?
UUH...
IT HURTS...
I'M SO PATHETIC!

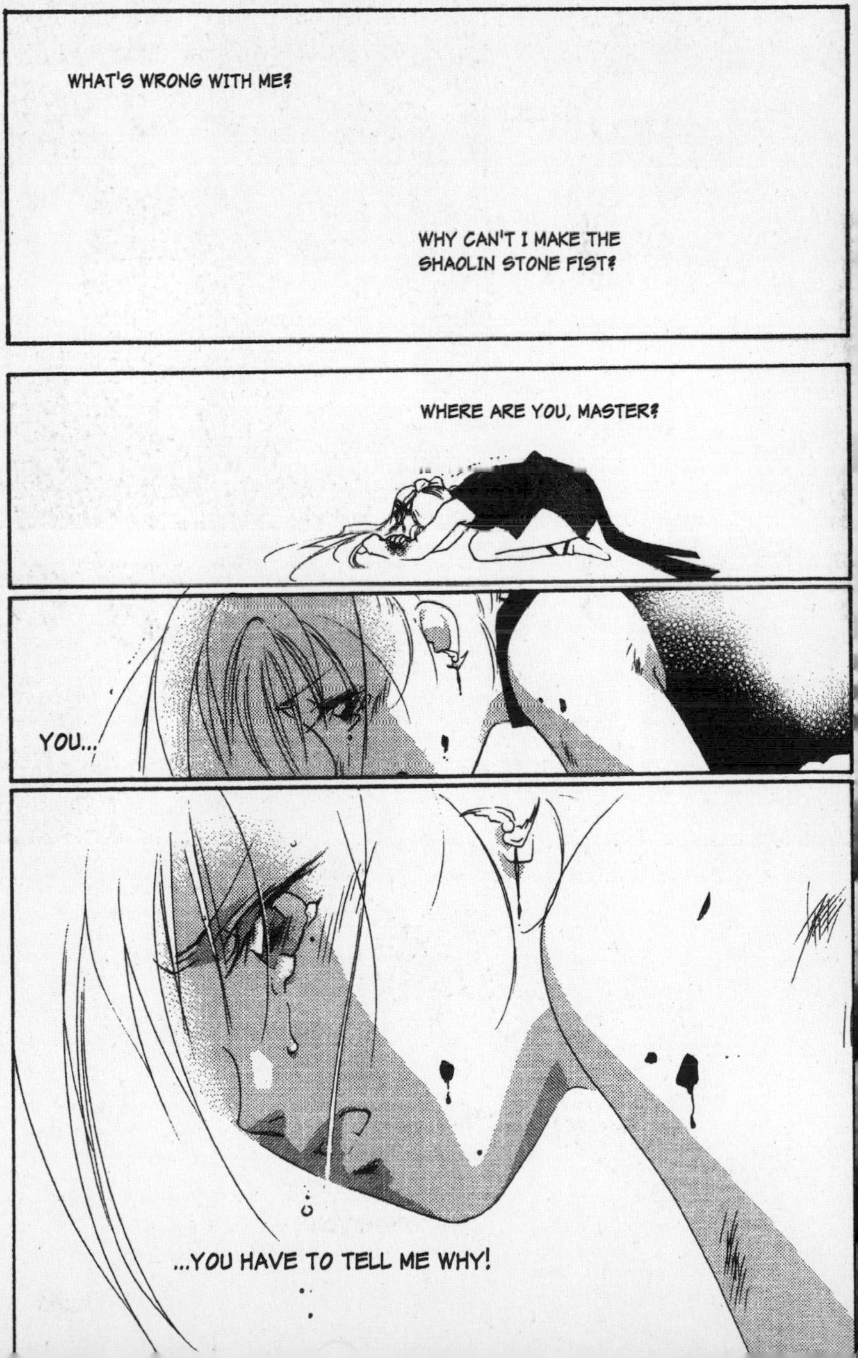
WHAT'S WRONG WITH ME?
WHY CAN'T I MAKE THE SHAOLIN STONE FIST?
WHERE ARE YOU, MASTER?
YOU...
...YOU HAVE TO TELL ME WHY!

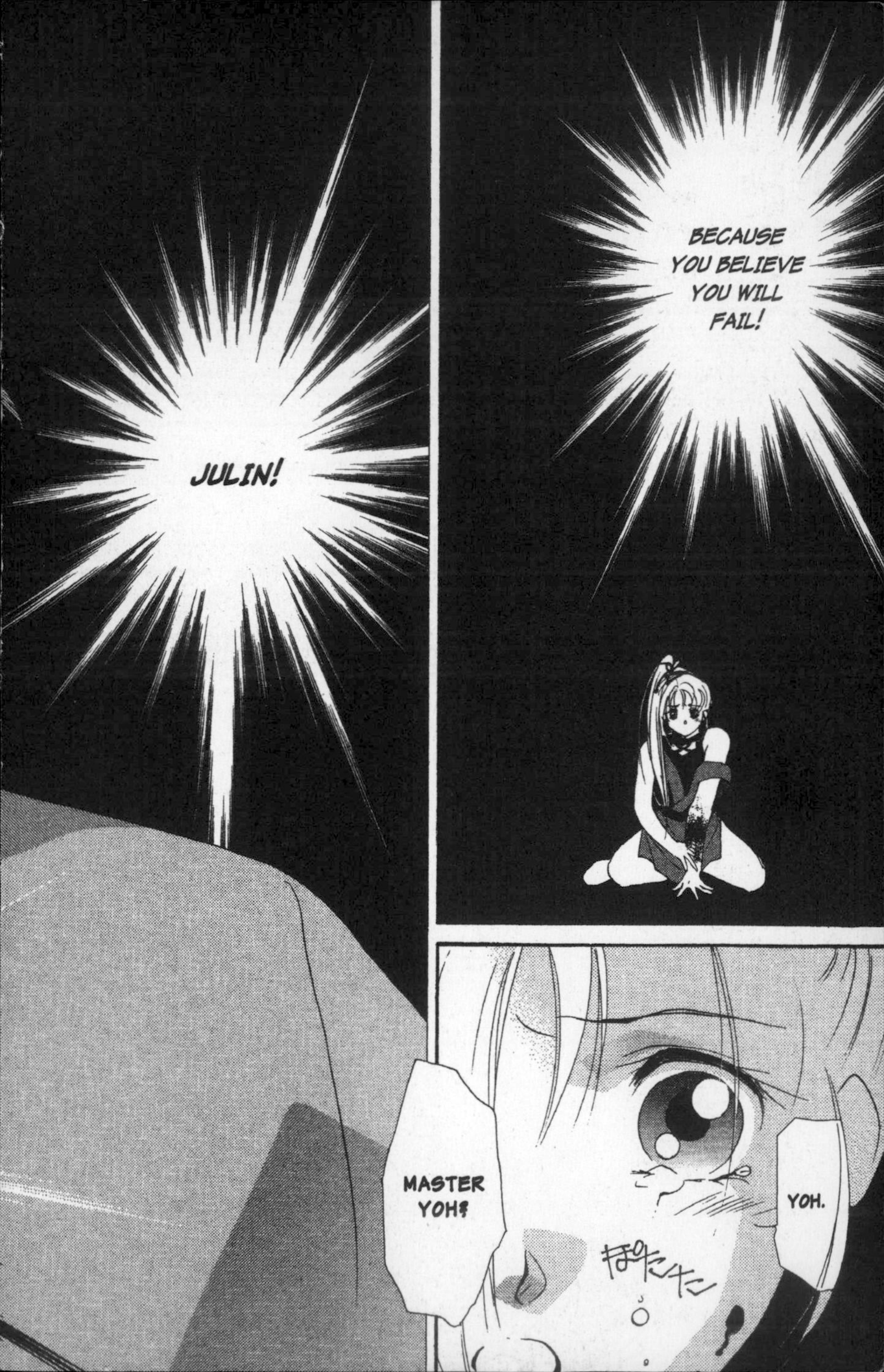
BECAUSE YOU BELIEVE YOU WILL FAIL!
YOH.
MASTER YOH?
JULIN!

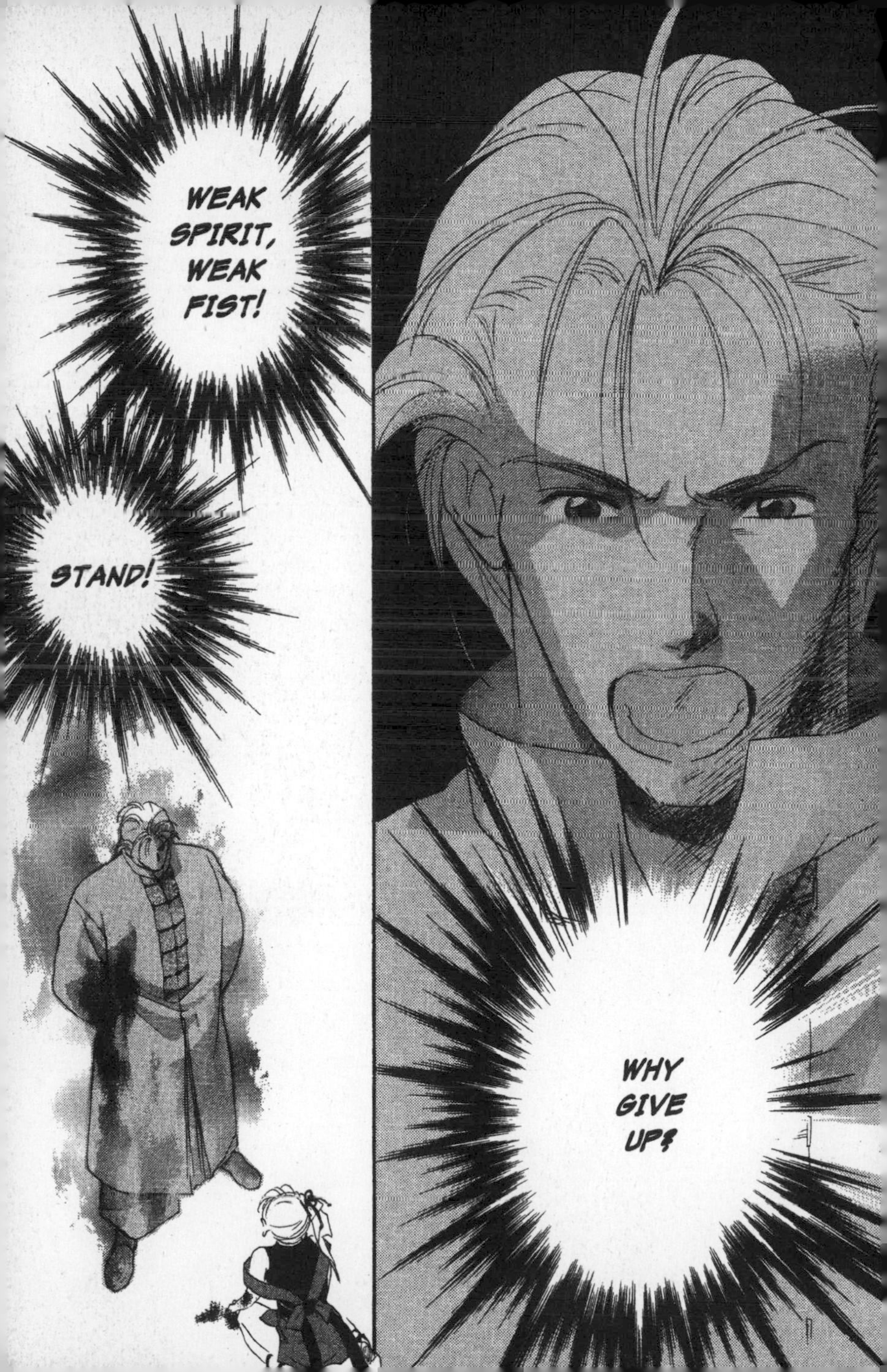
WHY GIVE UP?
WEAK SPIRIT, WEAK FIST!
STAND!

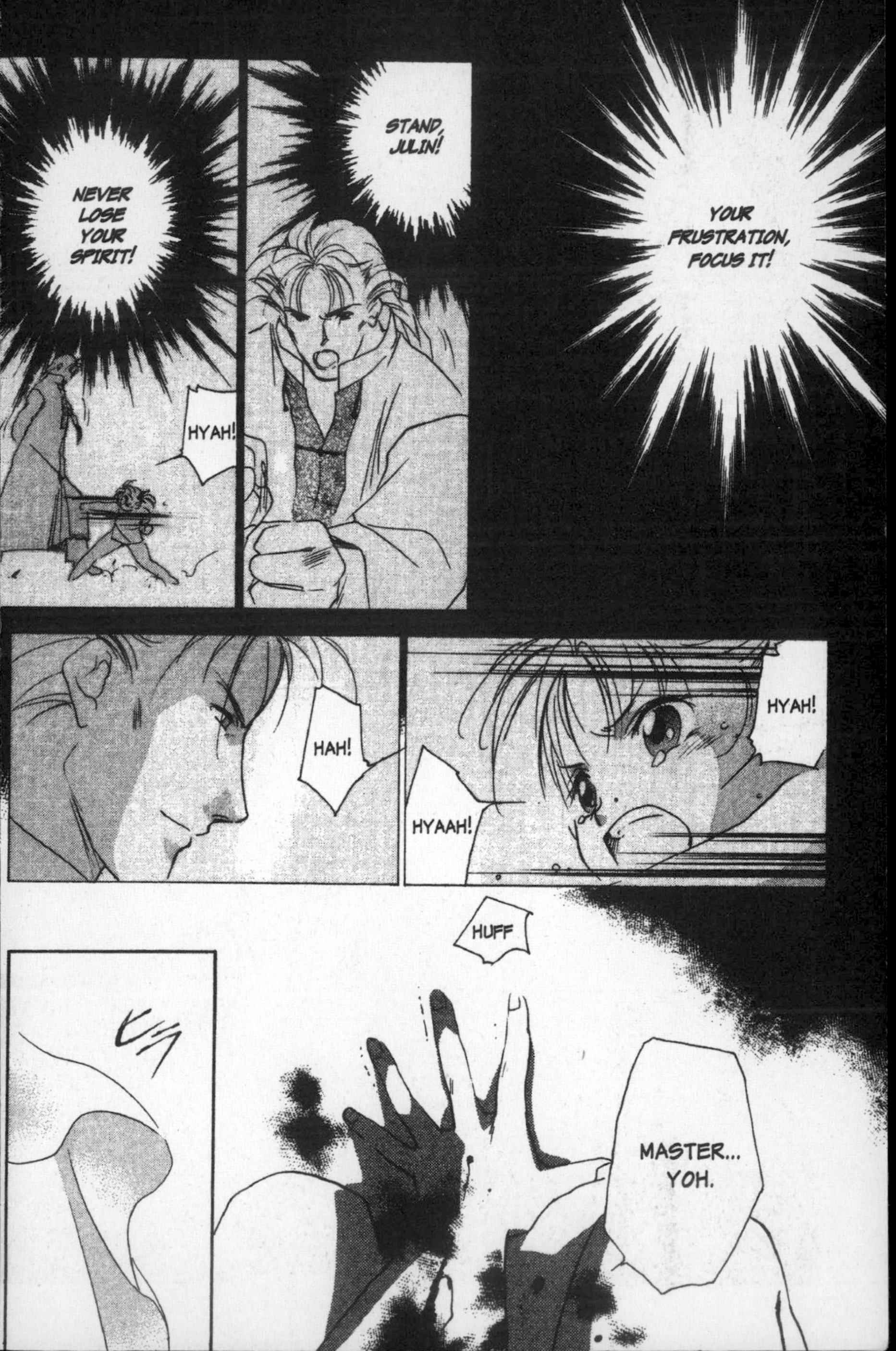
YOUR FRUSTRATION, FOCUS IT!
STAND, JULIN!
NEVER LOSE YOUR SPIRIT!
HYAH!
HYAH!
HYAAH!
HAH!
HUFF
MASTER... YOH.

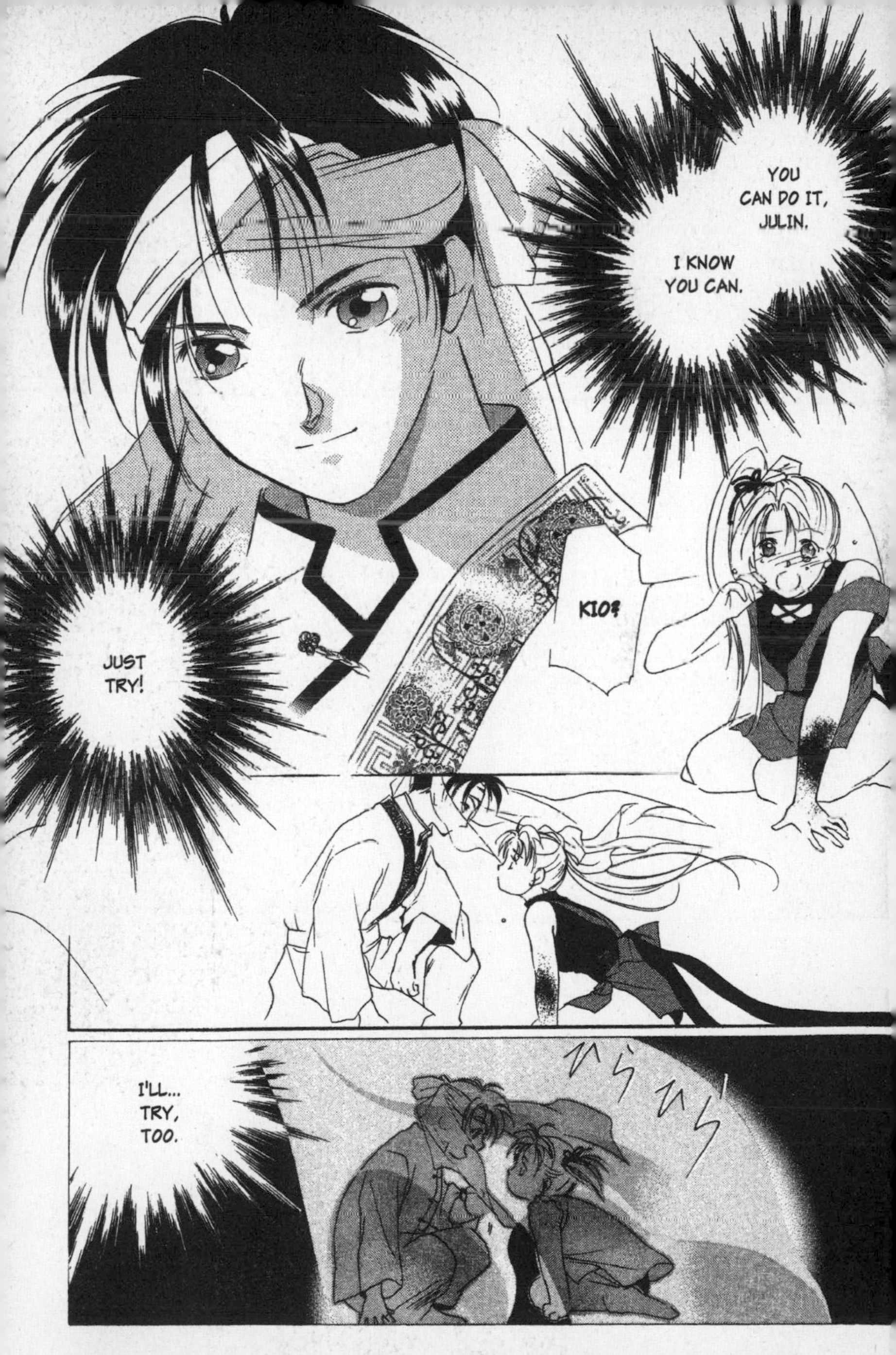
YOU CAN DO IT, JULIN.
I KNOW YOU CAN.
KIO?
JUST TRY!
ひらひら
I'LL... TRY, TOO.

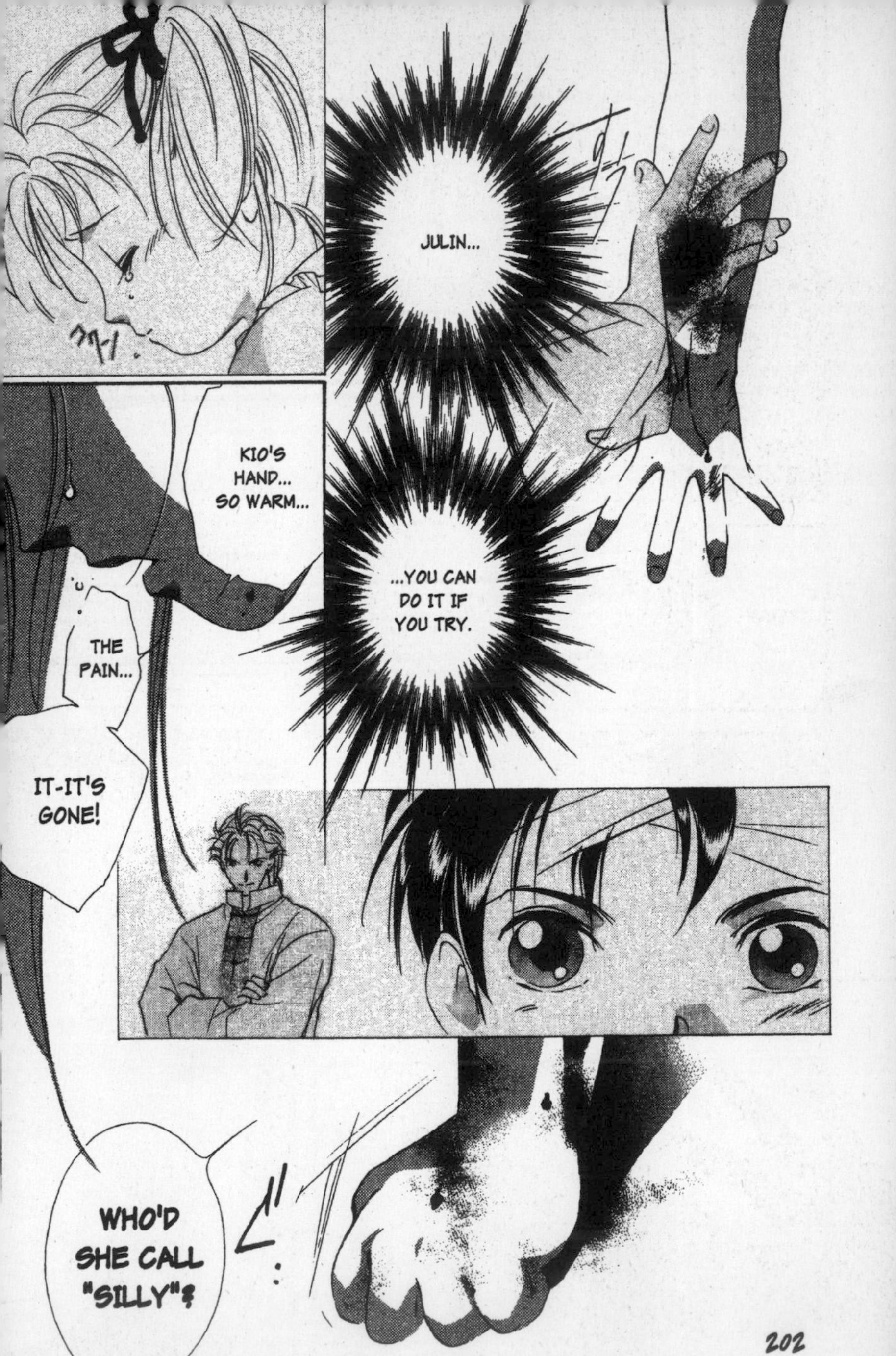
JULIN...
...YOU CAN DO IT IF YOU TRY.
KIO'S HAND... SO WARM...
THE PAIN...
IT-IT'S GONE!
WHO'D SHE CALL "SILLY"?

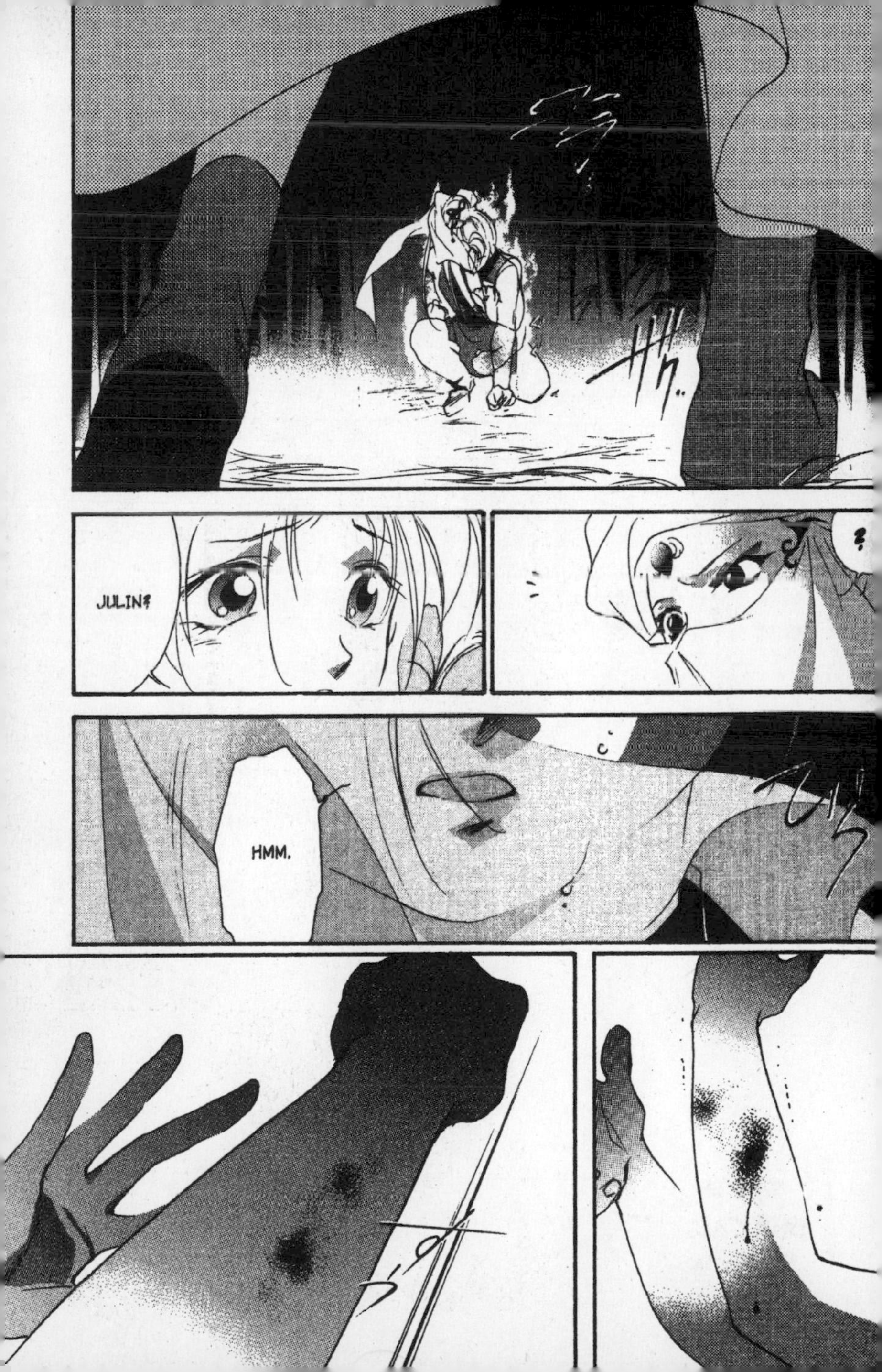
JULIN?
HMM.

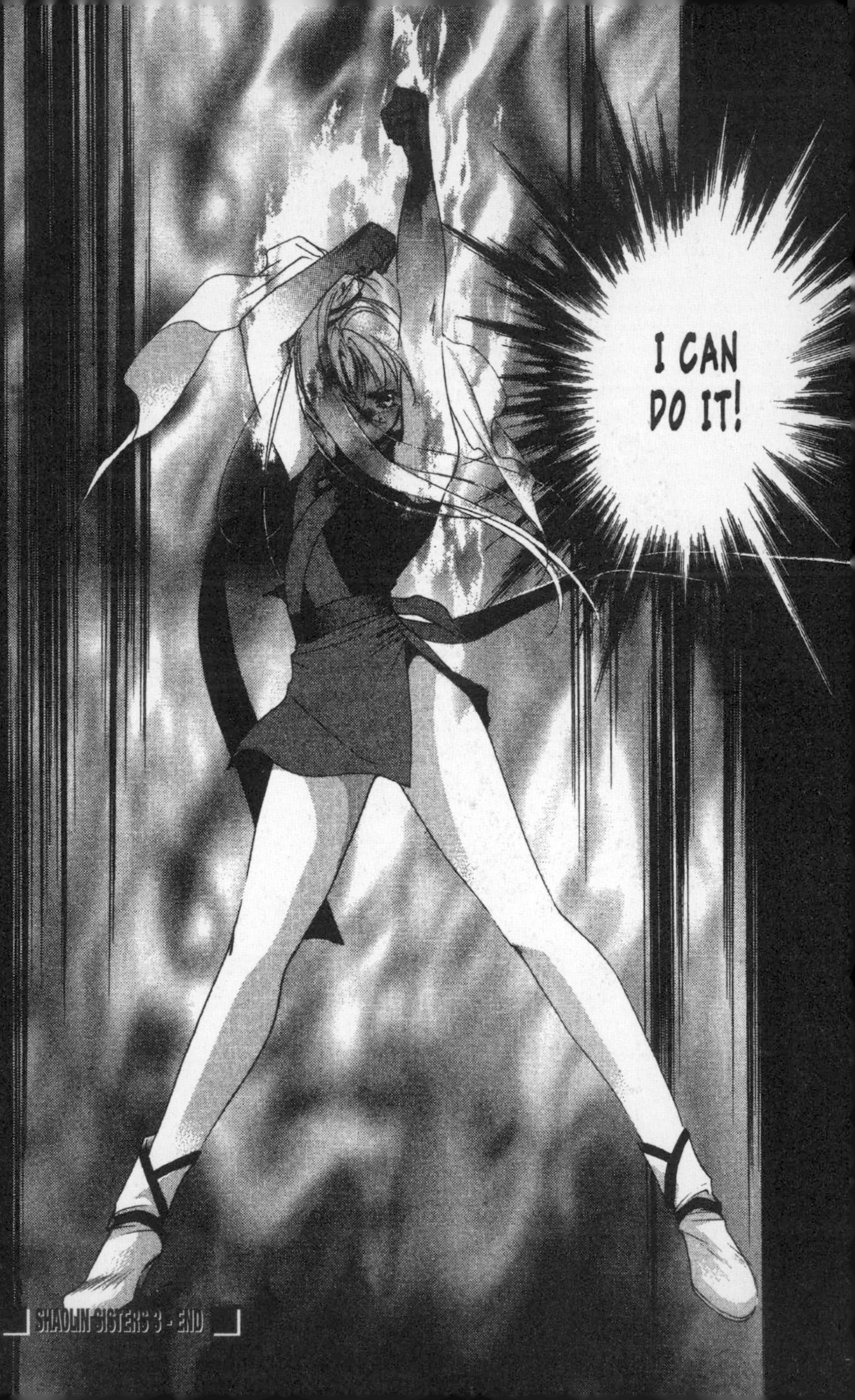
I CAN DO IT!
SHAOLIN SISTERS 3 - END

IN THE NEXT VOLUME

of

SHAOLIN SISTERS

Now that Julin is filled with resolve and focus, she's more determined than ever to recapture the bells. But will the Shaolin Sisters make it to Drake's mountain-top lair before Bai Wang does? Find out in the next exciting volume coming soon!

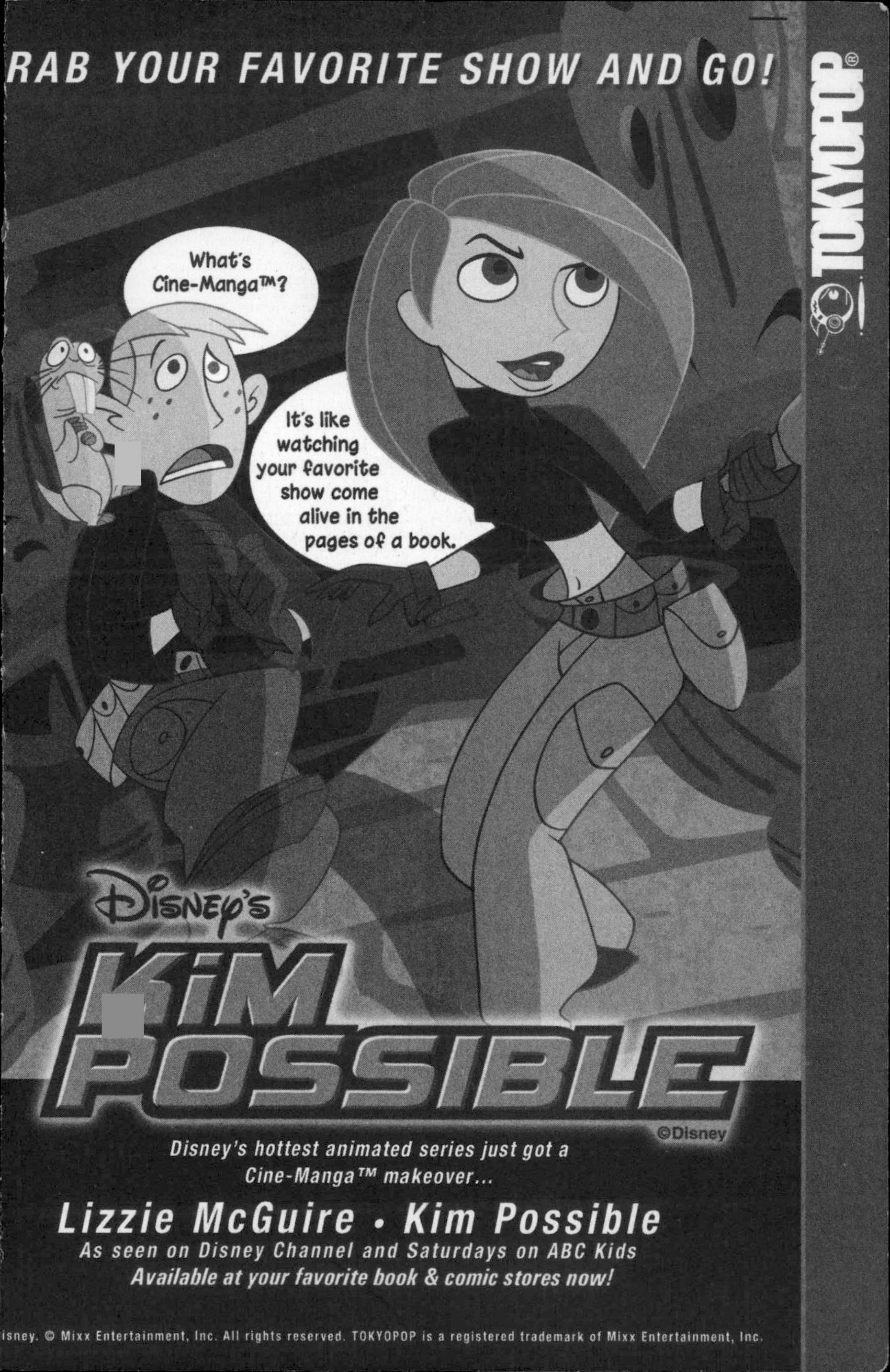
RAB YOUR FAVORITE SHOW AND GO!
TOKYOPOP®
What's Cine-Manga™?
It's like watching your favorite show come alive in the pages of a book.
Disney's
Kim Possible
©Disney

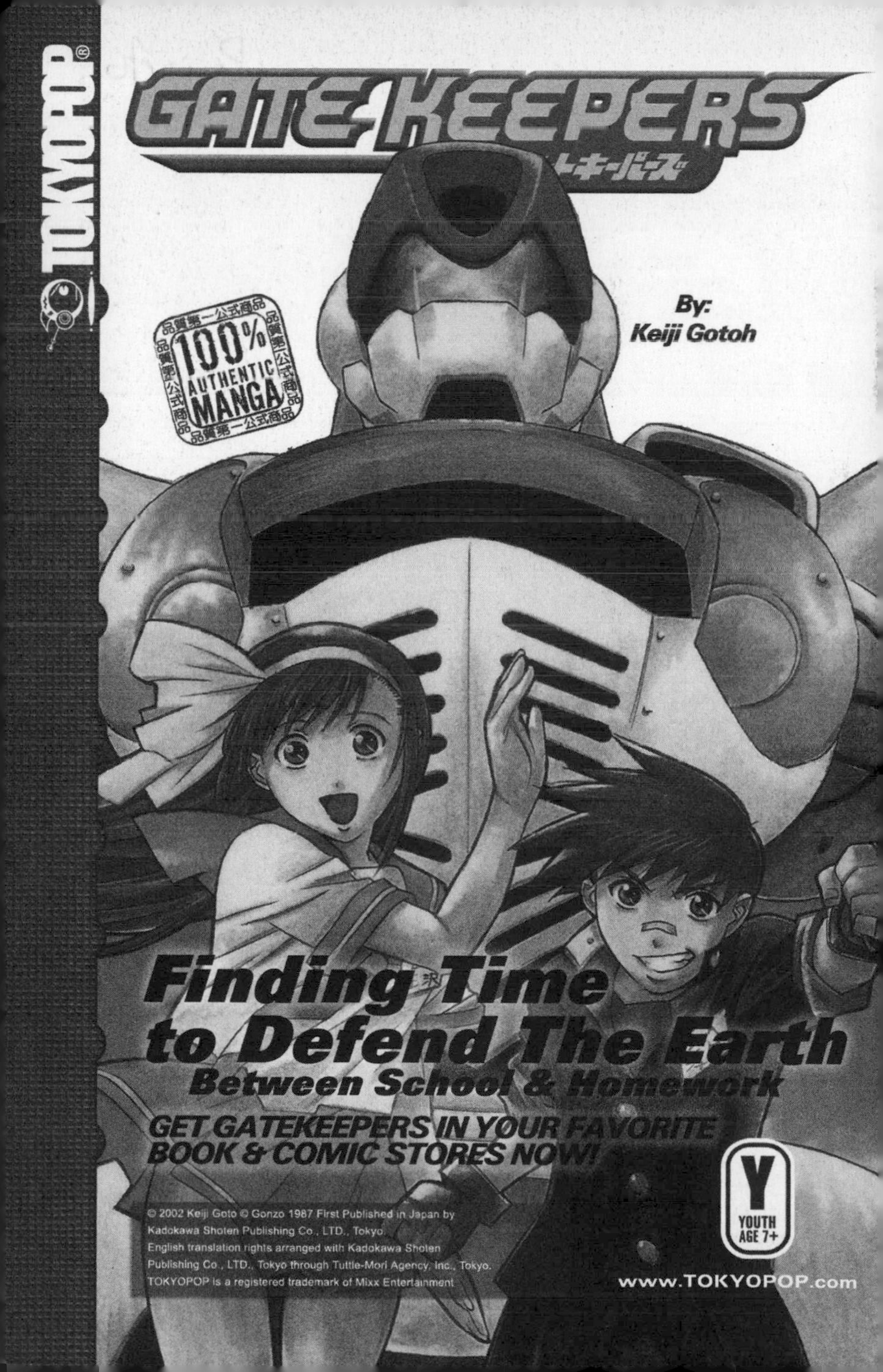
TOKYOPOP®
GATE KEEPERS
By:
Keiji Gotoh
100% AUTHENTIC MANGA
品質第一公式商品
Finding Time to Defend The Earth
Between School & Homework
GET GATEKEEPERS IN YOUR FAVORITE BOOK & COMIC STORES NOW!
Y
YOUTH AGE 7+
© 2002 Keiji Goto © Gonzo 1987 First Published in Japan by Kadokawa Shoten Publishing Co., LTD., Tokyo.
English translation rights arranged with Kadokawa Shoten Publishing Co., LTD., Tokyo through Tuttle-Mori Agency, Inc., Tokyo.
TOKYOPOP is a registered trademark of Mixx Entertainment
www.TOKYOPOP.com

PLYAG

STOP!

This is the back of the book.
You wouldn't want to spoil a great ending!

This book is printed "manga-style," in the authentic Japanese right-to-left format. Since none of the artwork has been flipped or altered, readers get to experience the story just as the creator intended. You've been asking for it, so TOKYOPOP® delivered: authentic, hot-off-the-press, and far more fun!

DIRECTIONS

If this is your first time reading manga-style, here's a quick guide to help you understand how it works.

It's easy... just start in the top right panel and follow the numbers. Have fun, and look for more 100% authentic manga from TOKYOPOP®!